TEN YEARS

AMONG

THE MAIL BAGS:

OR,

Notes from the Diary of a Special Agent

OF THE

POST-OFFICE DEPARTMENT.

BY J. HOLBROOK.

WITH ILLUSTRATIONS.

PHILADELPHIA:
H. COWPERTHWAIT & CO.
1855.

This Work

IS RESPECTFULLY DEDICATED TO THOSE OFFICIALLY CONNECTED WITH THE MAIL SERVICE OF THE UNITED STATES.

PREFACE.

THE idea of preparing the present work was suggested to the author by the universal interest manifested in regard to the class of delinquencies to which it relates, and the eagerness with which the details of the various modes adopted in successful cases to detect the guilty parties, have been sought after by all classes. He was also induced to undertake this series of narratives by the hope and belief that while it afforded interesting matter for the general reader, it might prove a public benefit by increasing the safety of the United States mails, and fortifying those officially connected with the post-office and mail service, against the peculiar temptations incident to their position, thus preserving to society some at least who, without such warnings as the following sketches contain, might make shipwreck of their principles, and meet with a felon's doom.

It has been said that whoever acts upon the principle that "honesty is the best policy," is himself dishonest. That is, policy should not be the motive to honesty, which is true; but taking into view how many there are who would not be influenced by higher considerations, it is evident that whatever serves to impress on the mind the inevitable connection between crime and misery, if not between honesty and happiness, will aid in strengthening the barriers against dishonesty, too often, alas! insufficient to withstand the pressure of temptation.

The author has endeavored to enforce these truths in the following pages, and he relies for the desired impression on the fact that they are not dry, abstract precepts which he presents, but portions of real life; experiences the like of which may be the lot of any young man; temptations before which stronger men than he have fallen, and which he must flee from if he would successfully resist.

The most elaborate treatise on rascality would not compare in its effects on the mass of mankind, with the simplest truthful narrative of a crime and its consequences, especially if addressed to those exposed by circumstances to the danger of committing offences similar to the one described.

Two objections to the publication of a work like the present, occurred to the author as well as to others whom he consulted, and caused him to hesitate in commencing the undertaking. First, the possibility that the detailed description of ingenious acts of dishonesty, might furnish information which could be obtained from no other source, and supply the evil-disposed with expedients for the prosecution of their nefarious designs. Second, the danger of again inflicting pain upon the innocent relatives and friends of those whose criminal biography would furnish material for the work.

In reference to the first of these objections it may be said, that, although descriptions of skilful roguery are always perused with interest, and often with a sort of admiration for the talent displayed, yet when it is seen that retribution follows as certainly and often as closely as a shadow; that however dexterously the criminal may conceal himself in a labyrinth of his own construction, the ministers of the law track him through all its windings, or demolish the cunningly devised structure; and that when he fancies himself out of the reach of Justice, he sees, to his utter dismay, her omnipresent arm uplifted to strike him down; when these truths are brought to light by the record, an impressive view will be given of the resources which are at command for thwarting the designs of dishonesty, and of the futility of taking the field against such overwhelming odds. And in addition to the certainty of detection, the penalty inflicted for offences of this description is to be taken into the account. Doubtless many employés in Post-offices have committed crimes of which they never would have been guilty but for a mistaken idea of security from the punishment to which they were making themselves liable. It is well for all to be correctly informed on this subject, and to know that offences committed against this Department are not lightly dealt with. Information of this character the author has fully supplied.

Again—Comparatively but few of the secret modes of detection are exhibited, and he who should consider himself safe in evading what plans are here described, will find to his sorrow that he has made a most dangerous calculation.

As to the second objection above mentioned, namely, the danger of wounding the feelings of innocent parties, the author would observe that fictitious names of persons and places are generally substituted for the real ones; thus avoiding any additional publicity to those concerned in the cases given. And furthermore, he ventures to hope that few of the class to which this objection refers, would refuse to undergo such a trial of their feelings, if by this means a wholesome warning may be given to those who need it.

There are other wrongs and delinquencies connected with our postal system, of a mischievous and immoral tendency, and of crushing effect upon their authors, which, although not in all cases punishable by statute, yet require to be exposed and guarded against. Descriptions of some of the most ingenious of these attempts at fraud, successful and unsuccessful, are also here held up to public view.

It was the author's intention to give two or three chapters of an historical and biographical character,—a condensed history of our post-office system, with some notice of that of other countries, and brief biographical sketches of our Post Masters General. But matter essential to the completeness of the work in hand, as illustrating the varieties of crime in connection with post-offices, has so accumulated, that the chapters referred to could not be introduced without enlarging the volume to unreasonable dimensions; and the author has been compelled to limit his biographies of the Post Masters General to a short chronological notice of each of those officers.

THE POST MASTERS GENERAL.

Under the Revolutionary organization, the first Post Master General was Benjamin Franklin. He was experienced in its duties, having been appointed Post Master of Philadelphia in 1737, and Deputy Post Master General of the British Colonies in 1753. He was removed from this office, to punish him for his active sympathies with the colonists; and one of the first acts of their separate organization was to place him at the head of their Post-Office Department. It is a singular coincidence that this eminent philosopher, who cradled our postal system in its infancy, also, by first bringing the electric fluid within the power of man, led the way for the electric telegraph, the other great medium for transmitting intelligence.

The necessities of the Revolutionary struggle, demanded the abilities of Franklin for another sphere of action. Richard Bache, his son-in-law, was appointed to succeed him as Post Master General, in November, 1776. He was succeeded by Ebenezer Hazard, who subsequently compiled the valuable Historical Collections bearing his name. He held the office until the inauguration of President Washington's Administration.

In relation to the several Post Masters General, since the adoption of the Federal Constitution, the author regrets that he is compelled, contrary to his original intention, to confine himself to brief chronological notes. The succession is as follows:—

1. Samuel Osgood.—Born at Andover, Mass., Feb. 14, 1748. Graduated at Harvard College in 1770. A member of the Massachusetts Legislature, and also of the Board of War, and subsequently an Aid to Gen. Ward. In 1779, a member of the Massachusetts Constitutional Convention. In 1781, appointed a member of Congress; in 1785, first Commissioner of the Treasury; and Sept. 26, 1789, Post Master General. He was afterwards Naval Officer of the port of New York, and died in that city Aug. 12, 1813.

2. Timothy Pickering.—Born at Salem, Mass., July 17, 1746. Graduated in 1763. Was Colonel of a regiment of militia at the age of nineteen, and marched for the seat of war at the first news of the battle of Lexington. In 1775, appointed Judge of two local courts. In the fall of 1776 marched to New Jersey with his regiment. In 1777 appointed Adjutant-General; and subsequently a member of the Board of War with Gates and Mifflin. In 1780 he succeeded Greene as Quarter Master General. In 1790 he was employed in negotiations with the Indians; Aug. 12, 1791, he was appointed Post Master General; in 1794, Secretary of War; and in 1795, Secretary of State. From 1803 to 1811 he was Senator, and from 1814 to 1817, Representative in Congress. Died at Salem, June 29, 1829.

3. Joseph Habersham.—Born in 1750. A Lieutenant Colonel during the Revolutionary War; and in 1785 a member of Congress. Appointed Post Master General Feb. 25, 1795. He was afterwards President of the U. S. Branch Bank in Savannah, Georgia. Died at that place Nov. 1815.

4. Gideon Granger.—Born at Suffield, Ct., July 19, 1767. Graduated at Yale College in 1787, and the following year admitted to the Bar. In 1793 elected to the Connecticut Legislature. Nov. 28, 1801, appointed Post Master General. Retired in 1814, and removed to Canandaigua, N. Y. April, 1819, elected a member of the Senate of that State, but resigned in 1821, on account of ill health. During his service in that body he donated one thousand acres of land to aid the construction of the Erie Canal. Died at Canandaigua, Dec. 31, 1822.

5. Return Jonathan Meigs.—Born at Middletown, Ct., in 1765. Graduated at Yale College in 1785, and subsequently admitted to the Bar. In 1788 emigrated to Marietta, Ohio, then the North Western Territory. In 1790, during the Indian wars, he was sent by Gov. St. Clair on a perilous mission through the wilderness to the British commandant at Detroit. In the winter of 1802–3, he was elected by the Legislature the first Chief Justice of the Supreme Court of the new State. In October, 1804, he was appointed Colonel commanding the United States forces in the upper district of the Territory of Louisiana, and resigned his judgeship. In the following year he was appointed as one of the United States Judges for Louisiana. April 2, 1807, he was transferred to the Territory of Michigan. In October following he resigned his judgeship, and was elected Governor of the State of Ohio, but his election was successfully contested on the ground of non-residence. He was chosen at the same session as one

of the Judges of the Supreme Court of the State; and at the next session as United States Senator, for a vacancy of one year and also for a full term. In 1810 he was again elected Governor of Ohio, and on the 8th of December resigned his seat in the Senate. In 1812 he was re-elected Governor. On the 17th of March, 1814, he was appointed Post Master General, which he resigned in June, 1823. Died at Marietta, March 29, 1825.

6. John McLean.—Born in Morris Co., New Jersey, March 11, 1785. His father subsequently removed to Ohio, of which State the son continues a resident. He labored on the farm until sixteen years of age, when he applied himself to study, and two years afterwards removed to Cincinnati, and supported himself by copying in the County clerk's office, while he studied law. In 1807 he was admitted to the Bar. In 1812 he was elected to Congress, and re-elected in 1814. In 1816 he was unanimously elected by the Legislature, a Judge of the Supreme Court of the State. In 1822 he was appointed by President Monroe, Commissioner of the General Land Office, and on the 26th of June, 1823, Post Master General. In 1829 he was appointed as one of the Justices of the Supreme Court of the United States, which office he yet holds.

7. William T. Barry.—Born in Fairfax Co., Va., March 18, 1780. Graduated at the College of William and Mary. He was admitted to the Bar, and in early life emigrated to Kentucky. In 1828, he was a candidate for Governor of that State, and defeated by a small majority, after one of the most memorable contests in its annals. Appointed Post Master General March 9, 1829. In 1835 appointed Minister Plenipotentiary to Spain, and died at Liverpool, England, on his way to Madrid.

8. Amos Kendall.—Born at Dunstable, Mass., August 16, 1789. Graduated at Dartmouth College in 1811. About the year 1812 removed to Kentucky, and in 1815 was appointed post master at Georgetown, in that state. In 1816 he assumed the editorial charge of the *Argus*, published at Frankfort, in the same State, which he continued until 1829, being, most of the time, State Printer. In 1829 he was appointed Fourth Auditor of the United States Treasury; and, May 1, 1835, Post Master General. He resigned the latter office in 1840, and has, since the introduction of the electric telegraph, been mainly employed in connection with enterprises for its operation. He is yet living.

9. John Milton Niles.—Born at Windsor, Ct., August 20, 1787. Admitted to the Bar in December, 1812. About 1816 he removed to

Hartford, and was one of the first proprietors of the *Hartford Times*, and had charge of its editorial columns until the year 1820. In 1821 he was appointed Judge of the Hartford County Court, which office he held until 1829. In 1826 he represented Hartford in the Connecticut Legislature. In April, 1829, he was appointed post master at Hartford; which he held until December, 1835, when he was appointed United States Senator to fill a vacancy, and in the ensuing May was elected by the Legislature for the remainder of the term. In 1839 and 1840 he was supported by his party, though without success, for the office of Governor of the State. May 25, 1840, he was appointed Post Master General. In 1842 he was elected United State Senator for a full term. Mr. Niles is yet living.

10. Francis Granger.—Born at Suffield, Ct., Dec. 1, 1792. Graduated at Yale College in 1811. Admitted to the Bar in May, 1816. He was elected a member of the New York Legislature in 1825, and again in 1826, 1827, 1829, and 1831. In 1828 he was a candidate for the office of Lieutenant Governor, but was defeated; and in 1830 and again in 1832, he was run for Governor, with the same result. In 1834 he was elected to Congress. In 1836 he was a candidate for Vice President, and received the electoral votes of the States of Massachusetts, Vermont, New Jersey, Delaware, Ohio, Indiana, and Kentucky. He was again elected to Congress in 1838 and in 1840. Appointed Post Master General March 6, 1841, but resigned the following September. His successor in Congress thereupon resigned, and Mr. Granger was again elected to that body. On the 4th of March, 1843, he finally retired from public life, but is yet living.

11. Charles A. Wickliffe.—Born at Bardstown, Kentucky, June 8, 1788, and was admitted to the Bar at an early age. He was twice elected to the State Legislature during the war of 1812. He twice volunteered in the Northwestern Army, and was present at the Battle of the Thames. In 1820 he was again elected to the Legislature. In 1822 he was elected to Congress, and was four times re-elected. During his service in that body, he was appointed by the House as one of the managers in the impeachment of Judge Peck. Upon leaving Congress, in 1833, he was again elected to the lower branch of the State Legislature; and, upon its assembling, was chosen Speaker. In 1834 he was elected Lieutenant Governor of the State, and in 1839, by the death of Gov. Clark, he became Acting Governor. He was appointed Post Master General, September 13, 1841. In 1849 he was chosen as a delegate to the Constitutional Convention

of Kentucky; and, under the new Constitution, he was appointed as one of the Revisers of the Statute Laws of the State. He is yet living.

12. CAVE JOHNSON.—Born, January 11, 1793, in Robertson Co., Tennessee. His opportunities for education were limited, but made available to the greatest extent. In his youth, he acted as deputy-clerk of the County, his father being clerk. He was thence led to the study of the law. In 1813 he was appointed Deputy Quarter Master in a brigade of militia commanded by his father, and marched into the Creek nation under General Jackson. He continued in this service until the close of the Creek war in 1814. In 1816 he was admitted to the Bar. In 1817 he was elected by the Legislature one of the Attorneys General of the State, which office he held until elected a member of Congress in 1829. He was re-elected in 1831, 1833, and 1835. Defeated in 1837. Again elected in 1839, 1841, and 1843. Appointed Post Master General, March 5, 1845. In 1849 he served for a few months as one of the Circuit Judges of Tennessee; and, in 1853, was appointed by the Governor and Senate as President of the Bank of Tennessee, at Nashville. He is yet living.

13. JACOB COLLAMER.—Born at Troy, N. Y., about 1790, and removed in childhood to Burlington, Vt., with his father. Graduated at the State University at that place in 1810. Served during the year 1812, a frontier campaign, as a lieutenant, in the service of the United States. Admitted to the Bar in 1813. Practised law for twenty years, serving frequently in the State Legislature. In 1833 he was elected an Associate Justice of the Supreme Court of the State, from which position he voluntarily retired in 1842. In the course of that period, he was also a member of a convention held to revise the Constitution of the State. In 1843 elected to Congress to fill a vacancy, and re-elected for a full term, in 1844, and again in 1846. Appointed Post Master General March 7th, 1849. In 1850 he was again elected a Justice of the Supreme Court of Vermont; and in 1854 he was chosen United States Senator, which office he now holds.

14. NATHAN KELSEY HALL.—Born at Skaneateles, N. Y., March 28th, 1810. Removed to Aurora in the same State in 1826, and commenced the study of the law with Millard Fillmore. Removed with the latter to Buffalo in 1830. Admitted to the Bar in 1832. Appointed First Judge of the Court of Common Pleas in 1841. In 1845 elected a member of the State Legislature, and in 1846 a member of Congress. He was appointed Post Master General July 20,

1850; and, in 1852, United States Judge for the Northern District of New York, which office he now holds.

15. SAMUEL DICKINSON HUBBARD.—Born at Middletown, Ct., August 10, 1799. Graduated at Yale College in 1819. He was admitted to the Bar in 1822, but subsequently engaged in manufacturing enterprises. He was Mayor of the city of Middletown, and held other offices of local trust. In 1845 he was elected a member of Congress, and re-elected in 1847. He was appointed Post Master General September 14, 1852. Died at Middletown October 8, 1855.

16. JAMES CAMPBELL, the present Post Master General of the United States, was born September 1, 1813, in the city of Philadelphia, Pa. Admitted to the Bar in 1834, at the age of twenty-one years. In 1841, at the age of twenty-eight, he was appointed Judge of the Common Pleas Court for the City and County of Philadelphia, which position he occupied for the term of nine years. In 1851, when the Constitution of the State was changed, making the Judiciary elective, he was nominated by a State Convention of his party as a candidate for the Bench of the Supreme Court of the State, but was defeated after a warmly contested and somewhat peculiar contest, receiving however 176,000 votes. In January, 1852, he was appointed Attorney General of Pennsylvania, which he resigned to assume the duties of Post Master General. He was appointed to that office on the 8th of March, 1853.

INTRODUCTION.

A MAIL BAG is an epitome of human life. All the elements which go to form the happiness or misery of individuals—the raw material, so to speak, of human hopes and fears—here exist in a chaotic state. These elements are imprisoned, like the winds in the fabled cave of Æolus, "biding their time" to go forth and fulfil their office, whether it be to refresh and invigorate the drooping flower, or to bring destruction upon the proud and stately forest-king.

Well is it for the peace of mind of those who have in temporary charge these discordant forces, that they cannot trace the course of each missive as it passes from their hands. For although many hearts are made glad by these silent messengers, yet in every day's mail there is enough of sadness and misery, lying torpid like serpents, until warmed into venomous life by a glance of the eye, to cast a gloom over the spirits of any one who should know it all; and to add new emphasis to the words of the wise man, "He that increaseth knowledge, increaseth sorrow." But until they are released from their temporary captivity, the letters guard in grim silence their varied contents. Joy and sorrow as yet have no voice; vice and crime are yet concealed, running, like subterranean streams, from the mind which originated, to the mind which is to receive their influence. The mail bag is as great a leveller as the grave, and it is only by the superscription in either case, that one occupant can be distinguished from the other.

But leaving these general speculations, let us give more particular attention to the motley crowd "in durance vile." If each one possessed the power of uttering audibly the ideas which it contains, a confusion of tongues would ensue, worthy of the last stages of the tower of Babel, or of a Woman's Rights convention. Indeed matters would proceed within these leathern walls, very much as they do in the world at large. The portly, important "money letter," would look with contempt upon the modest little *billet-doux*, and the aristocratic, delicately-scented, heraldically-sealed epistle, would recoil from the touch of its roughly coated, wafer-secured neighbor, filled to the brim, perhaps, with affections as pure, or friendship as devoted as ever can be found under coverings more polished. Would that the good in one missive, might counteract the evil in another, for here is one filled with the overflowings of a mother's heart, conveying language of entreaty and remonstrance,—perhaps the traces of anxious tears,—to the unwary youth who is beginning to turn aside from the path of rectitude, and to look with wishful eyes upon forbidden ground. Need enough is there of this message to strengthen staggering resolution, to overpower the whispers of evil; for close by are the suggestions of a vicious companion, lying in wait to lure him on to vice, and to darken the light of love which hitherto has guided his steps.

In one all-embracing receptacle, the strife of politics is for a time unknown. Epistles of Whigs, Democrats, Pro and Anti-Slavery men lie calmly down together, like the lion and the lamb, (if indeed we can imagine anything lamb-like in political documents,) ready, however, to start up in their proper characters like Satan at the touch of Ithuriel's spear, and to frown defiance upon their late companions. Theological animosity, too, lies spell-bound. Orthodoxy and Heterodoxy, Old and New School, Protestant and Catholic, Free Thinkers and No Thinkers, are held in paper chains, and cease to lacerate one another with controverted *points*. Nor in this view of dormant pugnacity, should that important constituent, the Law, be left out of sight. An opinion clearly establishing the case of A. B. unsuspectingly reposes by the side of another utterly subverting it, thus placing, or about to place, the unfortunate A. B. in the condition of a wall mined by its assailants, and counter-mined by its defenders, quite sure (to use a familiar phrase,) of "bursting up" in either case. And the unconscious official who "distributes" these missiles, might well exclaim, if he knew the contents, "cry havoc, and let slip the dogs of war."

But we come to another discord in our miniature life-orchestra. Those all-embracing, ever-sounding tones, which lie at the two extremities of the "diapason of humanity," namely, Life and Death, here find their representatives. Here lies a sable-edged missive, speaking to the eye as the passing bell speaks to the ear, telling of blighted happiness, a desolate home, and loving hearts mourning and refusing to be comforted because the loved one is not; while close at hand and perchance overlying the sad messenger, is the announcement of another arrival upon the stage of life—Our First—and though it is as yet behind the curtain, not having made its bow to the world at large, is an important character in the green room; and the aid of that convenient individual, Uncle Sam, is invoked to convey the information of its advent to a circle of expectant friends, as highly favored as that select few who are sometimes invited to witness a private performance by some newly-arrived artist, before he makes his appearance in a more public manner.

Nor should we omit at least a passing notice of the humorous aspects of our Bag. Physiognomy will not go far in aiding us to determine as to a given letter, whether its contents are grave or gay. A well-ordered epistle, like a highly bred man, does not show on its face the emotions which it may contain. But in what we may call the lower class of letters, where nature is untrammeled by envelopes, and eccentricity or unskilfulness display themselves by the various shapes and styles in which the documents are folded and directed, there is more room for speculation on their internal character; and it is the author's intention to furnish some rare specimens of unconscious humor of this kind, for the delectation of his readers.

As we contemplate the wit, fun, humor, and jollity of all sorts, which lie dormant within these wrappages, we are tempted to retract our commiseration for the imaginary official whom we have supposed to know the contents of the letters in his charge, and therefore drag out a miserable existence under their depressing influence. At least we feel impelled to modify our remarks so far as to say that in the case supposed, his days would be passed in alternate cachinnations and sympathizing grief. He would become a storehouse of wit, a magazine of humor. For there is much of wit, humor, and jollity running through these secret channels, that never is diffused through the medium of the press, but flows among the privacies of domestic circles, adding life to their intercourse, and increasing the attractions of social fellowship, like some sparkling stream, both refreshing and adorning the landscape through which it takes its course.

We leave the further development of this prolific train of thought, to the reader's imagination. Yet the imagination can devise no combination more strange than those which may be found every day within the narrow precincts of which we have been speaking; and the same may be said of the Post-Office system at large, interwoven as it is with the whole social life of civilized man.

The laws of the land are intended not only to preserve the person and material property of every citizen sacred from intrusion, but to secure the privacy of his thoughts, so far as he sees fit to withhold them from others. Silence is as great a privilege as speech, and it is as important that every one should be able to maintain it whenever he pleases, as that he should be at liberty to utter his thoughts without restraint. Now the post-office undertakes to maintain this principle with regard to written communications as they are conveyed from one person to another through the mails. However unimportant the contents of a letter may be, the violation of its secrecy while it is in charge of the Post-Office Department, or even after having left its custody, becomes an offence of serious magnitude in the eye of the law; and as the quantity and importance of mail matter is continually increasing, it has been found necessary to adopt means for its security, which were not required in the earlier history of the Post-Office. One kind of danger to which the mails were exposed before the days of railroads and steamboats, namely, highway robbery, is now almost unknown. The principal danger at present to be apprehended, is from those connected with their transportation and delivery, and a system of *surveillance* has been adopted, suited to the exigency of the case, namely, the creation of Special Agents, who have become a fixed "institution," likely to be essential to the efficiency of the Department, as long as any of its employés are deficient in principle or honesty. The origin of this Special Agent System will be given elsewhere. It is sufficient to say here, that the curious developments of character, and combinations of circumstances, which will be found in the following pages, were mainly brought to light by the operation of this system, as carried out by one of its Agents. "Ten years" of experience have given the author (or at least ought to have given him) an ample supply of material for the illustration of nearly every phase in Post-Office life. His principal difficulty is the "*embarras des richesses;*" yet he has endeavored to select such cases as are not only interesting in themselves, but well calculated to benefit those for whose use the present work is especially designed.

CONTENTS.

CHAPTER I.

CHAPTER II.

CHAPTER III.

CHAPTER IV.

CHAPTER V.

CHAPTER VI.

CHAPTER VII.

CHAPTER VIII.

A NIGHT IN A POST-OFFICE.

CHAPTER IX.

CHAPTER X.

STOPPING A POST-OFFICE.

CHAPTER XI.

CHAPTER XII.

CHAPTER XIII.

CHAPTER XIV.

OBSTRUCTING THE MAIL.

CHAPTER XV.

CHAPTER XVI.

CHAPTER XVII.

DETACHED INCIDENTS.

CHAPTER XVIII.

FRAUDS CARRIED ON THROUGH THE MAILS.

CHAPTER XIX.

POST-OFFICE SITES.

TEN YEARS

AMONG

THE MAIL BAGS.

CHAPTER I

No "Ear-Biters" employed—The Commission—A whole School robbed—Value of a "quarter"—Embargo on Trunks—Unjust Suspicion—The dying Mother—Fidelity of Post Masters—A venerable pair of Officials—President Pierce assists—A clue to the Robberies—The Quaker Coat—An insane Traveller—The Decoy Letters—Off the Road—The dancing Horse—The Decoy missing—An official Visit by night—Finding the marked Bills—The Confession—The Arrest.

In the fall of 1845, information was received from the Post-office Department at Washington, of extensive depredations upon the mails along the route extending from Boston to a well known and flourishing inland town in one of the New England States, accompanied with the expression of a strong desire on the part of the Post Master General, that prompt and thorough efforts should be made to ferret out, if possible, those who were concerned in these wholesale peculations.

It so happened that the gentleman at this time at the head of the Post-office Department, had not been a very ardent believer in the necessity or usefulness of "Secret Agents," so called. In fact, when he entered upon the duties of his office, he dismissed the entire corps of this class of officials, and notwithstanding the urgent calls of the public, and the dissenting views of his most experienced Assistants, he steadily refused to re-employ them, excepting temporarily, and in special cases, until near the close of his official term. Justice to that honest and thorough-going officer, however, requires some mention of the causes which controlled his decision in this important matter.

While he was a Representative in Congress, a violent onslaught was made upon the system of Special Agents, for the reason (as was alleged,) that they were neither more nor less than so many political emissaries, supported at the public expense; and in consequence of their secret, and therefore commanding position, possessing, and often exerting an undue and improper influence against those opposed to them in politics. Believing this charge to be unjust, he took up, in the House of Representatives, the defence of this Special Agent system, and called for proof in support of the accusations of violent partisan conduct brought against these Agents.

Those who know him will be able to judge of his mortification and displeasure when it was distinctly proved that in one instance a Special Agent relieved his pugnacious propensities by getting into a regular fight at the polls, and damaging one *poll*, by biting off an ear attached thereto; the poll aforesaid being the property of a political opponent.

It was also shown that this sanguinary Agent inserted a dirk knife between the ribs of another antagonist, thus performing a sort of political phlebotomy, with the intention, doubtless, of relieving the patient of some portion of his superabundant Whig or Democratic blood (whichever it might have been) and thereby bringing him to a rational view of public questions.

This, and some other equally reputable cases of interference in elections, having been fully established, it is not wonderful that strong prejudices should have arisen in the mind of the future Post Master General against this class of officers, although such disorderly and disgraceful conduct was clearly the fault of the individuals who indulged in it, and not of the corps or system, with which they were connected. And I would here say, in justice to this body of Agents, that many of them were gentlemen of intelligence and discretion, who would be far from countenancing such proceedings as have just been mentioned.

When, therefore, in the year above designated, the writer found himself in possession of a Special Agent's Commission, signed by the same gentleman, as "Post Master General," and rendered impressive by the broad seal of that Department, which represented a 2.40 steed rushing madly along, with a post-rider on his back, and the mail portmanteau securely attached,—when he received accompanying instructions to look into the alarming state of things on the route aforesaid—his leading thought and ambition was to satisfy the distinguished Tennessean that a Special Agent could catch a mail robber by the ear quite as readily as a political antagonist, and apply the knife of justice to those whose case required it, with at least as much courage and skill as could be displayed in the matter of disabling belligerent "shoulder hitters" at the ballot boxes.

How much the result of this first investigation, after the restoration of the "ear-biters" (as they were then sometimes facetiously called,) had to do with the radical change in opinion and action, noticeable in certain quarters, as to the utility and indispensable necessity of this "right arm" of the Department, it may not be advisable, nor indeed modest, to inquire.

The depredations in the case thus placed in my hands for investigation, were seemingly very bold, although from the length of the route, and the number of post-offices thereon, the rogue had no doubt flattered himself that it would take a long time to trace him out, even if Government should condescend to notice the complaints which he might suppose would be made at head-quarters. It is also possible that he was encouraged to this course of rascality by the belief that the Department had no officials whose particular business it was to be "a terror to evil-doers," and that he could easily elude the efforts of those no more experienced than himself in the crooks and turns through which every villain is compelled to slink.

The letters stolen were principally addressed to the members of a large and flourishing literary institution, situated in the town already mentioned, and embracing in its catalogue pupils of both sexes from almost every section of the Union. So keen was the scent of the robber, that, like an animated "divining rod," he could indicate unerringly the existence of gold, or its equivalent beneath the paper surface soil, and he "prospected" with more certainty, though less honesty, than a California miner. From all the mail-matter passing through his office, he would invariably select the valuable packages, abstracting their *material* contents, and, as it afterwards appeared, committing the letters to the flames. "Dead men tell no tales." Neither do burnt letters.

The results of this system of robbery, as regarded those who suffered by it, were somewhat peculiar. The abstraction of an equal amount from the members of a business community, might have inconvenienced some, but would have made little perceptible difference in the course of business. The temporary deficiency would have been as little felt, on the whole, as the withdrawing of a pail-full of water from a running stream. The level is quickly restored, as supplies flow in.

But when the victims of dishonesty are youth pursuing their studies at a distance from home, and depending on remittances from their parents and friends for the means of discharging the debts which they may incur, the case is widely different. Here the stream is dammed up somewhere between its source and the place where the waters ought to be flowing, and the worst description of drought—a drought of money—ensues.

All sorts of consequences, in the present instance, followed this state of things. The school became, in this particular, like a besieged city, cut off from supplies from without, while its inhabitants lived on under an ever increasing pressure of difficulties, which made premature Micawbers of the unfortunate aspirants to that temple which is so artistically represented in the frontispiece to Webster's spelling book, as surmounting the hill of Science, and animated by the figure of Fame on the roof, proclaiming through her trumpet a perpetual invitation to enter the majestic portals beneath.

The possessor of money, received, under these circumstances, a greater degree of consideration than is usually accorded to the millionaire in the world at large. The owner of a "quarter" had troops of friends, and became purse-proud on the strength of that magnificent coin. Happy was he who had unlimited "tick;" to whose call livery-stable keepers were obsequious, and with whom tailors were ready to in*vest*, having faith to believe that the present dry aspect of the financial sky would be succeeded by refreshing showers of "mint-drops" from the paternal pockets. Some of the young ladies who had invoked the milliner's assistance in defiance of the poet's line—"Beauty unadorned, &c.," occasionally received hints respecting the settlement of their trifling accounts, which materially diminished the pleasure that they would otherwise have felt in the contemplation of their outer adornments. Bonnets reminded them of bills, and dresses of duns.

The more juvenile portion of our scholastic community, too, felt the pressure of the "hard times" which some invisible hand had brought upon them. In early life, the saccharine bump is largely developed, but unlike other organs described by phrenologists, this is within the mouth, and is commonly called the "sweet tooth." Those luxurious youth who had hitherto indulged the cravings of this organ *ad libitum*, or as far as they could do so without the knowledge of their teachers, found the wary confectioners unwilling longer to satisfy their unsophisticated appetites, without more "indemnity for the past" if not "security for the future," than they had yet furnished.

So these victims of raging desire were compelled to retire hungry from untasted luxuries, not without sundry *candid* expressions of their feelings toward the obdurate retailers of sweets, and *tart* replies from those individuals. Their only consolation was to revel in dreams in which the temple of Fame was supported by pillars of candy, with a protuberant pie for a dome; while her trumpet was converted into a cornucopia from which unfailing streams of sugar-plums were issuing.

But such annoyances and inconveniences as have been enumerated were trifling, compared with other consequences which resulted from this prolonged and systematic robbery of the mails. It is hard for one who never had his word doubted, to learn by unmistakeable indications that his story of money expected and not received, is disbelieved by an impatient creditor, who perhaps hints that the money has come and gone in some other direction than that which it should have taken. The honorable pride of some was wounded in this manner, and much ill-feeling arose between those who had hitherto regarded each other with mutual respect.

The term of the school was just closing, and worthy Mrs. K., who had several of the pupils as boarders in her family, being blessed with a rather large organ of caution, refused to allow one or two to leave (who did not expect to return the next term,) without depositing some collateral security for the payment of their board-bills. Those luckless youth had written again and again for the money necessary to settle their accounts in the place; but their entreaties were apparently unnoticed and unanswered. They were in the condition of Mr. Pecksniff's pupils, who were requested by their preceptor to ring the bell which was in their room, if they wanted anything. They often did so, but nobody ever answered it. It very naturally seemed almost incredible to Mrs. K. that the parents of her boarders should neglect to provide for the various expenses which arise at the close of a school term, especially as these pupils were not to return. So the good lady felt bound by her duty to herself to lay an embargo upon their trunks, and she further took occasion to observe that if they hadn't been so much horseback riding, &c., during the summer, her bill could have been settled. This of course provoked an angry retort, and suspicion smouldered on one side, and resentment flamed out on the other, until the whole mystery was unravelled.

In another boarding-house, inhabited by pupils of both sexes, it had been customary for some of their number to get from the post-office the letters and papers sent to them, and this duty had lately devolved, for the most part, on one person, Henry S., who was a relation of the post master, and, from other circumstances, had frequent occasion to visit the office. As he returned almost empty-handed of letters from day to day, his disappointed fellow-boarders at first wondered at the silence of their friends, then suspicion began to work in their minds; and since the post master was a man of unsullied honor, and entirely reliable for honesty, they at length reluctantly admitted the supposition that Henry S. must be the delinquent.

Acting on the ground that S. was the guilty one, his fellow-boarders gave orders to the post master, forbidding the delivery of their letters to him. So the next day, when he presented himself at the office, he was thunderstruck by the information that he had lost the confidence of his fellow-pupils, and that they would no longer trust their letters in his hands.

"It can't be," exclaimed he, "that they suppose I took their letters."

"I guess they do," said the old post master; "but I think they had better be sure that there were letters coming to them, before they suspect you."

"Oh, now I see why they have acted so strangely, lately, just as if they didn't want me around. I never once thought that this was the reason of it."

From that time, he withdrew himself as much as possible

from the society of his fellow-pupils, stung by a sense of their injustice, and cherishing anything but amiable feelings towards them; yet he did not escape sundry taunts and flings at his character for honesty, from the maliciously disposed. And although those who had regarded him with suspicion, frankly acknowledged their error when the true culprit came to light, yet it was long before he could entirely forgive them the deep mortification they had caused him.

Nor were such cases as this the worst that occurred.

There was a boy in the school, "the only child of his mother, and she was a widow." The lad was quick in intellect, amiable in disposition, and a general favorite throughout the institution. He loved his mother with a strength of affection not often surpassed, and it was fully responded to, by his tender parent. The frequent visits which she made him during his residence at the school had given her opportunities to become acquainted with many of her son's young companions, as well as with his teachers, so that she was quite well known in the little community.

Let us place ourselves at the residence of Mrs. E. (the lady in question,) some hundred miles away. She is lying upon a sick-bed, from which she will never arise. Let us listen to the conversation between her and her attendant.

"Has the train come up yet, Mary?"

"Yes, ma'am, it passed a few minutes ago, but Charley hasn't come."

"Of course he hasn't, he would have been in my arms before this, if he had."

"Perhaps," suggests Mary, "he will be here by the next train."

"God grant he may," groans the dying mother. "It is now more than a week since they first wrote to him, telling him that I was very sick, and requesting him to come immediately. Oh, what *can* keep him away so long? I fear he is sick himself. Some one must go to-morrow, and find out what it is that keeps him from me. I cannot die without seeing him once more."

While this mother was struggling with disease, and with that "hope deferred" that "maketh the heart sick," her son was pursuing his daily round of studies and amusements, anticipating with delight his return home at the close of the term. We may imagine the grief and distress of the poor boy when his uncle, who came for him, told him how the friends at home had written to him twice, each time enclosing him the requisite funds to bear his expenses home, that there might be no delay from *that* cause. And how his mother's only wish, as she now lay rapidly sinking, was to see once more her beloved Charley.

Off they went, the boy and his uncle, on iron wings,—but the wing of the Death-Angel was swifter, and before they arrived at the place of their destination, had cast its awful shadow over the mother's brow.

It will easily be believed that the failure of so many letters to reach those for whom they were intended, excited no small degree of uneasiness in the minds of the parents and friends of the pupils; and in some instances, such was their alarm and anxiety, that journeys of hundreds of miles were undertaken in order to learn why their letters were not received, and why they heard nothing from those to whom they wrote; for the unknown author of all this trouble and confusion, in order to prevent discovery, often destroyed the letters passing both ways.

I cannot here refrain from saying a few words respecting the heinousness of such villanous conduct on the part of post masters or their employés. Leaving out of sight the fact that they are sworn to do nothing contrary to the laws, in their official capacity, and that if they incur the guilt of a breach of trust, they also become guilty of perjury, it should be considered that the well-being of community in all its relations, domestic, social, commercial, and literary, depends on the fidelity with which they discharge the duties of their office.

Much confidence is reposed in them by the public, and I am happy to say, that in comparatively few instances is this confidence misplaced. But in consequence of the circumstances just mentioned, an amount of evil, terrible to contemplate, may be the result of an abuse of trust, which may seem trifling to the guilty perpetrator. The law considers no abuse of the trust reposed in those connected with the post-office as slight; but with a jealous regard for the good of community, provides penalties commensurate with the greatness of their crimes, for those whom neither common honesty, nor honorable feelings, nor moral principle can withhold from the commission of such deeds.

But we will resume the thread of our story.

It may seem strange that the disorders which I have partly described, should have continued so long before the Department was informed of the state of things; but in regard to this, I would say that frequently such failures of correspondence go on for some time, and work much mischief before the post master is apprised of the troubles existing in his vicinity, as he of course is not expected to know what letters are sent to his office, in the absence of complaints made directly to him. It should be stated here, for the benefit of those not informed in these matters, that it is made part of the duty of a post master to report promptly to the Post-office Department all complaints of the loss of any valuable letters said to have been deposited in his office. In the case I am narrating, the failures in the delivery of letters became at length so general, that complaint was made to the post master of the town, and information communicated directly to the Department at Washington.

Having received a commission from the Post Master General as before stated, with orders to investigate this case, I proceeded at once to the place in question, having first been assured of the entire reliability of the post master in charge there; and if looks could ever be taken as the index of the man, I needed no other assurance of his honesty. I found an old gentleman who had numbered his three-score years and ten, a veteran in the service, having held the post which he then filled, "from time immemorial." He looked the worthy representative of that class of men, whose moral principles are applied to the discharge of public duties as strictly as to those of a private character,—men like that high-minded worthy, who, when his son attempted to help himself to a sheet of paper from a desk containing public property, rebuked him thus: "Take some paper from *my* desk, if you want it. *That* paper belongs to the United States."

It is generally necessary in investigating cases of depredations, to inquire into the honesty of the clerks in the offices to which we direct our attention; but in the present instance, such a precaution was uncalled for, since the only assistant of the old post master was his wife, a venerable, motherly matron, of about his age, who had aided him in his official duties, and had been his help-meet in the household for many, many years.

The correspondence of a generation had passed through their hands, and they were enabled to note the changes in the number and appearance of the letters which were placed in their charge during the long period of their incumbency,—changes produced by the increase of population, the freer intercourse between distant places, and the facilities for epistolary communication, which had been progressing ever since they had assumed the responsibilities of their office. At first few letters were transmitted but those of a sturdy, business-like appearance, written on coarse paper, and sealed with wafers of about the dimensions of a modern lady's watch,—wafers that evidently had in charge matter of weighty import, and were mighty embodiments of the adhesive principle. Then, as Time and Improvement advanced, and the *cacoëthes scribendi* became more generally developed, documents appeared of a milder grade, and of a more imaginative aspect, not only representing the cares of business life, but indicating, by the fineness of their texture, the laboriously neat and often feminine character of their superscriptions, and the delicacy of their expressive waxen seals, that Love and Friendship, and the interests of domestic circles, were also beginning thus to find utterance.

Our worthy pair, having been connected with the postal department during such a large portion of its existence, had naturally come to feel much interest in whatever concerned it, and of course were especially anxious that no blot should come upon the reputation of the office in their charge, and that the delinquent in the present case should be brought to light and to justice.

The old man was slow to believe that a fraud had been committed by those connected with any office in his neighborhood, as he thought he could vouch for the character of every one of his brother post masters with whom he was acquainted, and the information which he gave me respecting them seemed to exonerate them, so far as his opinion could do it.

My first proceeding at that point, was to examine the books of the office, by which it appeared that Boston packages were received only once or twice a week, while they had been sent daily, according to the records of the Boston post-office.

After passing over the entire route several times *incog.*, and taking as minute a view of the several offices as it was in my power to do without incurring the danger of being recognised, I concluded that my duty required me to seek an interview with the United States District Attorney, whose functions were then discharged by no less a personage than Hon. Franklin Pierce, now President of the United States. On laying the whole matter before him, he expressed much regret at the seeming implication of the "Granite State" in such acts of dishonesty and systematic fraud; at the same time confidently expressing the belief that the incumbents of two or three post-offices, to which I felt satisfied the difficulty was confined, could not be the guilty parties, as they were personally known to him.

Although I greatly respected his judgment, yet I ventured to suggest the possibility that his desire to think well of his acquaintances might have led him to view the characters of some of them in a too favorable light. So, in order to establish more firmly their trust-worthiness in my estimation, he kindly went over to the State-house, where the Legislature was in session, and confidentially consulted the representatives from each of the towns in question.

One of the members thus consulted, and who readily endorsed the favorable opinion of the Attorney, happened to be *a brother of the post master who had done all the mischief,* as it was afterwards ascertained. I have reason to believe, however, that this gentleman was not aware of his brother's delinquencies, and that he was incapable of doing anything to countenance or forward such dishonorable practices.

One of the lost letters contained several twenty dollar notes on one of the Boston banks. On the occasion of a public Exhibition, held at the close of the term, in the Academy before referred to, a large number of visitors from abroad were collected together, and as money at such a time would be circulating in the town more freely than usual, it seemed not unlikely that one or more of those bank notes might find their way into the current of business, and furnish, by their identification, some clue to the perpetrator of the robberies. With this hope, I inquired privately of several merchants in the place, whether they had recently taken any such bills, and learned from one of them that, about two weeks before, at the time of the Exhibition, several of those or similar bills had been offered for exchange by a stranger, which fact would perhaps have attracted no particular attention, were it not for the absence of any apparent object in this exchange. The imperfect description of the stranger which I obtained, agreed tolerably well, as far as it went, with that of Mr. F., post master in the town of C., where was one of the offices through which the many missing packages should have passed.

The most decided mark of identity which was furnished me, was a brown overcoat, cut something after the Quaker style, which my informant remembered to have been worn by the stranger for whose accommodation he had exchanged notes similar to those described. Deeming it unsafe to inquire of any neighbor of the suspected post master whether he possessed such a coat, I adopted the expedient of attending, on the following Sabbath, the church of whose congregation he was a member, for the purpose, of course, of listening to a good sermon, not forgetting, however, under the scriptural license furnished in Luke xiv. 5, to look about now and then for the Quaker coat and its owner,—a wolf in sheep's clothing. I observed the frequent characteristics of a country congregation,—a noisy choir, a gorgeous display of ribbons and other "running rigging" by the fairer portion of the audience, and a peculiarly ill-fitting assortment of coats, but never a Quakerish garment. By the time the preacher had drawn his last inference, I had drawn mine, namely, that it is easier to identify a man by his face than by his coat, inasmuch as he cannot lay aside the one, while he may the other. The day, indeed, was remarkably mild, and few overcoats made their appearance. Mr. F. was present, however, at both services, as I afterwards learned, and occupied a seat in the choir,—a *base* singer, probably.

I have now to mention one of those singular coincidences which are so frequently brought about, as if with the design of aiding in the exposure of crime, and of pointing out its perpetrators with unerring accuracy. The numerous instances which are every day occurring, illustrative of this principle, leave us no room to doubt its truth. "Murder will out," and so will all other crimes. Let the guilty one envelope himself in a seemingly impenetrable cloud of secrecy; let him construct, ever so cunningly, the line of his defences, sparing no pains to fortify every exposed point, and to guard against every surprise; yet some ray of light, darting, like the electric flash, he knows not whence, will pierce the darkness which surrounded him; some hidden spark will kindle an explosion, which will bury him and his works in ruin. "Trifles light as air" harden into "confirmation strong as words of Holy Writ."

Assuming that the aforesaid coat, if it had any connection with the author of the robberies, was probably manufactured at the only tailoring establishment in the place, I happened in there on Monday morning, and inquired of the presiding genius his price for a respectable overcoat, intending in some roundabout way to find out whether he had made one like that which I was in pursuit of.

"That depends," replied he, "on the material and style of making."

While continuing a desultory conversation with him on the subject of coats, their various shapes and styles, &c., my eye fell upon a small slip of paper pinned to the sleeve of a garment hanging near the door, and on approaching it, I found the name W. F. written upon the paper.

"That coat belongs to Mr. F., our post master," remarked the knight of the goose. "It was a trifle too small, and I have been altering it."

Its color, unusual length, and peculiar make, were circumstances almost conclusive to my mind of the identity of its owner with the individual who had been exchanging the twenty dollar notes.

I bid the tailor good morning, feeling pretty well satisfied that I had laid the foundation of a more important *suit* than any which his art could furnish.

The distance from this place to the town where the academy was situated, was about twenty miles, and the next thing to be done was to ascertain whether F. had been there within a week or two. A little reflection suggested a tolerably safe and direct mode of ascertaining this fact, which was, to see the merchant before referred to, as being cognisant of the passing of the twenty dollar notes, who had already been partially informed of the object of my former inquiries concerning them; and to request him to address a line to Mr. F., inquiring whether he recollected seeing a person, apparently insane, in the stage-coach, while on his way home after the Exhibition. This certainly could do no harm in case he was not present on that occasion, while if he had been, he would very naturally confirm the fact in answering the question proposed. The next mail brought a reply to the effect that he did not return home by the stage, but in his own private conveyance, and therefore saw no such person as the one inquired about.

I had thus made a beginning in laying a foundation for the superstructure of evidence which I was endeavoring to raise; a foundation, of which a tight coat was the corner-stone. If Mr. F.'s outer garment had not required alteration, I should, up to this time, have failed in establishing a most important fact, viz., his probable identity with the individual who passed the bank notes; and as long as this point was involved in much uncertainty, I should hardly have felt prepared to push my researches with much energy or hope.

The following facts were now in my possession: Mr. F. was in the same town where the Exhibition was held, and upon that occasion; his general appearance corresponded to that of the person who had then and there exchanged the notes; and his position as post master gave him sufficient opportunities to have committed the robberies. All this seemed to authorize and require more definite and concentrated measures on my part.

In the mail from Boston, which was to pass on that route on the following day, sundry tempting-looking packages might have been found, which were not altogether valueless in a pecuniary point of view, and would assuredly have been missed had they been stopped anywhere short of their place of destination. In other words, these packages were what are called *decoy letters,*—a species of device for entrapping the dishonest, which will always be effectual, and whose detective power the shrewdest rogue is unable to withstand. The utmost sagacity will never enable one to distinguish between a decoy-letter and a genuine one, so that the only way of securing safety from these missives is to let all letters alone. The coat of arms of Scotland—a thistle, with the motto "*Noli me tangere,*"—would be an appropriate device for these paper bomb-shells.

This set of packages, however, passed the suspected point

in safety on this occasion, and several times afterwards, for the very good reason, as it subsequently appeared, that, in the absence of the post master, an honest person overhauled the mails.

The snare was laid once more, and with better success.

Upon a certain day, as the mail was leaving Boston, a letter containing some fifty dollars, in good and lawful money, duly marked and recorded, that it might afterwards be identified, was placed in the package of letters for the post-office which had suffered so many losses before, and to pass through the office over which he of the tight coat presided. This package was watched by the Special Agent for the distance of seventy miles or more, until it had arrived unmolested within ten or fifteen miles of the suspected office.

About this time I again fell in with General Pierce, who kindly offered to act in concert with me until the result of that day's experiment should be decided; he taking the stage which was to convey the mail, and I intending to follow after by private conveyance, both to meet again, and to examine the contents of the bag after it had passed the office at C. The object of this temporary separation, as my readers will readily see, was to prevent the possibility of any recognition of my person, which might have been incurred had I been seen traveling with a gentleman so well known as the Hon. Mr. Pierce. Much curiosity would inevitably be manifested to know whom the U. S. District Attorney had with him, and speculations on the subject might approach too near the truth for the interests of public justice.

The united efforts of the sixteen legs which impelled the "leathern conveniency" containing my friend, the Attorney, were soon too much for the four that hurried along "Cæsar and his fortunes;" and the first-mentioned vehicle ere long was "hull-down" in the distance. I had often been over this route before, yet in some incomprehensible way, either by turning off too often, or not turning often enough, I got upon the wrong road, and came near making a bungling job of it. Pressing

4*

on as fast as possible to get a glimpse of the stage once more, I had driven furiously for several miles, until, becoming convinced that I was not likely to overtake it though I should go in that direction till doomsday, I halted at a farm-house which stood near the road, and addressed a man who apparently had been engaged in cutting wood in the yard, for he stood, axe in hand, with an unsplit log lying before him. The sound of my wheels had undoubtedly arrested his attention. Dropping his axe with alacrity, he lounged up to the fence, and leaned his elbows upon it, evidently prepared to refresh himself after his bodily toil, with a little social intercourse.

"Is this the road to G.?" said I.

"What are yer in such a darned hurry for, now," replied my interlocutor. "I've heerd them air wheels of yourn a rattlin, rattlin, this half hour by spells, and I don't bleive I've cut the vally of an armfull of wood all that time. I do'no what She'll say."

Here he glanced uneasily over his shoulder towards the house, as if he feared *Her* awe-inspiring presence.

"But, my friend," I remonstrated, "this don't tell me anything about the road. I *am* in a hurry, and no mistake; and I'll be much obliged to you, if you will give me a short answer to a short question."

"Wal, if that's all you want, mebbe I can 'commodate yer. 'Taint no use keeping on this ere road. Ef you should drive ever so fast on't, you couldn't never git to G. Cause it don't go there! Wal, you wanted a short answer, so I'll give it to yer. That are beast o' yourn hes some good pints. Wal, ef you want to git to G.—lemme see,—never bin on this road afore, hev you?"

"Of course I haven't," replied I, somewhat testily.

"Then you wouldn't know nothin about the old Hoxie place; no, sartin you wouldn't. Wal, abeout two mild furder on, you'll come to a brick house with four chimblys, jist where another road comes in. You turn to the right by the brick house, and that'll bring you to G."

"How much further is it to G. this way than it is by the direct road?"

"Wal, 'bout four mild."

Upon this, I was about starting, when he called out, "I say, mister, don't you want to trade hosses? I——"

"What yer boout there, Jerry," exclaimed a shrill voice from the house, which could be no other than that of the redoubtable "She"—"not a stick of wood in the house, and you a loafin there on the fence. I tell you——"

Her further remonstrances were lost to me, but I doubt not that the luckless Jerry received a suitable reprimand for his delinquency.

Here I was then, having four miles further to go than the stage, and my horse beginning to show unequivocal signs of fatigue. As the stage driver knew nothing of our plan, the probability was that he would pass the next office long before I could arrive and examine the mail bag. In this emergency, I could think of nothing better than to leave horse and carriage at some place on the road, and obtain a saddle-horse, with which I might succeed in "coming to time." And after turning at the "brick house with four chimblys," I was gladdened by the sight of a tavern some half a mile beyond, to which I hastened with all practicable speed, and lost no time in inquiring whether I could obtain a substitute for my overdriven animal.

The landlord was prompt in answering my demand, and forthwith ordered his hostler to put the saddle upon "Bob." While Bob was being "got up," I found myself the object of many inquisitive looks from the assemblage of tavern loungers, to whom my arrival was a rather unusual windfall; for it was not every day that the intervals between drams were enlivened by such a comet-like approach. The team wagons and other vehicles which frequented the road, and whose motions were as methodical as those of the planets—the tavern being the sun of their system—produced no emotions in the minds of these idlers, like the unexpected appearance of an unknown body like myself, coming no one knew whence, and going no one could tell where. One of two alternatives seemed forced on them by the "hot haste" of my movements. The stranger was either a pursuer or the pursued. If he was the latter, what had he been doing? And if the former, of what had somebody else been guilty? These perplexing questions were settled in a manner apparently satisfactory to them, by the inquiry which I made of the landlord, whether he had seen a man pass that way on horseback, leading another horse, which I described minutely. The anxious audience at once jumped at the conclusion, as I had intended they should, that I was in pursuit of a horse-thief, which impression I took care to strengthen by sundry incidental remarks. It seemed necessary by some such device to prevent all suspicion of my real character and object, in order that if I failed in executing my design this day, the case might stand as well as before.

By this time "Bob" had been saddled and bridled, and issued forth from the stable, equipped for action, under the auspices of the hostler. He (to wit, Bob,) was a stout Canadian pony, rejoicing in a peculiarly shaggy mane, and a tail which was well calculated to add completeness to my comet-like character. He was strong of limb, and evidently quite as competent as any quadruped that could ordinarily be found, to carry me to my destination within the required time.

As soon as I was fairly in the saddle, some one among the small crowd assembled to witness my departure, gave a slight whistle and made a sound something like "he up," whereat the treacherous Bob went through a series of gymnastic performances highly gratifying to the select audience in front of the tavern, and occasioning a display on my part, of equestrian accomplishments which I was never before conscious of possessing. The pony elevated himself upon his hind legs so as to assume an almost perpendicular posture, giving me much the attitude of Napoleon as he is represented in David's well-known picture, "only more so." After standing thus for an instant, he commenced a rotary movement, still upon two legs,

and coming down, reared in the opposite direction a few times, before he saw fit permanently to resume the horizontal position, I, during this period of revolution, hanging by his neck (my *main* stay,) and losing off my hat in the ardor of my embraces.

While I was thus the sport of circumstances, the spectators indulged in various jocose observations, which then seemed to me exceedingly ill-timed and impertinent. One suggested that I was a Millerite, and was endeavoring to "go up" on horseback, at the same time expressing a desire to know what I would charge for an extra passenger; while another inquired what direction I proposed to take in my pursuit of the imaginary horse-thief; intimating a willingness to be in his place, so far as concerned any danger of being overtaken by me.

"Well done!" exclaimed the jolly landlord, as Bob reassumed his quadrupedal character.

"No, no," replied I, "there's too much *rare* meat in him for that."

Under cover of this sally, I made a triumphant retreat, the landlord leading Bob for a little distance, lest he should be inclined to repeat the entire programme. While thus engaged, Boniface explained the conduct of the horse, by informing me that he formerly belonged to a person who had taught him the trick, which he would always attempt to go through with when instigated thereto by such a sound as I heard when I mounted him. With many apologies for the occurrence, "mine host" let go the bridle, and I proceeded to find out what Bob could do with his whole force of legs. This performance was more satisfactory to me than his former one, and as we flew along, his tail and my coat-tails streaming in the air, I seemed to myself an embodiment of the design upon the seal of my commission, and was inwardly amused to think how soon the ideal post-rider and his steed had found their real representatives in the persons of myself and Bob.

In this style we dashed onward, and as I reined in my panting charger before the door of the hotel in G., the stage was just ready to start, the driver being seated on his official throne, whip and reins in hand, looking the picture of impatience. He would have been gone before this, had not the District-Attorney interceded for a short delay. This gentleman was standing in the door of the post-office, appearing very much surprised at my want of punctuality. A hasty explanation produced a smile, and the remark, that it was a "good joke."

A doubt which I suggested, as to the safety of examining the mail in the presence of the post master, was set at rest by my companion, who assured me that he was certain of the integrity of this functionary, and also informed me that he had been made acquainted with the object of our call, before my arrival. The post master being a merchant, there was, among the other miscellaneous articles which compose the stock of a country store, a fair assortment of gentlemen of leisure, sitting upon the counter, and reclining in graceful attitudes upon the boxes and barrels. Our unusual movements inspired them with unwonted vigor, and an ardent desire was manifested on their part to know what hidden mystery lurked within the recesses of the mail-bag, which we were about carrying to a room above, in order to be out of the way of observation. Two of these gentlemen, thirsting for knowledge, hastily formed themselves into a committee of investigation, and followed us up stairs, until they were summarily relieved from the discharge of their self-imposed duties by a peremptory intimation from Mr. Pierce, that we wished to be alone for a short time.

As soon as we had secured ourselves from intrusion, the bag was hastily unlocked, and its contents turned upon the floor. Each package was taken up, separately and carefully examined, but the all-important one, whose absence would indicate unerringly the guilt of the suspected individual, was not there! This was the most trying and responsible moment of all, as it is always found to be in such investigations—the moment when it is discovered that the trap has been sprung, and the rogue is almost within your grasp. For experience has shown, that missing a "decoy-letter," and establishing in a legal manner the guilt of the individual who is known to have intercepted it, are two very different things. Much caution is requisite in the management of these cases, in order to leave no loop-hole of retreat to the culprit. Too hasty movements might spoil all, by alarming him before he had put it out of his power to account plausibly for the detention of the letter; while a too long delay might enable him to increase materially the difficulty of obtaining direct evidence, by affording him an opportunity of disposing of the necessary proof,—the letter itself, and the contained money.

In the present instance, it was considered that a too speedy return to search for the absent package, might result in finding it in a perfect state, allowing of the explanation by the post master, that it had been left over by mistake in overhauling the mail, which would have put the case in a capital shape for a tolerably sharp lawyer to defend. We therefore concluded to allow several hours to elapse before making a descent upon the premises, the time being mainly occupied in drawing up the requisite papers, and procuring the attendance of a proper officer to serve them.

All things having been prepared, we started, at about nine o'clock in the evening, for the post-office in question. The office itself was in a small building, some twenty rods from the post master's house, and as we approached the premises, no light was visible, excepting in one of the chambers of the dwelling. There, accordingly, we directed our steps, and a few raps upon the door brought down the post master, light in hand, who at once recognised "Squire Pāarce," as he called the District-Attorney. This gentleman politely requested him to step over to the office, to transact some business, the nature of which he did not then explain. The post master expressed his readiness to accompany Mr. Pierce, remarking that he must first leave him a moment, in order to go to another part of the house for a lantern. Some such manœuvre on his part had been anticipated, and he was closely watched—in fact,

Mr. Pierce went with him—while absent on his errand, to deprive him of an opportuuity of secreting any money that he might have on his person.

On reaching the post-office, he was introduced to the Agent, whose first object was, to get an admission from him, that he was present when the mail arrived from Boston that day, that he overhauled it alone, and that he had at this time no packages on hand to go by the mail Northward the day following. These points having been ascertained, the subject of the numerous losses on that route was broached, and the fact plainly stated, that they had been traced to that office; which piece of information was received by the post master with the utmost apparent self-possession. Indeed, he seemed exceedingly surprised to hear of the various frauds which I enumerated, and professed entire ignorance that anything of the kind had occurred, assuring me that if such things had been done, my suspicions as to his office were utterly groundless.

"Do you receive much money in the course of your business, Mr. F.?" I asked.

"Some," was the laconic reply.

"Have you much on hand now, and is it here, or at the house, or where is it?"

"I don't know that my duty to the Post-office Department compels me to answer such questions—to strangers, anyhow," replied he, with an air of defiance.

"Then," said I, "*my* duty to the Department will require me to dispense with further interrogatories, and proceed to satisfy myself as to the present state of your finances in some other, and more direct way."

"Well, Squire," said he, turning to Mr. Pierce, "I want to know if you have brought this man here to bully me, on my own premises, and accuse me of doing things that I never thought of, to say nothing of his impertinence in inquiring into my private business affairs. Let him find out what he can about them. I sha'n't help him."

The District-Attorney assured him that all was correct; that his rights should be protected; and that he had better furnish the required information as to his means, and allow us to examine any funds he might have on hand. This, the Attorney suggested, would be the course which a regard for his own interests should lead him to adopt.

After much grumbling, and giving vent to his dissatisfaction by the remark, that "he didn't see why he should be picked out, and treated in this way," he reluctantly complied with my somewhat urgent request to be allowed to look at the money in his possession. Handing me his wallet, he awaited the result of the examination with all the composure he could command. He must have inferred, from what had been said, that it was in my power to identify whatever money he had that was unlawfully obtained, yet with the consciousness that he was thus open to detection, he did not flinch, nor betray but in a small degree, the heart-sinking that a knowledge of his perilous situation could not fail to produce. These were my first thoughts, but I afterwards had occasion to believe that he was not aware of the overwhelming proof against himself which he supplied as he passed his pocket-book into my hands. A hasty examination of its contents revealed unmistakable evidence of his guilt, for on consulting the description of the bills mailed that morning in Boston, to go some twenty miles above this point, every one of them was at once identified!

"Mr. F.," said I, "this money I saw placed in a letter in Boston, this morning, to go some distance above you; how came it in your wallet?"

For some time the unfortunate man was speechless. He had continued so long in his course of fraud, that the ground had begun to feel firm beneath his feet, when all at once this gulf opened before him, about to swallow up everything that man ought to hold most dear: character, liberty, the love and respect of his fellow men, and even property—a thing of comparatively little importance—for restitution would justly be required.

5

The words in which one of Milton's fallen spirits addresses a brother angel, might appropriately be applied to this victim of the lust of gold.

> "If thou be'st he;—but O, how fallen, how changed!"

Yes, indeed, how changed! He had occupied a high position in community, enjoying the confidence of every one; and had been elected to places of honor and trust by his fellow-citizens, before his appointment to this office by the general Government. What was he now? What would he be when it should be known everywhere that the exemplary Mr. F. had been guilty of a felon's crimes, and was likely to meet with a felon's doom? How could he ever face again his children, already deprived of one parent by death, and about to lose another by that which is worse than death? Ah! if crime presented the same aspect before its perpetration that it does afterward, how vast would be the diminution of human guilt!

The District-Attorney and Sheriff having purposely retired for a few moments, I took occasion to represent to F., in as strong a light as possible, the disappointments and distress which his unprincipled course had occasioned among the pupils of the academy, at the same time urging him, if he had not destroyed their letters, to produce them at once, that they might be forwarded to their rightful owners. He did not deny that he was the author of all the mischief; and stated that the letters he had taken had been destroyed, but that the money—several hundred dollars—was invested in real estate, and could be restored.

After I had ascertained these important facts, I consigned the criminal to the Sheriff's hands, in virtue of the warrant which had before been made out, as I have already mentioned. The Sheriff returned to the house with him, to allow him to make some preparation for a night's ride, and as they issued from the dwelling, I noticed that F. had on the identical Quaker coat, which had been to him what the robe of Nessus was to Hercules,—a garment bringing unforeseen destruction to its wearer.

The trial of the prisoner was held in due time, and its result furnished no exception to the truth of the Scriptural declaration respecting the way of transgressors.

Before closing this narrative, I should mention that measures were taken to secure the restoration of their money to those who had been defrauded by this man's dishonesty. It was, however, a slower process to heal the wounded feelings, to re-establish the broken friendships, and to reproduce the lost confidence, of which he had been the guilty cause. Whether he ever regained his lost reputation, I am unable to say.

A long course of upright conduct may and ought to obliterate the memory of former crime, but the commission of such crimes ordinarily raises additional barriers in the way of a virtuous life; and too often it were as hopeful a task to collect the fragments of a diamond which has just been dashed upon the pavement, and attempt to reconstruct it in its original beauty, as to gather up the remains of a ruined character, and endeavor to restore it to its former lustre.

CHAPTER II.

A competent Assistant—Yielding to Temptation—An easy Post Master—Whispers of Complaint—Assistant embarrassed—Application to his Uncle—The Refusal—Value of a kind Word—Resort to Depredations—Evidences of Guilt—Decoy Letter taken—The Bowling Saloon—The Agent worsted—The Restaurant—Bother of the Credit System—The fatal Bank-Note—Keen Letter to the Agent—The Arrest—The next Meeting.

THOSE who are connected in any way with the administration of the law, find their sympathies excited in very different degrees by the several cases which they have in hand from time to time. Although the ruin of character is to be deplored under all circumstances, yet it never gives rise to greater commiseration and regret than when it destroys more than ordinary capabilities for adorning and profiting society. Such were the capabilities possessed by Thomas L., the subject of the following sketch.

I have rarely, in my official capacity, come in contact with a young man who was more richly endowed with acuteness of intellect, brilliancy of talent, and fascination of manners; and in addition to these gifts of nature, he had received from a devoted mother those lessons of morality and religion which she fondly hoped would guard him from the dangers that might beset his path. Well was it for her peace of mind that she was removed to that world "where the wicked cease from troubling, and the weary are at rest," while yet her beloved son retained an unsullied character, and the respect of his fellow-men.

Such was the young man whose fall I have to record. His employer, the post master, was a man of ample pecuniary means, independent of the emoluments of his office, and, as is often true in similar cases, giving but little time or attention to the discharge of its duties. Nor was his immediate superintendence necessary, so far as concerned the details of business, for his young Assistant, though only eighteen years of age, kept everything in complete order, and so administered the office, with the occasional assistance of a younger lad, as to give perfect satisfaction to all who had dealings with it, and to render the angel-like visits of the post master a matter of very little consequence to the public. But this universal popularity, and the absence of supervision and of restraint, other than that supplied by his own conscience, were circumstances unfavorable to the preservation of his integrity, and laid him open to the temptations which so easily assail those of like character and similarly situated.

The most gifted and socially attractive are always peculiarly exposed to danger of this kind, and nothing short of firmly established principle can be relied on for safety. Doubtless, the truths which his departed mother had endeavored to impress upon his young mind often sounded their tones of warning in his ears; yet they were too weak to be heard in the roar of the stream which was bearing him along to destruction.

A few drops of water seem of little importance. They may sparkle as dew, they may form a rainbow; but when, united to others, they rush onward as a mighty torrent, sweeping everything before them, we may see how pleasing and often apparently trifling are the beginnings of evil, and how irresistible are its downward tendencies to those who put themselves within its power.

The usual enticements of a moderate-sized Massachusetts country village,—the sleighing parties, dancing schools, balls, refreshment saloons, bowling alleys, &c., conspired in this case to invite considerable expenditures, and the subject of this sketch, in his attempt to keep up with the course of extravagance and unthinking dissipation upon which his companions had entered, who could better afford the expense, found his means entirely inadequate to this end; but before making the discovery, he had been committed to the whirlpool of fashionable pleasure too far to extricate himself without much difficulty.

The first effects of this course began to show themselves in the frequent closing of the office in advance of the proper time, and the opening of it at irregular and often unseasonable hours. Whispers of complaint were heard on the part of business men, which, coming to the ears of the post master, were followed by some *gentle* remonstrances,—gentle they necessarily were, for circumstances already related had given the boy too much consequence (rendering his services, as he well knew, quite indispensable) to allow him to bear patiently anything like a "blowing up" from his too easy employer. For a time, however, this remissness ceased, and like some noble ship struck by a heavy wave and brought to a momentary stand, while driving onward to shipwreck, this promising young man appeared to pause in his dangerous career, and for a while all seemed to be going on well. But the improvement was only temporary. The importunities of his companions, innocent perhaps of any vicious design, again diverted his attention from business, and he was soon fairly in the old track of pleasure-seeking, regardless of the sacrifice of time or money.

Having the entire control of the post-office funds, and not being required to account for the money collected till the close of the quarter, he at first ventured to use these funds in a limited way, to pay the more urgent demands upon him, trusting, as he afterwards expressed himself, that "something would turn up," he knew not what, to enable him to replace the money before the quarterly settlement with his confiding employer. As the time approached, he discovered with dismay that the deficiency amounted to some seventy-five dollars.

How to make this good was a perplexing question, which occupied his daily thoughts and disturbed his nightly slumbers. He was proud-spirited, and up to this time, had enjoyed an unspotted reputation. Discovery must be averted at any rate.

At this juncture, the thought of some property which his widowed mother at her death had left for him in the hands of a relative living at a distance, came to his relief, and he resolved to lose no time in applying for aid in that direction. A frank and full statement of his real situation would no doubt have brought him the desired aid, but, as will be seen in his letter of application to his uncle, he was induced to give a false reason for his need of funds, and the cold, business-like reply which followed, is such as would naturally be expected from one who had no sympathy with the weaknesses of youth, and no disposition to inquire with a kindly interest into the affairs of his young relative. Had this reply been different in its tone, it might have drawn out the requisite explanation, and have effectually prevented what afterwards occurred.

Here are the letters :

E——, Mass., February 16th, 1849.

My dear Uncle,

I am in need of some funds, say seventy-five dollars. I have foolishly loaned about that amount in small sums to a friend at school here, upon whose word I thought I could depend, when he promised me he could replace it at any moment I desired. I shall consider it a great favor if you will accommodate me.

Your affectionate nephew,

THOMAS.

To this the following reply was received :—

New York, February 19th, 1849.

My dear Sir,

Your letter of the 16th inst. is before me, soliciting the sum of seventy-five dollars. This singular request has very much surprised me, as in the first place I have no available means in my hands belonging to you, and besides, if I had, I should not be in a hurry to relieve you from the embarrassment which you seem to be in, as it may learn you to be more cautious in future.

I have understood that your compensation is ample for your support, if you are economical; but if you lend your money to spendthrifts, and get swindled out of it, it is your own affair. This is the opinion of

Yours, &c.,
HENRY S——.

It can be imagined how much a response of this description was calculated to open the heart, or invite the confidence of the unfortunate Thomas. His pride felt sorely the repulsive tone which his uncle adopted, and the supposed disgrace of making an unsuccessful application for money, to say nothing of the slurs cast upon his own discretion, and the honor of his companions. At this critical juncture in the character and affairs of the young man, such a cold rebuff was like a death-blow to all purposes of future fidelity and honesty; and as I listened to this part of the instructive narration, I could not but feel that the uncle, by withholding needed sympathy and aid, was in some degree responsible for the after course of his erring nephew.

All hope of assistance in this direction having been abandoned, desperation suggested a further departure from honesty.

"It is but a little more risk," whispered the fiend. "Take enough to make this quarter's account square, and you will come out right somehow before another settlement."

Weakened conscience was unable to withstand the pressure of circumstances, and the plausible scheme proposed for relief. So, money letters, which heretofore had been perfectly safe, were emptied of their contents to meet the present exigency.

Indications not to be mistaken, that some one was robbing the mails in that vicinity, soon began to appear, though among all the complaints, not one referred to the loss of any letter mailed at or addressed to the office at E. They all related to important letters posted at other offices, but passing through E., and it was not until all sorts of tests and experiments had been tried in vain at other points, and every other mode of operation exhausted, that the Agent took up temporary quarters at the private residence of an acquaintance, from which, without being observed, he could overlook this office, hitherto the least suspected on the route.

The opportunity afforded after dark of taking a glance at the interior of the office and its principal occupant, through the glass boxes in front, was of course properly improved, and this little experiment furnished, as the result showed, an important clue to the whole matter; for on the first evening's watch, I discovered what I deemed evidence of the clerk's guilt.

Stepping silently and unnoticed into the vestibule of the office, and gaining a position whence I could observe his motions, I distinctly saw him thrust what appeared to be a letter into the stove, afterwards taking up a wallet from the table and placing it hastily in his pocket. I must have made some slight noise, for after doing this, he suddenly turned and looked sharply in my direction.

This may have been nothing more than the instinctive glance of distrust which those who have not the entire control of themselves are apt to cast around after doing something that they would dislike to be detected in.

However it may have been, thinking that he had discovered me, I stepped boldly up to the "general delivery," and inquired for a letter for "Robert Marshall, railroad contractor," taking occasion to observe him closely as he was engaged in running over the letters. He seemed confused, his hands shook a little, his face was flushed, and his voice was inclined to tremble, as he replied that there was "nothing for Robert Marshall." I attributed all this to fear lest his previous movements might have been observed, and left the office, strongly suspecting that Thomas L. was the author of the depredations in question.

A few experiments in the way of "decoy letters," mailed

so as to pass through that office, soon converted suspicion into certainty. One of these letters, containing sundry bank-notes, disappeared, and one of the notes was traced directly back to his hands. How this was done, the reader will probably insist upon knowing, and it is my intention to gratify this thirst for information, although in so doing I shall be compelled to reveal a degree of unskilfulness in the game of ten-pins which would deter the most sanguine gamester from betting on my head.

In the basement of the hotel was a bowling saloon, which, as I had ascertained, the suspected clerk was in the habit of visiting in the evening, after closing the post-office, and this fact suggested my plan. I might have arrested and searched him at once, but I thought it the better way to watch the money exchanged by him, in the hope that some of the missing bills might thus come to light.

For if he should chance to have none of these about his person, a search would spoil all, by putting him on his guard, whereas if he should offer none of them, no harm would be done, and things would remain *in statu quo*.

With these views I made a confidant of the landlord of the hotel which contained the bowling saloon, and agreed to meet him there early in the evening for a "roll," and arranged that in case the young man came in as usual, my partner should excuse himself, and substitute L. in his place, to oblige a stranger, who, of course, was rolling merely for exercise.

My design in making this arrangement was to fasten the expense of the evening's recreation upon L. by a brilliant and overpowering display of my skill in bowling, calculating that he would probably pass some of the stolen money in payment. This was my programme—how it was executed I shall proceed to show.

"Mine host" and I had been rolling perhaps half an hour, when a fine-looking, well-dressed young man entered the saloon, whom I at once recognised as L. The landlord and myself happened to be the only ones then engaged in playing, as it was rather early in the evening for the appearance of most of those who resorted there; so L. watched our game for a while, till the landlord, looking at his watch, remarked that he had an engagement which must be attended to immediately, and turning to L., said,

"Here, Tom, you take my place with this gentleman, for I've got to go away."

"Enough said," replied Tom. "I am always on hand for most any kind of a *ball*."

As I looked at the pleasing features and intelligent countenance of the young man, a pang of sorrow shot through my heart, to think that over his head the invisible sword of justice was even now suspended. But such reflections are unprofitable, inasmuch as they tend to unfit one for the discharge of painful duty. So I dismissed them as far as I could, and applied myself to my double game—

> "Rolling down at once, by a double stroke,
> A man, as well as a pin."

The first roll of my new antagonist shook my faith in the feasibility of my plan, for the ball went clattering among the wooden platoons like the grape-shot at Balaklava, and in an instant ten *block heads* bit the dust.

"A rather bad beginning," thought I; "but I don't believe he can do that again."

Comforting myself with this reflection, I applied all the practical and theoretical skill I was master of, to vanquish my experienced foe. I called to mind my long dormant and slender knowledge about the angles of incidence and reflection. I considered the nature of resultant forces, and the effect which a ball impinging on pin A would have upon the uprightness of its neighbors, B, C, &c. I thus devised theoretical "ten strikes," which (doubtless from some defect in the reasoning) would fall short of my ideal standard by as much as four or five pins; and on several occasions, the ball strayed almost innocuously through the ranks, prostrating only one or two of the outposts. I had a few transient gleams of light when my adversary grew somewhat careless, perhaps from continued success; but darkness soon returned upon my prospects, and I saw in my mind's eye the money coming from my pocket and not his.

We held but little conversation during the progress of our game, for my thoughts were preoccupied with my ultimate object, and L. made no great effort to overcome my taciturnity; yet some casual remarks were made which showed that he identified me as the person who inquired for letters for "Robert Marshall, railroad contractor."

After playing thus for some time, he invited me to take a glass of ale, which proposition I gladly accepted, as it would give me one more chance to know something about the contents of his pocket book. I began to think that my toils were nearly over, and as we stood imbibing the fluid, I could hardly wait until the glasses were emptied, in my impatience to see the bank-note produced which was to settle at once the bill, and him.

Delusive anticipations! The credit system interposed to crush my hopes, for L. said to the bar-tender, "Put it down to me, Jim."

As "Jim" put it down, *I* felt put down, and followed my companion back to the alley as humbly as if we had changed places, and I was the suspected one.

"Come, Mr. L.," said I, after we had resumed our game, "you play so much better than I that you will be safe in giving me some little advantage. Just allow me twenty on a 'string,' and let me see if I can do any better at that."

"Very well, sir," said he, "I will do it, although I am afraid you will be too much for me."

But I was not, and after playing until the establishment closed for the night, I found myself under the disagreeable necessity of paying some three dollars for the privilege of being thoroughly defeated, deducting the benefit received from more than two hours' hard work!

One other expedient suggested itself, namely, offering in payment a twenty dollar note, in the hope that the proprietor, finding it inconvenient to make change, would call on the victorious clerk to accommodate him, and thus would bring to light the missing bills. But this device also failed.

I did not yet "give up the ship."

"I don't know how it is with you, L.," said I, "but I feel rather empty about the epigastric region, after such a pull as you have given me, and I should think you might afford to treat a fellow."

"Well, I don't care if I do," said he. "*I* feel a sort of gnawing under my vest. Come up stairs, and we'll get something."

To this I replied that I was tired of the noise, and would rather go to some more quiet place. He readily assented, and led the way to a neighboring restaurant. We ensconced ourselves within one of the curtained recesses, and here I devoted myself to the consumption of as much "provant" as my digestive organs could dispose of, with the intention of running up as large a bill as possible, in order that a bank-note might be offered in payment, and the desired proof of my companion's guilt secured. I saw through the corner of my eye that he seemed to be studying my physiognomy, and the thought came into my mind that his readiness to "treat" was owing to his wish for a good opportunity to find out something more about me. We had begun to talk about various kinds of occupations, and he inquired,

"Is not your business a profitable one, Mr.—Marshall, I believe?"

I acknowledged the name, and said that my business was anything but a profitable one.*

"Isn't it a rather ticklish one, now-a-days? so much rascality you know."

---

* See Act of Congress establishing the compensation of Special Agents.

"Yes, but I mean to look out sharp for rogues, and to be pretty sure that I deal with people I can trust."

"I have a very good situation in the post-office," said he, "but I sometimes wish to be where I could have more variety —some kind of business that would require me to travel."

"You had better be contented where you are," replied I; "this seventeen-year old fever never did any one much good. If you are faithful in your present place, you will have no trouble in getting a better situation a few years hence."

To this he made no reply, and the conversation dropped.

After I had appeased "the sacred rage of hunger," and added some works of supererogation in that line for the furtherance of my object, we emerged from our retreat, as "the iron tongue of midnight" was tolling twelve, which sounded to me like the knell of my companion's doom, for I felt confident that the time had now come for the *denouement* of the two-act drama which we had been playing that evening. It seemed extremely improbable that there should be here any accommodating "Jim" to score down the little bill for future settlement. But there was. We went up to what was then the bar, but in these temperance times would be called the "office," and L. said to the presiding genius, with a familiar and confident air, "Just charge that to me, and I'll make it all right."

"Rather all wrong," thought I.

As we passed out into the darkness of the night and stood for a moment on the steps, I thought I discovered, by the faint light of a street lamp, my companion observing me with scrutinizing glances, thus seeming to indicate a suspicion on his part that our rapid acquaintance and companionship had not been without some design, which he was desirous of penetrating. Indeed a fear of this produced anything but agreeable reflections after we had separated, and I had retired to my lodgings. Could it be that a suspicion of my real object had prevented him from paying for the ale, and settling the bill at the restaurant? It seemed possible, certainly, yet under other circumstances I should have thought nothing of the occurrence, and he seemed to be satisfied with the "dodge" of the "railroad contractor."

Then came a doubt as to the wisdom of the policy I had adopted, in allowing him to be at large, instead of arresting him at once on the disappearance of the decoy letter. Several days had elapsed since it was taken, and the probability of finding any part of its contents upon him, hardly seemed to warrant a resort to that course now; so, on the whole, I concluded to persevere in the cautious line of policy with which I had commenced.

In the course of a conversation which I held with the aforementioned landlord, on the following day, the fact came to light that he had a claim against L., for money loaned. It occurred to me that an urgent application for its repayment might accomplish the desired object, and I requested the landlord to assist me in this way. He readily complied, and after a second appeal the debt was discharged, and among the money, which I lost no time in comparing with the description of that purloined from the letter, was a five dollar note that I at once identified as one of the stolen bills.

Notwithstanding this overwhelming evidence as to the origin of the mail depredations on this route, there were good reasons for further delay in making the arrest, especially as it seemed unlikely that the person detected would know anything of his real situation for a few days. During this interval, I found it necessary to visit a neighboring city. The reader may judge of my surprise at receiving, two days afterwards, a letter, of which the following is a copy:—

Sir,

I have ascertained, no matter how, that you are the "railroad contractor" whom I met in the basement of the hotel in this place a few evenings since, and who partook of my hospitalities afterwards at M——'s saloon. Also that you entertained and perhaps still entertain some doubts of my honesty, as a clerk in the post-office here.

I am sorry you had not the candor to say as much to my face, and thus afford me the opportunity of satisfying you as to my standing and character among those who have known me best and longest. You are welcome, sir, to all the advantage you obtained in your underhanded dealings with me on the occasion referred to; if, however, you cannot prostrate private character faster than you can ten-pins, I think I have but little to fear at present.

Yours, *not* very respectfully,
THOMAS L——.

To J. Holbrook,
Special Agent, P. O. Dept.

How this clue to my official identity was obtained, I failed to discover at the time, and have been no wiser on that point at any period since. Nor was it of much account, as the information, from whatever quarter derived, came too late to be of any avail, and after he had exposed himself by passing the money which had been placed in the mail to detect him. When he was preparing the above epistle, congratulating himself on my want of skill at prostrating "private character," little did he think that I had already achieved a sweeping "ten-strike" in his own case!

The necessary complaint was made, a warrant issued, and the unfortunate young man taken into custody by the U. S. Marshal. I shall never forget the indescribable look which he gave me as he entered the office of the U. S. Commissioner, for a preliminary examination. It was the first time we had met since the memorable roll and supper, and the quondam "railroad contractor" now first appeared to his eye transmuted into the formidable "Special Agent."

There was little surprise in his look, but an expression of mortified pride and anger, as he addressed me in a low tone,

"I thought I should meet *you* here!"

"Well, Thomas," said I, "I don't know as you will believe me, but, I assure you, I heartily regret that you are brought to this pass, and if the ends of justice could be answered, I should be the first to let you go free."

"Perhaps you would," replied he, moodily. "It's easy enough to say so."

"But," I remarked, "I want you to take a reasonable view of the matter. You cannot think me so destitute of common humanity as to wish to place any one in such an unpleasant position, much less a young man like yourself, so capable of better things."

He appeared to be somewhat impressed by the earnestness with which I spoke, and answered in a softened tone,

"I suppose I ought to believe you, but it seems hard to be entrapped in the way I have been."

"It may be the best thing that could have happened to you under the circumstances," said I, "and I sincerely hope that it will prove so."

I was desirous of making him see that I was actuated in the course I had taken by no motive other than a wish to discharge my duty faithfully, and therefore left him for the time to consider what I had said, confident that a little reflection would calm his ruffled temper, and lead him to a correct view of the case. In this I was not mistaken, and when I urged him to make a confession on the ground of justice to others, and his own interest, he "made a clean breast" of it, and gave in substance the account of his downward course, with which the reader is already familiar. He expressed much regret and penitence, and a mournful satisfaction that his mother was not alive to know of his disgrace.

It seems unnecessary to pursue the subject further. The force of the lesson it is calculated to teach would not thus be increased, and the feelings of some might be harrowed up, who should rather receive sympathy and consolation.

CHAPTER III.

Business Rivalry—Country Gossiping—Museum of Antiquities—New Post Master—Serious Rumors—Anonymous Letters—Package detained—Bar-room Scene—*Ram*ifications of the Law—First Citizens—Rascally Enemies—Lawyer's Office—Gratuitous Backing—Telegraphing—U. S. Marshal arrives—The Charge—The Fatal Quarter—Enemies' Triumph—The Warrant—Singular Effects of Fear—A Faithful Wife—Sad Memories—The Squire's Surprise—All right.

THE jealousies and rivalry often existing between persons of similar occupations, which supply the truth contained in the old proverb, "Two of a trade can never agree," are fostered and strengthened in small towns to an extent which is not as conspicuous, and perhaps not as frequently observed in larger places. For this general spirit of emulation and strife is greatly aggravated by the interest that almost all the inhabitants of small communities feel in the sayings and doings of their neighbors.

This interest is too often manifested by reporting from one to another hasty and ill-considered speeches, which should be suffered to die where they are born; but thus set in motion by careless tongues, for the benefit of itching ears, they roll on like snow-balls, and attain a size and shape hardly recognisable by those who gave them their first impulse.

An incidental, but an important consequence of these circumstances, is the ready formation of parties about almost every quarrel that may arise in such a village. The tranquil surface of country life is in this way disturbed, like that of a still lake by the plunge of a stone into its bosom, and the resulting waves, in both instances, extend indefinitely in every direction.

The bustling little town of H. was not exempt from the evils at which I have glanced, for the half-dozen shopkeepers who supplied the inhabitants with their necessaries and luxuries, fully exemplified the truth of the proverb above quoted. Their rivalry, however, was not exercised by and toward one another impartially, but it was rather a contest between the old, established merchants of the place, and one whose coming was of a comparatively recent date. It was, in short, a competition between Old and Young America.

The old school merchants affected to look with contempt on their younger brother and his goods, suggesting that, however alluring his prices and commodities might be, his customers would find to their cost, that "All is not gold that glitters." Hints were thrown out about calicoes that "did from their color fly," and sugar that was not entirely soluble in hot water. It was also darkly intimated that B. (the merchant in question) couldn't stand it long at the rate he was going on, rashly keeping his assortment full all the time, instead of cautiously waiting until an article was ordered, before he sent for it. This sort of thing would never do. It was sure to bring him to ruin.

On the other hand, the enterprising B. ridiculed the clique of "old fogies," as he termed them, and characterized their establishments as "Museums of Antiquities." In accordance with the spirit of the age, he lined his shop with vast handbills, printed on type of stupendous size, so that he who runs might read; with such headings as "The only Cheap Store!" "Fresh and fashionable Goods at Low Prices!" "This Stock of Goods bought within the present Century!" and other wonderful announcements, which drew the susceptible public within his doors to a greater extent than was agreeable to the feelings or the interests of his "slower" competitors.

And as if all this was not enough, by way of climax to his prosperous course, B. received the appointment of post master. The post-office, as a matter of course, always brings an increase of business to the store where it is kept; and in the present instance, B. did not fail to secure all the advantages arising from his position.

And so successfully did he manage his affairs, with this additional impetus, that one or two of his opponents, finding many of their customers deserting them by reason of the superior attractions of the "new store," abandoned the field in disgust, determined, however, to lose no opportunity of undermining the object of their jealousy, or at least of injuring his prospects.

Rumors, detrimental not only to his reputation as a man of business, but to his character as a post master, soon got abroad. How they originated, no one knew; whether they had any foundation in truth, no one could say. The baseless reports which malice invents, have no more permanent effect upon an upright character, than have flying clouds upon the mountain which they may temporarily obscure; and it is only when rumors are weighted by truth, that they can injure materially the object at which they are aimed.

> "Honor dwelling in the heart,
> Welcome friends or welcome foes.
> Whensoe'er it doth depart,
> Smiles are weak, but strong are blows."

Anonymous letters were despatched to the Post Master General, expressing a want of confidence in the management of the office, and hinting at something of a more criminal nature than mere official carelessness and neglect; but as such complaints are always disregarded when unaccompanied by responsible names (being considered the result of personal rivalry or malice), nothing was done in the premises.

These unknown correspondents, however, did not cease from their machinations, and it soon came to the ears of the obnoxious post master, that he had been assailed at head-quarters; unjustly, as he claimed. So he lost no time in repelling the "vile slanders" through the medium of sundry long-winded communications to the Department, the burthen of which was, that business rivals had done it all; and that the ridiculous stories which had been set afloat, originated entirely in the unworthy design of building up their authors on the ruins of his good name. And in the most indignant terms he courted, and even demanded, a careful investigation of his official acts and his private character.

These various communications on both sides were all referred to the Special Agent, that he might establish either the truth or the falsity of the charges made against this post master.

The first step was to obtain a private interview with some of the complainants, who were traced out by means of the specimens of their handwriting furnished by the letters they had sent to the Department.

They readily admitted themselves to be the authors of those documents, after having been assured that the Government had no other object than to ascertain the truth, and to protect the rights of the citizens who had an interest in the post-office. I gave them to understand that the Department required something more than mere assertion as a ground for decided action; and suggested, that if those charges were well founded, which represented the loss of valuable letters posted at that office, their truth could be shown by furnishing a list of such letters, and a statement of all the facts, by the parties immediately interested.

As had been stated, the accusers of B. proved to be his rivals in trade, and their active friends, animated and impelled by that bitter competition of which I have already spoken.

In addition to the causes to which I have alluded as especially influential in country places, to produce such a state of feeling, may be mentioned a sectarian spirit, the bane of many small villages, creating needless prejudices, dividing the community into discordant fragments, and forcing a man to stand, in a degree at least, not on his own merits, but on the preference of the sect with which he may be connected. This sentiment is in some measure natural, and unavoidable. Similarity of opinion tends to create favorable prepossessions toward those who thus agree, but is ever liable to produce an exclusive feeling which does injustice to all concerned.

Thus arises much of the sympathy and preferences which are so strongly felt in small communities, especially towards merchants and professional men.

Dr. Wilkins goes to our meeting, therefore he is a good doctor, whatever other folks may say. Mrs. Garfield, the trader's wife, is *such* a good woman, and did so much in fixing up our church and the vestry, that we must all "patronize" her husband, and sustain him against his enemies, who oppose him solely on account of his activity, and that of his family, in building up "our society." Dr. Wilkins may not be eminently successful in the treatment of his patients, and Mr. Garfield may be far from remarkable for his moderate prices, yet their enthusiastic friends stick to them through thick and thin.

All these things must be taken into the account in pursuing investigations like those which I had just commenced, and due allowance made for the disturbing forces acting on the minds of those who undertake to furnish the required information. The rubbish of selfishness and gossip must be thrown aside, and only those statements regarded which are corroborated by sufficient evidence.

Acting upon this rule in the present instance, but willing, in justice to the accused as well as to the public, to follow up even the accusations of open enemies, I instituted careful inquiries in the right quarter, which soon established the fact that there was a screw loose not far from that post office, if not directly in connection with it. But for some weeks previous, no letters had been disturbed which were deposited in or addressed to this office, the failures having been confined to the mails which passed through it and were there assorted. This circumstance rather confirmed suspicion than otherwise, for the post master being aware of the complaints sent to Washington, would consider it necessary to use greater caution in carrying on his depredations (if he were guilty,) especially in regard to the class of letters taken. But in such cases, as in those that come under the supervision of medical art, various applications are required according to the changes in symptoms and circumstances.

For instance, I might perhaps have worked to this day in the ordinary line of experiments, such as depositing special test letters in that office, or sending them to be delivered there, and all to no purpose. They would, for a time at least, have been the object of special care, and particular pains would have been taken for their safe dispatch; while if dishonesty really existed, it would seek out and avail itself of such opportunities as would not be likely to betray it, or to attract the attention of the self-constituted "vigilance committee," which had already sounded the alarm.

With such views, I adopted a species of "decoy" which I thought best suited to meet the exigencies of the case. In the first place a document was prepared addressed to an imaginary firm at Rouse's Point, New York. It read as follows:

Boston, March 20, 1850.

Messrs. Baxter & Clark,

Gentlemen,

Herewith you will receive twenty-five dollars and fifty cents, the balance of my account, and for which you will please send me a receipt as soon as convenient.

When does either of your firm intend to visit Boston? I like the articles you last sent me very much better than the former ones, and so say my customers,—will send you another order before long.

Very Respectfully Yours,

F. P. Crane, Jr.

Bank notes of a small denomination were used to make up the twenty-five dollars named in the letter, and two American quarters enclosed, to make it more attractive; both bills and specie having been marked, and a full description of them taken.

Another letter, written in a different hand, addressed to a lady, and containing nothing of value, was also prepared and placed in a note envelope, to accompany the above *business letter*. Here is a copy of it:—

Boston, March 19, 1850.

My Dear Cousin,

Since you visited us, we have experienced important changes. Our family is pretty much broken up by George's death. Father and mother depended so much on him to manage our out of doors affairs, that they don't feel like keeping house any longer, and have gone to boarding, and as I shall not have any particular household cares, I expect to be floating about, like many others of the sisterhood of old maids, ready to make myself generally useful.

Perhaps I may inflict a visit on you in the course of the summer, and help you to take care of *that baby*. I can't stop to write any more, for we are hardly settled after moving. Father and mother send love to you and husband.

Your Affectionate
SARAH.

My object in sending this second missive was to prevent any suspicion that otherwise might arise in regard to the money-letter. For it might reasonably be presumed that the accused post master would be on the watch for anything that could by any possibility compromise him; and a solitary letter containing funds, passing through his office, might "give him pause," in case he should have any desire to appropriate its contents.

Both letters were directed to Rouse's Point, N. Y., regularly post-marked at the Boston post-office, and the post bill also made out for Rouse's Point. But on the outside wrapper was purposely written the name of the office which I wished to test. This would excite no suspicion, for mistakes such as this appeared to be, do sometimes occur in the hurry of making up the mails. Instead of putting the package into the mail, however, I conveyed it myself to a point near the town of H., and saw it placed in the pouch just before it reached that office.

The question now to be settled was, whether on taking off the wrapper (marked "H." as the reader will remember,) and finding the enclosed letters directed to another place, he would forward them to their address, as was his duty, or would appropriate them to himself, believing that they had come there in consequence of a mere accident, and that if he should see fit to take possession of them, the circumstances of the case would effectually conceal his crime, and render search unavailing.

It may be said that this was carrying temptation too far. By no means. What degree of integrity should be reasonably required, let me ask, of a person in the service of the public, occupying a responsible position like that of a post master? upon whose fidelity depend the prompt and safe transaction of business, and the security of many other interests of social life. Will a valetudinarian virtue answer the purpose? a virtue strong against weak temptations, but weak against strong ones? The man whose principles cannot withstand every degree of enticement to dishonesty, is unfit for any place of trust.

Furthermore, the combination of circumstances which I have just described, might occur in the experience of any post master throughout the country, and the sufferers by the unfaithfulness of an official so tempted, would hardly be satisfied with being told that he could have resisted any ordinary enticement, but that such an opportunity was too good to be lost.

It should be borne in mind that up to this time, the party whose character was involved in these investigations and experiments, was totally unaware of the visits of the Agent to his neighborhood.

The *mis-sent* package referred to, arrived at the office in H. on the evening of the day that it left Boston, and should have been remailed and forwarded on the following morning; but a close examination of the contents of the mail-bag soon after it left H., failed to bring to light the hidden treasure. No package for Rouse's Point made its appearance.

This, however, did not make out a clear case against the "persecuted" official, neither did it justify his arrest.

It occurred to me, on failing to find the letters referred to, that the wrapper in which they had been enclosed, might have been used in sending off other letters that morning, it being the custom in most of the smaller offices, as a matter of economy, to use the same wrappers several times by turning or reversing them. A short search produced the paper in question, which I removed from the package it enclosed, and substituted another in its place.

Here was an additional proof that the decoy package had reached the office at H., and had been opened, as the new address upon the wrapper was in the post master's hand-writing. He could not therefore say that he had never received such a package at his office, or should he make such an assertion, as he would be very likely to do if he were guilty, the production of this envelope would shut his mouth, and go far to prove his evil intentions.

But the case, at this stage, was very far from being a clear one against him, and he yet had a chance, if he were an honest man, of coming out triumphant over the efforts of malice, and the wiles of his "persecutors."

The removal of the wrapper and its use in enclosing other packages was all natural enough, being, as I have said, agreeable to the frequent custom in such small offices, and even the non-appearance of the Rouse's Point letters might yet be accounted for on the supposition that he had laid them aside to be forwarded, and had forgotten them; or that not observing the name of the town to which they were addressed, he had placed them in the "general delivery," where they might at that moment be lying unmolested.

Desirous of affording the suspected man a fair chance to

prove his innocence in this matter, if that were possible, and acting in accordance with the above-mentioned charitable suppositions, I allowed two other opportunities of remailing the letters to pass, but after searching in vain for them on both occasions, I resolved to wait upon the post master and talk over freely and frankly the subject of his enemies' attacks, believing that he would not for a moment dream that I had any connection with the missing package, even if he had purloined it,—a calculation which afterwards proved to be perfectly correct.

Accordingly I proceeded to the hotel at an early hour in the morning, intending not to seek an interview with him till after breakfast, and while waiting in the bar-room I overheard the following conversation. For convenience' sake I will indicate the different speakers by letters of the alphabet.

Mr. *A.* (to C. just entering the room.)—"Good morning, Mr. C. Are you 'armed and equipped as the law directs' to go over to F?" (a neighboring town.)

C.—"You mean by that, I suppose, whether I have laid in enough cigars to last till I get there, and patience enough to hold out till I can get back."

A.—"It will be a tedious business, that's a fact. Here's nobody knows how many going over from this town; no end to the witnesses, and no end to the case, *I* don't believe; at least not this term of court."

"Yes," broke in a rough-looking bystander, "the court 'll set and set, and never hatch out nothin' but a parcel of goslins for the lawyers to pluck."

A.—"We can't dispute you, L., for you've been one of those same 'goslins,' I believe."

L.—"No I haint, I've been a darned sight wuss,—a great goose. I swow it makes me mad with myself whenever I think on't."

"Come, daddy L.," spoke up a free and easy specimen of Young America, "tell us about that great law-suit of yours. I never heard all the particulars."

"Wal, young man," returned L. solemnly, "I'll tell you all

about it, hopin' it'll be a warnin' to you never to have nothin' to do with the law.

"About fifteen, mebbe sixteen year ago, afore you'd got through hollerin arter your mammy, I used to keep considerable of a lot of sheep, and one year I bought a ram that I'd taken a fancy to jest because he was sech an all-fired big feller, and had sech thunderin' curly horns. I got him pretty cheap, and arter I'd had him awhile, I found out the reason on't. He was the darndest buttin', jumpin' feller that ever *I* see. There couldn't a calf nor a colt nor nothin' about his size come into the pastur where he was, but what he'd be arter it and knock it into a cocked hat if he could git a lick at it. Fact, he pretty much killed two or three likely calves that I had, but the colts was mostly too lively for him. He couldn't often hit 'em.

"Wal, I kinder hated to kill the feller, he was such a buster, so I shet him up in a little three-cornered lot so's to have him out of the way till the calves was killed off or had got bigger. But what did the rascal du but go to buttin' agin the stone wall that kep him out of neighbor Bliss's patch o' rye; and afore he'd bin there tew days, he knocked a hole in't and got into the rye. It was a kinder out of the way place where the lot was, so he had a chance to stay there all night, and 'praps a little longer. Anyhow, when Bliss found it out, he was hoppin' mad.

"He's rether techy any time, but he'd bin a braggin' on this ere field o'rye, how he was goin' to beat the hull town on it, and to have that old ram a nibblin' and trottin' threw it, and a spilin on't, sot his dander up. I was willin' to a' paid him suthin' for damages, but his charges was tew hot for me. Told him I'd see him darned afore I'd be imposed upon in that shape. Wal, he said he'd sue me, and sure enuff he did.

"We kept a lawin' on it considerable of a spell. Fust the court gin him his damages; then I 'pealed, and the case kept a gettin' put over somehow or other, till the 'all wool *suit*,' as the lawyers got to callin' it, come to be a standin' joke, and I was heartily sick on't. Wal, finally we contrived to settle it, and arter payin' Bliss about what he fust asked, I had my costs to see tu, and I went to Squire Sharp, my lawyer, to see what *he* was a goin' to charge me for his *sarvices,* as he called it. He was jest as smilin' and clever as a baskit o' chips.

"'Take a seat, Mr. L.' says he, 'I'll find your little account in a minit. Pleasant mornin', sir, good growin' weather.'

"Wal, I set down and found out purty soon that I'd got 'bout fifty dollars to pay for his *sarvices,*—blame 'em!

"'Now,' says I, 'Squire, that air's a good deal o' money for a man like me tu pay, and I don't blieve I can raise it all tu wonst. P'raps you'd take part out in *pro*duce, jest ter 'commodate.'

"'Oh, yes,' says he, 'Mr. L., I'll take anything you've a mind to bring.'

"'So,' thinks I, 'I'll git red of one plague by the means;' and I went home and got the old ram and carried him up to the Squire's house.

"'Good mornin', Squire,' says I, 'I've brought the fust instalment on my little account.'

"'The deuce you have,' says he, 'what do you suppose I'm going to do with that old buck?'

"'Donno, Squire,' says I, 'all I know is that you said you'd take anything I was a mind ter bring, and this ere ram is *legal tender,* anyhow.'

"Wal, he saw he was kinder stuck, so he 'greed to take it, and 'low me five dollars.

"I heerd arterwards that the Squire put the ram into an empty hog-pen, to keep him until he could sell him, but the darned critter went over the top on't, and tackled Miss Sharp, the Squire's wife, that happened to be a stoopin' down, weedin' her posies in the gardin, upsot her, and then put arter little Jim, one of her boys, and floored him, and ended off with knockin' down a crazy old well-curb, pitchin' into the well, and breakin' his neck, or drowndin' himself, I donno which.

"That's the end of my experience in law. The old ram cost me, fust and last, about a hundred dollars."

After the conclusion of this instructive narration, the general conversation, which for the time had been suspended, was resumed, and I gathered from what was said that the post master was one of the principal witnesses in the trial above alluded to by Messrs A. & C.; that arrangements had been made for an early start, as the place where the court was to be held was some twelve or fifteen miles distant, and that the hotel where we were was the place of rendezvous.

I observed narrowly every new-comer, and soon a well-dressed, intelligent-looking man, apparently about thirty years old, entered, whom I took to be the very gentleman I wished to see. My conjecture respecting him proved to be correct, for it was not long before some one addressed him, inquiring whom he had engaged to take charge of the post-office during his absence.

Deeming it unsafe to delay longer, I beckoned him out of the room, unnoticed by others, and in a friendly and familiar manner, introduced myself, taking care to throw him off his guard by remarking, that being in that vicinity I had concluded to make him a call and satisfy myself whether the complaints made to the Department respecting him were just or otherwise, adding that in many of these cases similar complaints had their origin in personal disagreements, or business rivalry.

"I am delighted to see you," he replied. "I am gratified that the Department has at last authorized some one who is impartial, to look into its matters here, and if I can have a day with you, I will convince you by the testimony of the best men of all parties, that the stories detrimental to me are the invention of enemies, who seem determined to put me down if possible. But they haven't succeeded yet, and what's more, they can't succeed. Things have come to a pretty pass when a man can't carry on a more flourishing business than his neighbors, without being set upon and slandered out of his life.

"I am summoned to-day to attend court, but if it is inconvenient for you to wait till my return, I shall run the risk of being in time to-morrow, with my testimony, as this business is of vital importance to me and mine, and must not be neglected, come what may."

"It *is* very important," I replied, "and my advice is to risk the displeasure of the Court, and ask some of your friends to explain your non-appearance."

He concluded to follow my recommendation, and we walked over to the post-office, and retired within its sanctum, where we remained some time, combining pleasure with business, by inhaling the vapor of as good cigars as the mercantile department could furnish, while examining the post-office books, and the post master's general arrangements, and discussing various matters relative thereto.

My chief object was, if possible, to get a sight of the contents of the boxes where the two "decoys" should be if they had been mistaken for local letters, and placed in the "general delivery." The one enclosing the bank-notes and specie would come under the initial B., and this box contained quite a number of letters which I thought it unsafe to examine particularly. While I was endeavoring to devise some plausible mode of getting a satisfactory view of them, some one fortunately entered the store and inquired if there were any letters for John Barstow. All the B's were at once taken down by the post master, thus giving me exactly the opportunity I wanted of observing each letter, as he was running them over. The last one was reached, but the *mis-sent* document did not appear; so one important requisite for proving his innocence seemed entirely cut off.

Soon after, we started out to call on some of the "first citizens," as he termed them, but I readily discovered that the select few to whom I was being introduced, although evidently sincere in the opinions they expressed, were a little biassed in his favor by one motive and another; and that they were quite as likely to be deceived as those whose interests, perhaps, fully as much as their regard for a faithful administration of the post-office, had led them to scrutinize more closely the conduct and principles of our injured friend.

Among those of his backers on whom we called, was a lawyer of some note in that region, who had recently received a nomination for Congress from one of the leading political parties. On our way to this gentleman's office, the post master, as my readers will easily suppose, took care to inform me thoroughly respecting these important particulars. Squire W. was evidently a tower of strength to him, and he spared no pains to impress upon me the great truth, that whomsoever the Squire thought fit to endorse, possessed irrefragable evidence of an immaculate character. We fortunately found the would-be future M. C. in his office, no other person being present than a law student, also a warm friend to my companion, who quickly withdrew, owing probably to some silent intimation from one or the other of the gentlemen present, that his room was, for the time being, better than his company.

This was not, by the way, the post master's first visit here to-day, for he had stopped in as we were passing in the morning, leaving me a moment for that purpose, on which occasion he doubtless suggested our visit, and the importance to him of a pretty strong backing.

He appeared immensely delighted to think that he had been able to bring me, a "green" Agent, upon whom his character with the Department depended, into contact with one whose assurances were to dispel all the clouds that lowered about his head, and reveal him to the community with the double effulgence of injured innocence and undimmed integrity. This pleasing prospect seemed to beget an exuberance of spirits which rather astonished his friend, the Squire, as I judged by the occasional expression of his countenance.

"Now, Squire," said the post master, slapping him gently on the back in a persuasive manner, "I want you to tell this gentleman just what you think about the opposition made to me in this village. You know we have always been opposed in politics, and of course you are entirely disinterested in the matter. All you want is to have the office here well managed. You have heard all about the charges that some of my rascally enemies have made against me, and I believe I told you the other day, that they had sent complaints on to Washington. We'll see how their slanders turn out when the Agent here gets through with investigating the matter. All I want is the truth."

"Yes, yes, I see," said the Squire, clearing for action, by putting an extra stick into the stove, and materially lessening the contents of a good-sized snuff-box that stood upon the table. "It's just as my friend B. says, Mr. H——," continued he; "we've always belonged to different parties in politics, and are connected with different religious societies,—in fact, we don't seem to agree on anything of that sort. But I never mean to allow such things to affect my estimate of a man's character, and I hope I shall always be ready to do any one justice, however he may differ from me in opinion.

"The case, Sir, stands thus: Here is a young man fortunate enough to be possessed of more industry and enterprise than some of his neighbors, and accordingly succeeds in business better than they do. Their envy is excited, he incurs their ill-will, and they attempt by slander to ruin his character. I don't think any of them would lose by exchanging characters with him. No, Sir," (fortifying his position with another pinch of snuff,) "all these charges are utterly without foundation, save in the brains of those who produced them,—a narrow foundation enough, in all conscience, for anything.

"I have, perhaps, as great an interest in the proper management of the post-office here as any one, as I receive and send through it probably more important correspondence than any other man in town; but I have never had cause to complain, and, so far as I know, everything has gone right."

Here a moment's pause followed, which the lawyer improved by replenishing the stove and his facial promontory. The post master cleared his throat, gave the Squire an approving nod, and rocked back and forth upon the hind legs of his chair, picking his teeth in a nonchalant way, apparently much at his ease.

"By the way, Squire W.," he broke out, rather suddenly, "perhaps the gentleman would like to hear about that letter that Marshall mailed here to go to New Haven, Ct., and which was misdirected to New Haven, Vt."

I replied, that I should be happy to hear any statements that would throw light on the subject in hand.

"Well," said the Squire, "there was a great handle made of that affair. You see, this Marshall is a careless, absent-minded genius, and he wrote a letter, into which he put fifty dollars for his old mother in Connecticut, and it didn't get there. Well, he came and consulted me about it, and wanted me to sue B. here, for the money.

"'Why, Mr. W.,' said he, 'I'm confident that B. has got it. People say he can't be trusted, and I believe it now.'

"'But see here, Marshall,' replied I, 'there are twenty offices or more between this place and the one where you sent your letter; and it is, to say the least, quite as likely to have been purloined anywhere else as here. You had better wait a few days, and I will make inquiries, and do what I can to find out whether B. knows anything about it. If it should appear at all probable that he does, I can assure you that I will not hesitate to sue him.'

"So I put off matters for a little while, and before Marshall got very urgent again, the lost letter turned up in the New Haven, Vt., post-office; no one being to blame but the very man who had made all the fuss! The enemies of our friend here, who had all the time been chuckling to think they had him on the hip, felt flat enough, I assure you, when the letter came to light, for they would rather have paid over the fifty dollars themselves, than to have lost this chance of confirming their accusations against him."

This turn in the conversation gave me an excellent opportunity of trying the nerves, or the innocence of the post master, without exciting his suspicions in the least; so I remarked,

"The New Haven, Vermont, post master must have been an honest man, or this money letter might never have been seen again; as no one would have thought of looking there for it, and if they had, it wouldn't have been very easy to prove that it ever went there."

Here I glanced at B., but his countenance betrayed no consciousness that my observation was designed to hit him, and with an aspect of unruffled coolness, he proceeded to say,

"That New Haven case reminds me of something very similar, which happened in this office only a day or two ago. A package of letters came here from Boston, which were intended for a town in New York. By the way, Mr. Agent, I wish the next time you are in the Rutland office you would request the mailing clerks to be a little more particular in addressing their wrappers, as our packages, both of letters and papers, frequently go astray, while those for other offices sometimes come here. Surrounded, as I am, by so many prying and fault-finding people, failures caused in this way are likely to be seized upon to make me trouble."

I replied, that I would try to bear his request in mind, being all the time well satisfied that it was a device adopted to turn attention from the *mis-sent* package, to which he had unguardedly referred, and to prevent further allusion to it, which might awaken suspicion, and even betray guilt. He was indeed treading on dangerous ground. His voluntary admission, that a package similar to my decoy package had been in his hands, and that he had noticed the name of the place to which the letters were directed, was all that was wanting to confirm my belief that they had been purloined, since I already knew that they had not been forwarded from his office.

After our worthy legal friend had exhausted every illustration, and brought to view every fact at his command, corroborating his very high estimate of the post master's character, both personal and official, and had given the "enemies" the extremely low and degraded position which they, as maligners of spotless worth, and conspirators against tried honesty, ought justly to assume,—in short, after he had said, if not done, all that even the object of his advocacy could have desired, I proposed an adjournment for dinner, more for the sake of securing in that way an opportunity of telegraphing for the United States Marshal, than for administering to the wants of the inner man. The victim of calumny and myself separated at the door of the Squire's office, agreeing to meet again soon after dinner; and while he was dispatching his meal, I was dispatching a telegraphic message, which ran thus:—

"———, Esq., U. S. Marshal:

"Come here by first train. I will join you at the depot, and explain business."

Just as I had left the telegraph office, I was addressed in a very private and mysterious manner by a substantial-looking citizen, whom I had before observed eyeing me very closely. He wished to know whether I was the United States Mail Agent.

I informed him that such was the title of my office.

"Then I want an opportunity for some conversation with you about this business of the post office. I suppose you are here to examine into this affair, and are willing to hear both sides. There are some things in connection with the matter, which I think you ought to know."

"I was just going to the hotel for my dinner," said I. "Government officers must eat, you know, as well as other people, and for a while after dinner I shall be engaged; but if what you have to communicate is of importance, I will endeavor to confer with you before I leave town."

"I hope you will; and allow me one word now. I understand that you have been closeted with Squire W., and I want you to know something about his position in this matter. Everybody allows him to be an honest and a sincere man, but the fact is, he has been very active in effecting the removal of the site of the post-office from the other side of the river to its present location, and could hardly be called a disinterested witness in such an investigation as you no doubt intend to give the subject."

How far this dig at the Squire was just, I could not then certainly know; but a glance at his law dispensary and the post-office, distant from each other only a few rods, both being a good quarter of a mile from the old post-office site, gave some plausibility to the intimation that the Squire's interest and love for justice, happened in this instance, to run in the same direction.

My presence in the village had become pretty generally known, as appeared by various unmistakable indications, particularly some not very flattering remarks which I overheard at the dinner-table, such as "a one-sided affair," "consulting interested persons," "don't know how he expects to find out the truth," and the like; all of which I pretended neither to hear nor to notice. It was very evident that our man of letters hadn't many friends in *that* house, for those of its inmates and frequenters who were not in some way influenced by rival interests, were no doubt more or less disaffected by the removal of the post office from that immediate neighborhood.

As I was one of the last to leave the table, the usual cloud of tobacco smoke had taken possession of the bar-room, and was enveloping its occupants in an atmosphere

"Darkly, deeply, beautifully blue,"

when I entered the apartment devoted to the production of this mollifying vapor. The narcotic herb seemed to have lost its ordinary soothing power, for the company then and there present bestowed upon me glances cool and scrutinizing enough to dispel effectually any inclination I might have had for indulging a short time in the delights of social intercourse. So I seized my overcoat, and passed out; and this movement was the signal for a spasmodic giggle by the entire assemblage, in which the landlord joined, as I supposed, for I distinctly recognised his grum voice just as I closed the door, uttering, in a contemptuous tone, the following remark, "I guess the Agent don't like tobacco smoke!"

I was little disturbed, however, by these and sundry other indications that I was not establishing a reputation for impartiality and shrewdness with a majority of the citizens. If I were to listen to all they might be ready to tell me, I should be spending valuable time to no sort of purpose, for the proofs of the post master's delinquency which I had thus far obtained were derived, not from them, but from himself, and it was in that direction only that I could reasonably expect to obtain conclusive evidence of his guilt, for all the accusations which his enemies had sent to the Department had been supported by nothing better than the opinions of those who made them.

If I failed in securing what I expected from the course I was pursuing, it would then be time to see what other proof could be procured from different quarters; and until the result of my investigations should be known, I was content to rest under the cloud of misapprehension which appeared to be gathering about me, knowing that thus I could best serve the interests of justice, and that time would set me right with those who were now disposed to look on me as one whose mind had been preöccupied by the artful tales of the post master and his friends.

I must confess that I was somewhat amused to think what a complete metamorphosis my character would undergo in the eyes of almost every member of this little community, when the truth should come to light. I had sufficient confidence in the uprightness and candor of the Squire, to believe that he would readily acquit me of trifling, in the course I had pursued with him, and that he would acquiesce in the adoption of whatever measures the public interest might seem to have required. Nor was I in this instance the victim of misplaced confidence, as will hereafter appear.

The post master and myself soon met again at the post-office, when cigars for two were produced, and as we sat smoking them, I could not avoid a feeling of melancholy, at seeing him apparently so cheerful and happy, and sincerely regretted the necessity that compelled me to persist sternly in a course which would assuredly end in the blight of his hopes and the ruin of his character.

He was evidently certain of having fully established his innocence, and of having inspired me with some of the contempt for his persecutors which he felt himself. "We have met the enemy, and they are ours," seemed to be the language of his looks and actions, if not of his lips. The sky over his head appeared bright; the clouds, to his eyes, had dispersed; and he dreamed not that the roar of the next railroad train would be to him like the peal of thunder which accompanies the lightning's quick and deadly bolt. Yet I consoled myself with the reflection that my motives were such as should actuate every public officer in the discharge of his duty, and that I was not responsible for the consequences which might follow the carrying out of plans judiciously devised for this end,—an end which, in an important case like this, fully justified the means.

This train of thought was interrupted by the post master, who rather abruptly asked,

"Well, Mr. H., I suppose you have satisfied yourself about this affair; and, if it isn't asking too much, I should be glad to know what sort of report you are going to make to the Department?"

I was unprepared for this, and I confess I was for a moment nonplussed. But I evaded a direct answer, by relating what I had heard and seen at the hotel, and how displeased they all were with me for not giving them a chance to be heard in the course of my investigation. And wishing to divert his mind still further from the troublesome point on which he had touched, I ventured upon a few remarks about the painful and often disagreeable duties of a Special Agent, introducing, by way of embellishment, an anecdote of Post Master General Collamer.

In the course of a conversation between that officer and one of the western Special Agents, the matter of an increase of salary, among other things, was briefly discussed. Says the Agent,

"You know, Sir, that many times we are called upon to do things which can hardly be made to square with the code of honor; and in fact, we sometimes have to resort to downright duplicity and deception."

"Well, well," replied Judge Collamer, "I suppose you find yourself perfectly at home at that!"

This diversion answered the purpose, and nothing further was said about my intended report. Just as I had fairly extricated myself from this ticklish position, a messenger from the telegraph-office appeared, with a reply from the Marshal to my dispatch, which response I managed to read without the least suspicion of its nature on the part of the individual who had such a momentous interest therein.

The contents of the dispatch were simply, "I will leave by first train."

After having been introduced to a number of other swift witnesses for our friend, who *happened in* at the post-office, and holding some conversation with them on the all-absorbing theme, the iron horse's shrill neigh announced the approach of the train by which the Marshal was to arrive; and without much ceremony I took my leave, to meet him at the depot, promising to return again. He was the first man to alight on the platform, and was soon made acquainted with the business in hand. We thought it best that he should go directly to my room at the hotel, where I was presently to join him, in company with the post master; and ten minutes more found us there, sitting around as pleasant a fire as ever irradiated and comforted with its genial warmth, such a trio of officials. I had introduced the Marshal by his proper name and title, yet the announcement produced no visible effect upon the unsuspecting post master. He seemed as cool and unembarrassed as if he had been in the habit of forming the acquaintance of United States officers every day. This rather astonished me, as it did the Marshal, and he (the Marshal) favored me with a glance and a slight motion of the head, which intimated that, in his opinion, I had mistaken my man.

I had set it down as a fixed fact, that the appearance and introduction of the Marshal in his own character, would at once excite the apprehensions of the post master, and lead to inquiries from him which would render it comparatively easy for me to enter upon that decisive course of questioning and examination which the present advanced state of the affair required. But all my calculations were frustrated by this unexpected move on the part of my antagonist, and I was left *in statu quo*, so far as regarded any help I had hoped for from him. In this condition of things, all that remained for me was to make a bold push at once, and break the ice as speedily as possible. So, turning to the post master, I thus addressed him:

"Were you, Mr. B., at home, last Monday evening, when the Boston mail arrived?"

"I was," replied he, after some hesitation.

"Did you open and assort the mail yourself on that occasion?"

"I did."

"And did you find a package of two letters, mailed at Boston, and addressed to Rouse's Point?"

Here, for the first time, a change came over his countenance; and, after a moment's reflection, he answered very firmly, that he did not recollect any such package.

"One of the letters," continued I, "contained twenty-five dollars in bills, and fifty cents in specie, and the other contained no money, and was addressed to a lady."

8 *

He listened attentively, and repeated that he did not see any such letters as those I had described.

"Well, Sir," I observed, "we must now trouble you to show us the money you have about you."

He readily complied with this requisition, by handing me his pocket-book. It was well filled, but among a tolerably large roll of bank-notes, none of those included in the decoy letter appeared. His knowledge of the absence of these important witnesses against him, easily accounted for his promptness in submitting to the examination, and as he received the wallet from me again, and returned it to his pocket, his air of assurance, which for the moment had been dimmed, reäppeared in all its native lustre, and with an assumed expression of wounded pride, he requested to know if he was to understand that I suspected him of interfering improperly with the letters I had been inquiring about. To this I answered,

"Yes, Sir; you *are* so to understand me; and further, that I believe you have robbed and destroyed those letters!"

The Marshal was looking on all this while, evidently somewhat incredulous as to the justice of my accusations, for he had long known by reputation the young man against whom they were made, being an acquaintance of the family, and always supposed him to be an enterprising, honest person. Indeed, he told me afterwards, that he really thought, to use his own expression, that I "had put my foot in it." In fact, I began to think myself, that however certain B.'s guilt might be, it was likely to prove more difficult than I had supposed, to establish the fact legally.

One thing, however, remained,—to examine a quantity of specie, which I knew he had in his pocket, as he had frequently exhibited it during the day in the way of making change at his office. This also, amounting to some six or eight dollars, was promptly produced at my request, and laid on the table.

"Now," thought I, "the last card is dealt; let us see whether it will turn up a trump."

The evil spirit, which so enticingly leads people into scrapes, and is so reluctant to get them out again, true to its fatal instincts, had safely preserved the evidence of guilt in the present case. A moment's inspection of the different coins, brought to light one of the identical pieces which had been placed in the missing letter! It was thus described in the original memorandum to which I referred: "American quarter—dot over left wing of eagle; slightly filed on lower edge under date, 1850."

"Here is one of the quarters," said I, holding it up, "that was in the Rouse's Point letter,—marked and described in my memorandum, so that I could swear to it anywhere."

"Well, Mr. H.," said the post master, "I suppose this circumstance appears to you very strongly against me, and perhaps it is. But I should like a few moments' private conversation with you, if you have no objection."

Agreeably to this hint, the Marshal retired; but the post master remained silent for a while, resting his chin on his hand, and gazing into the fire with a countenance overshadowed by dejection and discouragement. The gloom on his features grew deeper and deeper, but at last he roused himself, and looked me full in the face, saying, in almost despairing tones,

"*Can* anything be done to save me? Oh, Mr. H., for heaven's sake, put yourself in my place for a moment! Think what it is to fight as I have fought for years, to defend my reputation against enemies who wanted to pull me down, and build themselves up on my ruins; and after holding my ground so long, to be blown to pieces, as it were in an instant! How they'll all exult! There's old P.; I can see just how he'll look, shaking his old fox head. 'Ah, I knew something was rotten all the time!'

"What can you do to get me out of this trouble? I can't have it so; I *must* have something done to save me from becoming the laughing-stock of my enemies."

"But," said I, "your enemies, as you call them, could have

done you no harm, if you had not supplied them with weapons yourself."

"That may be," replied he, mournfully, "but I assure you that this is my *first* offence. I had never dreamed of meddling with letters till this Rouse's Point package came in my way; but it didn't seem as if it could ever be discovered, so the temptation was too much for me."

(It is a curious fact, by the way, that almost all the cases of post office robbery we meet with are "first offences;" even those whose boldness indicates some little previous experience in such things.)

"What," inquired I, "did you do with the bills that were in the letter?"

"I sent them away," replied he, "the same day that I took them. Now, I've told you frankly all about the affair, and I hope you will contrive some way to save me from disgrace and ruin. Couldn't the business stop here, if I refund what I have taken, and resign my office as post master? I should be willing to do more than that, if it should be necessary."

I assured him that I had no power to make any such arrangement, and that I must leave the matter with the Marshal, who I supposed would be under the necessity of serving the process.

Thus speaking, I stepped to the door, and called that gentleman into the room, who proceeded forthwith to read the warrant issued against B. During the reading of that instrument, a sudden change came over the countenance of the unfortunate post master. He turned pale, and would have fallen, had I not prevented him. The Marshal and I assisted him to a bed that stood in the room, where he lay for a long time, prostrate in body and mind.

As I stood over him, attempting to revive him by the use of such means as were at hand, I thought how great must have been the shock which had so overpowered his faculties. His strength of body, and pride of soul, were, for the time, laid low. What a pity that he had not possessed the right kind of pride; not merely the ambition to rise above the machinations of his enemies, and put them under his feet, but the pride that despises a mean action, and dreads a crime more than its consequences. Such a feeling would have been a safeguard; but I was sorry to observe that, while he was confessing his guilt, the thought of his enemies' triumph over him was uppermost in his mind.

He had now somewhat revived, and wishing to calm his exasperated feelings, (which I supposed were in some measure the cause of his present condition,) by turning his thoughts to another channel, I inquired of the Marshal, in a rather low tone, whether he had any family.

"He has a wife, I believe," was the reply, and in a moment B. was saying to himself, his eyes still shut,

"Jane, Jane, what will *you* think? Don't despise me, if you can help it."

He went on for some little time in this strain, displaying a high regard for his wife's affection and good opinion, and an apprehension that he might have forfeited them by his misconduct; an apprehension utterly groundless—so far, at least, as regarded affection, for the undying flame of love in a true woman's heart cannot so be quenched.

Mrs. B., as I afterwards learned, was a most estimable woman, whose influence had doubtless been of great benefit to her husband. Alas! that the power of his good angel could not have triumphed over the temptation to which he yielded!

When he had recovered sufficiently to walk about, the Marshal took him in charge, and conveyed him to a neighboring town, where the United States District Judge resided, for examination. His friends, who were highly respectable, were informed by telegraph of his arrest, and gave the required bail for his appearance at trial.

Thus we have traced out an important part of the career of one whose character was laid low, not by his enemies, but by his own hand. And whenever I pass through the pleasant town which was the scene of these transactions, a shade of melancholy comes over me, entirely at variance with the general cheerful appearance both of the place and the surrounding landscape.

On one of the last occasions that I was in that vicinity, the train on which I was traveling stopped for a few moments at this station. It was a delightful summer's day, and if the objects which met my eye, as I gazed up and down the street, had not been, many of them, monuments to me of a melancholy history, I should have thought that the place yielded in beauty to few of the villages which adorn New England. But a stranger occupied the store where the unfortunate B. maintained the contest with his rivals; the post office was in other hands; and I was just turning away from a scene that suggested nothing but unpleasant reminiscences, when Squire W. emerged from the station-house, and cordially addressed me. This was the first time I had seen him, since our memorable interview in his office.

"Good morning, Mr. H.," said he; "how is the rogue-catching business now? I suppose you have disposed of a good many since you despatched B. so summarily. When I first heard of his arrest, feeling sure of his innocence as I did, I don't know that I should have been much surprised if you had come after me next; and I felt a little sore, to tell you the truth, to think that my endorsement of him had so little weight with you. But I have since seen that you were perfectly right about it, though I am sorry that poor B. should have turned out so badly."

Here the iron horse began to manifest indications of impatience, and shaking hands with the worthy Squire, we went our several ways.

CHAPTER IV.

High Crimes in low Places—Honest Baggage-masters—Suspicious Circumstances—Watching the Suspected—Shunning the Dust—Honesty Triumphant—An Episode—Unexpected Confession—The Night Clerks—Conformity to Circumstances—Pat the Porter—Absents himself—Physician consulted—The Dead Child—Hunting Excursions—"No Go"—Pat explains his Absence—His Discharge—The Grave-stones—Stolen Money appears—The Jolly Undertakers--Pat at the Grave—More Hunting—Firing a Salute—Removing the Deposits—Crossing the Ferry—Scene at the Post Office—Trip to Brooklyn—Recovery of Money—Escape—Encounter with a Policeman—Searching a Steamer—Waking the wrong Passenger—Accomplices detained—Luxuries cut off—False Imprisonment Suit—Michael on the Stand—Case dismissed.

Public confidence in the United States Mail, and in the integrity of those connected therewith, never perhaps received a severer shock than that which it suffered from the extensive robberies committed in the Summer and Fall of 1853, by Pat R., at that time a night porter in the New York Post Office. The range of *his* ambition was by no means commensurate with his humble station in life and the post office, and his menial occupation did not repress aspirations which could render him a fit rival to such men as Swartwout and Schuyler, both by the extent of his schemes of villany, and the success with which they were carried on.

He was no petty thief, content with doing a small but comparatively safe business at filching, or at least, satisfied to begin with the "day of small things;" but he had hardly taken the oath of office before its strength was tested, and it proved no greater restraint to him than a spider's thread to a wild buffalo. He at once plunged into the tempting field which lay before him, and grasped with a greedy clutch at every opportunity to enlarge his increasing store of ill-gotten wealth. He would sometimes add thousands to his hoard in a single night, and carried on these bold depredations for some time unsuspected, not because he was *above* suspicion, but because he was *below* it.

In other words, after these robberies had been pretty satisfactorily traced to the New York office, it was necessary to establish the innocence, so far as these losses were concerned, of a large number of clerks, before suspicion fairly rested on the guilty party. Thus, when the investigation was commenced, he was buried up, so to speak, beneath so many protecting layers, all of which were removed before he came to light. I will not attempt to give any idea of the quantity of labor necessary in this and similar preliminary investigations.

Some of the numerous complaints made to the Department and the post master of New York, involved large sums of money. Among them was a package of $2000 in bank-notes, mailed at Middletown, Conn., for Philadelphia, Penn. Another of $1800 from Bridgeport, Conn., to Zanesville, Ohio. Still another of $1400 from Joliet, Ill., to New York, and many other smaller sums, from $50 to $1000; also drafts, notes, checks, &c., to an enormous amount in the aggregate. None of these valuable remittances had been seen by any persons properly interested in them, after they had passed out of the hands of the senders.

Doubtless to those unacquainted with such matters, it may not prove much for the efficiency of the Special Agent to state that the thefts were occasionally repeated even after he had entered upon this investig-tion. But the Agent employed in this instance always preferred to catch the rogue, rather than frighten him, thereby leaving innocent parties under the ban of suspicion, as well as destroying all chances for the recovery of the property already stolen. And the benefits and propriety of that course were fully realized in the result of the important case under consideration.

As "it is the last straw which breaks the camel's back," so it is often the stealing of the last letter which aids in bringing to light the depredator of former ones.

I propose here to relate some details, which may be interesting, of the means taken to "narrow down" and trace out those extensive robberies, not so much on account of anything novel or original, adopted at this or any other stage of the investigation, as to demonstrate the value of a character that is proof against trying temptation; and the dangerous position of those who are not at all times thus fortified, although they may be innocent of the particular offences charged.

With but few exceptions, the mails in which the missing letters and money packages should have been conveyed to New York, would have come from the East by the express night trains, over the Boston and New York Railroad. Upon those trains, the mails were in charge of the baggage-masters, the regular mail or "route agents" being confined to the way mail-trains running at different hours of the day. A variety of circumstances, besides their good reputation, conspired to avert suspicion from these baggage-men. The mails were in "through bags," and it required a mail-key to obtain access to their contents; and besides, the robberies could not well be perpetrated in that way without collusion between several persons,—the express agents, and the conductors, all reliable men, having occasion often to visit the baggage car, which was always well lighted.

Accompanying the night express trains there were also "through baggage-masters," so called. Their duty was performed by two persons, one of whom left Boston and the other New York on each evening.

On privately consulting the officers of the railroad company as to the running of these men, it appeared that about all the losses had happened on the nights of one of them : a discovery which, as had been shown by experience in similar cases, was by no means conclusive, and yet of too much importance to be overlooked.

The individual thus involved knew me well, and it required no little manœuvring to get over the route as often as was necessary, without being observed by him. One night when thus endeavoring to avoid him, a very amusing incident occured.

The regular conductor soon after leaving Springfield, was taken suddenly ill, and procured the services of this identical baggage-master for a short distance, unknown of course to me. I was sitting curled up in the corner of the saloon of the first passenger car, when the door opened and the well known call of "Tickets, gentlemen," apprised me that he had found me out before I had recognised him, or at least had discovered that I was "aboard." But I made the best of it, simply remarking that there was the least dust there of any spot on the train.

Up to this time my ground of suspicion was mainly confined to the coincidence already mentioned between the dates of losses, and his presence on the cars. The investigation had not proceeded far, however, when another matter came to light, which increased suspicion in that quarter.

A citizen of New York called on me and stated that recently, just as the night train was starting from the depot in Canal Street, he handed this same baggage-master a letter containing money, which he asked him to take charge of, not having time to carry it to the post-office. He at first declined, on the ground that the conveyance of letters out of the mail was illegal, but finally proposed to receive it, and, if possible, to get it into the proper bag through one of the small openings between the staples. This was the last that was ever seen of the letter by the sender or his correspondent. The former having called on the baggage-master, had been told that the letter was crowded into the right mail-bag, as promised; but the statement was not believed, and the circumstance happening in the midst of other troubles on the same line, seemed to constitute an important step in the progress of discovering the author of all this mischief.

A very shrewd acquaintance of the man of trunks, in Boston, was confidentially employed to ascertain something of his habits, and the state of his finances. After a fair and faithful trial, he reported to me, that the aforesaid superintendent of baggage was "as steady as a model deacon, and as poor as a country editor within fifty miles by railroad, of a large city." And that "although always ready, like many other clever fellows, to partake of the hospitality of his friends when strongly urged, yet you might as well try to get a smile out of a dead man without the use of a galvanic battery, as to induce him to spend a dollar unnecessarily."

The justice of this report was speedily confirmed, and the problem for the thousandth time satisfactorily worked out, that suspicion never yet injured a really honest man, although seemingly well founded in the outset.

Connected with the mailing of one of the large money packages already described, were circumstances which made it necessary, as is often the fact in a series of robberies, to investigate it as an isolated case, unconnected with the theft of the other packages and letters, none of which would go into or pass through the office in which this one was deposited.

The statement of the cashier went to show that he took the package to the post-office himself, and handed it to a clerk who happened to be alone in the office, and but a short time before the mail left for New York. This was confirmed by the clerk's own statement, and by his entry in a book kept for the registry of valuable letters and parcels. About the habits of this clerk, and his manner when examined, there was nothing which appeared in the least to implicate him. The cashier thought it out of the question that anything could be wrong

there. The young clerk was a member of his sabbath-school class, from which he was never absent, and he believed him to be "all right."

And yet he had an excellent opportunity to have kept back the package, and the temptation would indeed have been a dangerous one to older and more strongly fortified persons than he was. I determined, therefore, to put him to the test of a direct charge of having purloined the package, which I lost no time in doing, intimating that a confession and restoration of the money was his first duty. But he met the charge fearlessly, and firmly asserted his innocence as to the important remittance in question. The faithful monitor within, however, would not let him rest there. Believing, probably, that I knew more about other transactions of his than the one I had accused him of, he addressed me as follows:—

"I mailed that bank package, and know that it left our office. What could I have done with so much money, if I had been bad enough to have taken it? And I *was* just bad enough! I am willing to tell you all I have done, and will very gladly restore the ill-gotten funds, for they have made me miserable."

I will omit the details of this unexpected confession, but the first case owned was the $40 letter that had been handed to the through baggage-master, to be crammed into the locked mail-pouch, the failure of which letter, as has been already shown, had given so much force to suspicions against him!

By way of corroborating this part of his admissions, at my request, he described the address of the letter, the kind of money it contained, and to complete the identity, he mentioned that it came there loose in the mail-bag.

This discovery relieved the baggage-man amazingly, and at the same time aided me in deciding at what point the heavy losses had occurred; for if the large package started from this office, and was not disturbed on the cars, it must have been stolen in the New York or Philadelphia office, where it was destined.

Another fact transpired about this time, which assisted still further in locating these alarming robberies. Among them was one of a letter mailed by the cashier of a bank in Vermont, for an office in one of the Western States, and enclosing a quantity of the notes of that bank. The bills had peculiar marks upon them. They all found their way back to the bank through the usual channel of redemption, within a week of the time they were mailed; hence, of course, the letter could not have gone beyond New York. Besides, it was sent to that office for distribution, and the post bill was on file there, and described this identical letter, by its unusual rate, and as being prepaid by stamps. In all the other cases, the post bills were not to be found, either in New York or other distant post offices, and they must have been taken with the packages themselves.

The fact that the night mails had suffered chiefly, warranted me now in confining the investigation principally to the night clerks. They were generally a worthy and reliable class of gentlemen, some of them having held this responsible station for many years. In the inquiries and examinations which I was obliged to make, I found some instances of conformity to circumstances and limited means, that would confer credit on any men, or any age.

But it will perhaps be said, that cunning men may be dishonest, and yet keep their ill-gotten gains out of sight; surrounding themselves with the appearances of frugality and even poverty. This may be so sometimes, temporarily, but it is nevertheless a fact that rogues *steal money to spend it*, and for the comfort and ease which they *expect* it will confer, which expectation, however, never is realized. For it is the universal rule that money, or any other property not honestly obtained, "bites like a serpent, and stings like an adder;" and realizing the fabled vulture of Prometheus, unceasingly feeds on the undying life of him who steals, not fire from heaven, but a baser thing from earth.

The sad experience of thousands who have thought them-

9*

selves cunning enough to cope with the shrewdest officers of justice, will show that however artful and ingenious may be the devices adopted, there are ways enough to meet and expose them. Honesty is, therefore, not only the best policy, but the only safe and impregnable barrier against suspicion, detection, and misery.

Pat R. was appointed as a night porter, at the urgent solicitation of a prominent, and at that time, somewhat influential citizen of the First Ward. He was recommended as a robust, athletic man, just suited to the drudgery which somebody must undertake in such an office, of attending to the lifting, handling, and removing of heavy mails. In that capacity it was not expected that he would discharge any of the more responsible duties of a regular clerk, such as making up and assorting mail-matter; but the labor of the office accumulating, he gradually added to his nightly employments that of "facing up" the contents of the midnight mails, after they had been emptied out, and separating the letter from the newspaper packages. Had this last fact been furnished me at an earlier date, by the head clerk of that department, this troublesome investigation would probably have been sooner brought to a satisfactory termination. But, supposing from Pat's position and legitimate duties, that he had not the requisite opportunities for committing depredations, he was about the last one to be looked after. And when I did conclude to extend my particular attentions to him, I was somewhat startled by the discovery, from an examination of the "time register"—a book in which each clerk is required to enter his name and the time of his arrival at and departure from the office—that Pat had not been on duty for nearly a week! This was of course known before to the then first clerk of that department, but the sickness of the absentee, and the death of one of his children, which had been alleged as an excuse, (through another porter,) seemed to be a plausible and satisfactory explanation.

But the Agent thought otherwise, under the circumstances,

and deemed it best, at all events, to ascertain in a careful way its truth or falsity.

By the aid of a reliable day clerk, who lived in Brooklyn, in the neighborhood of Pat, I learned the name and general standing of the physician whom he had employed. An interview with him, supposed on his part to be for the purpose of ascertaining whether Pat was a man of strictly temperate habits, and in all respects fit to be employed in a post office, confirmed the part of his story relating to the child's death, but disproved the rest of it, about his own illness. But the doctor went the whole figure in regard to Pat's good character and fitness for any place which was not too intellectual. I could see, however, that my referee cared more about keeping a paying customer, (all professional charges, as he stated, having been fully liquidated up to that date,) than for posting me up in any matters that would jeopardize so good a situation, where all the monthly payments were in hard and legal currency.

By this step I obtained the first tangible justification of my suspicions against Pat. He had assigned, in part at least, a false reason for his absence. At about the same time, I consulted one of the Brooklyn penny-posts, whose beat took in Pat's residence, and who reported that he had on several occasions recently met him with a gun on his shoulder, apparently starting on a hunting excursion.

He was very poor when he entered the office, and by way of testing his ability to live without work, it was arranged with an agent for procuring laborers for a Western railroad, to call on him, and offer him a chance to go to Illinois as foreman of a gang of hands. But it was "no go." His health was too precarious for that.

Thus matters went on for some time longer, when one day, very much to my surprise, Pat entered the post master's room, and with a woe-begone look, and most melancholy tone of voice, commenced apologizing for his apparent neglect of duty. I was busily engaged in writing at the time, and so continued, hoping that he would not recognise me, as it afterwards appeared he did not.

"Misther Fowler," says he, "I wish to spake to your honor about meself. Ye see, sir, I've been unfortunate, and didn't come to me task; and the cause is, sir, that I've been sick meself with a terrible diarrhœe (placing his hand on his abdominal region,) and what is more painful than that (still keeping his hand in the same position, instead of changing it to the region of the heart,) I have buried a darling boy, your honor; and sure isn't it enough to turn the brain of a poor divil? Ah, may the like on't niver happen to yourself, sir!"

And a big tear rolling down his cheek, attested the *sincerity* of his grief.

A momentary fear that the post master might intimate something of our suspicions, was speedily relieved by his shrewdly remarking that he was sorry for his (Pat's) misfortunes, and that he had no fault to find, except that he ought to have sent more particular word as to the cause of his detention.

Pat thanked his employer, and backing out of the room, promised to be at his post that night.

"Well, what do you think of him?" inquired the postmaster.

"I think," said I, "that if he *is* the robber, and can come here and appear in that way, he is smarter than either of us. But we shall see."

For the week following, but few of his movements were unknown to me. His duties at night were very indifferently performed, and the hours during the day usually improved by the other night clerks for rest, were by him devoted to dissipation; so that, before half the night had passed, he would often be found in some out of the way place, fast asleep.

His discharge (which he no doubt desired) was thought best, in order to throw him upon his own resources, with the hope of bringing to light some of the stolen funds, if they were still in his hands. Much of the money, which amounted in all to some $8000, could be identified. The Middletown package of $2000 consisted of small bills, put up in parcels of $200 each; and upon every bill there was a mark by which it could be readily known. Up to this time none of the money contained in this package or the others, except that mentioned as coming from Vermont, had found its way to the banks by which it was issued.

One day, about noon, I observed Pat's giant-like form crossing Broadway, and for more than an hour I followed him without his knowledge, until he brought up in a stone-cutter's establishment. As I passed and repassed the door, I thought I observed him paying over some bank-notes to the occupant. After he had left, I stepped in, and was soon in possession of three $5 notes of the Middletown (Ct.) Bank, with which he had paid for the *grave-stones* of *"his darling boy!"* The bills were clearly a part of the $2000 Middletown package, being of the same denomination, and exhibiting the same unmistakable marks.

This accidental meeting, at once supplying a key to the mystery, was one of those misfortunes that so often befall criminals at some point of their guilty career, and even when they imagine themselves perfectly successful, and permanently secure against the possibility of detection.

I must here tell the reader a secret, explanatory of a question that naturally arises, namely, why, with such overwhelming proof in my possession, an arrest was not at once made. It was simply because he would have gone clear before any tribunal, had I depended on the case as it then stood. The bills of the $2000 package were all marked as stated, but unfortunately a large amount, with precisely the same peculiarities, was in circulation at this very time, though not supposed to be in that vicinity. Had the arrest taken place then, and the cashier been summoned to testify on the point of identity, he would have said that he put *such* bills into the Philadelphia package, but could not have sworn that they were some of the identical notes.

Besides, it was no unimportant part of this difficult business, to effect a return of the funds, as far as possible, to the pockets of the victims of these robberies.

The scarcity of live game in any direction within several miles of Brooklyn, and Pat's supposed want of experience in the use of the "shooting iron," suggested the possibility that his frequent excursions to a neighboring wood had some other object than hunting. Possibly it might be the guarding of his hidden treasures.

Therefore, on a bright October morning, I concluded, if possible, to know more upon this point, and, disguised in the garb of a shabby-looking hunter, with a gun and dog borrowed of a friend for the occasion, I strolled off in the direction in which Pat had so often been in the habit of going. Before fairly reaching the woods, he and two of his companions passed me in a rough-looking vehicle, and soon after turned from the main road into the burial-ground. From a somewhat secluded spot, I could watch their movements tolerably well, and it soon became apparent that at least one of the objects of this trip was to place the marble stones—the payment for which had so singularly betrayed him—at the grave of his deceased child.

The whole party were evidently under the effects of the "critter;" and the prospect seemed to be, that they would soon have occasion to mourn the departure of other beloved *spirits*, for the jug circulated freely, and a more jolly set of fellows, considering the lugubrious nature of their errand, is seldom met with.

But when they arrived at the spot where the child was sleeping, their mirth grew less boisterous, and Pat in silence commenced his labor of love; and as he proceeded in his melancholy task, I could see that he refused to join his companions in further potations, for although their respect for the place, or for their friend's affliction, seemed to overcome for the time their rum-inspired loquacity, they did not cease to resort to the jug for strength to enable them to bear his

grief, while sitting in the cart waiting for the completion of the task which brought them there.

At length the little white stones stood in their places, showing, by the short distance between them, how brief was the passage from the cradle to the grave, of the being whose whole history, so far as concerned the world at large, was inscribed on these marble pages.

A parent's heart, however, bears a different record; and after Pat had adjusted the turf about the little grave, and given the finishing touches to his work, he stood and gazed for a moment upon the resting place of his child, thinking— of what? Perhaps of the contrast between the guilty living and the innocent dead. Perhaps a flash from conscience glanced across his mind. At least he exhibited some external signs of emotion, for as he turned away to join his unconcerned companions, he brushed away a tear, and with it, perhaps, the softening influences that were at work upon his heart.

The trio once more seated in the vehicle, Pat no longer refused the fluid consolation that his companions proffered him. They by turns levelled the jug at the heavens, taking observations with the mouth rather than with the eyes, and as the last member of this astronomical corps elevated the instrument, its near approach to the perpendicular showed that a vacuum was well nigh formed within its recesses. What discoveries they made, except "seeing stars" in general, I cannot say, for they immediately turned their course towards home.

This was the last that I saw of Pat that day, but the next time he started on his accustomed tramp, two days after, he had at least one attentive spectator of his rifle exercise; and although I failed on this occasion to discover the precise place of his deposits, owing to my fear of alarming him, the opinion was strengthened by what I saw, that they were still resting quietly within a thick piece of woods, embracing some three or four acres, where he spent several hours that day. During this time, I was not more than a quarter of a mile from him, yet not a single report of his gun did I hear. Presuming that he had seen me at a distance, I now and then let off a charge innocent of lead, and occasionally betrayed the dog into a tolerably ferocious bark, by making him "speak" for a small cigar case which, held at a respectful distance from the animal, might easily have been mistaken by him for a well-cooked morsel of meat. This stratagem I thought necessary to carry out the idea of a busy and enthusiastic huntsman. But this little essay at hunting yielded me no game of bipeds, feathered or otherwise.

Soon after this, a rumor that several of his neighbors were preparing for a removal to the West, led me to fear that Pat also might have similar intentions, and that on the occasion of his last visit to the woods, he might, after all, have withdrawn the deposits. It was therefore deemed unsafe to delay longer in bringing matters to a crisis. But the manner of doing this, and of conducting the arrest, so as to accumulate evidence of his guilt, and at the same time recover a part or the whole of the funds, was worthy of much caution and study. If I went with an officer directly to his house to make the arrest, he might be absent at the time, and, getting notice of our visit, effect his escape. His family or accomplices, if he had any, would of course be aware of our movements, and perhaps secure the spoils, unless they were secreted immediately upon the premises. Then I should be left with only the proof already mentioned: that he had had an opportunity of purloining the $2000 package, and had passed three bills supposed to have been contained therein; together with some other less important circumstances.

The only safe and discreet course seemed to be to secure him when alone, and by that means keep his family ignorant respecting his arrest, until every effort had been made to get possession of the money. Accordingly I procured the aid of an officer, and at an early hour in the morning, we took up our quarters in a private dwelling in the neighborhood, where we could overlook Pat's house, and patiently waited for him to make his appearance.

It happened to be one of his lazy mornings, and he did not venture out until near ten o'clock, and then, very much to our disappointment, in company with another individual, unknown to either of us. A moment's consultation resulted in the decision to follow them at some distance, in the hope that they might separate, but with the determination not to lose sight of Pat again, and to take him into custody that day at all hazards. We had not gone far, however, before he looked over his shoulder, and although at least two squares from us, and a number of other persons were passing and repassing at the time, he no doubt recognised the officer, for after proceeding but a few steps further, he and his friend turned and came toward us.

Believing that we were discovered, and that Pat was making for the house to look after the safety of the treasures, a stratagem was hastily arranged to throw him off his guard, and at the same time to separate him from the stranger, who was so much in our way. It matters little what this scheme was, provided there were no actual misrepresentations involved. Suffice it to say, it was quite successful, and his companion resuming his walk towards Brooklyn City Hall, the rest of the party were soon on their way to New York.

At the ferry, and while waiting for the boat, Pat suddenly became quite restless, as if he had for the first time connected me with the scene in the post master's room. He walked back and forth upon the dock, and several times halted and leaned on the railing directly over the water, with one hand in his breeches' pocket, as if he contemplated throwing something overboard. But I remained closely at his side, wherever he went, and kept him engaged as much as possible, in remarks about the weather, the growth of Brooklyn, and other common-place matters.

We had soon crossed the ferry, and were seated in an omnibus, moving slowly (who ever went in any other way by that conveyance?) up Broadway. Pat had by this time grown very taciturn, and no doubt began to suspect that his escort was not entirely prepared to fight for his personal liberty. In fact, he must have fully decided in his own mind that we were no very consistent friends of the "largest liberty," in his case at least, when one of us pulled the leather strap, to give the usual signal for a halt. This was just as we had reached the head of Cedar street, on which the post office is situated, and before we had arrived, by several blocks, at the place where he at first supposed he was going to call, for a much more agreeable purpose than that of being confronted with the charge of extensive mail robbery.

As he alighted from the "slow coach," he halted for a moment, as if inclined to have some better understanding before proceeding further, especially as we turned our faces in the direction of the post office. He possessed physical strength enough to have put an end to our troubling him any further, but Broadway at midday is no very favorable place for such an attempt; and besides, he no doubt hoped that all might yet come out right. After being told that he was wanted at the post office on some private business, he went there peaceably.

Once alone with him in a private room, the time had fully arrived for deciding—not as to his guilt, for of that I was fully satisfied—but what were the chances of proving it, and of inducing him to disgorge his plunder.

"Patrick," said I, "you are detected in your robberies of the night mails in this office, and the first question I wish you to answer is, can you restore the money, that it may be returned to those you have robbed."

He received the accusation with a look of surprise, but without any manifest trepidation.

"I am an honest man, thank God," he asseverated, "and I'll defy all ye can do to me; and it's nither ye nor the divil that can scare me, so it ain't," at the same time drawing himself up into an attitude of defiance.

"I don't wish to scare you, Pat," I remarked. "I am

sorry on account of your family that you should have so abused your trust while employed in this office. But that is neither here nor there. I want you to hand over the seven or eight thousand dollars you have got so wrongfully. You passed some of the $2000, from the Middletown package, to Mr. G., for the grave-stones, you know, and I have the bills in my pocket."

"And it's trouble enough that I've had," he replied, "with the sickness of meself, and the death of little Pat, and now ye'd have me father all the thievish tricks of the whole office, would ye? Ye'll find, if ye look sharp, that it's another that's got the letters ye speak of; for sure haven't I seen him, while 'facing up,' throw something under the counter, among the waste paper, and then go looking there agin, after his task was done? And wasn't they large, thick parcels that he dumped under the table?"

I have never had a doubt that he was then describing the exact process by which he committed his own depredations.

"Very well," I answered, "you will soon see who is answerable;" and calling the officer, who had remained outside the door during the conversation, Pat was notified that his person must undergo a thorough search—and it *was* thorough.

Among the contents of his wallet were some forty dollars that agreed very well with the description of the kind of money mailed at Joliet, and also the receipt for the aforesaid grave-stones. On examining his hat, which he had taken off on first entering the office, and placed at some distance, on the top of a secretary, there appeared, snugly stowed away under the leather lining, $165, all in fives of the Middletown Bank, with the well-known marks on each bill! But even this discovery produced but little impression on him; declaring, as he did very promptly, that he could show where he obtained that money; and no doubt he could!

Pat was left in charge of two suitable persons, and the remainder of the day was spent by the officer and myself in searching his house and premises for the balance of the missing funds, which was done without giving any information to his wife of the real object of our examination, or the unpleasant situation of her husband. The woods were also thoroughly ransacked, though the chances appeared to be, that the booty had been removed to the house or vicinity, as he went directly from home that morning, having a part of the funds about his person, with the design, as it was afterwards ascertained, of purchasing tickets for himself and family, and several others, to Illinois.

But our researches were unavailing, and I returned to the post-office somewhat disappointed; for the proof was not yet sufficient to convict him, on account of the impossibility of identifying the bills with certainty, as I have already mentioned.

Before leaving, I had made known to him our intention to search his house, and when we returned, he for the first time showed signs of great uneasiness, and walked the room constantly, evidently anxious to know if his treasures had been discovered. His anxiety was natural enough, for it turned out that the whole of the money was secreted in the house, and that at one time during the search, I was separated from its hiding place, only by a half-inch board!

But Pat remained immovable, so far as any confessions were concerned; and it was thought advisable, at this juncture, to call into requisition the influence of the person at whose urgent solicitation Pat had obtained his situation in the post-office. An interview between them was speedily arranged, but the accused, for a while, still continued stoutly to deny his guilt. Subsequently, however, he inquired of the post master whether, in case he produced the money, he would have his liberty. The post master assented, so far as to promise no prosecution on *his* part, and Pat finally agreed to go with us on the following morning, and point out the place of deposit, but insisted that H., his friend and patron, (just referred to,) should be of the party.

Fully impressed with the importance of securing Pat as well

as the property of his victims, I now obtained a warrant, which was at once placed in the hands of one of the U. S. Deputy Marshals, who agreed to be in the immediate vicinity of the mail robber's residence, but to delay the arrest till he received a signal from me that all was ready, and after the funds were fairly in our possession.

Accordingly, a hack was ordered to be at the post office at an early hour the next morning, and we (the post master, myself, Pat, and H.) were soon crossing the ferry to South Brooklyn. Ten minutes' ride brought us in front of Pat's house, where we all alighted. Here matters took a turn wholly unexpected to me, for Pat insisted that no one but his friend, H., and himself, should go for the money, which he said was buried in the yard behind the house. To this I objected, but Pat stood firm, remarking, that it would attract too much attention if all hands went, and that if his request could not be granted, he should make no further disclosures, and we might as well go back to New York.

The post master and myself having at that time confidence in H., I took him aside and told him Pat must not be allowed to escape, on any account, and that if he went alone with him, he must promise to be responsible for his safe and speedy return with the money, to all of which, H. readily assented, claiming to have complete control over his man, and promising to have him back in a few moments. With this understanding they both passed round the house, and I started to give the Marshal the signal that the time for his services had arrived.

Not more than three minutes had elapsed before I returned in company with that officer, and H. was seen coming towards us, with a small box under his arm, but *alone.*

"Where is R.?" I inquired.

"He went into the house, through the back yard," was the response.

Taking the box from H., and handing it over to the post master, to be taken to the carriage, we at once passed into the house, but no Pat could be found. On applying to H., to know what this meant, he explained by saying, that as soon as the box was handed to him, Pat hopped over the fence into his back yard, and entered the house.

After some further search, he could not be found there, and H. proposed that we should not then appear too anxious to secure him; repeatedly promising to have him forthcoming at any moment, after the excitement had passed by a little. Returning to the carriage, we started for New York, counting the funds as we rode, which amounted to $4473. Much of it was in the original parcels of bank-notes, of one hundred and two hundred dollars each, enclosed in the usual straps of paper, with the amount of each package marked thereon, in the figures of the cashiers and others, which greatly assisted afterwards in the identification.

The author of all this mischief managed to elude the most secretly and cautiously executed plans for his arrest. It was, however, pretty well ascertained that he occasionally visited his home during the night season, and one night he was discovered at a late hour, by a local policeman (who had been employed to watch for him,) emerging from the front door of his house. They saw each other at about the same instant, and the policeman made an effort to seize him; but Pat was well armed, and was in the act of pointing a gun at the officer, when the latter, knocking it aside, presented a revolver and snapped it, the cap, luckily for the miserable fugitive from justice, only exploding.

The noise had attracted the attention of two of his friends, who it appears were just leaving the premises, and who were also well armed, and in the confusion which ensued, aided by the darkness of the night, Pat managed to get clear again.

The next attempt to arrest him was undertaken in consequence of private information that his family, together with a brother and other relatives, had purchased tickets for the West. The buying of an extra ticket more than was required for the party entering their names, authorized the belief that it was obtained for Pat himself, who would probably join them at some point on the route. They were to leave on a certain evening, by one of the Albany boats, which usually made no landing between the two cities. On this occasion authority was obtained for the boat to touch at Poughkeepsie, to receive on board the Special Agent and two United States Marshals. With this sleepless corps of officials there was no lack of handcuffs, revolvers, &c., nor of firm resolves to take the culprit at all hazards, if he was on the boat, and to arrest his wife and one or two others, believed to have been his accessories after, if not before, the fact.

The night being still and cloudless, at about midnight the well-known sound of a steamer's paddles was heard, and soon the huge form of the "Hendrick Hudson" was seen looming up in the distance, her numerous signal and other lights, as she changed her position from time to time, appearing like some brilliant constellation, and making a most beautiful display.

As she approached, for a time there appeared no perceptible change in her course, but when nearly opposite the landing, she suddenly veered toward us, and in a moment her guards were chafing against the ends of the pier; and without waiting for the gang-plank, we were on board before the wheels had fairly ceased their motion. The engineer's bell sounded the signal for going ahead; and we about the same time commenced our search through the floating palace.

As we progressed through the spacious cabins, a chorus of discordant sounds saluted us from their sleeping occupants.

It is curious, by the way, to see how the levelling influence of sleep shows itself in establishing a sort of equality between different individuals, in respect of the noise they make in the world. Your modest man, who, in his waking moments, avoids all display of his vocal or other powers, no sooner comes under the influence of the drowsy god, than his modesty deserts him; he blows his trumpet with as much sonorousness as the most impudent of mankind. The most retiring person I ever knew, was remarkable for being outrageously vociferous in his slumbers.

The redoubtable Pat, however, was guiltless of contributing to the volume of sound aforesaid; nor was his physiognomy discoverable among the sleeping or waking occupants of the cabins, so far as we could see. And as for any discoveries we made that night, or any good that our trusty arms did us, we might as well have been encircled in the "arms of Morpheus." At one time, however, we thought our night's work would prove a successful one, for on hastily consulting the clerk as we boarded the steamer, he informed us that a man answering tolerably well the description of the object of our search, had paid his fare to Albany, and was snugly stowed away in berth No. 54, in the forward cabin.

The revolvers and "ornaments" were hastily examined, and the plan adopted of delegating one of the trio to proceed quietly to No. 54, and, under the pretence that its occupant was in possession of the wrong berth, to ascertain, first, if he was really the veritable Pat.

As I was the only one who could readily identify him, this duty fell upon me; and leaving my fearless associates at the top of the stairs, with instructions to rush to my aid, in case I took off my hat, with almost breathless anxiety I made a descent into the cabin, and in a few seconds stood in front of the berth designated by the clerk.

"Hallo, stranger," I called out, at the same time gently shaking him, "haven't you got the wrong pew?"

An inhuman sort of a grunt was all the reply I could at first obtain, but after repeating the inquiry, and increasing the force of the punch, he leisurely turned over.

"And what the d—l do you want?" says the lodger, "bothering a gentleman in this way? Is it my pocket-book, oı my boots, you're after?"

It wasn't Pat's voice at all, nor was it his face, which I at that moment got a glimpse of, by the aid of a lantern in the hands of one of the servants who was passing. As I saw preparations making for "turning out," and was satisfied that I had waked up the wrong passenger, I thought it prudent to withdraw before matters progressed further in that direction.

None of the suspected party were on board on that occasion.

The telegraph was resorted to after our arrival in Albany, and word transmitted to us in that way, that the party we were in search of would certainly go up the river by the boat on the following night.

The next morning we were at the wharf, and by an arrangement with the officers of the boat, we were enabled to see every person who went ashore, as they passed through a half-opened door at the after-gangway, in giving up the passage tickets. The net was well spread this time, and though we did not pick Pat up, we secured the whole party of his traveling friends, including his wife and two children. The Marshal took them in charge, and without much ceremony or explanation, conducted them to a hack which had been provided for their special accommodation. They were very soon after escorted to the police station, and a subsequent examination of their persons and effects afforded no additional light, except that among the baggage of Mrs. R. was found a lot of scrap gold, which a dentist of Philadelphia mailed to a New York firm, and which had never reached that firm. On the strength of this discovery, she was afterwards indicted as an accomplice of her husband, and committed to Brooklyn jail, where she remained for several months, her two children staying with her, at her own request.

Although she undoubtedly knew the precise locality of her "liege lord," and probably could have procured her own liberty by making it known, yet she remained firm, and to the last steadily refused to give the least information, insisting, moreover, that she was ignorant of the post office depredations at the time they were going on, and that the stolen property found in her possession was placed in one of the trunks without her knowledge. Possibly it was so, as some of Pat's wearing apparel was found there also.

The remainder of the party, three in number, were detained at Albany. It was deemed necessary that they should remain there a while, but the Chief of Police was instructed not to treat them strictly as prisoners, but to allow them to lodge at the station; and an arrangement was made for them to eat at a neighboring restaurant, at the expense of Government.

The proprietor of the aforesaid restaurant finding, however, that they were disposed to abuse that privilege, by imbibing too freely, and selecting from the bill of fare whatever was choice and expensive—and especially as the contract for this portion of his customers was not very clearly defined—took the precaution to erase from one copy of the bill of fare all articles of a rare and expensive kind, which corrected list, by the third day, embraced but one or two plain dishes. This brief programme was sure to be thrust before them as often as they called for anything to eat, though a verbal announcement of "coffee" was added at the regular morning and evening repast. Having also some faint recollection of the discussions in the public papers about reforms in the Navy, and dispensing with the "grog rations," he compromised the matter on that head, by allowing the men "two drinks" a day, and no more; that being, in his estimation, a proper Government allowance.

As sufficient legal evidence could not be procured, to show that they really aided and abetted in the robberies, they were notified that their bills would no longer be paid by the Post Office Department; and declining to continue their journey to the West, tickets were furnished them to return to New York.

Soon after their arrival in the city, they fell in with a tolerably smart specimen of a lawyer, whose indignation at the unheard-of proceedings against them, of course had nothing to do with so mercenary a motive as that of getting a fee out of them; and by his advice a suit was promptly brought against the Special Agent and the two Deputy Marshals, for false imprisonment!

The cause was "set down" for trial in the Marine Court, and came off in the course of a week or two. A waggish spectator remarked that he could not see why it was brought in the Marine Court, unless it was because the complainants were "half seas over" when stopped at Albany.

A very brief synopsis of this trial will, I think, prove worth a perusal.

On the part of the prosecution, the complainants themselves were the witnesses—all three of them genuine sons of the Emerald Isle

Separate trials were asked and granted, and that of the Special Agent was first taken up.

Michael D. was duly sworn, but instead of mounting the witness's stand, with one bound and a broad grin, he was inside the Judge's desk, and seated in the chair usually occupied by one of the Associate Judges! A burst of laughter followed, in which his Honor, as well as the spectators, joined. The officer in attendance on the Court was quickly alongside of Mike, and with considerable difficulty removed him to the witness' stand. Here he fixed his eyes intently on me, perhaps to keep watch, lest I should attempt to run away, considering me his prisoner at last, and evidently chuckling within himself at the thought that the time had now come to put me on as limited allowance, so far as variety went, as he had been restricted to while in Albany.

Order being now restored, the counsel commenced interrogating the witness.

"Michael, were you on your way to Illinois, from this city, on the 20th instant?"

Witness.—"Was I in Illinoi? and sure I niver was in me life; and if that spalpeen of an Agint beside ye says I was, he lies, bedad he does!"

Notwithstanding the loud calls of "stop, stop," by his lawyer, he went through with the sentence, and stood, a thumb in each arm-hole of his vest, looking defiantly at me, and apparently ready for the next question.

The Court.—"Now, Michael, you must not be in such a hurry. Try and understand what is said to you thoroughly, before answering. I shall not permit any indulgence in the use of harsh names to any of the Government officers, or to any one else in Court."

Witness.—"And didn't they stop me, and trate me the same as a male thafe, your Honor?"

The Court.—"Well, that's what we want to find out; but you must not talk, only when you are questioned; remember that."

Counsel.—"I will put the inquiry in another shape. Were you a passenger on board the steamboat for Albany, on any night during the present month?"

Mike remained speechless for a moment, staring at the Judge in the most penetrating manner. That functionary finally broke the silence,

"Well, why don't you answer?"

Witness.—"And sure, your Honor, didn't you just tell me to remain spacheless when questioned?"

Court.—"*Only* when questioned, I said."

Witness (to the counsel).—"I *was* on the stameboat, and the Agint there knows it, so he does; and them other big feeling chaps there (pointing to the Deputy Marshals) knows it too. And I'd like to see 'em try to delay me in that way agin," at the same time looking fists, if not daggers, at those innocent officials.

Here the patience of the Court, as well as the counsel, became well nigh exhausted, and it was suggested that Michael should stand aside for the present, as the same facts could be proved by another and more intelligent witness.

The new witness went on to describe the affair from the commencement, including the detention at Albany. The cross-examination, however, showed that so far as any "imprisonment" was concerned, it was literally "false."

It was shown that all had the "freedom of the city," while in Albany, having frequently visited some "distant" connections—*distant* about two miles from the police station—and had been well boarded, away from the station, at the public expense. That in fact they could have gone anywhere they chose, a few hours after their arrival in Albany, or on any succeeding day.

After listening to the circumstances, and the motives which led to the detention of these men, and to the testimony of one of the police officers at Albany, in relation to their treatment while there, the Judge summarily dismissed the case, remarking that, in the first place no "imprisonment" had been proven, and that, even if it had, he should probably have sustained the officers in the discharge of what they considered their duty, in endeavoring to ferret out and punish the authors of important crimes against the laws of the land.

The trial I have just described was but one of many incidental occurrences which took place in the course of the attempts made to arrest Pat R.; occurrences, both tragical and comical, which would here find a place, did not the limited space render that impossible.

In closing the history of this case, it will be sufficient to say that, in the course of our investigations, the innocence of many suspected persons was established; restitution made to the sufferers by Pat's villany, so far as their losses could be satisfactorily traced to him; and the Post-Office Department were rid of one of the most daring and unscrupulous mail robbers that ever disgraced the service. He is not even now as secure in his hiding place as he perhaps imagines himself to be.

If there are those (as there is reason to suspect) who shared with him in such of the spoils as were not recovered, they also, even if they escape the punishment which they merit from their fellow men, will not always elude the pursuit of conscience, nor avoid the retribution which she will most surely inflict upon them.

CHAPTER V.

An infected District—A "fast" Route Agent—Heavy Bank Losses—Amateur Experiments—Dangerous Interference—A Moral Lecture—The Process discovered—An unwelcome Stranger—Midnight Watching—Monopoly of a Car—Detected in the Act—The Robber searched—His Committal—A supposed Accomplice—The Case explained—Honesty again triumphant—Drafts and Letters—A long Sentence—Public Sympathy—A Christian Wife—Prison Scenes—Faithful to the last—An interesting Letter.

THE literary reputation of one of the oldest and most celebrated seats of learning in New England, was once temporarily overshadowed by the "bad eminence" that it attained in the eyes of all within a distance of fifty miles in every direction, who attempted to transmit valuable matter through the mails. The period during which this state of things existed, was in the months of January and February, 1854. Throughout those months a fatality attended all money-letters designed to pass through the place referred to; the like of which has seldom been known in the history of the Post-Office.

As well might one have attempted to send a valuable letter across the Maelstrom, as to get it safely past the fatal point. This point was like the lion's cave in the fable, *into* which many tracks entered, but *from* which none were seen to return. And the lion, whoever he was, had an insatiable and indiscriminating appetite, for he consumed the supplies coming from three or four neighboring counties in the State, and like a feline Oliver Twist, continually "asked for more."

The effects of these numerous losses, of course, were not

confined to the vicinities of the sufferers, but were felt in remote portions of the country.

But the loss of money and the consequent inconvenience, were not the only results following this wholesale robbery. Perhaps no series of mail depredations ever spread so widely the cloud of suspicion over those connected with the mail service. All the route agents, post masters, post-office clerks, and mail messengers, whose spheres of duty lay within the infected district; all these officials felt the severity of the test of character, which existing circumstances applied. Such a state of things as that which we are describing, often serves as a thunder-shower, to clear the moral atmosphere. Half-formed purposes of roguery are, for the present at least, laid by; those already guilty of peculation on a small scale cease from their operations; all wait in breathless suspense for the *denouement* of the drama; and when the bolt falls, and the offender is smitten down, they breathe more freely; and such a catastrophe is not unfrequently the turning point in the life of some young man, who has hitherto been vacillating between good and evil.

The arrest and punishment of another inspires him with salutary fear of similar results in his own case, should he venture upon a like course.

And the effect of such occurrences upon those who have never turned aside from the path of rectitude, is no less decided.

These are the times that "try men's souls." It is a hard thing for one to bear up for weeks and months under a load of suspicion, though conscious of innocence; but this is a still harder task, if he has nothing between the eyes of the public and his inward rottenness but the thin shell of a decent and false reputation. No man can know to its full extent the value of a good character, until he has been through some "fiery trial," in which nothing but such a power could have saved him from ruin.

Yet those who at the time of which I speak, were most firm

in conscious integrity, did not escape the stings of annoying suspicions, and significant insinuations.

"Could it be a certain Route Agent?" confidentially asked an officious individual, perhaps quite too willing to start such a suspicion, the aforesaid Agent having, in pursuance of general instructions, denied him the privilege of the mail car. "I saw him," continued our virtuous friend, "sporting a fine turn-out only last Sunday, and they do say that he is rather *fast* for a young man on so small a salary. It wouldn't surprise me much if they should find that the trouble is there."

Unfortunately for this theory, so well founded on the basis of a Sunday "turn out" and a "they say," the "fast" young man could not have had access to one in a dozen of the lost packages.

This is a specimen of the endless surmises and conjectures that were thrown out in the progress of the affair, much to the annoyance of numerous post masters' clerks, and other officials, whose honesty, aided by the strenuous efforts of the Special Agent to arrive at the truth, carried them through the ordeal triumphantly; and left their accusers, particularly the man who couldn't ride in the mail car, rather "chop-fallen," and possibly not a little disappointed.

The banks within the infected district, suffered in the loss of drafts, &c., to the amount of at least two hundred thousand dollars, while scarcely a business man in either of the two or three cities within range of the prevailing disorder, escaped the vexatious and often injurious consequences of the depredations then going on, for the robber did not stop to select his booty. Indeed, he could not have done so, had he wished it, as the reader will hereafter see.

An investigation of the case was ordered by the Department, and carried on with as much energy as prudence would permit; yet in the midst of it the robberies continued unchecked. Hereupon some of the bank officers grew very impatient, as the victims of depredations are apt to do, if they are not made acquainted with every step that is taken in the delicate process of narrowing down the investigation.

When I had been on the trail for nearly a week, one of those gentlemen—an excellent financier, but by no means profoundly versed in the mysteries of human nature—in his imprudent zeal to find out *something*, took matters into his own hands, and came near spoiling all by alarming the robber, without detecting him. He prepared a sort of decoy letter, as he called it, well filled with pieces of tissue paper, about the size of bank-notes, and this tempting package he addressed to a cashier to whom several of the missing letters had been directed. This fell into the hands of the robber, but the experiment was rendered harmless by the fact stated by himself after his arrest, that he never stopped to read or examine any letters, except to ascertain whether they contained money. It will never be known, probably, how much good advice the criminal lost, when he committed this *tissue* of deception to the flames, for the worthy cashier, in his well-meant zeal, supplied the place of bank-notes in the decoy package with what he doubtless considered of more value, namely, a moral lecture to the delinquent, displaying in vivid colors the folly and wickedness of his course, and closing with the warning that if he took *that* letter, he would surely be detected!

The ingenuity and shrewdness of this device cannot be too much admired. The threat contained in the letter was so well calculated to throw the culprit off his guard, that if he had read it, he would no doubt have fallen an easy prey to such cunning machinations! It was of course expected by the deviser of this scheme that the package would be preserved by the person who stole it, in order to afford the necessary evidence of crime! The pieces of tissue paper could easily have been identified, and he would naturally preserve the accompanying document with as much care as Job was ready to show to the "book" which he wished his adversary to write!

Such interference as this, with an important investigation, is never warranted by any considerations whatever. The commander of an army who has laid all his plans for surprising an enemy, would feel under very slight obligations to any officious friend, who, in his impatience and ignorance of the course intended, should alarm the foe by some hasty and ill-advised attack.

Thus is it in the investigations to which we refer. Secrecy is all-important to the successful issue of the plans that may be devised; and volunteer services, especially from persons destitute of experience, are quite as likely to aid the criminal as to assist those who are endeavoring to detect him.

This digression has been made principally for the sake of protesting against such interference as that above mentioned, and of inducing others to abstain from similar unwarrantable experiments.

Notwithstanding the uneasiness of our amateur detective officer, and the remarkable skill displayed by him (as he supposed) in that capacity, considerable progress had already been made by means much safer than those which he adopted, if not more ingenious.

There were but few points to which suspicion could be reasonably directed, as there were but few places where the stolen packages would have centered. Each of these points was closely watched. A section of rail road, some thirty-five miles in length, over which most of the robbed mails must have passed, seemed, for a time, to satisfy the conditions of the problem to be solved, but this hypothesis was overturned by the fact that on one and the same night, packages were taken from mails which had passed each other on this road, in opposite trains, on separate tracks, and at a high rate of speed.

The mail messengers employed to convey the mails to and from the several railroad depots at central points, were carefully looked after, but all appeared right among them. And as for the post-offices, there were not more than two out of all affected by the numerous losses, through which half a dozen of the lost letters would have passed.

There was however, one man who had not thus far been

included in the investigation, chiefly because in the discharge of his ordinary duties as baggage-master, at a central station or junction where mail carriers were provided by the rail road companies, he was not supposed to have even a temporary charge of any of the mails. But while watching one of the mail carriers on a certain evening, as he was conveying a number of mails from a city post-office to the cars, the Agent observed him placing them in charge of the aforesaid baggage-master, prior to the arrival of the train by which they were to be forwarded.

After they had thus been committed to his custody, he was seen to throw them carelessly into his baggage room, and enter the room, closing the door behind him. After a lapse of several minutes, he came out, piled the bags upon a barrow or baggage truck, and wheeled them to a point upon the platform, opposite which the approaching train was to stop. The unnecessary operation of placing the bags in the room, when the train was nearly or quite due, was a very suspicious circumstance, especially when taken in connection with the other movements of the baggage-master, and by means of the telegraph the post master of a neighboring city was requested to be present at the opening of that mail, to see whether certain letter packages arrived which were known to have been in the through mail pouch for his office that evening. The reply was, "opened mail myself, no letters for this delivery."

An hour and a half had now passed since the train had left, and if the mails had been rifled in the baggage room, sufficient time had been afforded the robber to have concealed or destroyed all the direct proof of his guilt upon this occasion. Hence no open action was then taken in view of the discoveries made. Besides, there was too much at stake to warrant the incurring of any risk on the strength of these facts.

The following evening the movements of the suspected person were again watched, the Agent having a better knowledge respecting the exact nature and value of a portion of the contents of the mail bags which were to be forwarded at that time.

Upon this occasion, the train was "on time," and the carrier a little later than usual, so the mails were placed directly upon the barrow, and wheeled by the baggage-master to an obscure part of the depot, more remote from observation, and less in the way of passers, than that where they were carried the previous night. After remaining there a short time, he rolled the truck and its valuable load back to the usual spot, in readiness for the train.

This strange manœuvre indicated still another and a bolder operation, but the probabilities were that he had been foiled in any attempt he might have designed to make, by a person whom I saw following him into his dark retreat to make application for baggage, as I supposed, for they both entered the baggage room, and soon came out, the stranger with a valise in his hand. This *contre-temps* excited in my mind no very amiable feelings toward its innocent cause, for I had concluded to bring the affair to a crisis at once, should the telegraph report anything missing from the mails. But the dispatch received that evening was, "All right," which confirmed my belief that my plans and those of the baggage-master had been frustrated by the stranger.

Another train from the opposite direction, and bringing mails for delivery at this point, were due at a later hour, and as there had also been losses from those mails, I decided to wait and see what usage they received on their arrival, which, owing to heavy snow-drifts somewhere on the road, was delayed till near midnight.

When the train came in and the baggage was disposed of, the mails were all carried to the baggage room instead of to the post-office, and, after putting out the gas-lights about the depot, the faithful baggage-master returned to his apartment.

Through a small swinging window designed for ventilation, opening into this room near the top, I could see a faint light, and from its unsteady motions, which showed that the lamp from which it proceeded was in the hand of some one moving it in various directions, I concluded that the occupant of the room was rifling the mails.

This was an exciting moment. My first impulse was to proceed at once to the door, demand admittance, and charge him on the spot with the crime of which I suspected him. But a slight distrust of my physical ability to cope with him single-handed in case of resistance, which would almost certainly follow if my suspicions were correct; and the lateness of the hour, rendering it improbable that I could obtain aid should it be necessary; these considerations prevented me from carrying out my first intention, and when the unconscious object of my scrutiny put out his light and left the depot, I went in an opposite direction to my quarters, determined, however, to give him but one more chance to continue his depredations.

The next night he robbed his last mail bag.

Obtaining a private interview with the Superintendent of the rail road, I for the first time laid the facts before him, for the purpose of securing some assistance in the prosecution of my plans which he only could render. I wished to provide a place of concealment in that retired part of the depot where the mails had been taken on the preceding evening; and as empty cars were frequently left standing over night upon some of the unoccupied tracks, it was arranged to leave a car near the place mentioned, for my exclusive occupancy. From the "loop-hole" of this "retreat" I could determine with some accuracy the nature of such mysterious movements as I had before witnessed in that vicinity.

Lest the baggage room should be chosen this time as the scene of operation, and thus my plans be defeated, a discreet friend was stationed near that point about the time that the mails were brought over from the office, in order to "head off" the suspected functionary.

For the purpose of allowing as much time as possible, the conductor of the train, which was to take that mail, had beer telegraphed to "come in a little behind time."

Certain money packages had been prepared, and everything being in readiness, I took my post of observation in the empty car just before the mails came from the post-office.

I had nót long been stationed, when I heard the familiar rumbling sound of the baggage truck, and in a moment more the baggage-master appeared, trundling along his load of mails, and coming to a halt upon the platform, within fifteen feet of my watchful eye.

That eye saw rapid work for a few moments! Hasty passes of the right hand between the mouth of one of the mail bags (as it appeared in the dim light to be) and the capacious pockets of a sack over-coat, showed clearly for what purpose the mails had been thus taken out of the way, and the well-known click of a mail-lock informed me that the operation was concluded, and that the moment had arrived for action on my part.

I think a rail road car was never emptied of its contents in a much less time than on the present occasion. And my very informal introduction to the wholesale dealer in goods in the "original packages," was about as sudden. In fact, he had hardly set down the barrow, after removing it a few rods to its usual position, before I was addressing him.

In the midst of the rifling process just described, I had seen him open the door of a small apartment near him, a light shining out for a moment while the door was open. And it occurred to me that an accomplice might be secreted there for the purpose of receiving the stolen property. Accordingly I remarked that I would like to have him accompany me for a moment into this room on private business, to which he readily assented, neither knowing me, nor having any suspicion of the nature of my "business," for otherwise he might not have so cheerfully complied with my request.

On opening the door I discovered a person within, who appeared to be wholly unoccupied, except in smoking a cigar. Thinking it probable that he was in some way connected with the robberies, I considered it prudent to obtain assistance be-

fore making known the object of this interview, and accordingly spoke to three or four persons who had been attracted to the place by the unwonted movements, requesting them to call one of the police officers, some of whom were generally in the vicinity of that rail road station.

During this delay, and in order to prevent any attempt at escape, I put a series of questions to the baggage-master, calculated to allay the suspicion which began to be strongly indicated by his looks.

"Did you," I inquired, "find, in this morning's train from H——, a pocket-book, lost there by a passenger? If we can recover the papers, the money is less of an object."

This seemed to relieve his fears considerably, and he replied in a cheerful tone,

"I have found no such thing. It isn't my business to go through the trains, but this man's," pointing to the other person present.

"Ah, it's my mistake. Did *you* see anything of a pocket-book," I asked, turning to the person indicated.

"No," was the answer; "have you lost such an article?"

I was relieved from the difficulty of this question by a rap on the door from the Chief of Police, who was the man of all others whom I wished to see.

As he entered, I intimated to him, in a whisper, what was on foot, and then turning to the baggage-master, without any preamble or formality, I requested him to hand me the mail-key, which he had in his possession.

"I haven't any mail-key," was the dull response. "Very well," said I, "then we shall have to search you."

He turned pale, and remarked, with assumed calmness, "I suppose I know what you want."

One of the side pockets of his over coat appearing somewhat distended, I commenced my investigations with that. The first article that appeared was the large package of letters made up that evening for delivery at the neighboring city, before alluded to, and the next dive brought to light a heavy distribution package for the same office. Several other packages of less size were afterwards drawn forth. After the search had been completed, the culprit was hand-cuffed, and lodged in jail within half an hour from the time when he had committed this last depredation.

After we had dispatched this part of the business, we turned our attention to the companion of the unfortunate baggage-master, who had been observing our proceedings with the utmost equanimity, though not without interest.

"That's rather hard on Ed," said he, as the door closed on the culprit.

"Yes," replied I, "it is. But I believe we must search you, for I think you are concerned in this affair."

"I never was searched in my life," said he, smilingly, "excepting when I've searched my own pockets, and then I never found much. Perhaps you'll have better luck; at any rate, it won't hurt me to have it tried;" and so saying, he laid aside his cigar, and presented himself to undergo the ordeal. But nothing was found to implicate him in any way.

I then expressed my fear that he might still be an accom plice, as I noticed the baggage-master open and shut the door of the little room, while rifling the mails that night.

An honest laugh followed this remark, and an explanation was given me, which satisfactorily accounted for the suspicious circumstance.

It seems that his dishonest companion, fearing that he would come out of the room and detect him in the act, had opened the door, telling him that he would have to be locked in till the train arrived, and turned the key on the outside. This passed for a joke, and the imprisoned person thought little of it, as he would have no occasion to leave the room until the train arrived, when it would be his duty to inspect the cars. It also appeared that this locking up trick had been played several times previously, no doubt for a similar purpose.

Thus, was an honest man subjected to suspicion, by circumstances beyond his control. A satisfactory explanation of them, however, was not beyond his power, and his experience goes to increase the array of testimony, to show the inestimable value of a clear conscience in all exigencies whatever.

The key of a private desk in the baggage room was taken from the robber, and in this desk was found about $40,000 in bank drafts, checks, &c., and more than a hundred rifled letters, which, as their post-marks showed, must have been the proceeds of one or two nights' robbery. Everything taken from the mails, except money, had been committed to the flames, as the criminal himself afterwards confessed. A large portion of the available funds which he had accumulated, was recovered and restored to the rightful owners.

In less than a week from this time, he was tried, and sentenced to the State Prison for the term of *twenty-seven years.*

The discoveries here detailed, gave rise to great surprise and excitement among all who knew the guilty individual, for he had sustained a good reputation for sobriety, honesty, and industry.

His innocent family received the warmest sympathy of the entire community, which indeed they deserved, for the culprit's wife was a sincere Christian woman;—a living exemplification of the religion by which she professed to be guided.

Some of the interviews at the prison between her husband, children, and herself, were painful to behold; yet, after the first terrible shock, (and how terrible it was, can be realized by those only who have seen a beloved one suddenly metamorphosed from a fancied angel into a "fallen spirit,") she became more resigned to the overpowering calamity which had overtaken herself and her children.

She had no reproaches for her sinning husband, nor did she allude in his presence to the sufferings which he had brought upon his innocent family; but her aim seemed to be, to induce him, by means of his bitter experience, to begin a new and a Christian life.

One day, when I called to see the prisoner, in company with a gentleman who was anxious to learn the fate of a package of valuable papers which he had lost, we found the afflicted woman sitting by her husband,—one arm thrown lovingly around his neck, and an open Bible lying in her lap. We apologized to her for the interruption. She looked up mournfully, a tear stealing down her wan cheek as she said,

"It is no matter. I was only reading to poor Edward." Then looking at him fondly, she continued,—"He has been a kind, good husband and father, and hadn't any bad habits or companions that I knew of; and I have often thought that if he only had religion, he would be perfect. And if this trial, bad as it is, will only make him a Christian, it will be all I shall ask."

Meanwhile her two little children were thoughtlessly playing about the door of the cell, unconscious of the ruin which had been wrought in the hearts and the prospects of their wretched parents. The youngest one, while we were there, tried to play at "bo-peep" with its father, but was immediately checked by the poor mother, who cried out in an agonized voice, "Oh Eddie, don't!"

Ever since her husband was sent to prison, this devoted wife has visited him twice a month, (having been furnished with a free pass by the officers of the rail road which passes near the prison,) and to judge by the report of those who have an opportunity of observing him every day, the prisoner has commenced that Christian life, to which the prayers and loving efforts of his wife were designed to lead him.

Nothing can be said that would add to the force of the lesson contained in the facts here narrated. If a life-time of imprisonment, and the blighting of the hopes and happiness of loved ones, do not show with sufficient impressiveness the result of crime, imagination will in vain attempt to supply the deficiency.

I append a letter received by me from the criminal, some time after his committal to the State Prison:—

W——, July 18, 1854.

Kind Friend—

For I must consider you as such, because through your instrumentality I have been saved, perhaps, from a worse fate than has befallen me. I think through this, I have been taught to see what a sinner I am. I am truly penitent for this crime, as well as all my disobedience to the just laws of God. I mean, through the help of Almighty power, to serve my Creator the remaining years of my life.

It is strange how I was tempted to do that crime. I never was inclined to do evil or keep bad company. In fact, I kept no company hardly, except that of my wife and little ones. Oh! how my heart throbs to break loose and join them! Look upon yours as you can in freedom, and think of me. It almost suffocates me to call them before me in my mind.

Oh, horrors! little did I ever think such a fate would befal me! I cannot tell why I did it, more than this—to pay my debts. How they did trouble me—how should I ever pay them? But this was not the way to cancel them.

I do not love money—not at all. I never desired to be rich, only to be square with the world. I became indebted by inexperience and pride.

I would tell you the little story of my life, if I could. My connections, except my father, are pious people. My mother was a good Christian, and died in the happy hope of Heaven. She called me to her bedside about two months before her death. That was the last time I saw her alive; and when she parted with me, she clasped me to her bosom, with these words—"My son, obey God and meet me in Heaven!" Oh! how full of meaning, and a mother's love.

But this is too painful. I cannot write of this.

You can imagine my feelings at this time. But the evil tempter has left me now, and I pray to God, never to return.

Do warn others of my sad fate, to shun the road to ruin.

God, in his infinite goodness, has looked upon me with compassion, and calmed my troubles in part. At least all that I have desired, He has done for me, or how could I have lived?

Will you not call and see me some time? Don't despise the thief; Christ did not.

Many thanks to your kind heart. Also please thank the Government Attorney, and the Post Masters of H——, and N—— H——. May God watch over and preserve you all.

Your unworthy servant,

E. A. S——.

CHAPTER VI.

Safety of the Mails—Confidence shaken—About Mail Locks—Importance of Seals—City and Country—Meeting the Suspected—Test of Honesty—Value of a String—A dreary Ride—Harmless Stragglers—A cautious Official—Package missing—An early Customer—Newspaper Dodge—Plain Talk—A Call to Breakfast—Innocence and Crime—Suspicion Confirmed—The big Wafers—Finding the String—The Examination—Escape to Canada—A true Woman—The Re-arrest—Letter of Consolation—The Wife in Prison—Boring Out—Surprise of the Jailor—Killing a Horse.

In our larger cities, and indeed throughout the country, there are thousands of persons engaged in the transaction of business, who if called upon would testify that in the course of their employment of the mails, involving in the aggregate the collection and disbursement of millions of dollars, no part of their correspondence, valuable or otherwise, had failed or had ever been delayed through any fault of the Post-Office Department.

Such, up to the year 1849, had been the experience—an experience extending through many years—of a firm in Northern New York, extensively engaged in manufacturing and real estate operations, which required the frequent transmission of heavy remittances between their place of business and New York City. For a long time they confined themselves to the use of drafts, checks, and other representatives of money, but as everything went on smoothly for years, they finally remitted money itself, in the shape of bank-notes, whenever convenience required, without bestowing a thought upon the insecurity or danger of such a course; and for a time the prompt acknowledgment of the receipt of the various sums thus sent strengthened their confidence in the safety of the mails, and the fidelity of their management.

Therefore the rifling of one money letter directed by them to New York caused but little alarm; but when this was followed in rapid succession by the loss of the contents of a second, third, and even a fourth, they began to think that there was "something rotten in the state of"—New York, and accordingly called upon the Post-Office Department for aid in ascertaining the locality, and detecting the perpetrator of these robberies.

The losses could not be attributed to misdirection, or any other of the long catalogue of causes not of a criminal nature, though occasioning much alarm and inconvenience. For in the present case the rifled letters had reached the parties addressed. They had been opened, robbed, and resealed.

The route over which the letters passed was a long one—some four hundred miles—and the first look at the case seemed almost to forbid the hope of success in its investigation; for it appeared probable that the robber might defy detection as effectually as "a needle in a hay-mow;" and a belief of this kind no doubt encouraged him in his course. There was, however, another fact in connection with the matter, as will presently be seen, of which he was ignorant, which might have caused him at least to hesitate in pursuing his designs, had he known it, for it very much curtailed the limits within which investigation was necessary.

The course of the mail on this route was, first to Ogdensburg, some sixty miles, by stage, the mail being overhauled at each of the intermediate offices, eight or ten in number. At Ogdensburg, all matter for New York was put into a "through bag," which was furnished with a brass lock, and not to be opened until its arrival in New York.

It may be well here to state that two kinds of locks are used in the mail service; the iron lock for short distances and upon routes where the mails are frequently overhauled, a key to which is in the possession of all the post masters and "Route Agents;" and the brass lock, used for greater safety only between large places and on important routes; the intermediate offices being supplied with their mail matter without the necessity of opening the through bag. Consequently the brass key is in the hands of comparatively few post masters, (only those who are connected with the offices where the through bags are opened,) and of none of the Route Agents.

The reader will see from this statement, and others hereafter to be made, that the robberies were probably committed somewhere between the first-mentioned place and Ogdensburg, and that thus it would be necessary to pursue the investigation only on the latter route, some sixty miles as has already been mentioned.

The *seals* of the rifled letters were important witnesses in this case. In the resealing, uncommonly large wafers of a peculiar shade had been used, as well as a particular kind of stamp, which circumstances satisfactorily proved that all the robberies were the handi-work of one person, and probably at a single locality. The letters had in each instance been detained somewhere one day longer than the time usually required for their passage over the route.

Now there are certain features or symptoms, so to speak, in cases of mail depredations which go far to assist one accustomed to their investigation in determining whether they have occurred in large or small post-offices, and to distinguish with tolerable accuracy, between city and country embezzlements. A city depredator seldom if ever confines his operations to letters passing over a particular route. Indeed he could scarcely do so were he to attempt it, for in the usual division of labor, a dozen letters arriving on separate days would be likely to be taken charge of by as many different hands, and if letters were passing each way on the same route, it would be still more difficult for the same person to purloin from both, as the receiving and forwarding departments are generally if not always entirely distinct.

Neither is it a city symptom to reseal and replace a letter after it has been rifled, for the reason, among others, that the depredator is not willing, after having succeeded in purloining it, to incur the additional risk of smuggling it back again. While in country or village post-offices, the thefts must in most cases be confined to one route, and there is more leisure and better opportunity for the resealing and returning process.

For similar reasons, the loss or robbery of a number of letters addressed to the same party or business firm, although arriving by different routes, would not necessarily place a city post-office clerk under suspicion, since he could scarcely have a motive for such a selection among the thousands of valuable letters coming into his custody. On the contrary, if he were disposed to be dishonest, he would be more likely to take A.'s letter to-day, B.'s to-morrow, and C.'s the next day. Neither would it, in the case just supposed, be probable that there was a rogue on each of the different routes. The theory which experience and observation have established, would be that the repeated embezzlements had been carried on by some dishonest messenger outside the office who had in his power only the correspondence with which he had been intrusted. At all events, such a conclusion would be fully justified by the very frequent discoveries of similar delinquencies in our cities and large towns.

The peculiar features in the present case showed quite plainly that neither the New York nor Ogdensburg offices were implicated, and that the depredations had occurred somewhere between the latter and the mailing office.

An important question now arose, namely, what postmaster between these points used wafers similar to those upon the rifled letters. Having entire confidence in the Ogdensburg post master, I requested him to write to each of the post masters on the suspected route, asking for information on indifferent subjects and requiring replies. One was requested to send a copy of the post-bill from his office to Ogdensburg of a certain date. Another was inquired of to know whether a letter remained in his office addressed to Timothy Saunders; another to know whether there was once a clerk in his office by the name of Philip Barton, and if so, where he was at present residing. In this way letters were obtained from all these post masters in the course of a few days, and the mode of sealing was in each case particularly examined. Upon one of these letters the large wafer was found! There was not only the kind of wafer, but the stamp identical with that used upon the rifled letters.

For a few days after this, the exterior of all the letters received at Ogdensburg, and which passed through the suspected office, were carefully examined to see if they had been disturbed. This examination showed plainly that a number had been opened, and resealed either with the large wafer, or by the use of the original seals, which of course were mutilated.

Careful inquiry of some who knew the suspected post master, showed that he was a merchant in good standing, against whom no charge of dishonesty had ever been preferred.

The next thing to be done was to visit a point beyond him, in order to pass decoy letters through his hands, on their way to the Ogdensburg office.

Accompanied by a citizen of Ogdensburg, whose services I had secured as a guide, I started in a private conveyance, and when we had arrived within ten miles of the office of the big wafers, we turned into a by-road so as to avoid passing through the village in which it was situated. At a short distance from the village upon the road aforesaid, we saw a sleigh approaching, (it was the month of December, and capital sleighing,) and as it drew near, my companion remarked that he believed its occupant was Mr. Willis, the very person we were endeavoring to avoid! My friend knew Mr. W. by sight, but was not sure that Mr. W. knew *him*.

We concealed our faces as well as we could under the circumstances, and passed at as rapid a rate as was compatible with the muscular powers of our Rosinante. It afterwards appeared that Willis was out on a collecting tour that day, and that neither of us were known to him, nor had he the least suspicion of our business.

The mail which had so frequently suffered the loss of its valuable contents, passed over the route in the night, leaving Fort Covington at about ten P. M. and reaching the suspected office a little before midnight.

An interview with the victim of the former losses, resulted in his preparing a letter containing one hundred dollars in bank-notes, addressed to the same New York correspondent to whom the other letters had been sent. A full account of the bills was taken, and the letter sealed with a *small* wafer. A post-bill was prepared by the post master at Fort Covington, and the letter enclosed in a wrapper directed on the outside to New York City.

For the first time it occurred to me that the *string* to be put upon the decoy package, might be made to play an important part in supplying evidence of crime. If the letter should be robbed, and then destroyed together with the wrapper, and the money secreted, no proof of the deed would remain excepting the circumstance that the package went into that office and never came out. But the most cunning depredator would never think of destroying a thing so insignificant as a string. So I concluded to make it available in the experiment about to be tried. Among my notes of this case, I find the following description—"A white cotton string, twelve inches long; a knot exactly in the middle, another an inch from one end, and another two inches from the other end,—the last-mentioned end dipped in ink."

The package, tied up with this tell-tale string, was then thrown into the bag, and we soon set out on our return in the mail conveyance. The road lay for the most part through thick swampy woods, upon whose grim silence the cheerfu.

sound of our sleigh-bells made but little impression. Nor did we possess any other means for dispelling the gloom around us than the red glow of a couple of cigars, with which we resisted the encroachments of Jack Frost, so far as our noses were concerned. These (the cigars, not the noses) must have appeared like feeble imitations of a pair of coach lamps.

We had passed over about half the distance through the woods, when an incident occurred serving at least to break the monotony of our ride. A dark object by the side of the road, made conspicuous by the snow upon the ground, attracted our attention and that of our horses, who attempted to halt, and required a smart application of the lash to induce them to resume their pace. A moment after we could distinguish the forms of two persons stepping nearer to the middle of the road as we approached them. Not a word was said by either of us, as we were too much engaged in speculating on the character of the unexpected apparitions, to indulge in conversation; but the driver had evidently made up his mind to forestall any nefarious designs which they might entertain. Requesting me to "raise up a little," he drew from the sleigh-box an instrument effectual to lay such phantoms, to wit, a revolver. There was, however, no occasion for its use, for the personages before us turned out to be two French Canadians too far gone in intoxication to be very formidable antagonists, had they entertained hostile intentions, which they were far from doing, as their energies were entirely devoted to maintaining a perpendicular position, and keeping somewhere within the bounds of the road. Their erratic course rendered it somewhat difficult to avoid running over them, but we finally left them behind, muttering "*sacre*" and staggering about in a very social manner.

When we had arrived at the village and were within a quarter of a mile of the office, I alighted from the sleigh and walked on, leaving it to overtake me, my object in this being to keep out of sight of the post master, whose suspicions might possibly be excited by seeing a stranger in the sleigh with the mail carrier, although the mail carriage occasionally conveyed passengers. Perhaps this was an excess of caution on my part. At any rate, it did no harm, and I prefer in all such cases to give a wide berth to possibilities.

Once more on our way, my mind was chiefly occupied with conjectures as to the result of that night's experiment, and in determining what steps were to be taken in case the money package had been abstracted. The post master himself had changed the mails on this occasion, the driver in the mean time having gone over to the hotel at my request, in order to afford the former a good opportunity for committing the depredation if he entertained any such design.

The distance to the next post-office on this route was about six miles, and nothing further could be ascertained respecting the condition of the package, till our arrival there. An excellent account had been given me of the post master at this place, and his assistant. The former boarded at the hotel nearly opposite the post-office, which was kept in his store. As he was crossing the street with the mail bag on his way to the office, I overtook him, made myself known to him, and under an injunction of secrecy, disclosed to him the object of my visit at such an unseasonable hour. I furthermore expressed a desire to examine the packages contained in the pouch.

"It may all be right," said he, "but I hardly think I ought to allow an entire stranger, especially at this hour of the night, to know anything of the contents of the mails."

I was glad to find in this gentleman such a degree of caution and faithfulness to his public trust, and I was disposed to test it a little further.

"Well, sir," I said, "if you are to obstruct an Agent of the Department in this way, while in the discharge of his duties, you will be reported at head quarters for removal."

"Can't help that," replied he, "I intend to go pretty straight while I am here, and if the Post Master General himself were to appear here and want to overhaul my mails, he couldn't touch them, unless he satisfied me that he was the very man. That's just as the case stands."

"Very well," I remarked, "the driver knows who I am, and if he says it's all right, I suppose that will do."

"Not a bit of it," was the decided answer; "he may be deceived as well as any one else."

I now drew from my pocket the official evidence of my authority, bearing the signature of the Post Master General, and the seal of the Post Office Department. After inspecting this document rather closely, the cautious officer observed that there was no mistaking the signature of N. K. Hall, and that he believed he must "give in."

I expressed my gratification at the fidelity which he had displayed, and in a moment more the contents of the bag were spread upon the counter. A careful search, several times repeated, failed to discover the decoy package. Its absence, of course, showed that it must have been stopped at the office which I had intended to test.

I informed the driver that I could go no further with him that night, and procuring another conveyance, I returned to look after the stolen letter, and its dishonest possessor. Directly opposite the post-office was the village tavern, and there I arrived about daylight, intending from that position to watch the post master, and introduce myself as soon as he entered his store.

After watching about an hour, I observed some one removing the outside shutters of the store windows, and was informed by the landlord that it was the proprietor and post master.

I deemed it important not to be seen by him until I had entered the store, when it would be too late to destroy or secrete anything that he might have taken from the mail the night previous. In this I was successful. When I opened the store door, he was stooping down near the stove, engaged in preparing "kindlings" for making his fire. I came upon him so suddenly that he started to his feet almost with a spring, and looked rather more flurried than one would naturally be who expected to see no more formidable a personage than some early customer for a codfish or a quart of molasses.

"Thus Conscience does make cowards of us all," thought I, as I observed his futile attempts to recover his self-possession. After returning my salutation, he resumed the occupation which I had interrupted, that of splitting up a knotty piece of pine; but in his embarrassment he endeavored in vain to strike twice in the same place, hitting the floor quite as often as the stick which he was attempting to dismember.

Several common-place questions and answers passed between us while he was thus engaged. With the view of giving a temporary relief to his nerves, and of ascertaining what part of the store was appropriated to the post-office, (for there was nothing of the kind in sight,) I inquired,—

"Is there a letter here for Albert G. Foster, Jr.?"

"No, there is no letter in the office for any one of that name," replied he, apparently much relieved by the inquiry.

"You must have a paper for me," said I, "will you look?" He dropped his hatchet, and I followed him into a counting-room at the further end of the store, which was devoted to the postal department. The transient newspapers were examined, but not a paper could be found for Albert G. or any other Foster.

By this time the gentleman had nearly recovered from the effects of my first sudden appearance, but the calm was destined to be only of short duration.

"Mr. Willis, you have been talking to an Agent of the Post-Office Department, who has been sent on here for the purpose of detecting you in your frequent depredations upon the mails passing through your office, particularly the letters of Messrs. A. & Co. And last night you repeated the experiment once too often. Now I want the letter that you then robbed, and the hundred dollars which you found in it. It is a shameful thing for any one, much more for a man of your standing and connections, to convert, as you have done, a position of public trust and responsibility into a sort of place of ambush, where you lie in wait for the letters of your unsuspecting neighbors, and other members of the community, and thus abuse the confidence reposed in you. It is worse than highway robbery."

He gazed intently at me for a few moments with a look designed to be one of surprise and injured innocence. The attempt was a miserable failure, however. Conscience would lend her aid to no such cloaking of guilt, but proclaimed it through the wavering of his eye, the forced expression of his countenance, and the general agitation which he vainly attempted to conceal.

"That is plain talk, sir, *very* plain talk," said he; "and I think you cannot know much about me or my standing in society, to come here and accuse me in the way you have done."

"Your standing," replied I, "can have but little to do with last night's transactions. I must have the hundred dollars, even if you have destroyed the letter; and it is also important that I should recover what you have taken from the mails on previous occasions."

"You seem to be sure that you are safe in making these charges, sir," said he; "but all you have yet stated is nothing but assertion without any proof."

Just then the front door of the store opened, and a pleasant voice was heard, "Breakfast is ready, father." A sweet little child stood in the door-way, and her innocent, careless face, contrasted strikingly with the anxiety which displayed itself in the features of her guilty father. Would that her voice could have called him away from the course of villany and dishonor which he had taken!

As her father did not at once reply to her, she came skipping up to him, and as she caught hold of his hands and playfully attempted to draw him along, he looked at her and then at me, with an expression that said as plainly as words could say it,—"Have you the heart to come between us, and destroy the happiness of my innocent family?"

I felt the force of the appeal, but was impressed still more strongly with detestation of the conduct of a man who could deliberately risk involving the members of his domestic circle in misery and disgrace for the sake of enriching himself at the expense of those who had confided in his integrity.

"I can't go now, my dear," said he, withdrawing his hands from hers, "I am very busy. Run along and tell mother not to wait for me."

So away tripped little Innocence, joyfully humming a simple air, and leaving us to deal with the grim question before us.

I now commenced a search among some waste papers scattered upon the floor and one of the tables, for the wrapper in which the decoy letter had been enclosed, but I could find it nowhere. I however continued the search, hoping to find the string, if nothing else; and my perseverance was rewarded by the discovery of the package at the back part of a drawer in a desk. The package appeared to be in a perfect state, except that the string was missing. Holding it up, I inquired of the post master, "What is this package doing here?"

"It must have been thrown out by mistake in overhauling the mail last night," replied he.

I removed the wrapper, and immediately found a full confirmation of my previous assertions, for the letter itself had been broken open, and the large wafer substituted for the original seal. In fact it had been served exactly like its rifled predecessors, and was now waiting to go forward to New York by the next mail. I also observed a quantity of the large wafers lying upon the desk, a few of which I secured for the purpose of comparison. The evidence of the string now became of little importance, but I wished to find it if possible, and after a few moments' search, I discovered it lying on the floor behind the counter of the store.

The probability is that after the mail had passed that night, he took the stolen letter to the store, and there opened it.

Against such overwhelming proof as this, it was worse than useless to contend. So thought the unfortunate post master, whose tone now changed considerably. He refunded on the spot the proceeds of the last night's robbery, and proposed to make over a portion of the goods in his store as security for the restitution of the amount previously purloined, if by such a step he could save himself and his young family (consisting of a wife and the little girl already referred to,) from the crushing effects of public exposure.

But this tender regard for the happiness and honor of his family came too late. Such considerations, if others are insufficient, ought to restrain one from the commission of crimes; and it has always seemed to me that when a man in the full possession of his faculties can thus compromise the comfort and peace of mind of his innocent family, he deserves little sympathy or pity from any quarter, however sincerely he may regret his folly.

Willis was arrested by a local officer, and taken before a Justice of the Peace in that neighborhood, who, notwithstanding the efforts made to impress upon him the importance of holding the accused for trial, fixed the bail at a few hundred dollars, which sum was readily furnished by responsible parties.

As several weeks were to elapse before the session of the Court, it was my intention to re-arrest him under a United States warrant, as soon as one could be obtained, but during the night he made over a portion of his property to his sureties, and hastily filling a few trunks with articles of clothing and other personal property, he decamped with his family to Canada, leaving behind a deserted home and a disgraced name.

As soon as the crimes of Willis became known in the town, universal sympathy for the wife of the criminal was felt and manifested. She was a refined and accomplished lady, connected with a highly-respectable family in a neighboring county, and had endeared herself to all who knew her, by her kindness and other excellent qualities. Like a true woman, she remained constantly at the side of her husband, after his arrest; overlooking all his offences in her devoted affection, and palliating them to others as far as she could, on the ground of pecuniary embarrassments.

Some weeks elapsed before a clue was obtained to his whereabouts. The deputy Marshal, to whom this business was intrusted, entered upon the search with great energy, and finally succeeded in arresting him, and conveyed him to Utica, New York, where he was examined before the United States Commissioner, who held him to bail in a large amount, for trial before the United States District Court. Being unable to obtain this heavy bail, he was sent to jail a few miles from Utica, to await his trial. His wife, on his second arrest, returned to her father's house. It was soon after this that she wrote him the following letter, which was left in the jailor's possession:

F——, Feb. 5, 1850.

My dear William,

It goes to my heart to feel that we are separated, even for a time, and above all, to think *what it is* that separates us. But, William, my love for you is such, that I had rather you were thus than dead.

"I ask not, I care not, if guilt's in thy heart,
But I know that I love thee, whatever thou art."

Oh! what strong temptation you must have had to struggle with, before you yielded to it! And I know that you meant to restore the money to those it belonged to, at some time or other.

I sometimes find it hard to elude Julia's artless inquiries. She wants to know "why Father went away with that man and didn't come back." Poor child! must she ever know that her father is in a ——? I can't write the word.

God forbid, my dear, that I should speak a word of reproach, but perhaps I can say in a letter what I might find it hard to say if I were with you. I am sure, William, that you have fallen into error for my sake and Julia's, but let me assure you, from the bottom of my heart, that I had far rather sink with you into the depths of honest poverty, than rise to affluence, leaving an approving conscience behind. Never think of me for a moment, I beseech you, as a wife whose wishes must be gratified at whatever expense, but reckon on me as one who will ever be ready to undergo any self-denial which the adoption of a straight-forward course may involve. I reproach myself that I had not been more free to confide to you my views on this subject before your misfortune. Had I done so, perhaps we might have been differently situated now. But the past cannot be changed. The future may be a new life to us, if we wish it; and shall we not?

As to the bail, I have strong hopes that it can be arranged before long. I hope to be with you as early as next week.

Julia sends a kiss to Father, and says, "Tell him I want him to come and see me and mother." I send the same for myself. Good night, my dear, and many good morrows.

Your affectionate wife,

ELLEN.

Not far from two weeks after the committal of Willis to jail, Mrs. Willis called one day late in the afternoon, and requested permission of the jailor to spend the night with her husband. This officer was a kind-hearted old gentleman, and the lady-like deportment of the applicant, whom he had seen on former occasions, had won his entire confidence. He made no objection, and his native gallantry, and sympathy for the lady, prevented a very thorough investigation of the contents of a large basket that she brought with her, which presented to his eye nothing but a goodly array of such delicacies as are not usually included in a prison bill-of-fare. So she was ushered into her husband's place of confinement, basket and all.

The jailor retired to rest that night with the happy consciousness of having done at least one kind act during the day, and slept soundly,—perhaps more soundly than usual—till morning.

When going his accustomed rounds, he noticed sundry shavings and chips of a decidedly new and fresh appearance on the floor outside of Willis's door. He further noticed that the door was partly open, whereupon he hastily entered the room in no small perturbation of mind. Nor was his disturbance diminished when he found that there was but one occupant of the bed, and that, the fair lady whom he had admitted the night before! She was apparently fast asleep, and although the spectacle was one of a picturesque description,

the old gentleman would have derived much more satisfaction from a sight of her liege lord. He looked in all directions round the room, with the vague idea that his prisoner might start up from behind a chair or table; but no such phenomenon occurred, and the conclusion forced itself upon him that he had been made the victim of misplaced confidence; in other words, that Willis had escaped by the aid of his devoted wife and her treacherous basket. An auger, concealed in its depths, had been smuggled in, and used in boring off the door-hinges, and now lay on the floor.

"Mrs. Willis," cried the now indignant jailor, "Mrs. Willis, I say!" But the slumberer stirred not, and he repeated the call in louder tones,—"Mrs. Willis, where's your husband?"

Rising up on one elbow, and looking about the room, apparently much confused, she replied,

"Where's my husband? have you taken him away without letting me know it?"

She steadily refused to give any information concerning the time or mode of his escape, and was equally careful not to deny that she furnished the means for securing his exit. She was therefore arrested and taken before an United States Commissioner, charged with aiding and abetting the escape of a prisoner; but such was the public sympathy in her behalf, that she was discharged from custody, and no doubt, soon joined her husband, who had proved himself so utterly unworthy of such an affectionate, devoted, and heroic companion.

Not long after this escape, a suit was brought in one of the lower courts, against a brother of Willis, to recover the value of a horse killed by hard driving on the night of Willis's disappearance. It was more than surmised that the two circumstances were in some way connected.

CHAPTER VII.

Startling Complaints—Character against Suspicion—The two Clerks—Exchanging Notes—The Faro Bank—Tracing a Bill—An official Call—False Explanation—Flight of the Guilty—The fatal Drug—The Suicide—Sufferings of the Innocent—The Moral.

THE close of the year 1839, and the opening of 1840, were marked in the Post-Office Department with frequent and startling announcements of the loss, by mail, of valuable letters from Southern Virginia, and Eastern and Northern North Carolina, directed to Richmond and other commercial cities farther North.

These cases, as they reached the Department, were duly prepared and submitted to the Special Agent for investigation. Search and inquiry were promptly instituted. But for a time the utmost vigilance failed to obtain any clue to the supposed embezzlements. The cases of loss continued to multiply; and at length the Agent's attention was particularly drawn to the Distributing Post-Office at P.

A circle of numerous facts pointed unmistakably to this spot as their center and focus. It was here that the lines of circumstantial evidence from every quarter converged and met. The post-office at P., therefore, became an object of special interest in the eyes of the Agent.

However, investigations in this direction proved at first no more successful than elsewhere. The high integrity of character for which the post master was distinguished, and the excellent reputation of his clerks, stood like a wall of adamant in the way of all evidence and all suspicions.

The Agent seemed destined to be baffled at every point. Yet a stern truth stared him in the face, and fixed its immovable finger over this Distributing office. Every missing letter, although reaching P. by various routes, had been mailed at points South of it for points North of it. Here they must all concentrate, and here only. It was therefore at this place only that all the losses could have occurred.

Several days were passed by the Agent in P. and the vicinity, quietly pursuing his investigations. No person knew the secret of his business. He became acquainted with the post master and his two clerks, studied their characters, and their social circumstances.

The first was a man of position and competence, whose honor no breath of calumny had ever dimmed, and who could not possibly have any motive for periling the peace and prosperity of his family by a dishonest course. Neither did the unflawed respectability of the clerks betray any chink or crevice in which to harbor a doubt.

The elder of these, and the superior in the office, was a young man of education and refinement. We will call his name Carleton. His face was frank, his eye steady and clear, his manners always self-possessed and easy. The Agent liked and admired him from the first. He learned too that he was a favorite with all who knew him—that his connections were among the first families in the State; and that by his talents and high-toned generous impulses, he had so far nobly sustained the lustre of his family name.

Another circumstance was greatly in Carleton's favor. Although descended from the "aristocracy," the fortunes of his family had run somewhat low in the later generations; and now, his father being dead, he devoted himself zealously to the maintenance of his aged mother, and the education and support of his only sister.

The junior clerk was a youth of minor pretensions. He was uniformly retiring in his manners. Although by no means a person of forbidding aspect, there was something measured and guarded in his movements, far less prepossessing than the free and chivalrous bearing of Carleton. This apparent prudence might arise from various causes. The Agent could not believe that it was the result of a secretive and dishonest disposition. If such was the case, however, that same discretion had effectually succeeded in covering the poverty of his moral character from public scrutiny.

Foiled at every point where he attempted to hang the sad burden of criminal facts, the Agent resolved upon striking a bold and hazardous blow. He sought a private interview with Carleton.

"Do you know," said he, "that I am here on very delicate and peculiar business?"

"I had not thought of such a thing," replied Carleton.

"Well, sir, I will tell you. I am convinced that you are the very man to assist me. If you will, you may do me and the Post-Office Department a signal service."

"I do not understand you."

"No, but you will. First, however, give me your pledge that what I have to divulge shall be held in strictest confidence and honor by you."

"Certainly," said Carleton, "if you wish it."

The Agent then stated the business that had brought him to P——. Carleton expressed some surprise, but cheerfully promised to afford the Department any assistance and information in his power.

"Have you mentioned the subject to Mr. B.?" he asked.

"Not yet; he is the nominal post master, it is true, but you have a far more intimate knowledge of the details of the office than he has. I have another reason for not speaking with him. I dislike to disturb his confidence until the establishment of strong proof renders it my duty to do so."

"You can speak to me with perfect plainness," said Carleton.

"I trust so," replied the Agent. "And I am sure you will do all you can to set me right, if I am going wrong. Nor will you, I am convinced, suffer me to injure an innocent person in your estimation. To come to the point, then, I wish you to open your inmost thoughts, and tell me if you regard it as possible that your fellow-clerk can be guilty of these depredations upon the mails."

"You shock me," said Carleton, not without emotion.

"Speak freely," continued the Agent.

"Why, I could almost as soon think of suspecting Mr. B. himself," exclaimed the other. "I believe Howard to be perfectly honest."

"Certainly, I know nothing to the contrary; and I sincerely hope your judgment is well founded. But," continued the Agent, "our public duty should not be altogether biassed by private opinion. You will not, therefore, fail to unite with me in tracing the embezzlements to their true source, no matter at whose door the blame may be laid."

"I will do all in my power," said Carleton. "Although I would be almost willing to pledge my own reputation that the losses have occurred outside of the office, I will use every exertion to discover any dereliction from duty that may come within my sphere of observation."

The Agent expressed his thanks for the clerk's ready promise of coöperation, and took his leave.

Meanwhile he did not neglect other measures that he had adopted for tracing the robberies. By a singular coincidence, within an hour after this conversation with Carleton, he was able to seize a certain clue, which he had long been in search of, and despaired of obtaining.

On his return to the hotel, the landlord thus addressed him:

"You asked me if I could give you any more large bills, in exchange for small ones. I think I can accommodate you this morning. I have a one hundred dollar bank-note, which, if you are sending money by mail, will be very convenient."

"Thank you," replied the Agent; "it will be a great accommodation."

The landlord passed the bank-note over the counter. One can imagine the Agent's secret triumph on discovering, at last, one of the very bills he was in search of, one that had been lost in a letter passing that post-office only a week before; and of which he had an accurate description from the Department.

Having made the purchase, he held the bank-note up to the light.

"I suppose you will warrant this paper to be genuine?" he suggested.

"There is no doubt about it, sir," said the landlord.

"Of course you know from whom you had it?"

"To be sure! I took it of one of my boarders this morning, Captain Wilkins."

"I have no doubt but the bill is good," said the Agent, putting it in his pocket. "You are sure you had it of the Captain?"

"O, yes! 'twasn't an hour ago he gave it to me."

"By the way, who is this Captain Wilkins? He's a very gentlemanly-appearing fellow."

"O, he's a capital fellow!" said the landlord.

"What's his business?"

"He keeps a faro bank."

To a Northern reader, the two clauses of this statement may seem inconsistent with each other. But allowance must be made for the freedom of Southern manners and society. To bet at a faro bank is considered no serious stain upon the honor and respectability of gentlemen in Southern cities. The keeper of a faro bank may pass, as we have seen, for a "capital fellow." But the Agent felt pained to know from what source the landlord had obtained the bill. Already a dark picture of temptation and crime arose before his eyes.

It is a significant and too often a tragical word—the Faro Bank!

Captain Wilkins had gone to ride. The Agent pretended to transact a little business, mailed two or three letters, and read the newspapers until his return. The rattling of a light-wheeled buggy before the hotel steps announced the expected arrival.

Captain Wilkins—a soberly-dressed and polite individual, whom one might have taken for a clergyman—stepped out of the vehicle, accompanied by a friend, pulled off his driving-gloves as he entered the house, and lighted a fresh cigar at the bar.

The Agent took an early occasion to accost him.

"Can I speak with you a moment?"

"Certainly," said Captain Wilkins. The two walked aside together. The Agent exhibited the bank-note.

"Did you ever see that paper before?"

"Yes, and very recently. I passed it with the landlord this morning."

"As the bill is of so high a denomination, you probably remember from whom you received it?"

"Perfectly well. I had it last night from one of the post-office clerks, who was betting at my bank, and for whom I changed it."

"May I ask from which one?"

"O, from Carleton. He is a reliable fellow. Have you any doubts about the bill?"

"No, if you are sure you had it of Carleton."

"I am sure of that."

"You could swear to it as the identical bank-note?" Captain Wilkins glanced at the paper again.

"It's the identical rag," said he; "I can take my oath of it."

This startling revelation gave a different phase to the business. The finger of discovery seemed to point directly at the senior clerk. Again the Agent, on leaving Wilkins, recalled Carleton's every look and word, in the conversation he had with him that morning. He could not recall the faintest indication of guilt. And he could not but hope that the young man was as innocent as he appeared; and that circumstances would prove him so. However, there was no way left but to follow the thread of evidence he had so far successfully traced.

He strolled towards the post-office, and found Howard there alone.

"Where is your brother-clerk?" he asked.

"He went to dinner about five minutes ago,—rather earlier than usual."

"Very well; perhaps you can do my business for me. I mailed a letter here this morning, which I would like to recover from the mails, if it has not already gone out." A description of the letter was given. All this was done to prevent Howard from suspecting the Agent's real business with Carleton. The letter had gone, as the inquirer well knew, and he left the office.

But now his pace was quickened. He knew not what might be the result of his interview with Carleton. It was a significant fact that he had gone to dinner at an earlier hour than usual. If guilty, what more natural than that he should take that opportunity of destroying any evidence of his guilt to be found among his papers at home?

The Agent had already learned where Carleton lived, and he hastened at once to his house.

The young man's mother received him in a truly lady-like and hospitable manner.

"He just came in," said she, graciously. "Sit down, I will have him called. He remarked that he had some trifling affair to attend to before dinner, and immediately went to his chamber. You may speak to him, Sarah."

"I have only a word to say to him," replied the visitor. "Perhaps it will be as well for me to go to his room, instead of calling him down."

"As you please. My daughter will show you the way."

Sarah, a beautiful and stately girl of eighteen, conducted

the caller to her brother's chamber, and knocked at the door. Presently Carleton appeared. A slight paleness overspread his features on recognising the Agent, but without losing his self-possession, he invited him to enter the chamber.

"I have strange feelings on seeing you!" he observed in a very natural tone of voice. "What you said to me about Howard, has troubled me more than I would have thought it possible. Take a seat. Do you smoke?"

"Not before dinner," replied the Agent. He made a rapid observation of the chamber, as he sat down. "You are very comfortably situated here."

"I have nothing to complain of. We live rather humbly, but we are not ambitious."

Carleton then spoke of his mother and sister, in a manner which touched his visitor deeply. Could it be possible, thought the latter, that he was destined to destroy the peace of that happy family? He shrank with indescribable repugnance from the performance of his duty; but it inexorably urged him to finish what he had begun, and he produced the fatal bank-note.

"Not to detain you," said he, "I have some question in my mind with regard to a bill I took this forenoon. I have been referred to you as the person who passed it. Will you see if you recognise it?"

Again the swift pallor swept over Carleton's face; but this time it was more marked than before, and his fingers trembled as he examined the bill.

"Certainly," said he, "I recognise it. It's a note I changed with Captain Wilkins last night."

"It also happens," observed the Agent, "to be a note which, according to an accurate description I have of it, was recently lost in the Southern mails. This is as painful to me, Mr Carleton, as it is unexpected; and I hope you will be able satisfactorily to account for the manner in which you obtained this money."

"It is still more painful to me than it can be to you," replied Carleton; "and heaven knows I heartily wish I could not tell how that bill came into my possession. I remembered it, after you left me this morning; and I had a presentiment that trouble would come out of it. I am afraid, sir," Carleton added, after some hesitation,—"I am afraid your suspicions of Howard will prove too well founded!"

"Do you mean to say, that Howard is responsible for that bill?"

"I will tell you all I know about it, sir. I yesterday sold a colt I had been training the past season. He proved too high-spirited for our use, and I preferred to own a horse my mother and sister would not be afraid to ride after. I sold it to a neighbor of ours, Mr. Fellows. He was to pay me one hundred dollars down,—and this is the money he gave me."

Carleton hesitated. The Agent begged him to proceed, as no time was to be lost.

"I was trying to recall the conversation that passed between Mr. Fellows and myself. It was to this effect:

"'I'd quite as lief you would give me small bills, if convenient,' said I, 'for I shall have several little sums to pay out of this in a day or two.'

"He replied that he could do no better by me, and added that he thought Howard would like to change it for me. 'How so?' said I.

"'You remember,' said he, 'that Howard bought a house lot of me, some time ago. The last payment came due yesterday. He seemed reluctant to part with this bill, and said if I would wait, he would give me specie for it in a day or two.' Something more was said about Howard's good luck in making payments for the house lot, so promptly, and so we parted."

"Where will I find this Mr. Fellows?" asked the Agent.

"I saw him not ten minutes ago enter a store in the village."

"You are sure he will corroborate your statement?'

'There's no doubt of it. He's a plain, practical man, who tells a straight-forward story."

"Come, then," said the Agent, "we will go and find him."

Carleton readily assented, and the two left the chamber.

"I've a little business to transact before dinner, mother," said the young man, as they passed out. "If I am not back in a quarter of an hour, do not wait for me."

But little difficulty was experienced in finding Mr. Fellows. He was such a person as Carleton had described; but he turned out to be very deaf, and the Agent deemed it expedient to retire with him and Carleton to some secure place, where their loud talking would not be overheard. The clerk proposed that they should make use of the private room of the post-office. The Agent readily agreed to this, for he was somewhat anxious to make sure of Howard; and he now resolved that the latter should be present at the interview. This plan was also proposed by Carleton, and when they had arrived at the post-office, the senior clerk informed the junior, in a low and serious tone, that his presence was requested in the private apartment.

"But who will attend in the office?" asked Howard.

"I'll speak to one of the clerks in the store; they accommodate us very often in this way," Carleton added, addressing the Agent. "It's only around the corner."

The thought struck the Agent that it would be safe enough to accompany Carleton. But to do so, it would be necessary to leave Howard, who, if guilty, might by this time have suspected the danger at hand. Besides, it seemed not at all probable that Carleton could have any motive for attempting an escape. His position in society, his family circumstances, his frank and manly demeanor,—everything tended to disarm suspicion. Furthermore, nothing could be more satisfactory than the story he had related of the manner in which he obtained the fatal bill. He was accordingly suffered to leave the office. As there were persons passing in and out, the Agent did not consider it proper to broach the important subject until Carleton's return.

But some minutes passed, and he did not reappear.

"I thought he said he had only to go around the corner," said the Agent.

"It is probable," Howard replied, "that the boys have gone to dinner. In that case, if your business is important, he has possibly gone to call the post master himself."

A quarter of an hour passed. Carleton had had time to walk to Mr. B.'s house and back, but still he did not make his appearance. The Agent grew uneasy. He waited five minutes longer, then resolved upon a decisive step.

"Mr. Fellows," he cried, in the deaf gentleman's ear, "did you ever see that bill before?" Fortunately, Mr. Fellows' sight was good, though his hearing was bad. He examined the paper without spectacles, and decided at once that he then and there saw it for the first time.

"Did you not buy a horse of Carleton yesterday?"

"No," said Mr. Fellows; "I have talked of selling his mother a pony, but I never bought anything of him."

The truth flashed upon the Agent's understanding. For his credit let it be declared, Carleton had played his game with a consummate art that would have deceived "the very elect."

No time was lost in obtaining traces of the young man's flight. The Agent judged rightly, from his character, that he would not attempt to leave town. He anticipated a more melancholy fate for the unhappy youth. Some inward prompting seemed to direct him to an apothecary's shop not many doors distant, and on inquiry he learned that Carleton had just been there.

"Which way did he go?"

"In fact, I am not certain he has gone," said the druggist. "He purchased some medicines, remarking that he wished to write out some directions for its use, and stepped into the back room. I have been very busy, and he may have passed out without my seeing him."

The Agent sprang forward. The door was locked upon the inside.

"What medicine did you sell him?" asked the Agent.

"Oh! you needn't be alarmed, he has studied medicine, and knows how to use these things."

"He knows how to use them too well! This door must be forced. His life depends upon it,—if it is not already too late!"

Too late, indeed, it was!

On breaking into the room, Carleton was found lying upon the floor, with an empty vial beside him, and an unfinished letter to his sister on the table.

In that letter he confessed his guilt, and besought his sister not only to support the mortal affliction he had brought upon her, with fortitude, but also to sustain and console their mother. The young man was not yet dead. Medical assistance was speedily procured, but all efforts to save his life proved unavailing. He was already past consciousness, and never spoke again.

A veil should be drawn to exclude the scene of horror, agony, and distress that awaited his family. The broken-hearted mother survived the tragical interruption of her late happy days but a few months. And though the sister was afterwards happily married, it is said that, from the date of her brother's disgraceful end, a continual cloud of melancholy rested upon her mind during the remainder of her life. She has since passed into that land where kindred souls are destined to meet again; and these allusions to her sad family history will give her no pain.

The secret of Carleton's lapse from virtue is soon told; and the lesson is one that every youth, who considers himself secure from temptation, should heed and carefully remember. The devil never boldly enters the citadel of rectitude, at the outset. He first walks around, and passes by; then holds a parley, and "makes the worse appear the better reason;" and ends by gaining permission to walk in just *once*, promising thenceforward to cease his solicitations, and keep aloof. But once admitted, he goes artfully to work to destroy all our defences, and before we are aware of it, he is a permanent occupant of the castle.

Such was undoubtedly Carleton's experience. He was not a hardened sinner. He was truly a man of generous and noble impulses. But little transgressions of the stern law of conscience had in his boyhood weakened his moral force, and prepared him for more serious offences. Then, in an unguarded hour, he formed an attachment for a fascinating, but gay and heartless woman, under whose influences his soul fell from the truth and purity of manhood. It was her hand which indirectly administered the deadly drug that destroyed his life. To meet her necessities for dress and dissipations, he resorted to the faro bank. Although fortunate at first, he afterwards lost extensively, and became pecuniarily embarrassed. He borrowed money, which he was unable to return. Only one course seemed open to him, to save his honor in the public eye. At first, he purloined cautiously and abstemiously from the mails, hoping, no doubt, that success at the faro bank would swell those unlawful gains, and cancel the necessity for further depredations.

But let us not pursue the sad topic. The end we have seen, and we will hasten to turn the last leaf of this melancholy chapter.

CHAPTER VIII.

A NIGHT IN A POST-OFFICE.

Midnight Mails—Suspected Clerk—A trying Position—Limited View—A "crack" Agent—Sneezing—"Counter Irritation"—The Night Bell—Fruitless Speculations—Insect Orchestra—Picolo introduced—Snoring—Harmless Accident—The Boot-black—A tenanted Boot—The Exit.

SOME years ago, the post-office of a prominent city in Western New York became involved in a series of mail depredations, and at length it was apparent that some one of three clerks who had slept in the office, must be guilty of committing them; but the fastening of the charge upon the delinquent was a thing yet to be accomplished. By various processes, the range of suspicion was narrowed down till it rested upon *one* of the clerks, and it only remained to get the *legal* proof of his guilt.

Packages were missed that were known to have reached the office by the midnight mails. The clerks took turns in getting up to receive these mails, each one performing his duty for a week in succession, the one who for the time attended to it, sleeping on a cot in the post-office *proper*, and the other two occupying a small apartment at some little distance from the main office, but connected with it.

It had also been ascertained that the packages were abstracted from a particular mail-pouch which arrived with many others about midnight, and remained unassorted till morning. On a certain occasion, when the suspected clerk was upon duty, an exact description of everything in that pouch was taken, upon the cars from the West, with the view of comparing the list of its contents with the post bills which should be found on the files of the office the following morning, these bills having heretofore disappeared with the packages.

As I had before this had good reason to know that magistrates and jurors in that section of the country very properly required pretty conclusive evidence for conviction in such cases, I determined, in addition to other expedients, to take the post of private watchman inside the office, for one night at least, that I might obtain, by ocular demonstration, sufficient proof against the guilty one, to satisfy the most incredulous court and jury.

One of the unsuspected clerks was sent away that night, and the other, in whom I had the utmost confidence, was apprised of my intentions. By him I was let into the office through a private door, before the object of our machinations had entered; and I was not long in selecting a suitable place where I could see without being seen, behind an open door leading from the post master's private room. This position could command (through the crack of the door) a fair view of the aforesaid cot and its occupant.

It was not long before the individual arrived who was to be honored with my scrutiny during the live-long night; and as he "wrapt the drapery of his couch about him," I could not avoid making a momentary comparison between the luxury about to be enjoyed by him, and the wearisome hours upon which I was entering. Well,

"Some must watch, while some must sleep;
Thus runs the world away."

Sitting in the public stocks,—watching with the body of a person who has died of some contagious disease,—being cornered by a bore, when you have an immediate engagement elsewhere,—waiting your turn in a dentist's office,—all these are somewhat trying to the nerves; but for a real test of their power of endurance, commend me to a stand behind a door, between the hours of 10 P. M. and daylight; the thermometer ranging from 80 upwards, all motion and sound being forbidden, under the imminent risk of being discovered in your hiding place, and forced to retreat ignominiously.

This is a faint picture of the situation of the author on the night in question. Zeal for the public good, and a cracker or two, alone sustained him through the tedious night watches.

The proverb says that "a great deal can be seen through a small hole." My sphere of vision, however, was rather limited, embracing only a portion of the adjoining room, faintly lighted by a hanging lamp, the cot with its sleeping burden, a table, and the dimly seen tiers of letter boxes forming a back-ground. Entirely in keeping with this scene of "still life," was the monotonous buzz of sundry flies of a rowdyish disposition, who, not content with tickling the noses of peaceable citizens, and otherwise harassing them during the day, must needs "keep it up" through the hours devoted to repose by insects of more steady habits. However, they might have been engaged in the praiseworthy occupation of soothing one another to rest by their "drowsy hum," for I myself began to feel its soporific influence, and to bless "the man who first *in*vented sleep," but anathematize (inwardly) him who was *pre*venting it.

I was roused from this sleepy condition by a slight irritation in the Schneiderian membrane; in other words, I began to feel a desire to sneeze. Now, sneezing is an operation which admits of no compromise. You must either "go the whole hog," or entirely refrain. Any attempt to reduce the force of the explosion is as unavailing as was the Irishman's effort to "fire aizy" when he was touching off the cannon. So the annoying inclination must be nipped in the bud, if I wished to preserve my secrecy inviolate, and prove that I was "up to *snuff*."

Accordingly I called to mind (as far as I was able) and

practised all the expedients of which I had ever heard, besides others entirely original, for allaying this titillation. I rubbed the bridge of the nose; I would have slapped myself on the forehead, had I not feared the remedy would prove worse than the disease in respect of noise. I instituted experiments in "counter irritation," by pulling my hair, pinching my ear, and thus diverting attention from the rebellious organ; and finally I succeeded in subduing this refractory member. The uneasiness I felt lest, after all, I should be compelled to wake the echoes of the building, as well as other more tangible creations, were in some degree dispelled by several hearty snores which proceeded from the sleeper, and, like the guns which announce the arrival of a vessel in port, gave evidence that he had arrived in the land of dreams.

Under the cover of this "*feu de joie*," I dispatched a cracker (not a fire-cracker) which I happened to have in my pocket, as my inner man began to feel the effects of my unwonted position and consequent weariness.

At about midnight, a sudden peal of the bell, pulled by the mail carrier, at a back door, aroused the sleeper, who started up, went to the door and received the mail, and, after a little delay, returned to his bed, not, however, to sleep as quietly as before, as he often rolled over from side to side, occasionally uttering a groan.

Having nothing better to do, I speculated on the cause of these phenomena. They might be owing, first, to heat, second, to a disordered stomach, or third, to an uneasy conscience.

As to the first of these supposed causes, it seemed improbable that his recent visit to the door in a very airy costume, should have had any tendency to increase the animal heat; and as regarded the second theory, my knowledge of his dietetic habits was too limited to furnish me with data for anything like an argument. If his short delay at the door after receiving the mail bags, was produced by any cause for which conscience might properly goad him, the last hypothesis might be correct,—but on the whole I was obliged to follow the ex-

ample of many profounder theorists, and confess that I didn't know much about the matter.

A combination of the stomach and conscience suppositions, might be an adequate solution of the question, for the slender salary of a post-office clerk hardly sufficed for more than three meals a day, and the inference from these premises would be rather easy that a fourth must have been at the public expense.

Here my reflections came to an untimely end, for the insect orchestra, of whose performances I have spoken, was reinforced by the addition of a picolo, in the shape of one of those minute specimens of creation commonly called mosquito, whose note, "most musical, most melancholy," blended with the trombone of the blue bottle fly in a manner rather more curious than pleasing. And the different sounds produced by these insects were no less unlike than their modes of approaching their victims; the latter, with bull-headed obstinacy, bouncing against your face in a blundering way, with apparently no particular object excepting that of making himself generally disagreeable, while the former, lighting upon you as delicately as a snow flake, proceeds with admirable promptitude and definiteness of purpose to take out his lancet, and, like some never-failing humorist, is always "in the vein."

The tones of this insect Æolian rose and fell for a little time at a distance, but I was speedily aware of its presence in immediate proximity to my ear, and apparently making a tour of observation around my head, whereupon I commenced a blind sort of defence by flourishing my hands as noiselessly as possible round the region invaded, to as little purpose, however, as the attack of regular troops upon a body of Indians; for in a moment the music ceased, and I felt the sharp prick which informed me that I was hit, and I instinctively inflicted an energetic slap upon the spot, by which my enemy was extinguished, and one bill at least effectually cancelled. This result was not attained without a report, which so violently broke the silence, that I stood for a moment in breathless suspense, fearing that the sound would penetrate into the realms of Morpheus, and that thus I might pay too dearly for my triumph. But the sleeper "made no sign," and I was again left to my solitary musings.

A small pistol which I had observed my sleeping friend place under his head, on going to bed, did not tend to increase the comforts of my position, for since he had become so restless, the thought passed through my mind that he might have heard some suspicious noise in my direction, and was feigning sleep, while on the watch for its repetition. If this were the case, the discovery of a supernumerary on the premises, might lead to a hasty assault on the supposed midnight prowler, and also a more rapid transfer of the contents of the pistol to me than would be either agreeable or wholesome, before I could offer any reasonable explanation for my presence behind the door at such an unseasonable hour.

After a while, however, a renewal of the snoring, which was occasionally echoed by the occupant of the adjoining room, assured me of the absence of belligerent intentions, and the buzzing of the flies before mentioned, with the ticking of a clock in the office, were the only additional sounds that broke upon the silence.

About two o'clock, a slight accident occurred to me, which, however, did no harm. In reaching for a pitcher of water that stood on the table near by, I knocked off a book, which must have been poised on the corner of the table. I immediately imitated, by scratching, the gnawing of a rat in the wall, so that if the falling of the book had aroused the sleeper, he would have attributed both the noises to the imaginary animal.

But few sounds outside the building were heard, save the occasional drunken shout of some votary of Bacchus, reeling home to disgrace his family with his presence; and the measured strokes of the city clocks, as they told off the long, long hours.

But the most ludicrous circumstance happened just about daylight,—that is, daylight outside, for within the office it was still dark, as all the blinds were closed. I was startled by a sudden rap on the door of the post master's room which opened into the main hall, soon followed by another even more energetic. The clerk in the bed-room jumped from his bed and passed by me to open the door. Fearing that I should be discovered, I darted into the bed-room without his knowledge, and before he had returned. The truth is, he was not more than half awake, and had forgotten me entirely. He had admitted a colored man to get the boots which required his polishing touch, and then returned to bed again.

This gentleman of color, who by the way proved to be a trusty porter employed in several of the offices in the building, proceeded first to the side of the cot to get the boots there, and then made for the bed-room, into which I had retreated. In feeling about the floor to find the remaining "leathern conveniences," he seized one of mine! "I've got my foot in it now," thought I; but by a gentle and dexterous movement I succeeded in withdrawing the exposed covering from his partial grasp, without his discovering the existence of a leg within. Whether it was fright at the touch of the tenanted boot, or something else, that made him leave the premises so suddenly, I have never been fully satisfied. I went out myself soon after, leaving both clerks sound asleep.

What occurred on that night beyond that which I have already described, or how the investigation terminated, I am confident the reader will not insist upon knowing, when I assure him that there are special reasons, affecting public as well as private interests, why I should make no further disclosures.

Though this was not the last night which I have spent in post-offices for similar purposes, yet I have never repeated the experiment under circumstances requiring quite so severe restraints, and such abridgment of personal liberty.

CHAPTER IX.

Throwing off the Cars—Fiendish Recklessness—The Boot-Tracks—A Scamp among the Printers—Obstruction removed—A Ruse—The Boots secured—"Big Jobs"—The Trial—Unreliable Witness—A Life-Sentence.

In the narrations of mail robberies which we have thus far given, their perpetrators, though bold and unscrupulous, have not often plotted the destruction of human life in order to further their projects. But in the case we are about briefly to relate, murder on a large scale was coolly contemplated for the sake of the facilities which would be afforded to the plunderers of the mail, by the confusion, distress, and preoccupation which necessarily follow the throwing of cars from a railroad track. The certain destruction of property and the probable loss of life which would be caused by the successful execution of their plans, were nothing to these atrocious scoundrels, as long as by these means plunder might be brought within their grasp.

Rather more than a year ago, on a certain day in March, the locomotive of a mail train upon one of the Western railroads was thrown from the track by a "T" rail, which was placed with one end against a tie, so that the other, projecting somewhat upward, was struck by the engine. This occurred near a city in one of the Western States. No one on the train was injured, and whoever placed the obstruction failed in accomplishing his purpose, if that was to rob the mail.

No person was particularly suspected of the deed, but

tracks made by a boot of peculiar shape, with rows of large nails around the soles and heels, were found in the soft clay in the neighborhood of the spot, and an impression of them was taken for future reference. On the same day the Superintendent of the road received a letter, of which the following is a copy.

Adrian, March 7, 1854.

Sir: I have for the last few days written five or six notes to send you, but as often I have changed my mind and concluded to let the information that I wish to convey you, lie buried in obscurity. But the late act of villany that was committed I may say within sight of our city, forces me to disclose to you information that I received a few days ago of the formation of a gang of rascals who have combined together to commit, I may say, wholesale murder, and other criminal acts, by obstructing the passage of trains and endangering the same on the M. S. & N. R. R. This gang of villains is under the management of two men that are now known to me. The subject came to my knowledge by an offer from them of a large sum of money if I would take part with them in their intended villany.

This I refused, and scornfully regarded their proposals to have anything to do with them. I further threatened to expose them if they should attempt at any time to carry their intentions into effect, and one of them said if I should ever disclose to any one their intentions, that it would be certain death to me. I cannot in this note explain to you the information I wish to convey in full; but should you answer by dropping a line in the post-office to me, I will, if you wish, disclose to you the names of the parties; in fact, I will give you all the information that I can of the parties and their intended plot, on condition that you will give a liberal reward. I would be able to point them out or describe them so that they might be arrested. I am satisfied one of them has in his trunk documents that would disclose the whole matter.

I hope you will keep this subject dark, as I am exposing myself to great danger by disclosing this to you, and would also expose the interest of the road by disclosing this subject to the public. Yes, such would make the road a terror to all.

As I cannot write to any satisfaction, should you wish to know further about the matter, let me know and I will go to your office any evening that may be convenient to you.

For the present I remain yours,

A. S——.

The author of this document (who here signs a feigned name) claimed to be a natural son of an English lord celebrated in literature, and assumed the name of his pretended father. He seems to have been a man of considerable shrewdness, though he did not prove to be quite shrewd enough to outwit the business men and officers of justice with whom he had to deal.

The Superintendent replied to the letter, requesting an immediate interview. To this B. (the person in question) returned an answer, stating that he had written to one of the leaders of the gang in New York, and that he would call on the Superintendent as soon as he had received a reply, which might give him further information.

Three or four days after this the interview was held, and afterwards another in the presence of the attorneys of the railroad company. On these occasions, B. repeated his story with some further details, and offered to assist in the detection of the scoundrels, if he could be assured of a sufficient reward. There were many suspicious circumstances about this person, both as respected his appearance and the statements which he made.

It did not seem very probable that any one should have so intimate a knowledge of the designs of the villains as he appeared to possess, without being, to some extent at least, involved in their guilt. Notwithstanding their suspicions, the officers of the road concluded to engage his services, with the intention of keeping a sharp lookout upon him. He gave the names of several persons as concerned in the scheme, and proposed to correspond with some of the leaders and draw from them disclosures which would cause their detection.

About this time he went to work in a printing office, and was observed to be irregular in his habits, being much out at nights. He had occasional interviews with Mr. S. (one of the Attorneys above mentioned,) rather respecting what he had *not* discovered than what he had, and sometimes showing letters that he pretended to have received, threatening his life unless he left the country. These interviews, however unfruitful they were in available information, led to a result which was not anticipated by the cunning B.

Had this individual narrowly observed all the surroundings of the lawyer's office, he would have seen a quantity of fresh damp sand strewed upon the walk in front, through which he was obliged to pass on entering. Of course he thought nothing of it; hardly any one would; but the impressions which his boots made on that sand were found to correspond exactly with those obtained from the clay at the scene of the railroad accident before mentioned!

One evening, about three weeks after the accident on the railroad, B. rushed into the office of the railroad company in breathless haste, and informed the Assistant Superintendent that he had been applied to by a certain person to put obstructions on the track a little West of the city, to catch the 9 P. M. mail train West; but had got away from him and hurried to the office to give this information. The Assistant Superintendent and others immediately went up the road about two miles, and found obstructions placed in the spot indicated, and removed them. When the train passed, the light in front of the locomotive showed several men running into the woods.

This was the third instance of attempted obstruction to the mail trains upon this road, within less than a month (one having occurred previously to that first mentioned, causing, however, but slight damage,) and it was ascertained that there were considerable amounts of money in the mail on each of those occasions.

It may be remarked in passing, that although B. had notified the company in advance, of actual obstructions, and had given the names of the parties concerned, yet no progress seemed to be made in detecting the guilty individuals. It was evidently his policy to obtain money from the company as the price of his disclosure, and yet to manage so that no discovery would result.

In the mean time, the Post-Office Department had been

informed of these facts, and an experienced and skilful police officer in Chicago was appointed Special Mail Agent to investigate the matter. He very soon came to the conclusion that whoever the other guilty persons might be, B. was "one of 'em" to all intents and purposes. As we have before stated, B. had said that one of the leaders was in New York, and at the request of the company's attorney, B. wrote a letter to him.

The Chief of Police of New York was written to, and requested to station an officer at the post-office to watch for and arrest the party who should call for the letter, but during the time which elapsed between the arrival of the letter and the officer who was to watch outside the post-office, the letter disappeared, and even before any one connected with the New York post-office had been apprised of the arrangement.

Four days afterwards, B. informed one of the company's attorneys that the man in New York had received the letter and sent him a verbal answer to the effect, that he had better write no more by mail, "as the letters might get lost." Mr. P., the Chicago police officer, went in company with a lawyer to New York, with the design of finding the man to whom the letter was addressed. Their efforts, however, though assisted by the Chief of Police, and the Special Agent for the New York district, were unavailing.

It was ascertained that he had paid his passage to Liverpool on the ship Washington, but having been asked a casual question by one of the officers of the vessel, concerning his relationship to a certain Englishman, he had forfeited his passage-money, and disappeared.

Having returned to the West, Mr. P., the government Agent, determined to arrest B., which he effected, and, without his knowledge, obtained possession of his boots, which had already supplied such important evidence against him.

He displayed much virtuous indignation, and talked largely

of his wealth, respectability, and high standing in society; but all this availed him nothing, and he was committed to jail.

Although he had arrested B., yet Mr. P. doubted whether he had sufficient evidence to convict him, and determined to condemn him out of his own mouth. Accordingly he made arrangements with a deputy sheriff of Milwaukie, to play the part of prisoner, and thus to obtain the rascal's confidence.

Agreeably to this arrangement, when B. entered the prison, he found the deputy sheriff already in his cell, apparently a fellow victim to the demands of justice. For about four weeks this gentleman was most of the time in the cell with B., representing himself as an "express robber;" conducting himself in such a turbulent manner that B. supposed the time of his absences was passed in the dungeon.

For some time, however, he failed in extracting any disclosures from B., who confidently expected that his connection with the railroad company would protect him. After he had been in prison about three weeks, B. was informed that his arrest had been made by an United States officer, who intended to make his boots convict him of obstructing the mail train, and that the railroad company were powerless to shield him from punishment for acts committed (as this had been) previous to his employment by them.

He now saw his danger, and, on returning to his cell with his supposed fellow prisoner, who had assumed the name of Harris, he manifested great agitation. Harris asked what was the matter. B. hesitated for a while, and at length exclaimed: "That rascally P. has stole my boots."

"What if he has?" replied the pseudo Harris. "They couldn't be worth much."

"They are worth considerable to me, I can tell you, for he means to send me to State prison with them."

"Send you to State prison? What in the world do you mean? How can your boots send you to State prison?"

"Why, he is going to show that they made the tracks that were found where the rail was put on the track East of Adrian."

"Well," said Harris, "that looks rather bad, but it isn't as bad as it might be. You'll get out of it yet, and I'll help you, if I can. I expect to get bailed out in a day or two, and if I can do anything for you, I will."

"You are the man for me," said B., "and I shall want you to come and swear on my trial that you saw a person by the name of A—— put the rail on, and that I wasn't there."

"But if you are innocent," replied Harris, "you will get clear; and if you are guilty, I don't believe I can help you."

"You must, by heavens," said B. "If you don't, I'm a goner!"

Here the conversation ended that day, but the next morning B. directed his fellow prisoner to testify that his name was Grover, and that on the night on which the obstruction in question was made, he went with A——, and saw him put the rail on the track. (So minute, by the way, was B.'s description of the place and the manner in which the obstructing rail was laid, that the deputy sheriff going there afterwards in company with Mr. P., easily found the spot, and identified the very tie under which the rail was placed, though it was the first time he had been there.)

"Well," said Harris, *alias* Grover, (who seemed to grow rapidly rich in names,) if I help you out in this way, what shall *I* get by it?"

B. replied: "If you get me clear I shall keep the confidence of the railroad company, and will introduce you to a set of good fellows who do nothing but big jobs, and my connection with the company will enable me to get you a position where you can pay yourself."

Having by such inducements secured (as he supposed) the aid of his companion, B. recovered his equanimity, and wrote as follows to one of the attorneys for the railroad company:—

"To return to the obstruction east of Adrian in regard to my boots such as I can prove by J S that I mentioned in my last, by him I can prove where I was that night, as also where my boots were, and as for the other man's evidence I am sure that I cannot be mistaken as to my success on trial or examination. I hope you will soon see Mr G again and be sure to have him at the time. As to the danger of my going to Adrian for fear I would fall into the hands of the engineers and firemen in that place, I will say for once and all, let me go to Adrian—& as to the danger of falling into the hands of rowdies I am not afraid of no! no! not if all the fiends of Pandemonium was to raise against me I will not shrink from anything as long as I am innocent or as long as I can have the protection of the law on my side Justice! Justice!! is all I claim and that I expect to have before a Court of justice and an independent & impartial Jury. if I can't swim there let me sink.

Res. yours & Others, A. S. B.

P. S. I will convince your Engineers & firemen that I was their friend, and that I have oftentimes run myself into danger for their safety, as well as that of the Company & the travelling public Yes & if they or the Co. have any feeling of gratitude in them I am sure that they will not show it by prosecuting me but first I must prove "*my title* clear" & that I can do so Hurra boys, &c., three times three.

Yours truly, A. S. B."

The railroad company could have no further doubt of his guilt. It was plain that he had entered their service to betray them; and though he had given the names of his accomplices, he had been careful not to catch them.

At his request he was removed to Adrian for trial. He told his counsel what he should prove by Grover; and was assured of an honorable acquittal.

At the trial, the counsel for the prosecution examined several witnesses in relation to the boot-tracks, which, for the time being, were as interesting to the legal fraternity, as are the ancient bird-tracks found in sandstone, to geologists.

The defence supposed that the counsel for the prosecution would there rest, and were confident that they had the game in their own hands, knowing, as they did, that the evidence thus far adduced was not sufficient to convict their client.

But the prosecution called "Wm. B.," (the deputy sheriff,) when, to the utter astonishment and dismay of the prisoner, his man Grover took the stand!

This unexpected transmutation at once dissipated the dreams of triumph and future villany in which he had been revelling; and as "Wm. B." testified to the facts in his possession, and the disclosures of the prisoner, this baffled scoundrel found the prop on which he had relied falling beneath him, and plunging him into that gulf from which he had made such desperate though vain efforts to escape.

He was found guilty on two indictments. On the first, he was sentenced to imprisonment for life, the judge remarking that he would suspend sentence on the other till the first had expired.

The interval between the pilfering of small sums and the deliberate plotting of wholesale murder for the sake of plunder, seems a wide one; yet no one who enters even the verge of the maelstrom of a dishonest course, can tell how far within the vortex he may be drawn by its ever strengthening current.

The case just related forms a culminating point in the series of villanies which we have recorded in this book for the benefit of those who, in defiance of the eternal laws of Providence, attempt to make the way of the transgressor easy.

CHAPTER X.

STOPPING A POST-OFFICE.

The Unpaid Draft—The Forged Order—A Reliable Witness—Giving up the Mail Key—A Lady Assistant—Post-Office Records—The official Envelope—Return of the Post Master—The Interview—Embarrassment of Guilt—Duplicate Circular—Justice secured.

ONE of the coolest and at the same time silliest pieces of post-office rascality that I have ever known, occurred a few years since in Rhode Island.

A small draft from the Post-Office Department having been presented by a mail contractor to the post master of P., payment was refused, on the ground that the office had been abolished some time before, and that there was little or nothing due the Department. No time was lost by the contractor in apprising the proper officer at Washington, of the non-payment of the draft, and the reason assigned therefor; when reference was at once made to the official records. They, however, failed to show the discontinuance of the office.

Here was a mysterious and singular affair, and a letter was accordingly despatched to the seemingly delinquent post master, requiring an explanation of his course. A reply to this was very promptly sent to the Department, to the effect that some months previous he had received from the Appointment Office formal notice that his office had been discontinued, accompanied by an order to hand over all the mail matter remaining on hand, together with the mail key, and other property of the Department, to a neighboring post master, and that he had of course answered the demand.

A re-examination of the books still showing the office to be a "live one," he was written to, and directed to forward the original document upon the authority of which he had shut up his office. The papers were duly forwarded, and sure enough, there was the "Order," signed with the name of the Second Assistant Post Master General, who was then at the head of the Appointment Office. It read as follows:—

Post-Office Department, March 28, 1846.

SIR,

The Post Master General having decided to discontinue the Post-Office at P——, from and after the expiration of the present fiscal quarter, you will, at that time, please hand over all mail matter, the mail key, and all other property belonging to the Department, to the Post Master at M——, on his presenting this order.

Very Respectfully,
Your Obt. Servant,
WM. J. BROWN,
2d Asst. P. M. General.

Although a tolerably fair imitation of that officer's handwriting, it was at once pronounced a forgery. My services, as Special Agent, were called into requisition, and all the facts, as they then stood, communicated to me. As speedily as possible I visited the scene of this perplexing and extraordinary official mystery. Arriving at the site of the late post-office, I found its former incumbent to be a highly respectable merchant, well advanced in years, and blessed with one of those countenances which, to a person at all accustomed to study character in that way, at once dispels all doubt and distrust. He was of Dutch descent, and, while intelligent on general subjects, was poorly "posted" in the arts and devices of cunning knaves. From him I received a full statement of the shutting up process, and obtained some additional facts, which afterwards furnished me with a clue to the whole mystery.

On one of the last days of March, Mr. G——, post master at another village in the same town, called on him in company with one of his friends, and presented what purported to be a copy of an order from the Department, directing him to close the office, and to give up the property in the manner already described. Of course the post master felt and manifested no little surprise, for the office had been established but about a year, and he had heard of no application or desire in any quarter for such a proceeding.

"It is all right, I suppose," said he, after carefully examining the "copy" which had been handed him without a word of explanation; "but I think, before I hand over the property, I ought to have the original order."

"Oh yes, it's all correct," responded the witness (who had seen the copy made from the spurious order, supposing that to be genuine); "I saw it compared with the original myself, and it's a true copy."

"But the quarter will not be ended till to-morrow," remarked the astonished official; "and, on the whole, I think I must refuse compliance, unless the original instructions are placed in my hands."

"Then I understand you as refusing to obey the order of the Department, do I?" said the applicant.

"Not at all," was the mild response; "I am perfectly ready to comply when I see the written command over the signature of the proper officer of the Department. It can be but little trouble to produce that, and I think, under the same circumstances, you would demand as much yourself."

"But do I not bring a reliable witness to prove that this is an exact copy of the original?" asked the visitor, impatiently.

"True, but my request is reasonable, and I think I will adhere to it," he replied; and the gentleman, with his companion, left the premises, simply remarking, "You will hear from me again, to-morrow." And sure enough, he did.

Towards sun-down on the following day, the abolisher of post-offices made his appearance, and, with an air of authority, without uttering a word, threw the extinguishing document upon the counter. The post master took it up, and after adjusting his spectacles, examined first the outside. It had the usual printed endorsement on the right hand upper corner, "Post-Office Department, Official Business," was properly franked by the Second Assistant, post-marked "Washington," and plainly addressed to the "Post Master, M——, R. I."

On withdrawing the letter from its covering, it had, sure enough, every appearance of genuineness, and no doubt remained that it was the official action of the Department. The post-office effects were accordingly put in shape as hastily as possible, and handed over. But

"The course of *knavery* never did run smooth."

Strong suspicions began to arise that the neighboring post master, before mentioned, was the author of the whole transaction, and when the knowledge of a motive on his part was supplied, his guilt became to my mind clear and positive.

It appeared that at the time of the establishment of the now defunct post-office, there was a tremendous opposition, in which he took an active and leading part, but the member of Congress for that District favored the application for the new office, and it was finally granted. Being but two miles from the old establishment, there was, as had been anticipated, a considerable falling off in the receipts of the latter. The snake was "scotched, not killed," or in other words, post master number one had bottled up his wrath, and was biding his time. The affair had now become with him a matter of pride as well as interest, and when joked, as he frequently was, about his defeat in the post-office contest, he was often heard to say that the new post-office was "short-lived any way."

He was quite an active, prominent politician, and when a new nomination for Congress was to be made, he thought he saw his way clear. He struggled hard for the selection of a personal friend, and succeeded, not only in the nomination, but in the election. But when the pinch came, the Honorable member failed him, and could not be persuaded to take the responsibility, for the new post-office had proved really a great convenience to many of his constituents and to some of his friends, personal and political.

With the advantage of this information obtained from the ex-post master and one or two other citizens of that vicinity, I proceeded to visit the office which at one gulp had swallowed up the other, without apparent injury to its digestive organs. The post master was absent, and the office in charge of his wife. This was a piece of good luck, for it would enable me to examine the books and papers to greater advantage, and what was better, to interrogate the lady and her lesser half separately. Two or three points were very important.

Might not some wicked wag in the Department, knowing all the circumstances of the case, have prepared the letter in question, and sent it as a hoax? This could be easily settled by referring to the account of mails received, for the record in that event should show the receipt of a free letter, either direct from Washington, or from the Distribution office at New York. Then another test, was a comparison of the "order," with the hand-writing of the post master. But the most troublesome point of all to reconcile, was, how the official envelope had been obtained, for that was beyond a doubt genuine.

Introducing myself to the lady assistant, who happened to be alone in the office, I remarked,—

"I am in pursuit of a letter which should have come here from New York in March last, and I wish to see if your New York packages, during that month, were all regularly received. Where do you keep your transcripts, the books, or sheets, you know, upon which you copy your post-bills?"

They were taken from a desk and laid before me. Turning to the record of the month in question, not a single free letter was entered as received at that office for the last two weeks in March, from any quarter!

"Who made the entries in this book?" I inquired. "My husband," was the prompt answer.

Having the general style of the "order" in my mind, I glanced over a few pages of the book, and observed several peculiarities in the formation of some of the capital letters which I had noticed in the (to this time) fatherless document. It was written in bluish ink, and so were the pages of the records made at about the same time,—a trifling circumstance to be sure, but yet a link in the chain of evidence. The wafer too, used in sealing, was strikingly similar in size and shade to those contained in a large box upon the desk. The "order" was on a half sheet of letter paper of different size and stamp from the wrapper enclosing it.

It now remained to establish some reasonable theory to account for his possession of a genuine official envelope. Some farther reflection supplied that theory which in the sequel proved to be the correct one. The date of the Washington post-mark I had before noticed, was very indistinct, in fact could not be made out, although the word "Washington" and "March" were tolerably plain. At that time the present style of envelopes were not much in use by the Department.

Could it not be an old wrapper, or the "fly leaf" of some former official document from head quarters? This idea was certainly favored by the fact that on one side it presented a ragged appearance as if torn from another half sheet; and if its fellow could be found on the premises, the two parts must necessarily fit together, and conclusively show that a branch of the Appointment office had really been temporarily established without authority of law, not far from that locality.

It was now late in the afternoon, and the post master still absent, though momentarily expected home. An invitation to take tea with the good lady, was the more readily accepted, from a desire to prevent any comparing of notes between them with respect to the inquiries and examination already made. At the table I ventured, for the first time, to broach the sub ject of the "stoppage" affair.

"I believe the last time I passed over this route, you had two post-offices in town," I remarked.

"Yes," was the reply, "but it made so much bother, and did so little good, that it was abolished some months since."

In her manner of receiving this remark, I could discover no proof of a participation in, or knowledge of the process by which the rival concern had been gotten rid of. And I might as well say in this connection as anywhere else, that I have never in my own official experience, known any instance of a wife or child being made an accomplice, partner or confidant, "before the fact," in the commission of serious post-office offences. Prying ladies have sometimes, however, from curiosity, rather than pecuniary considerations, exhibited a remarkable aptness in getting at the written contents of letters, without the consent or knowledge of the owners.

The cloth had not long been removed before the post master's approach was heralded by the scratching at the door of a large Newfoundland dog, the circumstance being at once noted by the lady as indicative of the safe return of her husband. In a moment more the sound of the horse's hoofs were distinctly heard, and as soon as the nag had been passed over to a boy we had left in the office, the post-office annihilator entered.

"My dear," says the affectionate wife, "you have got back once more." And with this salutation she announced her guest, as "a gentleman who had come to see about some post-office business."

He eyed me rather closely, and with a much less amiable expression than he assumed on learning that I was a near relative of his "Uncle Sam," which I saw it was essential to make known to him, in order to secure decent treatment; for he was decidedly savage in his looks and manners on the first introduction, taking me no doubt for some troublesome customer (as I eventually proved to be, by the way,) who had come to bother him about some trifling affair.

An intimation that I would like to see him at the post-office was sufficient. We soon found ourselves there alone, and I commenced interrogating him thus:—

"Did you receive notice from the Department in March last of the discontinuance of the office at P.?"

"I did, and was ordered to take possession of the property of the Department," he replied. "The old gentleman," said he, "rather hated to yield; but, when I showed him the documents, he caved in and made the best of it. The fact is, the office never ought to have been created at all."

"When did the order reach your hands?" I asked; "and do you remember the circumstance of its arrival in the mail?"

"I well remember all about it," said he; "I opened the mail that day myself, as usual. I think it was one of the last days in March. I shall never forget the astonished look of neighbor N., as he perused the order converting him into a private citizen once more."

"He wasn't satisfied with a certified copy of the unwelcome document, was he?" I remarked. "And, by the way, what was the object of serving a *copy* of the paper on him?"

"Well," he rejoined, with a slight embarrassment, "the fact is, I thought I had better retain the original for my own protection, in case of any fuss. He had to have it, however, before he would shut up shop."

At this juncture I produced the "order," and laying it before him, requested that he would turn to the entry of a free letter on his "mails received," at the time of the receipt of this one. The search was in vain, as I well knew it would be; and he undertook to explain that circumstance by claiming that official letters frequently came from Washington without wrapper or post-bill.

By this time he evidently began to construe my inquiries into a suspicion of his fraudulent conduct; and, as in all such cases, every attempt to extricate himself only made the matter worse.

"Come to think of it," said he, "I was absent from home the day that letter arrived, and on my return I took it from my private box where my letters are put," at the same time pointing to a pigeon-hole in a small letter-case over the desk.

"And would your wife open the mail in your absence?" I inquired.

Receiving an affirmative answer, I requested him to call her, taking care that they should hold no private conversation. Exhibiting to her the outside of the letter, I asked if she recollected taking it from the mail and placing it in the post master's box. They exchanged glances, and, on the second look towards him, I was just in time to observe a trifling nod of the head by way of intimating that she had better say yes. But she thought otherwise, and was quite positive that if such a thing had come loose in the bag, at any time when she opened the mail, she would have noticed it.

"To come right to the point," said I, "this document is disowned by the Department, and no authority has been given to any one to discontinue the other office."

A forced laugh from the post master followed this announcement, but the honest wife looked worried.

"Well," he answered, "if it did not come from the Appointment Office, then some mischievous clerk in the Department may have sent it as an April-fool hoax, as it was near the first of April; or some one may have slipped it into my private box unobserved, though no one could well do it unless it was the boy that you see about here."

"I see no motive that he could have had for doing it," I observed.

"But he might possibly have been hired to do it," was the reply.

In accounting for the envelope, it now became an important point to settle whether or not the post master had been in the habit of preserving all official circulars from the Department. If so, and this envelope had been torn from one of them, the remaining fragment might still come to light as his certain accuser. A search of the files showed the preservation of all such documents for two years previous, but nothing appeared to match the covering of the "order."

Still believing it was obtained in that way, I adjourned the investigation for a few days, and meantime applied to the Department for duplicates of any printed circulars that had been sent to this office, and the return mail brought me one that was so sent, but a few weeks previous to the fraud in question. Its absence from the post master's files, while all other similar documents had been carefully saved, was a strong circumstance to show that a part of it at least had been used for this dishonest purpose. But the damning proof was yet to come. In the printed words "Official Business," which were in capitals on the outside of the duplicate circular, there was a defect, or "nick" in the letter O, and the last S, in business. On comparing this with the covering of the spurious order, exactly the same bruises were found in the same letters, identifying the one with the other in the most positive manner, as the coincidence would be almost miraculous of the same type being battered in precisely the same way, upon circulars printed at different times.

Nor was this all. In folding the circular before the ink was fairly dry, some parts of the printed words in the body of it had "struck off" upon the inner side of the "fly leaf," which parts of words could, by a strong light, be distinctly observed upon several lines directly under each other. Referring to the printed page of the entire circular received for examination and comparison, a copy of which was known to have been sent to this post-office, *the same words were found to occur, and precisely in the same relative positions.*

Thus was the final link in the chain of evidence closed and riveted; a chain which held the guilty one in its unyielding grasp, and set at nought all attempts at evasion or escape, had he been disposed to make them. His only alternative was silence or confession, and of these he chose the latter.

A full report of all the facts above stated was made to the Department, and the tricky post master soon received an official letter from Washington, concerning whose genuineness the most sceptical could have no doubt. In this case, "the engineer was hoist with his own petard." In stopping his neighbor's office he was himself stopped; and, furthermore, received a reward for his misdeeds, the nature of which any future post-office stopper will learn by sad experience.

The defunct office was resuscitated, and its former incumbent reinstated in all the rights and privileges of which he had boon deprived by the treachery of his unscrupulous opponent.

Nothing but the most obstinate determination to carry his point, at all hazards, could have impelled this man to the extreme measures which he adopted for ridding himself of his rival. Forgery is a crime of sufficient magnitude, one would think, to deter from its commission any one that is not prepared to go all lengths in the execution of his designs. And the present case shows how far pride and self-will may carry a man who yields to their suggestions, and how small a matter may be sufficient to raise them to an irresistible height, and create a tide which may sweep away conscience, and honor, and all that is valuable in character, to say nothing of an enlightened regard to self-interest.

The man whose discreditable exploit we have recorded, paid dearly for his short-lived triumph; and whoever is in danger of suffering his pride or obstinacy to hurry him beyond the bounds of prudence and virtue, will do well to "sit down first, and count the cost."

CHAPTER XI.

Indian Depredations—The model Mail Contractor—Rifles and Revolvers—Importance of a Scalp—Indian Chief reconnoitering—Saving dead Bodies—Death of a Warrior—The Charge—A proud Trophy.

Sunset on the Prairie—Animal Life—A solitary Hunt—The Buffalo Chase—Desperate Encounter with an Indian—Ingenious Signal—Returning to Camp—Minute Guns—A welcome Return.

PREVIOUS to the year 1850 there was no regular mail service between the valley of the Mississippi and New Mexico and Utah Territories. In selling lands to settlers and taking these communities under the protecting care of the nation, the Government was bound in good faith to give them a regular mail. This, like all other mail service, is carried on without much regard to the question whether the actual receipts from the locality will be remunerative or not.

The commencement of this service in 1850, called out the energies of some of our most daring and enterprising business men. A tract of country nearly one thousand miles in extent had to be traversed, where there were no civilized inhabitants, and but one or two military posts.

The Indian tribes, finding their game disappear before the unerring rifle of the white hunter, and learning the taste of the luxuries of civilized life without the industry to procure them, became at first sullen and despairing, then hostile and revengeful. A detailed account of the "hair breadth 'scapes," the dangers, losses, and tragedies in encounters with hostile

Indians, in transporting the United States mails across these plains, would form one of the most remarkable chapters in the postal history of the world.

One mail contractor on the route from Independence, Missouri, to Santa Fé, by his success in transporting the mails safely, and his daring and diplomacy with the Indians, has become eminent among his countrymen, and dreaded by the hostile tribes whom he has encountered. The treachery so fatally prevalent in meetings between small bands of whites and these dark sons of the forest, and the cunning and boldness displayed in stealing the horses and cattle that belong to the "pale faces," have made it necessary that great caution should be used, and also that the Indians should be made to feel the force of that terrible weapon the modern rifle. The Indian has long since learned the superiority that the possession of "revolvers" gives to the white hunters. And he has also learned at what distance it is safe for him to approach the camp or the traveling party of his foes. They do not consider that there is much security in any distance less than three hundred yards, when well mounted and in rapid motion.

The honor attached to the possession of scalps, and the dismal forebodings attending the loss of a beloved chief, make all the tribes particularly cautious that their leaders shall not be too much exposed, and that their slain shall not fall into the hands of the enemy. A reckless daring displayed by a chief, always gives him honor with his tribe, and this is proportioned to the success which attends his efforts and skill, whether in the offensive or defensive.

The mail contractor before alluded to, is a man of great humanity as well as courage, and prefers making now and then a terrible example, rather than wage an indiscriminate warfare with tribes inveterately hostile.

After the tragic occurrences attending the capture and terrible death of Mrs. White, with several others in a party of California emigrants near Santa Fé, the Indians, emboldened by success, seemed to feel that they had the power and did not lack the will to drive all white travelers from the plains. Our "model mail contractor," in addition to the heavy responsibility of conveying from fifteen hundred weight to a ton and a half of the United States mails, often had intrusted to his care, coin and gold dust in considerable quantities, and the lives and effects of numerous passengers.

A usual "mail train" consisted of three covered wagons, with elliptic springs, each drawn by six mules, guarded by eight or ten men, and carrying perhaps as many passengers.

Thirty miles a day was a usual drive, and this gave several hours' rest in every twenty-four. By having plenty of Sharp's rifles, and Colt's six-shooting cavalry pistols, the entire company of men and passengers formed a terrible phalanx, able to fire three or four hundred shots without any delay in loading.

The Indians soon learned to *respect* these parties, and usually gave them a wide berth, not venturing to attack them though outnumbering them by more than ten to one.

Soon after the above-mentioned barbarous transactions near Santa Fé, the mail was on its way accompanied by the contractor himself. One morning, marks of hostile Indians were quite frequent. A large camp was passed where the fires still burned, and newly picked bones of buffalo and deer were scattered around.

In the course of the forenoon, several Indians were seen, and at the noon rest, their whole party was in sight, numbering apparently one hundred and fifty or more. The main body kept three or four hundred yards off, but one daring warrior, evidently their chief, would ride in a wide circuit, approaching sometimes within a hundred and fifty or two hundred yards of the mail wagons. He seemed to be reconnoitering; and though the mail party, passengers and all, did not exceed a dozen persons, there seemed to be little disposition to attack them. The chief—as he proved to be—was splendidly dressed; the long feathers on his head waving in the wind, and mounted on a milk white horse, he seemed the Murat of his nation.

A shield of raw hide, dried in the sun, quite common among the Indians, covered his entire person from his saddle to his neck. Though within rifle shot, his swift riding and the protection afforded by the shield, gave but little chance for a successful shot. In the most daring and impudent manner he rode several times in a semicircle, reducing the distance between his followers and the little band of whites, at least one half.

The mail contractor told his men to stand by their arms, and be ready for an attack. He then took his Sharp's rifle and lay down on the ground, resting his gun across a stone. He looked across the sights, and saw the chief "wheel his daring flight" within good gun range, but always on the full run with his head just in sight over the shield. Each Indian is provided with a rope or *lariat* made of hide, and this is fastened by one end around the rider's waist, and by the other to the saddle, that in the event of his being killed, the horse will drag off the dead body and thus prevent its falling into the hands of his enemies.

Some accident happened to the chief on the white charger; his stirrup broke, or something took place which obliged him to dismount. He was then about a hundred and seventy yards from the mail camp, and as he dismounted on the farther side, he was no fairer mark than before. It was easy enough to shoot down the horse, but that would accomplish nothing, as the chief was nearer to his friends than to his foes. It was evident that he must, to a certain extent, expose himself, when he mounted, and as he sprang up in his stirrup, his breast for a moment presented a fair mark.

The sharp ring of the rifle was heard, and the chief lay on the ground, while the blood sprinkled the snowy flank of the beautiful charger. He was shot through the heart!

The horse sprung, and the weight of the dead chief broke the *lariat* clear from the saddle. The consternation among the Indians was terrible. Drawing their knives and pistols, the mail carriers gave a yell, and charged directly at the whole array of Indians. The head of the little band, whose successful shot had so opportunely killed the chief, had given orders not to attack except on the defensive, but nothing could restrain them; and appalled as much by the daring bravery of the whites as by the sudden death of their chief, the warriors broke and fled.

The scalp of the unfortunate Indian was soon stripped from the skull, and, with its dark and flowing locks, formed a trophy of the short combat, and made the subject of a tale around the fireside of the bold and hardy pioneer.

We have room for but one more narrative of border life, and the perils of mail carrying in the backwoods; and this is also an incident in the life of our "model mail contractor."

At a period anterior to the events just related, the mail, with quite a number of wagons, was wending its way toward Santa Fé. The party were near the banks of the Cimmeron, and then in the country of the Arrapahoes. Large herds of buffalo were constantly visible, but no Indians had been seen for some days.

It was a beautiful afternoon in June, the slowly descending sun illuminating one of the grandest scenes in nature—a broad rolling prairie covered with verdure, and presenting one checkered field of animal life. Beautiful antelopes, that flew rather than ran, and scarce seemed to touch the earth; stately elks, with branching horns, gallantly guarding their gregarious herds, and the unwieldy bison, far more numerous than all the rest, numbering hundreds of thousands, and blackening the plain as far as the eye could reach. Our hero of many an Indian skirmish and numerous buffalo hunts, mounted his horse to go and select an animal from the vast herd, which should furnish supper for his party.

He was mounted on a fleet animal, but after getting fairly away from the train, he found he had omitted to put on his spurs. It was in a section of country where small streams form deep ravines, some of them nearly as abrupt, though not as deep as the awful *canons* of the Gila and the head branches of the Rio Grande. He singled out a fat buffalo cow, and drawing his "Colt," dashed on to get near and be sure of a fatal shot at the first fire. Not being able to spur his horse, the animal led him a rapid race, and taking a path, followed it down a dark ravine, where a slender stream gurgled idly between its banks.

His horse, accustomed to the sport, went faster and faster, and neared the buffalo at every spring, till she suddenly turned the corner of the bank, now near the bottom of the ravine, and some fifty or sixty feet below the level of the prairie. The path that led down the ravine was a gradual descent, and on each side were some scattering trees and bushes.

When the bluff was rounded in pursuit of the buffalo, the animal was but a few yards ahead, and then, for the first time, a fair mark. Our hero was nearly ready to fire, when *whiz!* went an arrow so near that there was no mistaking its sound, especially to one whose ear was practised in Indian warfare.

The arrow had scarcely ceased its whir, before a mounted Indian came down upon our buffalo hunter, from behind the bank of the ravine. His lance was poised in its "rest," with the butt of it firmly against his shoulder. The buffalo passed from sight, and the Indian instantly appeared; and before there was a moment for reflection, the "white hunter" had to "wink and hold out his iron."

The lance was a bright piece of steel, about twenty inches long, on a pole of some twelve feet in length. This murderous blade was aimed directly at his breast, and the two horses on a full run in opposite directions. Our contractor had nothing on but a pair of trousers, his red hunting shirt, and traveling cap.

The Indian, with the exception of some long feathers on his head, was naked to the waist. The savage observed the "law of the road," and took the right, and with one simultaneous and almost involuntary movement, the "pale face" dropped the bridle, and with his left arm parried the approaching blow by knocking the lance upward. The blade in its course ripped the hunting shirt, and tore the muscles from his shoulder; and simultaneously with this he fired his "Colt," and saw the blood spirt from the naked breast of the Indian. The slain warrior fell heavily to the ground, while the white man's horse turned suddenly to the right, and mounted the bank of the ravine, which was here so steep, that, having no longer a hold of the bridle, the rider came near tumbling backward.

The surface of the prairie was gained, and near two hundred yards measured off by the horse before the owner had time to gather his scattered thoughts. He attempted to grasp the bridle, but found his left arm quite powerless, not only from the wound on the shoulder, but the stunning effect of the lance on his fore-arm, near the wrist. With a rapid movement he plunged his pistol into the holster, and seizing the bridle with his right hand, drew up his horse and dismounted.

Every movement had been so rapid since going down the path into the ravine after the buffalo, until he emerged in safety on the plain, that he had not reflected a moment. He had done better; he had *acted.*

There now appeared five Indians, all mounted, and not more than two hundred and fifty yards from where he stood. He instantly formed his plan. His arms consisted of his revolver, and a double-barrelled English fowling-piece, one barrel loaded with ball, and the other with buckshot. He unstrapped his gun, kept himself on the farther side of the horse from the Indians, and as they seemed to be approaching him, he made his arrangements. He concluded to wait until they arrived within about a hundred and fifty yards, and then fire with his ball, and if possible, kill the foremost. The other barrel with the buckshot would then be "good" for two more, when he would have five loaded barrels of his "Colt," with only two foes. But the cowardly villains dared not attack him. Four of them retreated, and the other rode a little nearer to reconnoitre.

The Indian, believing he knew the character of his foe as that of an old hunter, was sure he was armed with one or more "six-shooters." He communicated his thoughts to his red-skinned brethren, by riding several times rapidly round in a circle, this being the sign given by the Arrapahoes when they meet white men armed with "revolvers."

Being satisfied with this view of their foe, and the taste they had had of his prowess, they turned their horses and disappeared down the ravine.

Danger was not yet over, and our friend was determined to be ready for whatever might happen. He rode slowly away for fifty or a hundred yards, and stopped. Thinking he had better have his arms in as good condition as possible, he dismounted and thought he would load the discharged barrel of his pistol. On looking, this trusty weapon was missing. The holster was entirely torn away, and the pistol gone. He went back where he had waited for the Indians, and there lay the pistol on the ground.

In his violent effort to put up the weapon and stop the horse while one arm was totally disabled, he had evidently thrust it in the holster so violently as to tear the leather away, and the weapon unperceived had fallen to the ground.

Having loaded the empty barrel, he again mounted. The sun by this time was just setting. The Indians and the long dark ravine lay between him and the camp, and he took a circuitous route to meet the train.

After going some four miles to the south-west, he came to the road. By the light of the moon he examined the track to see if his wagons with their broad tires had passed. There were no ruts but those made by the narrow-tired wagons of a Mormon train that was one or two days ahead of them. He then followed back, and mile after mile not a sound, not a person, not an animal, or a camp fire broke the vast solitude! But now he hears a gun directly ahead of him.

Another minute and another gun; yes, 'tis his own party camped out for the night, firing minute guns as a signal, and waiting with anxiety and fear for their absent leader. He soon rode up, and—in the words of the narrator, as he told us the story—" how the boys took me in their arms and hugged me ! They fairly screamed as I told them how I missed the buffalo but didn't miss the Indian. They took me on their shoulders and carried me three times round the camp. We saw no more of the Arrapahoes during the journey to Santa Fé."

Such have been the adventures and perils of carrying the mails between the far outposts of civilization, on our wild frontier.

CHAPTER XII.

Cheating the Clergy—Duping a Witness—Money missing—A singular Postscript—The double Seal—Proofs of Fraud—The same Bank-Note—"Post-Boy" confronted—How the Game was played—Moving off.

OUR collection of "outside" delinquencies would be incomplete, were we to omit the following case, which was investigated by the author not long ago, and in which not a little ingenuity, of the baser sort, was displayed. It will serve as a specimen of a numerous class of cases, characterized by attempts to defraud some correspondent, and to fasten the blame of the fraud upon some one connected with the Post-Office. We could give many instances of a similar kind, did our limits permit.

A person of good standing in community, who laid claim not only to a moral, but a religious character, was visiting in a large town on the Hudson river, about midway between New York and Albany. This person owed a clergyman, living in New Haven, Conn., the sum of one hundred dollars; and one day he called at the house of another clergyman of his acquaintance in the town first mentioned, and requested to be allowed the privilege of writing a letter there to his clerical creditor, in which the sum due that gentleman was to be enclosed. Writing materials were furnished, and he prepared the letter in the study of his obliging friend, and in his presence.

After he had finished writing it, he said to the clergyman, "Now, as the mails are not always safe, I wish to be able to prove that I have actually sent the money. I shall therefore consider it a great favor if you will accompany me to the bank, where I wish to obtain a hundred-dollar note for some small trash that I have, and bear witness that I enclose the money and deposit the letter in the post-office."

The reverend gentleman readily acceded to his request, and went with him to the bank, where a bill of the required denomination was obtained and placed in the letter; which was then sealed with a wafer, the clergyman all the while looking on.

They then went to the post-office, (which was directly opposite the bank,) and after calling the attention of his companion to the letter and its address, the writer thereof dropped it into the letter box, and the two persons went their several ways.

The letter arrived at New Haven by due course of mail, and it so happened that the clergyman to whom it was addressed was at the post-office, waiting for the assorting of the mails. He saw a letter thrown into his box, and called for it as soon as the delivery window was opened.

Upon breaking the seal and reading the letter, he found himself requested to "Please find one hundred dollars," &c., with which request he would cheerfully have complied, but for one slight circumstance, namely, the absence of the bank-note!

This fact was apparently accounted for by a postscript, written in a heavy, rude hand, entirely different from that of the body of the letter, and reading as follows:—

"P. S. I have taken the liberty to borrow this money, but I send the letter, so that you needn't blame the man what wrote it."

(Signed) "Post-Boy."

The rifled document was immediately shown to the post master, and in his opinion, as well as that of the clergyman, a daring robbery had been committed. The latter gentleman was advised by the post master to proceed at once to New

York, and confer with the Special Agent, and at the same time to lay all the facts before the Post Master General. He did so, and it was not long before the Agent had commenced the investigation of the supposed robbery.

In addition to the postscript appended, the letter bore other indications of having been tampered with, which at first sight would seem almost conclusive on this point. Upon the envelope were two wafers, differing in color, one partly overlapping the other, as if they had been put on by different persons at different times.

Notwithstanding these appearances, there were circumstances strongly conflicting with the supposition that the letter had been robbed. The postscript was an unnatural affair, for no one guilty of opening a letter for the purpose of appropriating its contents, would stop to write an explanatory postscript, especially as such a course would increase the chances of his own detection. And in the present instance, there had been no delay of the letter to allow of such an addition.

By a visit to the office where the letter was mailed, the Agent ascertained that it must have left immediately after having been deposited, and the advanced age and excellent character of the post master, who made up the mail on that occasion, entirely cut off suspicion in that quarter.

An interview was then held with the clergyman who witnessed the mailing of the letter, and from him were obtained the facts already stated. Concerning the writing of the document, and its deposit in the letter box in a perfect state, after the money had been enclosed, he was ready and willing to make oath, and had he been called upon he would have done so in all sincerity and honesty.

In reply to an inquiry whether he used more than one sort of letter paper, he informed me he had had but one kind in his study for several months, and at my request, immediately brought in several sheets of it. A comparison of this with the sheet upon which the *rifled* epistle had been written, showed that the latter was a totally different article from the first. The shape and design of the stamp, the size of the sheet, and the shade of the paper, were all unlike. Moreover, the wafers used at the bank, where the hundred-dollar note was obtained, and the letter containing it, sealed, were very dissimilar to either of those which appeared upon the "post-boy" letter.

From the consideration of all these facts, I was satisfied that a gross and contemptible fraud had been perpetrated by the writer of the letter, and lost no time in proceeding to the village where that personage lived. I called upon the post master and made some inquiries relative to the character and pecuniary circumstances of the person in question. From the replies made, it appeared, as I have already stated, that his reputation in community was good.

I thought it might be possible that in so small a place, I could ascertain whether he had lately passed a hundred-dollar note, as he would have been likely to have done, if it was true that he had not enclosed it in the New Haven letter.

Calling at the store which received most of his custom, I introduced myself to the proprietor, made a confidant of him to some extent, and learned that the very next day after that on which the aforesaid letter was mailed, its author offered him in payment for a barrel of flour, a hundred-dollar note on the bank from which a bill of the like denomination had been obtained, as before-mentioned, in exchange for the "small trash." The merchant could not then change it, but sent the flour, and changed a bill which he supposed to be the same, a few days afterward.

Armed with these irresistible facts, I proceeded to call on the adventurous deceiver of the clergy, who had attempted to make one member of that body second his intention to cheat another. "Insatiate archer! Could not one suffice?"

"Mr. T——," said I, after some preliminary conversation, "it's of no use to mince matters. The fact is, you did not send the money in that New Haven letter. You offered it the day after you pretended to mail it, at Mr. C.'s store. You see

I've found out all about it, so I hope you will not deny the truth in the matter."

I then gave him his choice, to send the hundred dollars promptly to his New Haven correspondent, or allow me to prove in a public manner, the facts in my possession.

Being thus hard pressed, and finding himself cornered, he confessed that he had prepared the letter which was received in New Haven—postscript, double wafers and all—before he left home, and that while crossing the street from the bank to the post-office, he substituted this for the one he wrote in the clergyman's study! He promised to send the money, and pretended to have suffered severely in his feelings, on account of this dishonest act.

There is no United States law providing for the punishment of such an offence, but public opinion and private conscience make nicer distinctions than the law can do, and often mete out a well deserved penalty to those who elude the less subtle ministers of justice.

In the present instance, the foregoing story was made public by direction of the Post Master General; and the author of the trick, unable to sustain the indignation and contempt of the community in which he lived, was compelled to make a hasty retreat from that part of the country.

CHAPTER XIII.

Young Offenders—Thirty Years ago—A large Haul—A Ray of Light.

THE facts of the following case were furnished me by a gentleman connected with the New York post-office. I will introduce him as the relator of his own story, taking some liberty, however, with the phraseology.

It is one of the too numerous class of cases, of which mere boys are the heroes, (if the term may thus be perverted,)—a class that is represented in this work, which would otherwise be incomplete, professing, as it does, to illustrate the various phases of post-office life, as respects persons of different ages and conditions. The present narration will show that our own times are not the only period fertile in juvenile rascality, but that the youth of thirty years ago were too frequently set upon evil.

At the time when the incidents occurred which I am about to narrate, (viz. in the year 1826,) it was the usual practice in the New York office to make up the morning's mails on the preceding evening, and to place them upon tables before they were entered on the "transcripts," (sheets or books in which copies of the post-bills are made,) and enclosed in wrappers. At this time a boy twelve or thirteen years of age was employed as assistant to one of the letter carriers, and generally arrived at the office at an earlier hour in the morning than the regular clerks. The nature of his duties made him well acquainted with the different species of letters, so that he could determine without much difficulty, from its general appearance, whether a letter contained hidden treasures or not.

So, by way of beguiling the time before the arrival of the clerks, or for the sake of a little improving practice, he one morning looked over the Eastern mail, which lay spread before him, and selected a letter addressed by the Cashier of the Farmers' and Mechanics' Bank of New York, to the Cashier of one of the banks in Boston, containing four thousand dollars in bank-notes of one thousand dollars each.

On the discovery of this "pile," the boy lost no time in "removing the deposits" to his own pocket, substituting for the bank-notes four pieces of paper of an equal size, cut from wrappers lying on the floor. He then resealed the letter and replaced it. The letter was forwarded by due course of mail, and when it was received at the bank, the Cashier discovered to his dismay that the money by some jugglery had been converted into brown paper; and the evident marks of breaking open and resealing, indicated unequivocally that some human agency had been engaged in working the spell.

Information of the loss was immediately conveyed to the New York office, much to the consternation and grief of all concerned, for this office had been considered a model one, and the clerks had taken pride in sustaining its character, to say nothing of their own; and now that suspicion was thrown among them by this daring act of dishonesty, which, from appearances, must have been committed by some one having access to the mails, they felt that all confidence in one another, as well as the confidence of community in them, would be greatly weakened, until the author of the deed should be discovered. It was suggested, indeed, that the robbery might have been committed in the Boston office, but circumstances rather favored the supposition that the guilt rested with New York.

The Post-Office Department at Washington was apprised of the facts in the case, and the attempts made to investigate the matter elicited a good deal of correspondence, which, however, produced no successful result.

Among other expedients, intimations were thrown out that a thorough search should be made of the residences and persons of the clerks, although it was not likely that the thief, whoever he might be, was so green as to keep the money for such a length of time, in any place where its discovery would be positive proof against him; and if the search were unavailing, the only result would be the infliction of mortification upon those who were innocent of the crime.

At this juncture, a ray of light appeared. It was then as well as now the practice of the assorting clerks to place the letters "missent" and "overcharged," in a box by themselves, and one morning a letter of this description was missent to this office, directed to Jamaica, L. I., which was accordingly placed in this box. On our return from breakfast this letter was found to be missing. As the boy before mentioned was the only occupant of the office during our absence, the disappearance of the letter naturally induced the belief that he had taken it. This second instance of delinquency assumed a double importance from the fact that the purloiner of this and the robber of the Boston letter, were in all probability one and the same person. Every exertion was therefore made to bring the truth to light.

One of the clerks was dispatched to Jamaica to ascertain whether the letter might not have been somehow received at that office, but his proposed investigations were prevented by the unofficial behavior of his horse, which, unmindful of the important business in hand, ran away, upset the carriage, and spilt out its contents. The clerk was so much injured as to be unable to proceed, and therefore returned without the desired information.

On the next morning, while the "drop letters" were being assorted, this letter was found among them and was identified. It had been broken open, examined, resealed, but not robbed of a draft for a large amount which it contained. Near the seal were written with a pencil the words "Picked up in Vesey Street."

The hand-writing was believed to be that of the suspected boy, and he was immediately charged with taking and breaking open the letter, which accusation he stoutly denied, but when he was assured that we knew his hand, that the words which he had written on the letter showed conclusively that he knew something of its whereabouts during its absence, and that it was our determination to investigate the matter thoroughly, his courage gave way, and he confessed opening the letter, but said he did not meddle with the draft which it contained, as he could make no use of it.

Having thus applied an entering wedge, I lost no time in turning to account the information already obtained, which I hoped would lead to the detection of the person who robbed the Boston letter. Indeed, I was entirely unprepared to admit the existence of two such rascals in the New York office, as such repeated instances of delinquency would imply, and was quite positive that the boy before me was the only culprit. I accordingly said to him, "Now, Samuel, I am glad for your sake that you have confessed your guilt in relation to this letter, and I hope you will be equally frank if you have been doing anything else of a similar nature. I strongly suspect that you robbed the Boston letter that we had so much trouble about, and if you did, the best thing you can do will be to confess it."

"No, sir," replied he, "I don't know any more about this Boston letter than you do, and I haven't touched any letter but the Jamaica one."

"It is useless," said I, "for you to make such assertions, in the face of the probabilities in the case. You have confessed that you stole one letter, and that renders it the more likely that you have robbed the other."

"Perhaps it is likely," returned he, "but I didn't do it."

"Well," said I, "take your choice. If you persist in your denial, you must meet the consequences, and you know that this kind of offence is punished severely; but if you will own up, I will engage that you shall get off as easily as possible."

By such considerations I finally induced him to acknowledge his guilt in relation to the Boston letter, and on being questioned further, he stated that he still had the bills, and offered to show me the place where they were concealed. I at once started off, accompanied by him as my guide. We took a course which soon led us out of the city, and along the banks of the East River.

The day was rainy, and a mist overhung the river and the land. As we plodded along through the mud and wet, the face of my young companion was shaded with a sadness which indicated that the external world harmonized in its gloom with the little world within.

For myself, I must acknowledge that the prospect of re-establishing lost confidence among my fellow-employés in the post-office, and of putting an end to the suspicion which had haunted almost every one, as well as restoring the stolen property to its rightful owner, produced in me an exhilaration of spirits strangely at variance with all that met my eye. But as we continued to go on and on, with no signs of approaching our place of destination, I began to query with myself, whether my companion might not contemplate giving me the slip, after leading me a wild-goose chase. I could not see, indeed, what motive he could have for such a proceeding, unless he wished to vent his malice on me as one who had been prominent in detecting his misdeeds.

But he kept on steadily, till, after going half a mile or so beyond the old Penitentiary, (a distance of about three miles from the post-office,) he turned from the road and stopped before an old wooden house, apparently uninhabited. The exterior showed signs of many years' conflict with the elements, in which it had been decidedly worsted. Moss had gathered upon the shingles, and the paint, of which there was here and there a trace, strengthened by a feeble contrast the dark color of the parts from which it had been entirely washed away.

Some of the windows were destitute of glass, and probably served as a mark for the "slings and arrows" of passing boys.

We entered the building, whose damp and musty-smelling air chilled me, heated as I was with my long and fatiguing walk, and ascending a flight of stairs, the boy unlocked the door of a room into which I passed by his request. The room contained no furniture but half a dozen chairs, a table, and an old bureau. This last he approached, unlocked, and taking out entirely one of the drawers, he showed another smaller one, which was behind the first when that was in place. Opening this, my eyes were refreshed with a sight of the four bills, of which I immediately took possession, and thinking it well to see what further discoveries I could make in this *terra incognita,* I found a little drawer, concealed like the first one behind another, and containing two or three hundred dollars in bills, which the precocious youth confessed to having purloined at different times from dead letters, which were usually *laid out* upon tables while the clerks were making up the dead letter account. It would seem that the boy thought no more of robbing a dead letter, than do the camp-followers of plundering dead men after a battle.

After examining the bureau as thoroughly as I was able, and finding no more of the ill-gotten wealth, I asked my companion whether he had any more money that did not belong to him, to which inquiry he returned a negative answer.

The place of concealment was certainly well chosen, for the old house would be the last place to which any one would think of going, who was in search for anything valuable. It seemed to me that it was a particularly fortunate circumstance that the discovery was made at this time, for he informed me that he had been accumulating the money found in the bureau with the intention of intrusting it to his uncle, for the purpose of purchasing some property in Newburgh. This would have been a rather large operation for a youth of his age! an operation even worthy of some specimens of Young America at the present day.

It seemed remarkable to me, as it doubtless has to the reader, that the boy should have such a remote and strange hiding-place. I afterwards learned that the house, the back part of which was occupied by a small family, belonged to an acquaintance of his, and that he used the room as a place of rendezvous, with some of his companions, and, as we have seen, as a receptacle for stolen money.

Having accomplished the object of my expedition, I returned light of heart, though heavy of limb, and communicated the facts as soon as possible to the Cashier of the Farmers' and Mechanics' Bank, and to the post master. The lad was at once arrested, tried, and found guilty, but in consideration of his youth, and his apparent ignorance of the extent of his crime, and the recovery of the property, he was sent to the House of Refuge for three years.

The boy's reformation was permanent, as I have been informed by one who afterwards knew him, when he had removed to a distant place, and established a good character. If this was so, (which there is no reason to doubt,) it furnishes an instance of the salutary effects arising from early detection in a course of crime, especially to those who are not yet hardened in iniquity. The whole case, also, shows the danger of allowing boys, with principles hardly established as yet, and destitute of that firmness which habit and perseverance bestow, to occupy responsible stations in large offices, where the apparent facility for the commission of crime and the temptations offered, too often subvert the honesty which has not yet ripened into a second nature.

CHAPTER XIV.

OBSTRUCTING THE MAIL.

A sound Principle—A slow Period—A wholesome Law—"Ahead of the Mail"—Moral Suasion—Indignant Passengers—Dutch Oaths—A Smash—Interesting Trial—A rowdy Constable—The Obstructors mulcted.

The proper adjustment of the various interests, great and small, which are involved in the every-day life of a nation like ours, is a problem not always very easy of solution, yet one of vital importance to the well-working of the social machine. Indeed, it has ever been an important part of legislation to determine the relative magnitude of different interests, both public and private, and to assign to each its proper place in the scale.

Republican principles require that the less should yield to the greater—individual convenience to public good. And an excellent illustration of the practical application of these principles by the wisdom of Congress, is found in the provisions which that body has made to secure the uninterrupted transmission of the mails.

It is unnecessary to enlarge upon the vast importance of punctuality in this branch of the public service. Time, as an element in business transactions, is increasing in value in proportion to the multiplication of devices for obtaining the greatest results possible from each passing moment. An hour in the present year, represents more—more business—more planning—more results of various kinds, than did an hour thirty years since.

To take, for instance, the matter of traveling. The state of things no longer exists which will permit public conveyances to take pretty much their own time in starting and in arriving at their destinations. That was a distressingly "slow" period, when horses were in their glory, and wayside taverns afforded comforts and luxuries which are poorly replaced by the eating, or rather devouring department of a rail road depot, where ravenous passengers, like the Israelites of old, are obliged to dispatch their repast, girded up for flight, at a moment's notice, instead of comfortably and deliberately sitting down under the auspices of "mine host," to a meal which deserved more respectful attention than could be given it in a less space of time than half an hour; the driver, meanwhile, being easy in his mind on the subject of "connecting," inasmuch as he, the *connector*, felt quite certain that the *connectee* would not leave him in the lurch, as "lee-way" of an hour or two was allowed, and often required, by the exigencies of traveling. But since, by the agency of steam, an hour swallows up thirty miles instead of four or five, minutes become correspondingly precious, and the locomotive infuses somewhat of its own energy into every mode of progression.

The inexorable hand of the rail-way clock waits not for dilatory drivers, and makes no allowances for detention, unavoidable or otherwise. Here comes in the application of our republican principle. If it were in the power of any one to delay the progress of the vehicle containing the mail, to suit his whim or convenience, the public interests would often be seriously interfered with; and, in order to prevent such contingencies, the following law was enacted by Congress:—

And be it further enacted, That if any person shall, knowingly and wilfully, obstruct or retard the passage of the mail, or of any driver or carrier, or of any horse or carriage, carrying the same, he shall, upon conviction for every such offence, pay a fine not exceeding one hundred dollars; and if any ferryman shall, by wilful negligence, or refusal to transport the mail across any ferry, delay the same, he shall forfeit and pay, for every ten minutes that the same shall be so delayed, a sum not exceeding ten dollars.

It is obviously right that the pleasure of an individual should not weigh for a moment in the balance, with the interests of thousands depending as they do, in a degree, upon the prompt transmission of correspondence. Were all the consequences of simply impeded delivery of important letters to be made known, the record would be a melancholy one indeed.

In crowded cities especially, through whose streets the mails are many times a day conveyed to steamboats and rail road stations, it is particularly important that all obstacles in their way should be removed; and pains have been taken to make the law on this subject generally understood, so that at the approach of the wagon bearing the magic characters "U. S. Mail," the crowd of vehicles which throng the busy streets, separate to the right and left, and do homage to that supreme power—the Public Good.

A curious trial under the law I have cited, was held in Boston before the United States Court, about two years since.

It appears that the regular mail-coach from Worcester to Barre, left the former place on the afternoon of January 8, about half past four, full of passengers, and ornamented, as well as distinguished, by the words "U. S. Mail," painted in conspicuous letters on both sides of the foot-board.

The passengers were beginning to develope those sparks of sociability which are elicited by the collisions with one another, and the stimulus to the brain resulting from sundry jolts inseparable from the vicissitudes of stage-coach traveling. In other words, the coach had proceeded about two miles, when, arriving at a place where there was some ascent in the road, it overtook three one-horse wagons, which made way for it to pass. Very soon, however, the two occupants of the hindmost wagon, (whom we will call Stark and Baker,) whipped up their steed, and rushed by the coach, like some saucy cutter shooting ahead of a seventy-four. After this demonstration, their horse, having gained four or five rods on the coach, subsided into a walk.

The correspondingly moderate movements which the driver of the coach was compelled to adopt, did not very well suit his views, as the icy road and his heavy load formed a combination of circumstances which rendered him anxious to make all possible speed, in order to fulfil the requirements of the U. S. Mail, as well as those of his passengers. But he was obliged to retain his humble position of follower to the wagon, for the road at that point was too narrow to admit of passing, and as no other means of attaining his object were at his command, he proceeded to try the effect of moral suasion.

"I say, you, there," shouted he to the obstinate couple in the wagon, who were smoking very much at their ease, and apparently busily engaged in conversation, "I wish you'd drive on faster, or let me go by you."

"Couldn't do it," replied the provoking Stark, "unless you'll race."

"It's none of my business to race," returned the driver; "all I want is to go on."

"Well, let's see you do it, then," said Stark, checking his horse still more.

They soon came to a wider portion of the road, and the stage driver attempted to pass the wagon, but was foiled by the dexterous manœuvring of Stark, who so accurately adjusted his motions to those of the stage-coach as to check-mate its presiding genius. Upon coming to a still wider place, the driver outsailed his persevering tormentor, and pushed on at a rapid rate, say seven knots an hour, indulging the sanguine hope that he was rid of his Old Man of the Sea. But this expectation was short-lived, for, on arriving at a curve in the road, where it was narrow and icy, he was compelled to "shorten sail," whereat Stark added wings to his speed, and

ran by the coach, directly afterward reining his horse into a walk as before.

A succession of similar manœuvres was kept up till the coach reached Holden, a distance of three or four miles, and during this time the facetious Stark, not content with these highly aggravating proceedings, added insult to injury by personal reflections on the skill of the driver and the character of his horses.

"Hallo, you driver!" shouted he derisively, "why don't you *drive?* If there's any of your passengers in a hurry, I'll take 'em on, and tell the folks that you'll be along in the course of a day or two."

To this the driver wisely answered nothing, but his tormentor did not profit by his example. After some ineffectual attempts on the part of the U. S. functionary to pass the wagon, which were foiled as before, Stark again essayed to beguile the time with a further display of his conversational powers.

"Guess your horses ain't very well trained to keep the road, are they? They seem to go from one side to the other as if they couldn't draw a bee-line. May be, though, they are kinder faint, and that's what makes 'em stagger about so. I'll try 'em."

So saying, he proceeded to open a bag which lay in his wagon; and, taking from it a handful of oats, he allowed the horses to come nearly up to him, when he held out the grain to them, calling "k'jock, k'jock," as if he was desirous of enticing them along.

Before this time, the occupants of the coach had become aware of what was going on, and were naturally highly indignant at the imposition practised on them by the audacious Stark and his fellow conspirator. One irascible gentleman did not bear the infliction with as much equanimity as his "guide, philosopher, and friend," upon the coach-box; but, every time that the wagon passed the coach, he popped his head out at the nearest window, and fired at the enemy a volley of reproachful epithets that could be likened to nothing but the "nine-cornered Dutch oaths," which on special occasions were wont to rumble through the gullet of William the Testy, at the hazard of choking that illustrious individual, as we are assured by the grave and matter-of-fact historian of New York.

The persevering repetition of the provocation at last excited a degree of rage in the breast of our peppery friend which could not be allayed by the expedients we have mentioned. He called out, "Driver, I say, stop and let me out, and I'll see whether this sort of thing will go on much longer. Why don't you stop? Do you suppose we are going to stand this for ever? How the deuse do you think we shall ever get to Barre, at this rate?"

The driver advised him to keep cool, telling him that very likely they would get rid of the wagon before long; with which opinion another of the passengers coincided, who knew the men, remarking that they belonged in Hubbardston, and would probably turn off at the road leading to that place. This road was beyond Holden, where the coach stopped at the public-house. Here the men in the wagon came up, and expressed a wish to exchange their horse for the four coach-horses, provided sufficient "boot" were offered them. To this impertinence the driver made no reply; but the fiery passenger intimated to them that, if they would come within his reach, he would give them *boot* enough to make their accounts *foot up* even.

After leaving the mail, the coach started out of Holden, preceded by the wagon, which dodged back and forth along the road as heretofore. They passed the Hubbardston road, but the men did not turn off; and, about a mile from Rutland, they made that once-too-often attempt which such mischievous individuals usually make somewhere along their course. The patience of the much-enduring driver had become finally exhausted; and, as the annoying wagon was in the act of passing him, at a rather narrow place in the road, he drove on without particular reference to that vehicle, and experimentally tested the relative strength of the fore wheel of the coach and the body of the wagon. The latter structure was "nowhere," or, to speak more accurately, it was resolved into its original elements; while the aforesaid wheel rolled away uninjured, bearing its share of the triumphant passengers.

The occupants of the smashed vehicle survived the "wreck of matter;" whether with a whole skin or not, does not appear, as the personal knowledge of the driver, as stated on the trial, was summed up in the words, "*I left 'em there!*"

In consequence of the proceedings which have been described, the coach arrived at Barre an hour and a quarter behind the time.

It having been thought advisable to prosecute these men for obstructing the mail, a suit was brought against them in the U. S. District Court of Massachusetts.

The evidence on the part of Government went to show that they must have known the character of the coach: that it carried the mail, for the words "U. S. Mail" were conspicuously painted on the coach; and the sign "Post-Office" was up at the place in Holden where the mail was taken out, and where they saw the coach stop. Also the men were known by sight to some of the passengers; and one of them had been a stage-coach proprietor, and the other had driven a coach. Indeed, one of the passengers, while they were at Holden, addressed Baker, whom he knew, by name, and told him "he should think that he had been in the stage business long enough to know better."

The passengers were unanimous in considering the case as clearly one of wilful detention.

The testimony for the defence was rather lame. The post master at Rutland testified that the mail from Worcester was due at 7 P. M., though he had known it three-quarters of an hour later. He thought it arrived, on the evening in question, at 5 minutes past 7; but could not say certainly that the 8th of January was the night when the mail arrived at that time, though he had no doubt of it, nor had he looked at his register since that night. In short, his evidence amounted to a rough guess, which could make no impression on the Gibraltar of opposing testimony furnished by a coach full of passengers, as well as other witnesses.

Another witness for the defence testified that Stark's horse was "smooth-shod," with the view of establishing the extreme improbability of the alleged performances, as the road was icy, and rapid motion therefore hazardous to an animal thus shod. But, as the quadruped in question was shown actually to have done the thing, this ingenious theory was set aside, although a slur was thus cast upon Mr. Stark's character as a prudent driver.

But the crowning shame of Stark's delinquency consisted in the fact that he was constable and tax-collector of the town of Hubbardston. History is not without instances of monarchs and others high in authority, who have descended to the indulgence of freaks inconsistent with the dignity of their station; and Shakspeare has immortalized the frolics of Prince Henry. But neither historian nor poet has hitherto been able to record of a constable and tax-gatherer that he amused himself with maliciously driving a smooth-shod horse, so as to obstruct the progress of the United States Mail.

This man, set to be "a terror to evil-doers" should have been a terror to himself; indeed we may conceive of him as smitten with compunction, and arresting himself—Stark the constable tapping himself on the shoulder. At least he should have arrested his own progress, before he fell from his high estate, and degenerated from a constable into an unlucky buffoon.

The questions for the jury were, First, Did these men obstruct the United States Mail? And, secondly, Did they do so knowingly and wilfully? If they did so obstruct the mail, then as a man is presumed in law to intend what is the natural and necessary consequence of his acts, in the absence of controlling testimony otherwise, the inference would inevitably follow, that their conduct in this affair was the result of "malice aforethought."

They were both convicted, and sentenced as follows,—Stark, the driver of the wagon, to a fine of thirty dollars, and Baker to a fine of fifteen; thus footing up the pretty little sum of forty-five dollars for their evening's diversion, besides the destruction of their wagon, which was taken into the account in determining the amount of the fines.

Thus ended this piece of folly, the record of which it is hoped will serve as a warning to any who may be disposed to try similar "tricks upon travelers," since they might not get off as easily as did the pair of worthies, whose brilliant exploit we have briefly sketched.

CHAPTER XV.

A dangerous Mail Route—Wheat Bran—A faithful Mail Carrier —Mail Robber shot—A "Dead-head" Passenger.

An old Offender—Fatal Associate—Robbery and Murder—Conviction and Execution—Capital Punishment.

Traveling in Mexico—Guerillas—Paying over—The Robbers routed—A "Fine Young English Gentleman"—The right stuff.

In the early annals of our country, many instances of mail robbery are found, some of which occasioned the display of great intrepidity and daring, as the perusal of the following pages will show.

While the country was yet thinly settled, and the mails were transported on horseback, or in different kinds of vehicles, from the gig to the stage-coach, often through extensive forests, which afforded every facility for robbery, the office of stage driver or mail carrier was no sinecure. Resolute men were required for this service, who on an emergency could handle a pistol as well as a whip.

Some thirty or forty years ago, a mail-coach ran in the northern part of the state of New York, through the famous "Chateaugay woods." The forest was many miles in extent, and common fame and many legends gave it the reputation of a noted place for freebooters and highwaymen.

One morning the stage driver on this route had occasion to examine his pistols, and found, instead of the usual charge, that they were loaded with *wheat bran!* A daring villain had, through an accomplice, thus disarmed the driver, preparatory to waylaying him. He drew the charges, cleaned the weapons, and carefully loaded them with powder and ball.

That afternoon he mounted his stage for his drive through the Chateaugay woods. There was not a passenger in his vehicle. Whistling as he went, he "cracked up" his leaders, and drove into the forest. Just about the centre of the woods a man sprang out from behind a tree, and seized the horses by the bit.

"I say, driver," said the footpad, with consummate coolness, "I want to take a look at that mail."

"Yes, you do, no doubt, want to overhaul my mails," replies the driver; "but I can't be so free, unless you show me your commission. I'm driver here, and I never give up my mails except to one regularly authorized."

"O, you don't, eh? well, here's my authority," showing the butt of a large pistol partly concealed in his bosom. "Now dismount and bear a hand, my fine fellow, for you see I've got the documents about me."

"Yes, and so've I," says the driver, instantly leveling his own trusty weapon at the highwayman.

"O! you won't hurt nobody, I guess; I've seen boys playing soger before now."

"Just drop those reins," says the keeper of Uncle Sam's mail bags, "or take the consequences."

"O! now your'e joking, my fine lad! but come, look alive, for I'm in a hurry, it's nearly night."

A sharp report echoed through the forest, and the disciple of Dick Turpin lay stretched upon the ground. One groan and all was over. The ball had entered his temple.

The driver lifted the body into the coach, drove to the next stopping place, related the circumstances, and gave himself up. A brief examination before a magistrate resulted in his acquittal, and highwaymen about the Chateaugay woods learned that pistols might be dangerous weapons, even if they were loaded with wheat bran, provided they were in the hands of one who knew how to use them.

Another exciting case occurred near Utica, early in the present century, when Western and Northern New York was a wilderness.

An old rogue, who had long been steeped in crime, finding his companions nearly all gone—the prisons and gallows having claimed their own—and his material resources nearly exhausted, sought for a profitable alliance. He succeeded in getting into familiarity with a very young man, son of a gentleman of standing and reputation, a worthy citizen and an honest man. These two laid their plans for robbing the mail. Considerable sums of money were known to pass constantly in the great mail running East and West.

Watching their opportunity, they stopped the coach one night when there were no passengers. The driver was bold and faithful to his charge, and made a stout resistance. They tied him to a tree, and opened the mail. Fearing detection and not obtaining much money, the veteran villain drew his pistol and shot the poor driver. As in most criminal transactions, fortune went against the perpetrators. They were both taken, and sufficient evidence being produced, they were sentenced to be hanged.

Though there was but one opinion as to the comparative culpability of the two individuals, no one could say but that both were equally guilty, in a legal sense, of the murder. Out of respect to the parents of the young man, great efforts were made to obtain a pardon, but they were unsuccessful.

Both the sentences were carried into execution. The circumstance gave rise to a thorough discussion of the policy, the humanity, and the right or wrong of Capital Punishment. One of the most powerful arguments ever made against the death penalty, was written by the father of the younger criminal, and obtained a wide circulation in pamphlet form.

In the summer of 1851, a company of travelers were seated in the mail stage that runs from Mexico to Vera Cruz. Marauding parties of *guerillas* had often stopped the mail, and when practicable, robbed the passengers. Sometimes returning Californians, and other travelers, gave these freebooters a rather warm reception.

On the present occasion there were but three or four passengers, some of whom were armed with small revolvers. Suddenly a party of mounted guerillas appeared, nearly a dozen in number, and at once stopped the coach and ordered the pas sengers out.

Either from fear or collusion, the drivers never interfere, but remain neutral. Probably, if they resisted, their lives would pay the forfeit. The passengers, supposing there was no hope of escape but to give up their watches and money, commenced "paying over."

A young English gentleman in one corner of the coach, immediately took up a double-barreled gun and shot the villain at the door of the coach, and then with the other barrel killed another of the party, by shooting him off his horse. He then drew a revolver, and jumped out. The other travelers concluded, like Wellington's reserve at Waterloo, that they might as well "up and at 'em," and, quite unprepared for such a reception, the freebooters—the surviving ones—fled with precipitation. The papers resounded with the praises of "this fine young English gentleman, all of the modern time."

His father was a distinguished member of Parliament, and soon had the pleasure of meeting his son, who had been abroad and shown that he was made of the right kind of stuff for a traveler in a dangerous country.

CHAPTER XVI.

The tender Passion—Barnum's Museum—Little Eva—The Boys in a Box—The Bracelet—Love in an Omnibus—Losses explained.

As Shakspeare, after having displayed Falstaff in his ordinary character of rascal and rowdy in general, represented him as a "lover sighing like furnace," so we, in the course of our researches among juvenile delinquents, find that they are sometimes the victims of what they consider the tender passion. And the ardor excited in their breasts is not always innocent in its effects, but, as in the case of "children of an older growth," sometimes leads to the commission of heinous crime, as is exemplified in the instance we are about to relate.

While the drama of "Uncle Tom's Cabin" was running at that Museum of Natural and *Un*natural History, commonly called Barnum's, four boys, the eldest apparently about fourteen years of age, were observed night after night occupying a stage-box in the theatre attached to that establishment, and watching, with admiring eyes, the movements of the young lady who represented "Little Eva." Boys are gregarious in their loves and hates, and it appeared that in the present instance, the three younger ones were not smitten with the aforesaid damsel, *per se*, but simply as friends or satellites of their older companion, accompanying him in that capacity, to encourage him, and witness his hoped-for triumph over the heart of the young actress, and possibly for the sake of sharing in the "treats" of various kinds which he dispensed to favored ones with a lavish hand.

Not content with sighing at a distance for the object of his affections, and on one occasion making a decided demonstration, by throwing a gold bracelet upon the stage, intended to encircle her arm, the enamored youth often watched for his charmer as she descended from the world of imagination to that of real life,—from the theatrical stage to that humble, but useful vehicle, an omnibus; and having ascertained which one was irradiated by her presence, he madly rushed after, and purchased, with the slight outlay of a sixpence, the enrapturing consciousness of being included within the narrow walls that held the mistress of his heart.

But "the course of true love never did run smooth." Sometimes unfeeling parents obstruct; sometimes "no" is a decided obstacle; but neither of these was the immediate cause of the rough "course" in the present instance. It does not appear that our stricken youth had ever approached near enough to his "bright particular star" to admit of any confidential disclosure of the state of his feelings; much less had he opened any negotiations with the "powers that be." The rocks on which he split were, the manager of the Museum and a police officer!

When the reader is informed that the lad in question was not the son of wealthy parents, and had, or ought to have had no other pecuniary resources than those which he derived from his occupation in the employ of a bookseller, he will readily conjecture whence came the means for the indulgence of such extravagance and folly as have been described. Such an unusual occurrence as the hiring of a stage box by a boy, for several nights in succession (the expense of which was five dollars a night), attracted the attention and the suspicions of the manager of the Museum, who sent for the police, and on searching the boys, an empty envelope, addressed to "S—— & Co., Fulton Street," the employers of our precocious young gentleman, was found upon his person. It was then ascertained that S—— & Co. had recently lost several money-letters, and the boy, being the person who took the letters out of the post-office for the firm, had appropriated the money to his own use. He was tried before the United States Court, and sent to the House of Refuge, where, it is to be hoped, he was cured of indulging his boyish whim at the expense of his employer's money and his own character.

CHAPTER XVII.

DETACHED INCIDENTS.

Bank Letter lost—The Thief decoyed—Post-Office at Midnight—Climbing the Ladder—An exciting Moment—Queer Place of Deposit.

A Post Master in Prison—Afflicted Friends—Sighs and Saws—The Culprit's Escape—How it was done—A cool Letter—A Wife's Offering.

Moral Gymnastics—Show of Honesty—Unwelcome Suggestion.

"A hard road to travel"—Headed by a Parson—Lost Time made up —A Male overhauled.

The Invalid Wife—The Announcement—A touching Incident.

During the whole of the author's official career, he has never been brought into physical conflict with any one, nor exposed to any great danger in the discharge of his duties. These duties have seldom called him to undergo "moving accidents by flood and field," excepting so far as severe weather, dangerous roads, fractious horses, or some other of the inconveniences and perils incident to the different modes of traveling, might be classed under that head.

An incident, however, once occurred while I was engaged in investigating a case of depredation, which may be worthy of record here, as it is not devoid of a certain picturesqueness, even aside from the extremely interesting circumstance (to me) that my head, for a short time, seemed to be in imminent danger.

The case referred to was that of the loss of a letter containing six hundred dollars, posted by the cashier of a Northern bank. The person, (a post-office clerk,) whom I suspected of being the robber, was detected in taking a decoy letter which was placed in his office after the loss of the one first mentioned. On the strength of this, I boldly charged him with the first loss, and insisted that he should restore the money. After the usual assertion of innocence, and some demur, he intimated to me that the spoils were hidden somewhere in the post-office.

This interview was held in the directors' room of the bank which had suffered the loss, and I immediately proposed that we should go over to the office and get the money. Accordingly we proceeded thither. It was then after midnight. As soon as we entered, my companion locked the door behind us, and preceded me, with a lantern in his hand. A remark which I made respecting the lonely appearance of a post-office at that time of night, drew from him nothing but a sullen assent, which put an end to any further conversational efforts on my part.

The room (or rather recess) in which he lodged, was over that part of the office devoted to the public, a space in front of the boxes, and access was had to it by means of a ladder inside the office.

The clerk rapidly ascended this ladder and I followed closely behind, without a word being spoken by either of us. The apartment, besides the ordinary furniture of a lodging-room, contained a few shelves of books, indicating some pursuit more creditable to their owner than those which had rendered my interference with them necessary. I had before been told that he was somewhat diligent in the cultivation of his intellect.

Setting down his lantern upon the table, he reached up and took down a rifle which was suspended to the wall, directly over his bed, a fit emblem for one engaged in *rifling* the mails.

Although the moodiness which he had displayed during our intercourse that evening, had not surprised me, yet I was by no means prepared to expect that he would resort to such extreme measures as his movements seemed to indicate.

I was uncertain what to do. "The better part of valor"

being "discretion," it was by no means clear whether this same discretion required me to rush upon him, or to make a precipitate retreat down the ladder, or to jump and disappear in the darkness below. There was evidently no time to lose, for the deadly weapon was already pointed in my direction, and its desperate owner was fumbling about the stock, as if, in the dim light, he could not easily find the lock.

Springing towards him, I seized the rifle by the barrel, remarking, that I wished he would not turn the muzzle upon me, and then I saw what he was attempting to do. He had crammed the stolen notes into the "patch-box" of the rifle, and was endeavoring to get them out, which he could not readily effect as they were tightly wedged in. I cheerfully volunteered to assist him, and by our united efforts, the debt was discharged instead of the rifle! In other words, I recovered the identical bank-notes, deposited in the office by the cashier several weeks previously, all in one hundred dollar bills.

The evidence furnished by the "patch-box," was of course amply sufficient to convict the depredator, had other proof been wanting, and he was recently sentenced to ten years' imprisonment in the State Prison.

An ingeniously planned and successfully executed escape of a mail robber from prison, occurred in Troy, New York, less than a year ago.

This person had held the office of post master in a place of some note in the Northern part of New York. He was a man of education, and connected by birth and marriage with some of the most respectable and influential families in that part of the State, and in the Province of Canada.

These favorable circumstances, however, did not prevent him from becoming seriously embarrassed in his pecuniary affairs, by which he was led, in an evil hour, to resort to mail depredations, continuing them until this course was cut short by his detection and arrest. As he failed to give the requisite bail, he was thrown into prison to await his trial, which was to take place in the course of a few weeks.

As the efforts which he and his friends had made to secure the intervention of the Post Master General for postponing the trial were unavailing, and the direct and positive proof against him made it certain that he would be doomed to at least ten years' imprisonment at hard labor, the desperate expedient of breaking jail seemed to be the only hook left to hang a hope upon.

He occupied a large room, adjoining that of the notorious murderess Mrs. Robinson, and had for his room-mate a person who had been committed for some minor offence.

He was frequently visited by his relations, whose high respectability exempted them from the close examination which should have been made by the jailor, to ascertain that they carried no contraband articles on their persons. Respectability in this case, as in many others, served as a cloak to devices from which rascality derived more benefit than the cause of justice.

These afflicted friends, in the course of their visits, contrived to supply the prisoner with the tools necessary to enable him to effect his escape from "durance vile." Sighs and saws, regrets and ropes, anguish and augers, were mingled together, supplying both consolation for the past and hope for the future.

The time selected for the escape was a Sabbath night. The first thing discovered by the jailor on the next morning, was a rope suspended from a back-hall window in the second story, and reaching to the ground, the window being open. On ascending the stairs, he found in the partition separating the mail robber's room from the hall, an opening about large enough to admit of the egress of a small person; and on entering the room but one occupant appeared, who was fast asleep; but the mail robber was gone.

It was with the utmost difficulty that the sleeper could be

aroused. He was evidently under the influence of some powerful narcotic, as was fully shown by his replies to the interrogatories of the jailor after he had sufficiently recovered from his stupefaction to understand what was said to him.

His story was, that on the previous evening he was complaining of a severe cold, whereupon his sympathizing roommate remarked that he had some medicine that was just the thing for such complaints, and offered to give him a dose, if he wished to try it. To this the unsuspecting victim of sharp practice assented; and the amateur "M. D." measured out a quantity sufficient for the purpose intended, first pretending to swallow a dose himself, in order to convince his patient that the medicine was perfectly safe.

One of the last things that the patient remembered on the night in question, was that about eleven o'clock he was affected by a very drowsy sensation which he could not overcome, and that he lay down on his bed to sleep. About this time his attending physician came to him and inquired "how he felt;" to which he replied, "very sleepy." His benevolent friend assured him that this was a "favorable sign," and asserted further that he would be "all right by morning." At the same time showing his solicitude for his companion's comfort by taking the pillow from his own bed and placing it under his head.

The cause of these phenomena stood revealed, in the shape of a vial labeled "Laudanum," which was found upon a table in the room. Near it lay a note addressed to the jailor, of which the following is a copy.

Sunday Night.

Dear Sir,

Intelligence of a very discouraging nature, informing me that my approaching trial is not to be postponed on any account, impels me to make my way out of this place to-night.

Before doing so, however, I have to thank you for your kindness to me. I am also indebted to Dr. M. for his attention to my comfort, and I regret that interests of the highest importance require me to take a step which may lead some people to find fault with you. All that I can say about that is, that I have been fortunate in eluding your vigilance as a public officer.

The effects I leave behind me should be sent by express to my friends in P——, who no doubt will pay all expenses incurred by me while I was with you. Any letters coming here may be forwarded to me at P——, that is, after waiting a week when my brother is to be at that place.

With a renewal of my acknowledgments for your goodness, I remain

Respectfully yours,

A. C. N.

To J. Price, Esq., Sheriff, &c.

Among the "effects," left behind, were sundry saws, files, and chisels of the best workmanship and materials; a large roll of putty, to have been used in concealing the saw-marks, in case a second night's labor had been required; and a valise containing a variety of books, wearing apparel, and letters received from his friend during his confinement. One of them was from his wife, a young, lovely, and accomplished woman. It is full of love, devotion, and Christian resignation, and ends as follows:—

"The dear baby is quite well, and is growing finely every day. She is a dear, beautiful child. Oh that God may keep her for us both, for she will make us so happy, she binds us so closely together.

"Here are some lines which I have preserved for some time. They have often comforted me, and I hope your feelings are such that they may comfort you."

"GOD'S WAY IS BEST."

This blessed truth I long have known,
So soothing in its hopeful tone—
Whate'er our trials, cares and woes,
Our Father's mercy freely flows—
That on his bosom we may rest,
For God is good, "His way is best."

Trouble without and grief within,
Are the sure heritage of sin;
And e'en affection's voice may die
In the last quivering, gasping sigh;
But what though death our souls distress,
'Twere better thus—"God's way is best."

Misfortune's dark and bitter blight
May fall upon us like the night;
Our souls with anguish may be torn
When we are called o'er friends to mourn;
But what assurance doubly blest,
To feel that all "God's ways are best."

Yes, glorious thought! in yonder sky
Are joys supreme which never die—
That when our earthly course is run,
We'll live in regions of the sun;
And there, upon the Savior's breast,
We'll sing for aye, "God's way is best."

It was a doctrine advanced by Mahomet, that all men after death were obliged to cross a fiery gulf, upon a bridge as narrow as a single hair. The good always succeeded in effecting their passage safely, while the wicked were precipitated into the depths below.

This idea might be extended to the present life, by way of illustrating the difficulties which beset those who follow a criminal course, and attempt to conceal the fact from the eyes of others. A step too far, or not far enough, this way or that, is sufficient to cause them to slip, and this kind of tight-rope balancing is a species of moral gymnastics, in the execution of which few are successful.

A specimen of this was once furnished me by a post master against whom serious complaints had been made to the Department, but who was not aware of the existence of such charges. In the course of several interviews which I held with him, I gave him not the remotest hint that I suspected his integrity, yet (probably on the principle of taking medicine when one is well, or thinks he is, in order to be better) he resorted to several somewhat original expedients to establish a character for honesty in my estimation.

The most striking of these was the following:—

As I entered the vestibule of the office one day, he pretended to pick up a ten dollar note from the floor.

After the usual morning salutation, he said,

"I am in luck, this morning. I just picked up here a ten dollar bill, and I must see if I can't find the owner;" and he forthwith proceeded to write a flaming placard, announcing the finding of "a sum of money" outside the delivery window, and to post it in a conspicuous place.

His singular manner, however, while speaking of the money, and while engaged in drawing up the notice, attracted my attention, and I became strongly impressed with the belief that the whole affair was one of those silly devices which are as effectual in preventing the detection of those who employ them, as is the device of the ostrich, in hiding his head under his wing, to conceal him from his pursuer.

It occurred to me, after a little reflection, that I had seen a well-known merchant in the place hand the post master a ten dollar note the day previous, in payment for postage stamps. This fact was confirmed by inquiries which I made of the merchant, who further informed me that he could recognise the bill if he should see it again, from the initials which it bore of a correspondent, who had sent it to him by mail a few days before. Having ascertained what these initials were, ("C. P.,") I took occasion to examine the note, (which the post master had rather ostentatiously laid aside in a drawer, to be ready for the *owner* whenever he should claim it,) and found the "C. P." upon it.

After the notice of the finding had been posted some twenty-four hours without the appearance of any claimant, I suggested to the *honest* finder, by way of annoying him a little in return for his attempted deception, that as the money was found within the post-office limits, the Department would probably require that it should pass into the United States Treasury, in the same way as funds contained in dead letters for which no owners can be found.

This view of the case did not seem to strike him favorably.

He looked blank, but attempted to pass it off as a joke, by saying that he didn't know that the post-office was a dead letter.

The next morning the placard had disappeared, and the post master informed me that a stranger had called late on the evening before, who claimed and described the bill, and to whom it was accordingly surrendered!

The termination of this case fully confirmed my opinion of the post master's double-dealing in relation to this affair.

It sometimes happens that the ends of justice are best secured by allowing criminals to go on for a time unmolested in their course, and even by affording them facilities for the commission of offences, which will be to them as snares and pitfalls. When means like these are adopted for the detection of crime, a temporary check to the operations of the suspected persons, from whatever cause arising, creates some additional trouble and anxiety to those who are endeavoring to ferret out the evil-doer, and provokes a degree of exasperation toward his unconscious abettor.

Such an untimely interference with plans carefully laid, and carried out at a considerable expense of time and effort, once occurred while the author was attempting to bring to light an unscrupulous depredator, in whose detection the public was much interested, as many had suffered by the loss of money sent through his office.

I had been hard at work for a week in pursuing this investigation, having for the third time passed decoy letters over the road on which the suspected office was situated, (the road being one of the roughest kind, about forty miles in length, and very muddy,) and was flattering myself that *that* day's work would enable me to bring my labors to a conclusion satisfactory to the public and myself, if not to the delinquent; when my hopes were, for the time, dashed to the ground by the innocent hand of the village parson.

And it happened in this wise :—

The mail carrier was instructed to throw off his mail, as usual, at the suspected office, and to remain outside, in order to afford the post master a good opportunity for the repetition of the offence which he was supposed to have committed, the Agent being all the time a mile or two in advance, in another vehicle, impatiently waiting to learn the fate of his manœuvres.

As the part of the road where I was stationed, was in the midst of woods, and the carrier had no passengers, no particular caution was needed in conducting the conversation, and before my associate had reached me, he called out,

"I guess you'll have to try it again; the Dominie was there and helped to overhaul the mail to-day."

The sportsman, who, having just got a fair sight at the bird which he has been watching for hours, beholds it, startled by some blunderer, flying off to "parts unknown;" the angler, who, by unwearied painstaking, having almost inveigled a "monarch of the pool" into swallowing his hook—sees a stone hurled by some careless hand, descending with a splash, and putting an end to his fishy flirtation;—these can imagine my feelings when the mail carrier made the above announcement.

"Confound the Dominie," involuntarily exclaimed I, "why couldn't he mind his own business?"

I examined the mail bag, but nothing was missing except the matter that properly belonged to that office.

But at the next trial, the parishioner did not have ministerial aid in opening his mail, and accordingly, probably by way of indemnifying himself for his forced abstinence, he not only seized the decoy package, but several others.

The following day, instead of overhauling the mail, he was himself thoroughly overhauled by an United States Marshal.

A man of such weak virtue, should hire a "dominie" by the year, to stand by and help him resist the devil, during the process of opening the mails.

Not the least painful of the various duties connected with the detection of crime, is the sometimes necessary one of revealing a husband's guilt to his wife.

I anticipated a severe trial of my feelings in making such a disclosure during the progress of a recent important case where the mail robber was in possession of a mail-key by means of which he had committed extensive depredations. He was at length detected, and has lately entered upon a ten years' term in the State Prison.

On his arrest he manifested much solicitude for his wife, fearing that the intelligence of his situation would overpower her. "She is in feeble health at best," said he, "and I am afraid this will kill her."

It was necessary, however, that I should see her in order to get possession of some funds, a part of the proceeds of the robberies, which her husband had committed to her keeping. Furnished with a written order from the prisoner, and leaving him in the Marshal's custody, I proceeded to call on the invalid, racking my brains while on the way to her residence, for some mode of communicating the unpleasant truth which should disclose it gradually, and spare her feelings as much as possible.

On my arrival at the boarding-house, the note was sent to the lady's room. It read as follows:—

My dear Susan:

Will you hand to the bearer a roll of bank-notes which I left with you.

EDWIN.

The lady soon made her appearance. She was young, rather prepossessing, and evidently in delicate health. Finding that I was the bearer of the note, she addressed me, expressing great surprise that her husband had sent a request so unusual; and with an air of independence observed that she did not "know about paying over money under such circumstances to an entire stranger."

Desiring not to mortify her unnecessarily by making explanations in the presence of others, I requested her to step into a vacant room near at hand, and after closing the door, I said in a low tone,

"It is an extremely painful thing for me, Mrs. M——, but as you do not seem inclined to comply with your husband's order, I must tell you plainly that the money was taken from the mails by him. There is no mistake about it. He has had a mail-key which I have just recovered, and has made a full acknowledgment of his numerous depredations. I beg of you to bear this dreadful news with fortitude. No one will think less of you on account of his dishonest conduct."

I expected to see the poor woman faint immediately, and had mentally prepared myself for every emergency, but, a moment after, *I* should have been more likely to have fallen into that condition, if astonishment could ever produce such an effect, for as soon as I had finished what I was saying, she stood, if possible, more erect than before, and with some fire in her eye, and one arm 'akimbo,' she replied in a spirited manner,

"Well, if he *has* done that, he's a dam'd fool to own it —*I* wouldn't!"

She gave up the money, however, soon after, and although the recklessness displayed in the speech above quoted seemed to make it probable that she was implicated in her husband's guilt, it afterwards appeared that this exhibition of "spunk" was due to the impulses of a high-spirited and excitable nature, which sometimes, as in the present instance, broke away from control, and went beyond the bounds of decorum. Such an ebullition of passion indicated, in her case, a less degree of moral laxity than it would have shown in one differently constituted.

In a subsequent examination of their apartment in search of other funds and missing drafts, a touching incident occurred, strikingly displaying, when taken in connection with the outbreak just mentioned, the lights as well as shades of an impulsive character.

During this examination, it became necessary to investigate the contents of a well-filled trunk, and this was done by the lady herself, under my supervision. After several layers of wearing apparel had been taken out, she suddenly paused in her work, and wiped away a falling tear, as she gazed into the trunk. Thinking that some important evidence of her husband's crimes was lurking beneath the garments remaining, and that her hesitation was owing to reluctance on her part to be instrumental in convicting him, I reached forward and was about to continue the examination myself, when she interposed her arm and said sobbingly,

"Those are the little clothes of our poor baby,—they haven't been disturbed since his death, and I can't bear to move them."

A second glance into the trunk confirmed her sad story, for there were the little shoes, scarcely soiled, the delicately embroidered skirts and waists,—all the apparel so familiar to a mother's eye, which, in its grieving remembrance of the departed child,

> "Stuffs out his vacant garments with his form."

A similar affliction had taught me to appreciate the sacredness of such relics, and I waited in sympathizing silence, until she could command her feelings sufficiently to continue the search.

She soon resumed it, and the contents of the trunk were thoroughly examined, yet none of the lost valuables were found therein.

CHAPTER XVIII.

FRAUDS CARRIED ON THROUGH THE MAILS.

Sad Perversion of Talent—Increase of Roguery—Professional Men suffer—Young America *at* the "Bar"—Papers from Liverpool—The Trick successful—A legal Document—Owning up—A careless Magistrate—Letters from the Un-duped.

Victimizing the Clergy—A lithograph Letter—Metropolitan Sermons—An up-town Church—A Book of Travels—Natural Reflections—Wholesome Advice.

The Seed Mania—*Strong* Inducements—Barnes' Notes—"First rate Notice"—Farmer Johnson—Wethersfield outdone—Joab missing.

"Gift Enterprise"—List of Prizes—The Trap well baited—Evading the Police—The *Scrub* Race.

An incalculable amount of talent is perverted to dishonest purposes, thereby becoming a gift worse than useless to its possessors, and a fruitful source of evil to the community. Such misemployed ability is like the "staff of life," turned by a magic worse than Egyptian, into the serpent of death. And the brilliancy which surrounds the successful development of some deep-laid plan of knavery—the admiration which it involuntarily excites, in the mind even of those who abhor the deed, and condemn the cunning designer, render such misdirected powers doubly dangerous, by exciting in the weak-minded and evil-disposed a desire to emulate such wonderful achievements, and to become notorious, if they cannot make themselves famous.

It cannot be denied that a considerable degree of talent is requisite to insure success, even in a course of knavery; and by success I mean nothing more than that longer or shorter career, which ends, if not always in detection, certainly in disappointment and misery. Success, then, in this connection, signifies putting off the evil day—a day which is as sure to come as any other day. Time is an enemy which no rogue can ever outrun.

Even such pitiful success as this is not within the grasp of small abilities. The possessors of such moderate endowments will find it emphatically true, that Honesty is the best policy for them, however brilliant and seductive a dishonest course may be.

When Shakspeare wrote, "Put money in thy purse," he probably did not intend to exhort any one to pocket another's money, but to confine himself to that which he actually possessed. But, judging by the number and variety of the ingenious frauds which are practised upon the community, the saying in question seems to have been adopted in its most unscrupulous sense as a principle, by sundry personages, more remarkable for smartness than for honesty. Not a few of these characters have selected the mails as the means of facilitating their designs upon the pockets of the public at large.

"But this sort of thing is becoming too prevalent," as a worthy magistrate was in the habit of remarking, when about to sentence some pick-pocket or disturber of the peace; and if the devices of the class of villains referred to continue to increase as they have done for years past, semi-annual sessions of the legislative branch of Government will scarcely suffice for the enactment of penalties to meet the increasing exigencies of the case.

There is no end to the gross swindles of this description now perpetrated or attempted, and requiring the utmost care and watchfulness on the part of the public to avoid being deceived by them. No class nor condition in society is exempt from these wiles; the most intelligent and shrewd being vic timized quite as often as the credulous and inexperienced.

Lawyers, clergymen, editors, farmers, and even post masters, have all in turn been swindled by means of facilities afforded by the post-office system, the frauds ranging in magnitude and importance, from imaginary papers of onion seed, to "calls" for ministerial aid in the momentous work of converting "a world lying in wickedness!"

It is with a view to put those who may peruse these pages on their guard, that a few rare specimens of the tricks of these "Jeremy Diddlers" are here exposed, most of which have come to light within a few months of this present writing.

The first that we will describe, was perpetrated quite successfully upon the legal fraternity, and some of the most distinguished members of that highly useful profession in the different States, will no doubt readily recognise the truthfulness of the picture, as it is held up to their gaze. This "dodge" may properly be entitled

YOUNG AMERICA PRACTISING *AT* THE BAR.

In January of the present year, the post master of Brooklyn, N. Y., called my attention to the fact that large numbers of letters were arriving at that office to the address of "William H. Jolliet," and that from some information he had received, he was led to believe that the correspondence was in some way connected with a systematic scheme of fraud.

Arrangements were accordingly made to watch the person who was in the habit of inquiring for the "Jolliet" letters, and the next time he called, which was in the evening, he was followed as far as the Fulton ferry, detained just as he was about to enter the ferry-boat, and questioned in reference to the letters.

The person thus interrogated was an exceedingly intelligent boy, about fifteen years of age, plainly but neatly dressed, and of prepossessing manners, particularly for one so young. When asked what he intended to do with the letters he had just taken from the post-office, he manifested great self-possession, and apparently anticipating trouble, without allowing an opportunity for a second question, he hurriedly asked,

"Why, what about this business? I have been thinking there might be something wrong about Jolliet's letters. I am a student in a respectable law-office in New York, and would not like to be involved in any trouble of this sort. I can tell you, sir, all I know about these letters."

As his explanation will hereafter appear in full, suffice it here to say, that he threw the entire responsibility upon a stranger whom he accidentally met in the Harlem cars. The story was told with much apparent frankness, and a gentleman passing along who knew the lad, and confirmed his statement as to his connection with a prominent law-office in New York, he was allowed to go at large, under a promise that at an appointed hour on the following day, he would call on the Brooklyn post master, explain the matter more fully, and put him in possession of facts which would enable the officers to arrest Jolliet, if that was thought best.

The appointed time arrived, but the young man did not. A rather voluminous package of papers, however, was sent as a substitute. These papers are so well worded, and so formally drawn up, that I will here introduce two of them *verbatim*. The reader will bear in mind that they are the production of a boy only fifteen years of age:—

New York, January 26, 1855, 12, M.

Post Master, Brooklyn, L. I.

Dear Sir:

Being detained by important court business from attending to my promise given to you yesterday to be at your office, I am obliged to write to you. I enclose a statement of facts which I think sufficient to get a warrant. It is sworn to by me before a Commissioner of Deeds of New York, authorized to take acknowledgments for the State.

I saw Mr. Jolliet yesterday evening. He does not suspect anything. I told him that the mails had not arrived when I was over to Brooklyn, yesterday; and, in course of the conversation, he told me *he would take a sleigh ride to Snediker's on Saturday.* Therefore, it is important you should *get a warrant, and take him upon that day.* He also told me he would have a white sleigh, a white robe, and a cream-colored pair of horses. You can easily know him. I will be over, if no accident intervenes, to-morrow, say about 11 or 12 o'clock. I tracked him to the Manhattan bar-room in Broadway, but could not find out his residence, as he stayed too late. I think he is connected with a gang of rascals who have made this kind of rascality their special business.

I am acquainted with the District Attorney in this city, and have thought of getting him to bring the case before the grand jury, and get a bench warrant out in New York against Jolliet, in càse you should think it advisable.

Meanwhile, I will remain still about the matter until I hear from you again.

Yours, very truly.

Annexed is the statement of facts alluded to above :—

Statement of Facts. A.

During the month of November or Decemoer, 1854, I became acquainted with a man whom I knew by the name of William H. Jolliet. He seemed to be about 25 or 30 years of age, and, by his dialect, of English parentage; he was genteelly dressed, and seemea to be a gentleman by his talk and manners. He came to know me from often seeing me on the cars of the New York and Harlem Rail Road, and often talking to me. I am in the habit of doing copying, &c., for pay, and therefore was willing to do anything in that way, under the usual circumstances—that is, for pay.

He asked me one day if I was a man of business. I told him I was. He then asked me if I could make a copy of a note he had in his pocket, and show it to him the next time I should meet him, and not to say anything about it to anybody. I told him I would. He gave it to me, and it was something as follows—that is, substantially :—

Brooklyn, L. I., Jan. 6, 1855.

Sir:

I have received a package of papers for you from Liverpool, England, with six shillings charges thereon—on receipt of which amount the parcel will be sent to you by such conveyance as you may direct.

Yours, respectfully,

WILLIAM H. JOLLIET.

I met him one or two days afterwards, and gave him his original, and my copy. He said it was very well done, but looked too much like a law-hand, and asked me if I couldn't write more of a mercan-cantile-looking hand. I told him I supposed I could. He then gave me my copy, and told me to buy some paper, and make as many copies as I could, and direct them one to each of the names he gave me on a list, and mail them. I told him I would. This was on a Saturday evening; and on Sunday afternoon I wrote about a hundred copies of them, and directed them and sent them. I met him on Monday, and he asked me if I had done it. I told him I had; he then asked for the list of names he had given me, and I handed it to him. He asked if I knew the names I had directed the letters to. I told him I did not, although I did well, my suspicions about him having been aroused by his request for secrecy.

On that Sunday on which I wrote the notes, I made up my mind to play traitor to him, by sending the notes as directed, and keeping all answers which he should get (he having told me to call for them at the Brooklyn Post Office), and then delivering them, with my evidence, to officer B——, in New York, whom I know well by reputation as a good officer, and an American in fact and principle. This was foiled by my disclosures to the Post Master of Brooklyn, on Thursday.

At the time he asked me to make the copies of the note, he gave me a five-dollar gold piece, to defray expenses. I have kept a copy of the list he gave me, and also of another which he had given me, and which I returned in the same way. I have mailed about 200 letters in all. At the time he ordered me to make the copies of the letter and mail them, he requested me to make a letter and direct it to him at Brooklyn, and mail along with the others. I did so, but I asked him what this was for, and he said he wanted to know how long it would take for a letter to go from New York to Brooklyn. But I did not believe him, and this formed part of the causes for my suspicions. I afterwards received the letter, I think it was Tuesday, and gave it to him. At the time of my first mailing the letters, I dropped, by carelessness, a list of the names of persons to whom they were directed, along with them. Could this list be got, it would tell us a great deal about the transaction, and then we could have a complete list of all the persons addressed. It was dropped in one of the three new boxes on the south-west corner of the New York Post-Office.

I have seen him since he first spoke to me about this affair, five or six times, (once on Friday, Saturday, Monday, and Tuesday, and twice on Wednesday, I believe.) He lives in Harlem, I think. I don't know anything further of interest, and close with the ardent wish, that a King's county officer will get the credit of catching one of the greatest scoundrels that ever lived, thereby ridding the community of him.

G. H. B.

City of Brooklyn,
County of Kings, ss.

G. H. B——, of the city of New York, student at law above named, being duly sworn, doth depose and say that he has read the foregoing statement, and knows the contents thereof, and that the same is true of his own knowledge.

G. H. B.

Sworn before me this
26th January, 1855.
B. T. B——,
Comr. of Deeds.

Being satisfied that a young lad of sufficient abilities to compose these documents in such a style, could not have been made the innocent dupe of any one, especially a stranger, I determined to lay the whole matter before his employer, a prominent member of the New York bar. He had heard nothing of it before, and was much pained to hear my narration, for he was warmly attached to the young student, who, up to that time had enjoyed his entire confidence, and for whose improvement and legal education he had taken unusual pains.

A moment's reference to the Law Register, a work containing the names and residences of all the members of the legal profession in every State in the Union, and to be found in almost every law office, showed the source whence he had obtained the list which had been "dropped by carelessness" into the post-office, for pencil marks appeared against the names of most of the *country* lawyers, but including none of those that had ever been correspondents of the firm with which he was connected!

The opinion that there was no accomplice, nor even principal, in the case, beyond the boy himself, was fully coincided in by his employer, and it was at once decided to call the lad up for a private examination.

I thought, as he entered the room, cap in hand, and with an air of perfect *nonchalance*, that I had seldom seen a more expressive and intelligent countenance. His high forehead, adorned with graceful curls of brown hair, his full and laughing eye, and the regular features of his face, seemed made for some better use than to delude unwary victims.

"George," said his employer, "what do these Jolliet letters mean, that you have been sending all over the country?"

Boy.—"I will tell you all I know about it, sir. Some weeks since, as I was coming in town one morning, in the Harlem cars, a man calling himself Jolliet——"

Agent.—"Stop, George, and hear me a moment before you go further. We don't want to hear that story. We know there is no such person as Jolliet, and if you go on with such a statement before Mr. F.," (his employer,) "your pride will render it harder for you to make the acknowledgments that I know you must come to. You have had no accomplice, and if you will bring me the Law Register, I will show you where you got the names of the lawyers to whom you sent the letters."

Mr. F.—"Now, George, you see that Mr. H. knows all about it, and I hope you will not attempt to deny the truth. I am deeply pained to find that you have been guilty of such misdemeanors; and I trust, for your own sake, that you will make a clean breast of it."

After a pause of a few moments, the young man acknowledged, that, being "hard up," he had resorted to this plan to obtain funds, and that he knew no such person as "William H. Jolliet."

Agent.—"How then could you have sworn to the statement you sent to the Brooklyn post master? You must have been aware that in so doing, you were committing perjury."

Boy.—"Ah! but I did not swear to it. My name is attached to the affidavit, it is true, but having prepared it beforehand, I spoke to the Commissioner just as he was leaving the officer, and he signed it, but in his hurry he forgot to administer the oath."

Agent.—"But that omission must have been merely accidental. Supposing he had required the usual ceremony, what would you have done?"

Boy.—"I have so often seen him omit it, that I took that risk. If he had insisted, I should have backed out."

Subsequent inquiry satisfied me that the Commissioner in question, having often had occasion to sign affidavits for the young man, in the course of the office business, was not always particular in administering the oath, and that it was no doubt neglected in the present instance.

The punishment inflicted in this case, was all that the most indignant victim of the fraud would have demanded; and there is reason to believe that a permanent reformation in the character of the young man has been the result; and that the rare talents which he possesses, will yet be found arrayed on the side of honesty and virtue.

Answers to the Jolliet letters continued to arrive from all parts of the country, for some time after the discovery of the fraud, as here related. The letters that had accumulated in the Brooklyn Post Office, were sent to the Dead Letter Office, opened, and subsequently returned to their respective owners, with their contents, accompanied by a proper explanation.

In nearly every instance, the dodge had been successful. The six shillings, or that amount in postage stamps, were duly enclosed; and, in some instances a dollar, to make even change, with directions for forwarding the mysterious package.

Such an unexpected notice had no doubt given rise in many cases to sundry visions of heavy fees, which were to flow in upon the fortunate correspondent of Jolliet, for conducting the business of some wealthy capitalist of the old world, who, attracted by his professional fame, was about to confide to him matters of great weight and importance—perhaps some complicated law-suit, the successful issue of which would bring him a wealth of reputation and money, compared with which the outlay of six shillings was an item too contemptible to be regarded.

Or some sanguine individual might scent out a legacy in the "package from Liverpool."

People were dying every day in England, whose heirs lived in this country. It was not very unusual for persons to inherit immense fortunes from those whose names they had never heard. It might make the difference of thousands of dollars to a man whether his name was Brown or White, when some possessor of one or the other name came to leave his property behind him. And it would be a pity to lose the chance of securing a handsome property for one's self, or the opportunity of acting as agent for somebody else, though the whole affair might prove but a hoax, and the chance of thus finding a fortune rather less than the prospect of drawing a prize in a "gift lottery."

It was amusing to peruse the letters which the Agent received from those who had been swindled, acknowledging the safe return of the letter and money which they had sent to Jolliet. Most of them were "well satisfied" when they sent the money, "that it was all a hoax," but then it was a small sum that he applied for, and they thought they would send it to the fellow for the ingenuity he had displayed in "raising the wind!" All, however, seemed very glad to get their money again, even at the risk of allowing such talent to go unrewarded.

Some wary old heads, too acute to be caught by such chaff, took the precaution to request Jolliet to call on their friends in New York, leave the package, and get the six shillings. Another directed that it should be left at the Express Office, the expenses paid there, and when the parcel arrived, the entire charges would be promptly met.

Two or three, not content with informing Jolliet that he had not taken them in, indulged in a somewhat sarcastic style of correspondence. The following are two specimens of this kind of reply:—

P——, Feb. 2, 1855.

Mr. Wm. H. Jolliet,

Sir:

I am in receipt of a note from you, informing me that you have in your possession a package for me from Liverpool, Eng., on which there is a charge of 6*s.* sterling, and which you will send to me on receipt of the above sum.

Sir, I cannot but think it a little strange that my large circle of friends and correspondents in Liverpool (a circle which may be represented thus, 0) should have thought it necessary for parcels which they send me, to pass through your hands, unless you have some connection with the friends aforesaid, unknown to me. Before I send you the *sterling* money, I should like answers of the like quality, to some or all of the following interrogatories:—

1st. Who are you?

2d. Who knows you?

3d. Who do you know?

4th. Is "Wm. H. Jolliet" the name given you in baptism?

5th. Wouldn't you receive less than six shillings, if you could get it?

6th. Do you think you have taken me in?

7th. After reading the above, please inform me whether you remain *Jolly yet.*

Not your victim,

JNO. S——.

H——, Jan. 28, 1855.

Sir:

I know I am ambitious. I have my aspirations. My fame may be extending. Perhaps it is. I had thought it was local; confined to this county, certainly to the State. But it seems that I am known abroad, and you wish me to pay the moderate sum of seventy-five cents for verifying the fact. Sir, I am an Anglo-Saxon. I rejoice in it. And I don't doubt that somewhere between Adam's time and mine, some of my progenitors have inhabited England. But I believe they have all died or moved away. So you see it isn't likely that I have any relations in Liverpool, whence came the package you say is in your hands.

In the next place, sir, living as I do in an inland town, I know little of those "who go down to the sea in ships." (David, Psalms, Cap. 107.) And all my particular friends are in this country, according to the best of my knowledge and belief. But no others than the individuals I have cited, would be likely to send me packages from foreign lands. It therefore follows, sir, that the aforesaid package is not *in rerum natura.* I shall be happy to receive from you any facts which may vitiate this conclusion.

Pending this, I remain yours, &c.,

ED. B——.

Mr. Wm. H. Jolliet.

We have allowed the lawyers to lead off in the melancholy procession of victims of rascality which we have undertaken to display to our readers; and it is our design, in marshaling our regiment of "the Great Deluded," to place the clergy second in order. Lawyers are (or ought to be) hard-headed, with little faith in mankind at large; while it is the general characteristic of clergymen to be soft-hearted, and to trust, sometimes "not too wisely, but too well," in the integrity of their fellow men. In addition to the weak points which they may have in common with all, and through which they are liable to be successfully assailed, the cultivation of that spirit of charity which "thinketh no evil" makes them slow in suspecting villanous designs on the part of others; and renders them an easy prey to those who are unscrupulous enough to use their unsuspecting disposition as a means of carrying into effect their own base purposes.

In making these remarks, we are far from wishing to cast any slur upon the native shrewdness or penetration of the clergy, which would be unjust to them, (for there are few keener intellects than those that are possessed by some who are members and ornaments of this body,) but our object is simply to mention some of the causes which often make them the victims of imposition. Many of them, especially those who live in the country, occupied as they are with the duties of their calling, in the retired life of the study, and in intercourse with the comparatively honest and virtuous community in which their lot is cast, are somewhat secluded from the world at large, and know little, except by report, of the innumerable forms of deceit and iniquity that people enact, who live outside of their own quiet boundaries. This is, perhaps, less generally true at the present time than it was years ago, before the increased facilities for communication had given equal facilities to rogues, who have chosen our large cities as a field for their nefarious operations, and have extended them, by means of the mails, to the remotest corners of the country.

The trick which we are about to describe was attempted on a large scale, and the trap set for unwary clergymen was sprung in almost every section of the country, with considerable success, though some of the intended victims were too wary to be thus swindled.

The trap alluded to was in the form of a letter, of which the following is a copy:—

New York, Sunday, March 18, 1855.

Brother P———:

Being at leisure this afternoon, and somewhat wearied rather than refreshed by the morning's discourse of our respected pastor, I have concluded to sit down and write you, though utterly unacquainted save in that sympathy which persons of like temperament involuntarily feel toward one another.

It is the apparent coldness and formality of our metropolitan sermons that has led me, by a pleasant contrast, to think of you. I heard you once, while passing through your place—a sermon that has many times recurred to my memory, though its calm piety and deep perception of human nature may be weekly occurrences to your congregation. I have several times thought it would be well for our church to call on you for a trial here. Our house is wealthy, and "up town," though that is no matter.

I had almost given up the idea, when it was forcibly returned to me yesterday by seeing a notice of you in the new publication of travels through the States; in which I see the writer has heard you, and was so impressed that he gives a strong description of you and your style, so well according with my views, that I feel confirmed in my opinion of you. You have probably seen it. And, aside from any vanity at praise in print, or any pain at his censure, (for he finds fault, too,) I think a preacher cannot too much study his style, in duty to his Master and his people, by learning all he can of his hearers' views of him, if not for the praise at least for the blame.

So you see I yet hope to sit under your ministrations. I wish you would write me, immediately, what you think of coming here, if I propose you. My bell has just rung for tea, and I close hastily, wishing you success in any field, and "many souls as seals of your ministry."

Yours, in the Lord,

A. D. CONNELSON.

P. S.—If you have not seen the notice of you, (in the book I alluded to,) I will get it for you. I believe it sells at a dollar and a half, or thereabouts.

I close in haste,

A. D. C.

Here is an instance of one who

"Stole the livery of Heaven
To serve the devil in."

The author of this production, which was lithographed, leaving only a space after the commencing word "Brother," for the insertion of the name of the person addressed, was signed in some copies as above, and in others by the name of "W. C. Jansing."

We can easily imagine the effect of such an artful, flattering epistle upon the mind of some unsuspecting and humble country pastor, whose chief ambition had hitherto been to minister to the spiritual wants of his little congregation, and who had never before indulged the thought of receiving a "call" to the attractions and responsibilities of a city pastor's life. He taxes his memory in vain to recollect upon what occasion any stranger, who might represent the devout Connelson, had been present during his Sabbath services, and in like manner fails to recall any reminiscences of the author, who, in his "Travels through the States," had also heard him, and was "impressed" so remarkably in accordance with Mr. Connelson's "views." His opinion of his own abilities having been elevated several degrees by the united testimony of two such competent witnesses, he begins to think that after all, it is not so very improbable that he should be thought of as a candidate for that "wealthy" and "up-town church."

"Was not the distinguished Dr. L—— called from as small a place as this, to the charge of a large city congregation? And I remember that his abilities did not use to be so much superior to mine."

With reflections like these, he works himself into a state of mind that would prevent any surprise, were he some day to be waited on by a committee from the church aforesaid, with the request that he would favor the congregation with a specimen of his preaching, with the additional view of securing the "pleasant contrast" to the "apparent coldness and formality of metropolitan sermons," that might result from his ministrations. At any rate, it would be gratifying to him to see for himself, what the traveling critic had said of him and his sermons; not that he cared particularly about the opinion, so far as he himself was concerned, but he would like to have his people know that their minister had attracted the attention of distinguished characters from abroad. So he replies to his spontaneous correspondent, intimating that he should have no objection to taking charge of the "up-town" church; and enclosing a dollar and a half, to purchase the book of travels, which he does, not without misgivings that he is sacrificing too large a portion of his slender salary, for indulgence in the anticipated luxury.

It is almost needless to add, that the dollar and a half went to the "bourne from which no *traveler* returns," and that our clergyman did not, in this instance, display "that deep perception of human nature," which so often recurred to the mind of the admiring Connelson.

The operations of this worthy were soon stopped by the New York post master, who, having received letters from some of the shrewder members of the reverend body, enclosing the above epistle, gave the matter in charge to the police, whose movements alarmed the rogue, and blew up the cheat, before many letters containing money had arrived. Enough came, however, to show that had he not been disturbed, he would have feathered his nest comfortably with the spoils of those whom he had plucked.

These letters, remaining uncalled for, became "dead" in due course of time, and were returned with their contents to their authors; doubtless refreshing the heart of many a sorrowing minister, who supposed that he had seen the last of his money, and had given up all hopes of receiving the promised *quid pro quo.*

I insert as a sort of epistolary curiosity, a letter addressed to Connelson by one of his intended victims, which was sent under cover to the New York post master, with the request that he would read and deliver it, if he knew the whereabouts of the person alluded to.

"F——, March 23, 1855.

"Mr. A. D. Connelson.

"Sir:

"I am in receipt of a communication from you, of the 18th inst., of whose flattering contents I have reason to believe that I am not the only recipient; as I am not ignorant of the fact that the art of lithography can be employed to multiply *confidential* letters to any extent. If, as you state, you have at any time heard a discourse from my lips, I regret that the principles which it inculcated have produced so little impression upon your actions, especially as it has 'many times recurred to your memory.'

"There are truths, sir, in addition to those you may have heard on the occasion referred to, (if there ever was any such occasion,) which, judging from the apparent object of your letter, it might be profitable for you to recall. I would recommend to your attention the truth contained in the following saying of the wise man:—'The getting of treasures by a lying tongue, is a vanity tossed to and fro of them that seek death.'—*Prov.* 21, 6.

"You have expressed a hope 'to sit under' my 'ministrations.' I trust you will be profited by the few words I now address to you, and if you feel any disappointment in failing to find the expected 'dollar and a half, or thereabouts,' you will have to console yourself with the reflection, 'How much better is it to get wisdom than gold? and to get understanding rather to be chosen than silver?'—

Prov. 16, 16. I give you the references to the passages quoted that you may ruminate on them at your Sabbath's 'leisure,' which I hope will hereafter be more profitably employed than in attempting to perform the part of "a wolf in sheep's clothing."

"Your well-wisher,

G. J. T."

"P. S. If you ever happen to pass through this place again, and to be detained over the Sabbath, your name, mentioned to the sexton, or indeed, to any member of my congregation, will secure you as good a seat as the house will furnish; and if you will inform me of your intended presence, beforehand, I will endeavor to suit my discourse to your *wants*, if not to your *wishes*.

"'Not what we *wish*, but what we *want*,
Do thou, O Lord, in mercy grant.'

"If, however, circumstances like some that I can foresee, if you continue in your present course, should prevent a visit to our place, I hope you will manage to be satisfied with the ministrations of the chaplain at Sing Sing, who, I understand, is an excellent, talented man. And I trust that you and your *traveled* friend will agree as well on the question of his merits as you have on those of others."

Further comment on this case is unnecessary; and we would only say that any one suspecting an imposture in any such mode as the foregoing, need not be prevented from indulging in a reasonable suspicion, by the charitable thought, "This person could not be such a rascal;" for it is a truth that should be well known and acted upon, that no amount of hypocrisy, deceit or audacity is too great to be practised by miscreants like those whose villanous devices are to some extent exposed in these pages.

THE ONION SEED TRICK.

"If you have tears, prepare to shed them now."

The next ingenious "dodge" to which I would call the attention of my readers, is one which might be styled double-barreled, inasmuch as it brought down both editors and farmers simultaneously.

The agricultural portion of community has been much exercised of late years on the subject of seed. Astounding stories have circulated through the newspapers from time to time, concerning the wonderful prolific powers of certain kinds of seed, and prices have in some instances been demanded for these choice varieties, which remind one of the times when a laying hen of the right breed would earn more per day for her owner than an ordinarily smart negro. It really seemed to be the belief of many enthusiastic persons, that seed could be brought, by careful culture, to a pitch of perfection that would almost render it independent of the assistance of mother earth, save as a place to stand on. The improved seed was to do it all. However desirable it might be to obtain seed which could be warranted under all circumstances to produce heavy *crops*, (which of course can always be done after a certain fashion, by feeding it out to fowls,) this "good time coming" will not be hastened, we apprehend, by the public-spirited efforts of "Mr. Joab S. Sargent," notwithstanding the glowing prospects held out in the following advertisement :—

FARMERS AND GARDENERS.—ATTENTION!

Spanish Onion Seeds.

The subscriber will send to any part of the United States and Canada, a paper of the seeds of the above superior Onion, on the receipt of ten cents (one dime.)

Farmers and Gardeners, see to it that you secure the best of seeds. For a mere trifle now, you can put money in your pockets and fat on your ribs.

Address, JOAB S. SARGENT,
266 Hicks St., Cor. of State,
Brooklyn, N. Y.

P. S.—Publishers of newspapers giving the above and this notice three insertions, calling attention editorially thereto, and sending marked copies to the subscriber, will receive by return mail three dollars' worth of the above seeds, or a copy of Barnes' notes on the Gospels, valued at three dollars and fifty cents, or two dollars cash Address plainly as above.

April 11, 1855.

Observe how adroitly the cunning Joab aims his thrusts at the most vulnerable spot in both classes of his victims. "Publishers of newspapers," in the plenitude of Joab's generosity, are to have their choice between the onion seeds, the gospel, and the ready cash, if they will but make known to the world the incomparable qualities of the genuine Spanish article. And many of these publishers "called attention to the same" with a will, as the following copy of one of those notices will show:—

"SOMETHING NEW FOR FARMERS AND GARDENERS.—See our advertising columns. If you want *large onions*, get the real *Spanish* seed—a change in the seed works wonders. We have seen bushels of onions imported from Spain of half a pound weight each, and as large as saucers."

It may be well to say here that no onion seeds, "Spanish" or other, were sent in compliance with the many orders which poured in upon the successful Sargent from all parts of the country, excepting that a few of those first received were supposed to have been answered by the sending of a few seeds of some kind, whether onion or grass, no one knew. Perhaps the recipients will discover in the course of time. The editors were equally unfortunate. Many of them selected the "Notes on the Gospels" in preference to the seed or the money, yet their wishes were not destined to be gratified.

Let us see how this tempting advertisement worked on the farmers and gardeners.

Here is farmer Johnson, whose boy has just brought in his weekly paper from the office, and who is proceeding to refresh himself after the labors of the week, with the record of what the world at large has been doing in the same time. He deliberately peruses the columns of his hebdomadal, dwelling with solemnity on the more weighty articles, and endeavoring to laugh over the funny ones, till, after having exhausted the "reading" department, his eye goes on in search of new advertisements, which he can distinguish at a glance, for he knows all the old ones by heart. His attention is arrested by the conspicuous heading, "SPANISH ONION SEEDS." He reads it over carefully, and studies every word, that he may be sure that he fully and correctly understands it; and then comparing it with the editorial notice of the same thing, he rapidly becomes convinced that Spanish onions must be great things, and that ten cents may be safely invested in the speculation. Visions of saucer-like onions rise before him; of prizes in Agricultural Exhibitions; and if he is an inhabitant of Connecticut, he fancies he sees the former renown of the ancient town of Pyquag, or Wethersfield, growing dim before the lustre of Spanish onions. Accordingly he sends the required dime to Joab, who proved to be like the elephant which had been trained to pick up coin from the ground and place it on a lofty shelf. Upon a certain occasion, a young gentleman was gratified by this performance, he having furnished a half-dollar for the display of the animal's skill. After the piece was safely deposited far out of reach, the youth requested the exhibitor to "make him hand it down again." "We never learnt him that trick," was the reply!

The enterprising Joab reaped an abundant harvest of dimes, and floods of papers poured into the Brooklyn post-office, each one containing his advertisement marked, agreeably to its conditions, and a few words written upon it by the editor, making his choice between the valuables promised by Sargent, and directing how to send the books, when they were the articles selected. These papers were of course charged with letter postage, and as the quantity which had arrived was becoming somewhat troublesome by its bulk, (since Joab took very good care not to inquire for *them*,) the post master sent to 266 Hicks Street, in order to notify him of the mass of news waiting for him at the office, as well as to make some inquiries in reference to the voluminous correspondence in which Mr. Sargent was engaged. But the person sent, returned with the report, "*non est inventus*," and the wary deceiver, having doubtless taken the alarm, came no more to the office to inquire for letters; so that although the rogue was "unwhipped of justice," a stop was put to his unrighteous gains. This case may serve as a warning to all, to look with distrust upon such advertisements emanating from unknown individuals, especially if the promises made are out of proportion to the "value received." In the present imperfect state of human nature, it is not common to find an individual offering through the papers most disinterested proposals for the good of people in general, without the fact coming to light sooner or later, that he had rather more prominently in view his own good in particular. And I will conclude with the following aphorism, —If you want onion seed, or anything else, send where you know you will not be cheated.

A GIFT ENTERPRISE.

The fraud of which I am about to speak, also depended in a great measure for its success on the fact that it could be carried on through the mails.

Gorgeous hand-bills were sent to the post-offices throughout the country, accompanied with requests to the different post masters to act as agents, and allowing them a liberal per-centage on all tickets sold. Those who read these handbills (suspended on the post-office walls,) and swallowed with expanded eyes and capacious throats the magnificent promises which they contained, could not determine by anything that appeared on the surface, whether "Dashall & Co." were real personages, or merely figments of the brain; and if the former, whether or not they were able and willing to meet their engagements.

The scheme certainly had as fair an appearance as any "Gift Enterprise," and the "local habitation" and "name," which were appended, gave more probability to the idea that the firm in question was not a myth but a reality. Thus it is evident that no one could have detected the fraud without entering into a course of investigation which would have involved more time, trouble, and expense, than most people would be willing to devote to the affair under the circumstances.

The following is a copy of "Dashall & Co's." list of prizes:

150,000 Presents to be given to the purchasers of the large and elegant engraving of the "Inauguration of George Washington, President of the United States," from the celebrated painting of David Paul Laurens. Price of engraving One Dollar, which includes a gift-ticket, entitling the holder to a chance in the following list of magnificent gifts.

The value of the presents, as appraised by a committee chosen for the purpose, is $146,000, as follows:—

A splendid Farm on the Hudson River, completely stocked, houses, &c.	$20,000
Stone Front Dwelling and Lot on Fifth Avenue, N. Y.	13,000
A magnificent *gold* Tea Service, property of the late G. Van Denton	4,000
Silver Wine Service	1,000
The Race Horse "White Raven"	8,000
Coach, Harness, and Horses, *a magnificent establishment*	3,500
30 Shares Central Rail Road Stock	3,000
200 Fine Watches, $100 each	20,000
10,000 Gold Seals and Charms	10,000
10,000 Gold Pens and Silver Holders	5,000
100 Boxes Best Cigars	500
100 Gold Guard Chains	1,500
A splendid Buggy	190
" Phaeton	1,000
A Horse, Harness, and Buggy, splendid affair	500
An elegant Dog, St. Bernard	100
Splendid Fast-sailing Yacht, "Spirit of the Wave"	4,000
The fast and trim pleasure Yacht, "Evening Bird"	1,000
A loan for 25 years	8,000
" "	5,000
" "	1,000
(all without interest.)	
1 Rosewood Piano	800
3 Mahogany Pianos	1,500
A Farm in Ohio	4,000
A Farm in Kentucky	3,000
A Farm in Pennsylvania	6,000
A Farm in Massachusetts	10,000

25,000 Vols. Poems. 11,000
Statue of "Cigar Girl," by Reeves 1,000

Also over 100,000 Paintings, Statues, Medals, Charts, Albums, Valuable Books, and Portfolios of Engravings, making in all 150,000 gifts, which will be distributed by a committee appointed by the Shareholders, and forwarded free of charge by the Public's obedient servants,

DASHALL & CO.,
486 Broadway, New York.

Whoever concocted the above list certainly deserves credit for the expansiveness of his views, the soaring flights of his imagination, and the nicety with which he adapted his various enticements to the different phases of human nature and life.

Was the reader of the hand-bill a "fast" youth? To him a dollar opened the prospect of "a horse, harness, and buggy,—splendid affair;" or "a splendid, fast-sailing yacht;" or "100 boxes best cigars;" or, as a companion to the above cigars, "Statue of Cigar Girl, by Reeves." Did the list of prizes attract the attention of a person agriculturally inclined? To him a choice of farms was offered in the varied regions of Massachusetts, Pennsylvania, Ohio, or Kentucky; or "a splendid farm on the Hudson River" awaited some fortunate individual, who had sufficient faith in good luck and "Dashal. & Co.," to purchase the one hundred and fifty thousandth part of a chance to secure that valuable property. The man of business was tempted by sundry loans "for 25 years without interest," and by "thirty shares of Central Rail Road stock." Through what "centre" this rail road ran, unless it was Dashall & Co's. office, the deponent sayeth not. Upon the man of literary tastes, one dollar might confer "an elegant selected library," while the lover of music was attracted by tl e offer of elegant "rosewood and mahogany pianos."

Nor was the fairer portion of creation forgotten, in the shower of gifts which was to fall on the 10th of March, 1855. The ambitious lady, who had long sighed for more splendid adornments to her table, could not read without emotion the promise of "a magnificent *gold* tea service, the property of the late G. Van Denton." As the lamented Van Denton was doubtless known, in the circle of his acquaintance, as a man of taste, the promised tea service must have been unexceptionable in that respect.

"Melodeons, Harps, Paintings, Albums, Portfolios of Engravings, &c.," formed a galaxy of attractions which drew many a dollar from fair hands.

The engraving of the "Inauguration of George Washington" appealed to the patriotic feeling of every American. What friend of his country would refuse to part with the paltry sum of one dollar, which would enable him to possess this transcendent work of art, copied from the "celebrated painting" of the no less celebrated "David Paul Laurens;" a blood relation, no doubt, of the departed "Van Denton."

Each ticket was so embellished with intimations of the rich gifts possibly in store for its holder, as almost to make him feel as if he were already driving a "blood horse," or taking his ease in the "magnificent residence on the Hudson."

The reader is by this time probably aware of the true character of "Dashall & Co.," and their magnificent scheme. The former were atrocious impostors, and the latter was only a bag of wind.

The suspicions of the New York post master were excited as to the character and destination of the numerous letters which came addressed to the aforesaid firm; and the Chief of the Police taking the matter in hand, a detachment from that body made a descent on 486 Broadway, where they found a respectable female of Milesian extraction, engaged in washing the floor; and observed an open window, through which the representative of Dashall & Co. had probably made his exit. There was no furniture of any description in the room; so, having secured neither "persons" nor "papers," the civil authority was compelled to beat a retreat, not without sundry remonstrances from the old woman, touching the invasion of her "*clane flure.*" She could tell them nothing about the firm, and only knew that she was sent there by the owner of the room to "clane up," which occupation she resumed, after imparting this information, with a vigor that threatened the immediate submersion of the intruders.

The parties concerned in this fraudulent transaction are supposed to have cleared upwards of fifty thousand dollars by the operation, which, allowing for the per-centage to agents and other expenses, proves conclusively that there was more than that number of fools existing at the time in this enlightened land. We would hope that those who were taken in by this cheat, will not be thus deceived again.

We trust that the foregoing record of knavery, whose contrivers were indebted, in some measure, for the carrying out of their plans, to the post masters who acted as agents, will have the effect of producing greater caution on the part of these officials as respects undertaking agencies for *unknown* individuals. It would seem that a proper regard for the public interest would prevent any post master from lending himself, even undesignedly, to a fraudulent scheme like this of "Dashall & Co." It would be easy to refuse to have anything to do with proposed agencies, whose principals were not known to the post master, or concerning whom satisfactory information could not be obtained.

The adoption of this practice would seriously interfere with the operations of the class of rogues who succeed in their villanous designs by making cats' paws of honest people in ways similar to that above described. I do not hesitate to say that thousands of dollars would every year be saved to those who are now swindled out of their money, if post masters were to take the course suggested, and refuse to allow hand-bills containing advertisements to be posted up in their offices, unless they were satisfied of the reliability of the parties sending them.

CHAPTER XIX.

POST-OFFICE SITES.

Embarrassing duty—An exciting Question—A "Hard Case"—Decease of a Post Master—The Office discontinued—The other side—Call at the White House—The Reference—Agent's Arrival—Molasses Incident—An honest Child—Slicking up—The Academy—Stuck fast—The Shoe Factory—A shrewd Citizen—The Saw Mill—A Tenantless Building—Viewing the "Sites"—Obliging Post Master—The defunct Bank—A Funeral Scene—The Agent discovered—Exciting Meeting—"Restoration Hall"—Eloquent Appeals—A Fire Brand—Committee on Statistics—Generous Volunteers—Being "put down" —Good-nature restored—The Bill "settled"—A Stage Ride—Having the last Word.

Of all the troublesome matters that have to be passed upon and decided by the Head of the Post-Office Department, the settlement of controversies involving the location of small post-offices, is undoubtedly the most perplexing, and difficult of adjustment.

By such cases we are forcibly reminded of attempts which we have witnessed in our younger days, to soothe the troubled breasts of an angry swarm of bees, destitute of a queen, and uncertain where to "locate." Whoever tried to settle the question before *they* settled, was pretty sure to get well stung for his pains.

The difficulty above referred to arises from the conflicting, contradictory representations made to the Department by interested parties, governed by as great a variety of motives as the number of individual whims and interests depending upon the settlement of the "vexed question." Notwithstanding the voluminous documents and geographical information usually tendered in these cases, those with whom the final decision rests, often find themselves perplexed beyond measure, to know what is for the true interests of a majority of the citizens —that being the only object aimed at by the Department— and deem it necessary, occasionally, to refer the subject to a Special Agent, with instructions to visit the neighborhood, make a personal inspection of the different sites proposed, and decide, if possible, what the public interest and convenience demand.

In some instances, where the emoluments of the office itself would not exceed the sum of fifty dollars annually, and where its entire abolishment would not prove any serious inconvenience, a whole neighborhood has been thrown into the most intense excitement, and feuds and animosities have been engendered which the parties concerned will perhaps carry with them to the grave.

But, like numerous other phases of post-office life, they furnish many admirable and instructive illustrations of human nature *as it is.*

During his experience, the writer has himself been frequently charged with the duty of becoming the medium for the settlement of local disputes such as have been alluded to; and a difficult and unpleasant duty has he often found it, though a better school for studying the selfishness and other hard points of the human character, cannot be desired.

But the Government official who is sent to ascertain the truth in one of these post-office disputes, will sometimes find himself about as much embarrassed as have been his superiors, and unless he is well posted up in the shrewd dodges and ingenious appliances that he will have to encounter, will find it quite as troublesome to give an impartial and just recommendation. Decide satisfactorily he cannot of course, for those whose ends are not answered are not only sure to grumble, but to charge all sorts of unfairness upon him in conducting the investigation.

The town of M., situated somewhere East of a line drawn across the map, from New York city to Whitehall, N. Y., but out of the State of New York, was recently the scene of one of these hotly contested controversies; and it is proposed to give an outline of the investigation, as it stands sketched among the author's official notes, under the head of a "Hard Case," with, of course, some additional comments and illustrations.

In extent of territory, the town referred to is about six miles square, and contains three small villages, one comparatively new, having sprung up at the rail road depôt near the West line of the town. The second, about two miles to the Eastward of this; and the third, about two miles still further to the East.

Village number two, in the order in which they have just been mentioned, had for many years been the site of the only post-office in the town, and continued in the uninterrupted enjoyment of this monopoly until the office became vacant by the death of the post master. This was the signal for a movement for some time privately contemplated and discussed within a limited circle composed of a few of the knowing ones residing in villages numbers one and three, which movement involved nothing less than the establishment of a post-office at each of those points, and the abolishment of the old established one at village number two.

A petition to that effect was hastily drawn up and circulated chiefly among those whose interests in the plan sought, would be apt to secure secrecy, due care being taken to say quite as much in favor of the new sites and against the old one, as the facts in the case would warrant. This petition was dispatched to Washington in charge of an influential person, whose hot haste for immediate action was rendered tolerably reasonable by the fact, that the decease of the post master left the community without any appointed guardian of its postal interests.

A fair case having been made out according to the meagre information before the Department, and the aforesaid bearer of dispatches not hesitating to supply verbally what seemed to be lacking in other forms, with one fell swoop of the pen of the Post Master General, the glory departed from village number two to its more fortunate rivals, numbers one and three; and by the same trifling operation, two very competent and suitable individuals were promoted from the condition of private and unassuming citizenship, to the dignity and responsibilities of deputy post masters of the United States of America!

When the news of this sad calamity reached the staid and peaceable villagers, who had thus been unexpectedly deprived of their ancient postal privileges, rest assured it was no favorable time for the organization of a Peace Society! Such oil would not still these waves! Their late beloved and popular post master had become a "dead letter," though properly "addressed," as was fondly hoped, by the heavenly "Messengers" who beckoned him away from other duties, to "wrap" and "box up"—and now even the post-office itself had been prematurely "taken away" also.

Not many suns had risen and set, however, before the other side of the picture was prepared and presented at Washington, and now the ball had fairly opened, with the orchestra in full blast. A formidable remonstrance had received the signatures of all the "legal voters," and, as was charged on the other side, of many whose elective rights were not so easily settled.

The customary accusations of unfairness, improper influence, stealing a march, downright misrepresentations, &c., were called in requisition to show the Department that this "outrage" on the citizens was unwarrantable; and the important trust of conveying this evidence to the seat of Government, fell to the lot of a certain gentleman well known among political circles in that section of the country, and supposed to possess a fair share of influence with the appointing power. He repaired to Washington, made his first call at the White

House, and labored hard to enlist the feelings of the Chief Executive in the case, but a few words from that distinguished official were sufficient to show that such interference in a comparatively unimportant matter could not reasonably be expected of him.

The President did however show his respect for his visitor, who happened to be an old personal friend, by escorting him down to the Department, and introducing him to the Post Master General. The Governor of the State was also in the case, the two United States Senators, and several of the members of Congress, as the files of the papers, *pro* and *con*, clearly demonstrated. Not that they felt any personal interest in the result of the controversy, but because their political relations with many of those who did, were such that they could not well resist their importunities to come up to their relief.

On patiently listening to the statements of the representative from the seat of war, and re-examining the documentary evidence, the Post Master General declined to reverse his former decision, but suggested sending one of the Department's Agents to investigate the whole matter. This course was adopted, and the responsibility thus transferred for the time being, to the shoulders of the to be author of "Ten Years."

For many days before he arrived upon the ground, the excitement both among the vanquished and the vanquishing, was at the highest pitch; information that such reference of the case had been made, having been conveyed to both parties on the return of the distinguished politician from the Capital.

Post master number one, however, could not await the slow process of that form of justice, so he dispatched a semi-official private note to me, nearly as follows, if my memory serves me:

Sir:

Will you please inform me if you have been instructed to visit this place in connection with our post-office controversy. If so, I would like to be informed of the time of your visit, as I wish to post you up as to certain parties here whose true position you ought to understand before their testimony in the case is heard.

Yours truly,

F. B. S———.

P. S.—If I knew when you are to arrive, I would be at the cars.

To this I simply replied that I could not fix upon the precise day, but would call upon him on my arrival.

One lovely afternoon of a lovely day in October, the "Agent" might have been seen alighting from the car at the rail road station at M., fully impressed, of course, with the difficulty of the task before him, but with a sincere desire to carry out, if possible, the intention of Government, and to mete out equal and exact justice to all parties.

A new and flourishing-looking store, the only one by the way in the neighborhood, with a small sign over the door, with the words "Post-Office" inscribed thereon, saved me the necessity of inquiring for post-office site number one. In a few moments I found myself in the presence of the merchant and post master, who proved to be a young man of prepossessing and business-like appearance.

A few questions on my part served to apprise him of the official character of the person by whom he was addressed, and also to cause his momentary neglect of a young customer for whom he was just then engaged in answering an order for a gallon of molasses. The little damsel who was there upon the saccharine errand, regarded me with open-eyed awe, having probably heard something of the Department in the course of the all-pervading Post-Office controversies of the last few months, and cast as many stolen glances at me as her modesty would allow, thus securing a mental daguerreotype, to be displayed for the benefit of her wondering parents, after her return home with the double load of news and molasses.

In his embarrassment at my sudden arrival, the post master forgot the molasses, and in a moment quite a torrent of the thick liquid had overflowed its bounds, and formed a pool upon the floor.

"Post master," said I, "you have left your molasses running over." In his eagerness to stop the leak, he went plump into the sweet puddle, with both feet, and any time that day his tracks might have been seen all over the store.

"Never mind," said he, "accidents will happen;" at the same time drawing his feet across some waste paper upon the floor. The young customer smiled, but during the running over process, she had said not a word, for by the means she was getting "scripture measure." She handed the post master a bank-note in payment, who, still laboring under considerable excitement, made her the wrong change, doing himself out of at least half the cost of the molasses, which, together with the loss of the surplusage, made it anything but a profitable business transaction for him.

But the little girl was honest. She counted and recounted the change that had been given her, and with that peculiar expression that in one like her attends the consciousness of an honest act, she threw it all back upon the counter, remarking, "You have given me too much, sir."

The countenance of the post master gave evidence by this time of not a little mortification at the occurrence of two such awkward blunders in the presence of a dignitary all the way from Washington; and in his hurry to turn my attention from them, he forgot even to thank the child for her honest conduct, as he returned her the change "revised and corrected."

But I did not. Wishing not to cast an implied censure upon sweet-foot, I passed to the piazza of the store, to throw aside the stump of an Havana, (or a "Suffield," as the case may have been,) and unobserved by him, handed her a quarter, which she acknowledged by a blushing smile, and a low courtesy.

Returning, I missed the post master for a moment, and stepping within sight of the floor behind the counter, I could distinctly see the molasses tracks going toward a small enclosure at the other end of the counter. It proved to be the apartment used for the post-office. Stepping a little further behind the counter, I spied my new and confused acquaintance, arranging the books, letters, and papers, apparently in great haste. Seeing that I had returned to the store and now observed him, he advanced towards me a few paces.

"I usually keep things in better order in the post-office," said he, "but I was away this forenoon, and my boy has got things a little mixed up."

"Never mind that now," I replied; "I am in something of a hurry, and want to enter at once on the business upon which I came. What is all this fuss that the people of the old village are making about the new post-office arrangements? By the row they are kicking up at Washington, the Department are almost led to believe there was something unfair in the means adopted to effect the change, and that they may have erred in their decision."

This plain and informal opening of the case seemed to restore his self-possession.

"Well, they have tried to make a fuss, that's a fact, but it's more spunk than anything else. You see this is a new village, and although there are not yet many buildings, business is fast centering here, and it's bound to be *the place*. The folks up there have to come to the depôt constantly, and if they only think so, can be just as well accommodated here. They hate to lose a good place to loaf in, that's all there is to it. They don't need a post-office no more than a rail road wants a guide post.

"They will tell you a great deal about their Academy, and talk big about other things. As to the Academy, it has got reduced, and most of the pupils who do attend, either belong to the upper village where they have a post-office now, or have to pass right by this door in going to school. But few of them being from abroad, they have but little correspondence any way. Then you will hear tall speechifying about a flourishing hat factory which perhaps did something once, but can hardly be said to be in operation now. I hear they claim to have three extensive stores in the village. Now if you will look for yourself, you will see two small affairs that don't both together sell half the goods that I do, and as to the third, it was closed some time ago, and if the owner went away in broad daylight, then common report does him great injustice."

After a few remarks in the same vein, in the course of which he waxed quite eloquent, he closed by offering to take me in his wagon and show me the other two villages. He had been standing quite still during the delivery of this speech, and considerable effort was required to raise his feet to go in the direction of his hat, the adhesive qualities of the syrup still holding out.

I thanked him for the offer, but said I must decline it, as I desired to avoid all cause of jealousy in my mode of investigation, and further remarked, that I would prefer to take a general view of all the localities, without the aid or explanations of any of the parties interested; and that after this had been done, I would give all hands a fair and impartial hearing.

"Very well," said he, "all we ask is fair play, but you will have to make a good deal of allowance for the extravagant statements of the leaders in the old village. I can prove that they have got democrats to sign to have the office restored, who are on our paper, and who say they were deceived when they signed theirs."

Having heard about enough of this, I had gradually moved along to the store door, when my eye rested upon a large wooden building near by, several stories high, and with an unusual number of windows, about the only building of any size in the vicinity.

"What is that?" I asked, at the same time pointing to it.

'That?—that is a shoe manufactory."

"How many hands are employed there?" I inquired.

Just then, a fine-looking, elderly gentleman, with an air which denoted that he had a right to do pretty much as he pleased, stepped upon the piazza, and was introduced to me by the post master as his father-in-law, not omitting of course to inform his respected relative that I was no less a personage than the identical gentleman expected from Washington.

"Ah," said he, "I am glad the Department has seen fit to send so competent a person to look into this business, and I hope, sir, it will be thoroughly done."

This was said in a gentlemanly, dignified manner, and he passed into the store without any further conversation. But the term "competent person," as applied to me, warned me that I should probably find it necessary to guard against "soft sodder" also, as one of the means of persuasion, and made me half suspicious that he might not be the impartial and disinterested individual that he appeared at first sight.

The suspicion was just, for I afterwards learned that he was a wealthy and enterprising whig citizen, owning a beautiful mansion and a good deal of other property in village number three, (one of the new sites,) and that he was the proprietor of a good share of the real estate at the depôt village; and further, that he had been mainly instrumental in getting the changes effected. His personal interests in them footed up as follows: A post-office established at the village of his residence, and a post-office at the depôt village, (where the store in which it was kept belonged to him,) and his son-in-law appointed post master! A shrewd Yankee operation that, though I could discover the adoption of no dishonorable means in securing these advantages. It was decidedly smart, though, and it isn't every body who could have successfully executed such a programme, after it had been arranged.

This interruption of the conversation between the post master and myself, came in just in time to stave off an answer to my question about the large building in view, and my friend no doubt considered that an effectual stop was put to further inquiries on that subject. But not so. Failing to discover any signs of thrift or vitality in or about the huge edifice referred to, I now repeated the inquiry.

"I was asking how many persons are employed in that shoe factory?"

Before I had fairly finished the sentence, however, he had darted into the store and returned with two Havanas, (?) saying, "Come, have a smoke, and let's walk over and take a look at the saw mill," which by the way happened to be in an opposite direction from the aforesaid shoe establishment.

I consented, however. The mill was in operation, and the stream, such as it was, kept up a pretty respectable roar, though you could hear yourself converse, I noticed, quite as easily as by the side of old Niagara just after a smart shower!

Feeling somewhat humorously inclined, owing to his persevering evasion of my researches as to the boot and shoe enterprise, I remarked as we stood observing the perpendicular thrusts of the saw through a submissive-looking log, "This is the *board*ing house spoken of in your post-office petitions, isn't it?"

He did not "take," however, but gravely replied that they *had* turned out stacks of boards since the mill was started, and that they had thought of keeping it running nights as well as days.

As I could conceive of no very direct connection between a saw mill and a post-office, and not caring to have too much saw dust thrown in my eyes, nor to countenance any log-rolling operation, I moved off toward the store again. But not a word was volunteered about the "factory," so I marched straight over to it, and trying one of the main doors, found it all fast as I had suspected. I was about to repeat the attempt at another part of the building, but the post master had now arrived on the ground, and his reluctant explanation saved me further trouble on that head at least.

"Owing to the hard times, it is not occupied now, but until lately it has employed some thirty or forty hands. They'll get agoing again soon, and intend to employ some eighty workmen. The suspension is only temporary."

"Worse off than the hat factory of which you spoke, at the other village," I observed. He made no reply.

Finding I could obtain no independent conveyance by which

24

to make the tour of observation through the other parts of the town, I accepted the offer of a young man who drove up to the store very opportunely, to whom the idea was suggested by the post master, and who, it was hinted, was in no way identified with this vexatious dispute.

During the first mile or so of our ride his neutrality seemed well sustained, but it began rapidly to disappear as we came in sight of the village which had been bereft of its post-office as well as its post master, his answers to my questions betraying a decided bias toward the "let well enough alone" policy as applicable in this case.

I did not propose to stop there at this time, but to pass through to the upper village,—but my suspicions that I had after all committed myself to the temporary keeping of one of the friends of the new sites, were fully confirmed when I found him taking a narrow by-way through the old settlement, poorly calculated to show off the place to much advantage.

"Look here," said I, "don't go through this hollow, but take a turn round by those spires, and let me see what they have got to brag about."

Coming to a halt, and backing round in a somewhat spiteful manner, during which manœuvre we came near upsetting, he soon came upon the route indicated.

Whether from a conviction that there was no use in trying to cheat me any longer, or from the study requisite for the invention of some new system of tactics likely to be more successful, he said but little more during the rest of our ride.

I subsequently ascertained that he and the scheme of getting two post-offices for one, rejoiced in one and the same paternity, or in other words, that his mother was the wife of the enterprising and wealthy gentleman before mentioned, and like a good and dutiful son, he "went in" for whatever favored the "old man's" interest.

Passing through one of the main streets of the middle or post-officeless village, I observed standing in front of a respectable, ancient-appearing mansion, a solemn-looking hearse, and a large number of other vehicles, indicating that funeral services were being performed within, and through the open windows and doors I could see the friends and mourners.

"A funeral, I perceive," said I to my companion.

A sullenly emphasized "yes," was all the notice vouchsafed to my remark.

"A fine-looking lot of horses collected here," I continued.

"Yes, pretty fair," he rejoined, without, however, withdrawing his attention from a large fly which was annoying our animal, and at the same time proving himself anything but an expert marksman by his repeated unsuccessful attempts to annihilate the insect with the lash of his whip.

"This accounts for my seeing so few persons in the streets," I remarked. "They must be attending the funeral."

"I suppose so," he answered, at the same instant striking the unlucky fly dead, which neither he nor bob-tail had before succeeded in choking off.

A quarter of an hour more found us at village number three, pleasantly situated upon elevated ground, and consisting of an old-fashioned country church, the fine establishment of the wealthy pioneer in this post-office enterprise, already referred to, a store, and a few other buildings.

The solitary merchant here was also the newly-appointed post master, a very worthy man from all appearances, though of course deeply impressed with the idea that the "balance of power" should not be disturbed by a discontinuance of the recently established office, and the restoration of the old one on its former site. And it appeared very clear that he had done all in his power to make the inconvenience of the late change fall as lightly as possible upon those more directly interested, for he had arranged to extend every accommodation in his power, and among other things to post a list of all the letters for distant sections of the town, upon the "meeting-house" door every Sabbath, and to keep his office open "between meetings," for the delivery of all mail matter which should be called for.

His brief history, as related by himself, brought to light the fact that he had served the Government as post master many years before, having originally been appointed, as he said, by "old Hickory" himself.

During half an hour's conversation, the information furnished at this point was generally of a candid and impartial character, though the explanations regarding a defunct bank, the remains of which stood within a stone's throw of the post-office, proved the most troublesome subject that was talked over. The expiration of its charter, if I mistake not, was given as the reason for its closed doors.

The measured tolling of the church bell attracted my attention. The funeral procession from the other village had reached the hill and was just entering the burial-ground, through the church-yard, and after a short interval passed out again on its return.

Having now obtained all the information I could in that quarter, I suggested to my escort that I was ready to move, and we were soon on our way back. About half way to the middle village, we came up with the procession, and followed along at a slow pace, in fact forming a part of the solemn cortege.

It had somehow leaked out that the "Post-Office Agent" was there, and along the whole line, hats and even bonnets could be seen projecting from the sides of such of the carriages as were provided with coverings. Compared with the post-office question, the grave was nowhere, and funerals were at a discount. Some of the most interested happened to be in the nearest vehicles to us, and when they discovered who my companion was, a number of the animals were suddenly relieved of a good share of their burthen. Several of the deserters fell in the rear, and without waiting for a formal introduction, began to discourse eloquently upon the subject of their post office grievances. I assured them that I would spend the night at the hotel in their village, where I would be happy to

Darley fecit
BOBBETT-HOOPER. Sc.

meet them and their friends, for the purpose of inquiry and investigation.

Many a head of a family, I think, was missed that evening from the tea tables, for although it was about the usual hour of that repast when I reached the hotel, the citizens came flocking in in great numbers, and filling the spacious audience room which the landlord had hastily prepared on hearing of my approach, to its utmost capacity, and even before I was fairly seated.

Most of them being still in the same dress in which they had attended the funeral ceremonies, the "customary suit of solemn black," they were about as well-looking a set of men as you will often see in country or city. A more excited and anxious group of faces, I am sure was never seen in a council of war on the eve of a great and decisive battle. Nor will I attempt to assert that I was wholly free from anxiety as to how I should acquit myself before this august assembly, as the representative and embodiment of the Government, on this trying occasion.

The scene, however, considered in reference to the real importance of the interests at stake, was richly ludicrous. I felt that the dignity of the Post-Office Department was for a time committed to my keeping, and I flatter myself that I succeeded admirably in sustaining it, though it required occasionally not a little effort.

One of the gentlemen whose acquaintance I had informally made in the rear of the funeral procession, did the honors in the way of introducing me to each of those who had assembled, and to such as came in in the course of that ever-to-be remembered evening—I should have said night, for it was not far from daylight, when I had listened to the last eloquent appeal in behalf of restoring to them their lost rights and privileges.

The whole thing was conducted in a way which, for parliamentary order and decorum, would have put to the blush the lower House of Congress near the close of the session; and I am not quite sure that the upper branch of that Honorable body, with an exciting subject in hand, could not have derived some useful hints from the manner in which business was there enacted.

The room, which I understand was soon after christened and is now known as "Restoration Hall," was about twenty-five feet by thirty, and for most of the time during this eventful meeting, I chanced to occupy the only rocking chair therein, at one side of the room facing the door. Considering that most of the company were my seniors by several years, that was hardly polite; but after several times insisting in vain that some one else should take the post of honor, I settled down without further misgivings.

Never did I so heartily regret my ignorance of the art of stenography as now; for a *verbatim* report of all that was here said, would prove the richest and most amusing part of this narrative.

After some general and desultory conversation, and considerable manœuvring as to who should lead off, the responsible task fell upon a somewhat venerable and prominent citizen, who, as I perceived from his "opening," had enjoyed the honor of representing the town in the lower House, as well as the Senate of the State. This gentlemen's indignation was so intense at the "shabby treatment" of the Government, that at first he seemed to question the propriety of condescending to enter into any argument or formal statement in support of a speedy restoration of the post-office.

"I feel myself mortified and humbled," said he, "that anything more should be required in this case in securing us justice, than a mere glance at this assemblage, which, leaving out the speaker, cannot be surpassed in respectability and intelligence, by any which could be so readily convened in any community."

(A general sensation, and a modest assent all round, so far as looks could indicate it.)

"You have before you, sir," continued he, "professional

men—men who have devoted all their lives to the training and education of youth,—farmers, mechanics, and merchants,—all of them, sir, men who know their rights, and knowing dare maintain them, sir. Many of them, and I for one, sir, differ with the Administration in politics; but I take it, sir, that has nothing to do with tho settlement of this business. Our Government will have arrived at a pretty pass, indeed, when it makes a distinction between a whig or locofoco community, in the granting of mail facilities."

The term "locofoco" proved for a moment a slight firebrand in the camp—a six foot, plain farmer-looking individual, who had not I think attended the funeral, and who, like the brave Putnam, had left his plough in the furrow, on hearing of a chance to fight—starting to his feet and interrupting the speaker,—

"Your Honor," said he, "I hope my whig friend, if he must speak of politics, will consent to call democrats by their right names. What would he say if I should apply the term 'federalists' to his side of the house?"

The first speaker was evidently preparing for a broadside in return for this interruption, but it was averted at once by the assurance volunteered on my part, that the question of politics would have nothing to do with this one; and that no harm was probably intended by the use of the objectionable designation; whereupon our agricultural friend quietly resumed his seat, his blood seemingly several degrees cooler than when he left it.

"You're right, sir, no harm *was* intended," good-naturedly responded the pioneer orator. "It came so natural to say locofoco, that I hardly noticed it myself. We all have one common object here, and the fact that neighbour B. is the only loco—I beg pardon—democrat, who happens to be present, should have suggested to me greater allowance for his sensitive feelings."

There was a general laugh at the expense of our lone

representative of the democracy, and the discussion resumed its more legitimate channel.

At a later period, a careful canvassing would have shown quite a respectable sprinkling of the political friends of the gentleman who took exceptions as above stated; and I have always mistrusted that he managed in some way to procure their special attendance, being evidently a little chagrined at the accidental exposure of the very meagre representation of his party at the commencement.

The gentleman having the floor proceeded :—

"I am satisfied the Post Master General would never have decided as he has, if he had waited for further information. And the indecent haste with which certain men acted in this matter, is a downright shame and disgrace. I doubt not, from what I can learn, that they had their petitions secretly circulating, as soon as the sickness of our late post master became known. Would to God he had lived to defeat their selfish and illiberal schemes! But an overruling Providence ordered it otherwise, doubtless for the accomplishment of some wise purpose!

"We are prepared to show you, sir, by the figures, (though we have seen that, in the hands of unprincipled men, figures *will* sometimes lie,) that three-fourths of the mail matter for the town belongs to persons of this village, who, by this wicked movement, are obliged to send a distance of two miles for their letters and papers."

Here was a strong statement, exhibiting a greater difference in the business and correspondence of the three villages than even the papers on the official files of the Department had claimed. I was therefore disposed to call for the proof, if it could be had, before proceeding further.

"Is there any way of getting at what you have just stated as a fact?" I inquired.

They were not to be caught napping, for the "Committee on Statistics" was on the spot, to meet any such exigencies that might arise.

A slight nod of the gentleman's head toward the corner of the room was promptly responded to by one of the company, whom I had observed listening more intently, if possible, than the rest, to the opening address.

He might be described as a gentleman about forty years of age, with sharp features, and withal as active and keen-looking a body as you will often come across. With a smile, and an air of self-reliance, he drew from his hat a bundle of papers of different shapes, from an inch wide to a full sheet of large size "cap," and, coming to the table, placed them upon it. A moment's search, during which not a word was spoken, produced the desired voucher, which was to confirm the truth of the three-fourths assertion. It proved to be a certificate signed by the assistant of the late post master, setting forth that, *in his opinion*, only about one-quarter of all the letters arriving at that office, during the last three months of its existence, went outside of a circle of one mile.

The ex-assistant himself, being present, was appealed to, but although he was willing, in general terms, to re-affirm what he had put upon paper, yet he failed to furnish any very satisfactory data upon which the calculation had been made. It was so much at variance with the allegations contained in the petitions for the new sites, that the impression could not be resisted that there had been truth-stretching somewhere.

"Should the office be re-established here," said I to the ex-assistant, "can the Department rely on the benefit of your experience in its future management, as post master?"

My object of course was to fathom, if possible, the depth of any personal interest he might have had in making the certificate referred to.

"Well, sir, as to that," he answered, his face a little flushed, "I hardly think I could attend to it; and besides, I may go to the West in the Spring, if not before."

My unexpected inquiry as to a suitable candidate for the office, produced a marked sensation. I observed that it had especially disconcerted the "Committee on Statistics;" why it did so the reader will learn in due time.

Apologizing to the gentleman whose speech had thus been interrupted, he resumed, but in a few moments came to an abrupt close on the arrival of two young gentlemen, both residing near village number three, and therefore, except to a few, supposed to have come as spies and reporters. A short consultation, in which I took no part, showed that they were, as I inferred, all right on the main question, notwithstanding their location. They were brothers.

If the actors in this scene had been engaged in a play upon the stage, these two new characters could not have been introduced in a more artistic or timely manner. What they had to offer was prefaced by a few words from the gentleman who had just terminated his formal discourse, informing me that they had magnanimously volunteered to come here and throw their mite into the scale, on the side of truth and right, and that private interest, even, could not blind *them* to the great injustice that had been perpetrated.

Their own testimony was very brief, and so was their stay, for, believing I had seen their names on one of the petitions asking for just what had been done, I unlocked my carpet-bag, and on referring to one of the original papers which for the time being had been placed in my hands, I there found both their signatures, quite conspicuous among the petitioners!

And I felt bound to give others a sight of them, too, if for no other reason, to impart to the "injured" members of that community a slight knowledge of some of the difficulties which the Post Master General and his Assistant often have to encounter in these and similar cases. It was all news to those present excepting to the two "magnanimous" gentlemen interested. They had doubtless supposed that the evidence of their double-dealing was very quietly sleeping in one of the snug and obscure pigeon-holes of the Appointment Office.

On coming into the room again, after a quarter of an hour's

absence at the supper table, I missed these two generous volunteers, and understood they left very soon after I withdrew. Their inconsistent course was afterwards explained to me in this wise: After they had signed for the change, and the papers had gone to Washington, it came out that the three Select-men of the town had united in a letter to the Department, on the same side of the question, all three of them happening to live nearer the new sites than the old one; and the brothers having become involved in a somewhat bitter quarrel with one of those officials, had determined to get on the opposite side, in the post-office struggle, and defeat their wishes if possible.

Among the speakers was the Principal of the Academy before alluded to; a very intelligent gentleman, and one of dignified appearance. His observations related mainly to the inconveniences resulting to the members of that institution from the want of a post-office. After he had concluded his remarks, I inquired,

"What is the present number of your pupils?"

Upon this, some one suggested obtaining a printed catalogue, and the "Committee on Statistics" forthwith disappeared in search of the required pamphlet. The zeal and efficiency of this gentleman may have had no connection with his desire to fill the office of post master, should the office be re-established. The reader will judge of this when he learns who was finally selected for that position.

After a few moments' absence, he returned with a copy of the catalogue.

Observing that it was for a previous term, I asked whether there were as many pupils now as at that time.

"The school is not quite as large at present," said the Principal; "but we expect even a larger number of pupils at the beginning of the next term."

The hint furnished me (as the reader will remember) by my official friend of molasses memory, in respect to the residences of the pupils, happening to occur to my mind, I ran my eye over the column containing that information, and found that, with few exceptions, they belonged in town. Consequently, unless they carried on a more extensive correspondence than is usual for such youth, the argument maintained by the Principal would lose much of its force. I made no allusion, however, to this discovery, and he soon closed his remarks, expressing the hope that the loud complaints of the distant (?) parents and guardians of the young ladies and gentlemen under his charge would soon be effectually hushed by the restoration of their former excellent mail facilities !

A few of those wise words, which, as Solomon assures us, are "as nails fastened by the masters of assemblies," were driven, in conclusion, by farmer G., who, as a person sitting near me whispered, was a Justice of the Peace. His remarks were characterized by much good sense, but an untoward circumstance occurred as he concluded, which interfered with the gravity of the proceedings as well as with his own centre of gravity. As the closing passage of his peroration fell from his lips, he also fell at the same instant!

There was a scarcity of seats upon the present occasion, and our oratorical friend had no sooner risen for the purpose of "pouring the persuasive strain," than his chair was appropriated by a fatigued neighbor, who "squatted" on the vacant territory, regardless of "pre-emption" or pre-session.

Unconscious of this furtive proceeding, Mr. G. went on with his remarks, and closed with the following sentence :—

"In conclusion, sir, I should like to know whether the people of this village are to be put down in this way?"—at the same time attempting to resume the seat he had vacated, in the full belief that it was still where he had left it. As facts did not bear him out in this opinion, he was obliged to yield to the force of circumstances, and had gained such a backward impetus before he discovered the treachery of his friend, that he descended to the floor with as much emphasis as two hundred pounds of bone and muscle are capable of producing under similar circumstances!

The illustration of his remarks was perfect. He thought that the inhabitants of the village were to be "put down" in an underhanded manner. Whether they were to rise again as rapidly as did he, remains to be seen.

"That strain again; it had a dying fall,"

thought I after the orator descended so suddenly from his rhetorical and personal elevation.

Business was for the moment swallowed up in a roar of laughter, to which the ex-Senator, the dignified Principal, the energetic dealer in Statistics, and the Agent, contributed; and even the fallen speaker, whose title to the *floor* no one was inclined to dispute, joined in the chorus.

The person who had caused this catastrophe, apologized to Mr. G. by remarking, "You got through quicker than I'd any idee of."

"Or I either," dryly returned Mr. G., brushing the dust from his inexpressibles.

This occurrence seemed the signal for adjournment, and all retired in good spirits, thanks to the gentleman who had thus, in spite of himself, been made the instrument of producing such a pleasant state of feeling.

A sort of informal levee was held on the following morning, when all the forcible things bearing on the subject in hand were said which had been forgotten at the meeting of the night previous, or were the result of after cogitations.

As the time drew near for leaving, I called upon the landlord for my bill.

"Oh, that's all settled," said he.

"Settled? by whom, pray?" I asked.

"Why, *they* told me not to take anything from you, as they would make it all right," he replied.

I called the attention of the landlord to the impropriety of such a course under the circumstances, since in the event of the restoration of the office to that village, it might be said,

"Oh, it's easy enough to see how that happened. They knew what they were about when they paid the Agents' hotel bill."

For such reasons I declined the courtesy, and insisted on paying the bill myself. The landlord finally yielded, remarking, "*they* won't like it when they find out that their directions were not followed."

Soon after, the stage arrived at the door of the hotel from a neighboring town, on its way to the rail road depôt, and this was to be my conveyance to that place. I took leave of such of the gentlemen as were standing about the piazza, and mounted to the seat upon the top of the stage, behind and above the driver's station. To this elevated position I was unexpectedly followed by the "Committee on Statistics," and another person whom I had not seen before. This move on the part of the former gentleman was probably made not only to secure my ear during the passage to the depôt, but to prevent the post master there from gaining any advantage over him in the time which would elapse between the arrival of the stage and the departure of the cars.

Being placed, like men in general, between the known and unknown,—the "Committee" on one side, and the stranger on the other, my attention, soon after we had started, was attracted to the former individual by sundry punches in the ribs, proceeding from his elbow, accompanied with ominous winks and glances towards my other companion, who was just then conversing with the driver.

"Look out what you say," whispered the vigilant Committee, "that fellow is a spy; he is one of the Depôt boys."

"All right," I replied, in all sincerity, for I was not sorry to find that my friend would be prevented by the presence of the "spy" from executing the design which he undoubtedly had, of catechizing me in reference to the report I should make to the Department.

Arriving at the station, I crossed over to the post-office, and there remained until the whistle of the locomotive was heard.

"Well, good bye, Mr. W—," said I to the post master, offering my hand.

"I think," said he, "that I will ride a little way with you, as far at least as the next station."

He accompanied me across to the depot, and as we stepped upon the platform of a car, we were followed by the "Committee" and one of his most interested friends, who had come over in the stage with us, an inside passenger.

These gentlemen were evidently bent on thwarting the plans of my saccharine associate, but he had in an important particular greatly the advantage over them, for, by virtue of his office, he was allowed the privilege of riding in the mail car, to which we at once proceeded, leaving our disappointed friends in the outer world, among the undistinguished crowd whom the conductor indiscriminately calls upon for "your money or your ticket."

My companion and his opponents alighted at the next station, to wait for the return train, and as the cars moved on, I observed that they were conversing together, the countenance of the former displaying a radiant appearance of satisfaction which plainly showed his triumphant state of mind.

I have no means of knowing what passed between them on their return, but it is altogether probable that the "Committee" and his friend employed the time in "pumping" or attempting to pump their associate, unless he took refuge in the mail car.

The investigation resulted in restoring the post-office to the center village, and in discontinuing the two others.

The reader will be pleased to learn that the "Committee on Statistics" received the appointment of post master.

CHAPTER XX.

HARROWFORK POST-OFFICE.

A gloomy Picture—Beautiful Village—Litigation in Harrowfork—A model Post Master—The Excitement—Petitioning the Department—Conflicting Statements—The decisive Blow—The new Post Master—The "Reliable Man"—Indignant Community—Refusal to serve—An Editor's Candidate—The Temperance Question—Newspaper Extracts—A Mongrel Quotation—A Lull—A "Spy in Washington"—Bad Water—New Congressmen—The Question revived—Delegate to Washington—Obliging Down Easter—The lost Letters—Visit to the Department—Astounding Discovery—Amusing Scene—A Congressmen in a "Fix"—The Difficulty "arranged."

THERE is no blessing bestowed upon us by a kind Providence, which man's selfishness may not pervert into a grievance. We have seen this principle illustrated in the use and abuse of post-offices, as often as in any other civil institution.

How society in the nineteenth century could exist without mail routes and the regular delivery of letters, it is impossible to conceive.

Imagine a town without a post office! a community without letters! "friends, Romans, countrymen, and lovers," particularly the lovers, cut off from correspondence, bereft of newspapers, buried alive from the light of intelligence, and the busy stir of the great world! What an appalling picture!

We have always thought that Robinson Crusoe and his man Friday might have enjoyed a very comfortable existence, had Juan Fernandez been blessed with a post-office. But think of a society of Crusoes and Fridays! nobody receiving letters, nobody writing letters—no watching the mails, no epistolary surprises and enjoyments, which form so large an element in our social life to-day!

But gloomy as the picture appears, we have many times thought that some very respectable and enlightened villages would be decidedly benefited, were the post office stricken from the catalogue of their institutions. This is a bone of contention, which often sets the whole neighborhood by the ears · and communities, which might otherwise enjoy the reputation of being regular circles of "brotherly love," break out into quarrels, contentions, slanders, litigations, and all sorts of unchristian disturbances.

The case of the town of Harrowfork, which I find recorded in my note-book, will most capitally illustrate the point under consideration. Harrowfork, by the way, is not the real name of the town, but a fictitious one, which we use for our convenience, to avoid personalities. It is located on the Eastern slope of an eminence, which overlooks one of the fairest of valleys on one of the most beautiful New England streams. The town was once a favorite place of resort with the writer, during the Summer season; and, although this was years ago, the pretty village is still fresh in his memory, with its green hills, its handsome residences embowered in the foliage of trees and vines—its rival churches, with their emulous spires pointing toward heaven; its shady roads, and magnificent prospects, looking far off upon the wide-spread valley, dotted with farmhouses, and beautified by the sinuous, glittering waters of the stream.

Its sunrises were particularly fine, and it has always seemed to me that the poet must have had them in his mind, when he penned the sonnet commencing

> "Full many a glorious morning I have seen
>   Flatter the mountain tops with sovereign eye,
> Kissing with golden face the meadows green,
>   Gilding pale streams with heavenly alchemy!"

It appears to us a strange dispensation of Providence, that such a perfect nest of loveliness should be invaded by inharmonious cat birds, and mischief-making wrens. But dissensions did creep in through the post-office. Up to a certain time, such universal peace prevailed among the inhabitants, that its two lawyers would have been beggared, had they not wisely resorted to farming, as a more reliable occupation than the occasional and precarious one of conducting some tame and straight-forward case, for a petty fee. But now the lawyers have enough to do, without turning aside from their regular profession; litigation is brisk and spirited in Harrowfork, and intricate and aggravated cases are numerous. Neighbors quarrel, church members sue each other, deacons go to law, the lawyers build fine houses, their families grow extravagant in dress—all owing to the post-office.

As long as old Uncle Crocker was post master, there was no difficulty. He seemed just the man for the business. He was looked upon as a part of the institution. Nobody thought of turning him out, more than they would have thought of petitioning for the removal of Harrowfork Hill.

But Uncle Crocker was not a permanent institution, notwithstanding the people's faith. One of his daughters married, and settled in the West. Excited by the report she made of the country, two of his sons followed her, and in the course of time, Uncle Crocker himself "pulled up stakes," retired from the post-office with honors, and migrated to the new territory.

As soon as the old gentleman's intention was made public, there was a slight flutter of interest in the community, in relation to the subject of a successor in his office. At first, if the name of a new candidate was hinted at, it was offered like Snagsby's expression of opinion in the presence of his wife—only as a "mild suggestion." But there was a good deal of partisan feeling latent in Harrowfork, and this was just the thing to develope it; and gently as the breeze had arisen, it freshened and increased, until it blew a perfect hurricane, that not only disturbed the whole county, but became troublesome even as far off as Washington.

At an early period of the excitement, the friends of an enterprising tradesman in the place had gone quietly to work, and procured his appointment to the office. It was quite a surprise to many of his fellow-townsmen, and no small sensation was produced when DEACON UPTON was announced as the new post master. Many were dissatisfied, of course, and although the deacon had always been known as a quiet, inoffensive man, he suddenly became the subject of derogatory remarks. The personal friends who had been instrumental in securing the appointment, formed a spirited minority in his favor, while all who had not been consulted in the premises, naturally felt bound to range themselves on the side of his critics and opponents.

To make matters worse, a Presidential campaign followed Mr. Upton's inauguration, and politics "ran high." The post-office became the great centre and source of excitement. People met, on the arrival of the mails, and glanced over the editorial columns of their newspapers, and talked over their grievances. At length the great crisis came. A change of Administration was effected. And as the health or sickness of the nation appeared now to depend entirely upon the post-office incumbent at Harrowfork, this subject received prompt attention from all parties.

All sorts of communications, full of absurd complaints, contradictory statements, imperative commands, and angry denunciations, were now poured in upon the Post-Office Department at Washington. To show what human nature is at such times, and also to designate how perfectly clear and beautifully pleasant the duty of the appointing power becomes, in the progress of the snarl, we will give a few specimens of these conflicting missives.

Here is one version of the story :—

To His Honor, the Post Master General, at Washington.

Sir:

Your Honor's humble petitioners, legal voters in the town of Harrowfork, respectfully submit the following *undeniable facts* for your consideration.

First, the person who now holds the office of post master in our place, is *totally unfit* for the business. He was got in by a clique of interested individuals, who used underhanded measures for the purpose, and succeeded in their object only by blinding the eyes of the Department to the real character of the man, and the wishes of the people. Not one man in fifty is in favor of the present incumbent; and those who are, turn out generally to be persons who seldom write or receive letters, and have little or no business in connexion with the post-office.

Second, the office is left during a great portion of the time in the charge of the post master's father-in-law, a worthy old gentleman, but whose sight has somewhat failed him; so that when persons call for letters or papers, he has first to hunt up his spectacles, which he has been known to be near five minutes in finding; then he has to go over with the letters, &c., very slowly, to avoid making mistakes, very often taking them out of the wrong box at that, and after all, giving the wrong letters to people, or giving them none at all, when the fact is, letters for them have perhaps been lying untouched in the office for weeks. Such cases are nothing uncommon.

Third, valuable letters have been lost through carelessness on the part of persons in the office, or from *less excusable* causes, of which we leave your Honor to judge. Letters containing money are particularly liable to miscarry.

Fourth, it is a fact which merits your Honor's special consideration, that, in consequence of the dissolute habits of the post master's nephew, who attends in the office evenings, a not very respectable gang of young men are encouraged to hang about the doors till late at night, making it very unpleasant for the more sober citizens to go there for their mails.

Fifth, the present post master is a deacon of the church, and very sectarian in his views. There may be no direct connection between this circumstance, and the fact that the religious newspapers of different sects from his own, are apt to be lost or destroyed in the mails, while the "Helmet of Truth," a paper to which he is commissioned to obtain subscribers, is always punctually delivered! Your Honor's petitioners state this only as a remarkable coincidence, which may however have some bearing upon the case.

In view of these stubborn and undeniable facts, we the undersigned, legal voters in the town of Harrowfork, humbly petition your Honor, that the present post master be removed, and a more suitable person appointed in his place.

We also beg leave to suggest to your Honor's consideration, the name of Josiah Barnaby, as a fit and reliable candidate for the office, and a person who would be sure to give more general satisfaction to the community than any other available man.

Trusting that the foregoing statements will receive your Honor's early attention, and such official action as the merits of the case demand, we remain

Your Honor's respectful petitioners.

Signed by { Aminadab Fogle, and thirteen others.

This was certainly a strong case, and it would seem perfectly clear that "his Honor" should straightway remove Upton and appoint Barnaby to fill his place.

But close upon the heels of the above petition, followed another of a very different character. The framers of the last also maintained that a change should be made, and adduced strong charges against Upton; but it appeared after all, that Barnaby was not the most reliable man.

"Such an appointment," said the new document, "would give greater dissatisfaction, if possible, than the old one has done. The said Barnaby is an infidel, who made himself very obnoxious to all right-minded citizens by his avowed disbelief in the Scriptures, and his contempt of the Sabbath, and the ordinances of religion. Your Honor's humble petitioners, therefore, submit that it would be an outrage upon the feelings of a Christian community to have such a person appointed to so important and responsible an office.

Furthermore, the undersigned take it upon themselves to affirm that it is not the wish of over four persons in our district that the said Barnaby should receive the commission. We understand the petition in his favor was drawn up by one Aminadab Fogle, whose name heads the list. Now it happens that the said Fogle is a brother-in-law of the said Barnaby, while at least three others in his (Barnaby's) favor are likewise connections of the family, and persons, like him, entirely destitute of religious principles. With regard to other persons who signed the petition, the most of them privately acknowledge that they did so, because they were urged, and could not refuse, without offending their neighbors.

Under these circumstances, the undersigned respectfully represent that they express the general feeling of the community, when they nominate Mr. Homer S. Clark as an eligible candidate for the office in question."

Then follows an eulogy on Mr. Homer S. Clark; the whole winding up with a grand rhetorical flourish, to the tail of which are attached some twenty-three names, representing the active "better class" of society in Harrowfork.

So it appeared that Clark was the right man; and undoubtedly the Department would have proceeded at once to invest him with the disputed honors; but before any action could be had in the matter, a candid representation from another party, strengthened by affidavits, served to cast "ominous conjecture" on the whole affair. This was a petition from the Upton party, wherein it was maintained, that of the two aspirants for office, Barnaby was the better man of the two, Clark having made himself very unpopular, by failing for a large amount some years before, going through chancery, and afterwards living in a style of elegance unbecoming a man who had dismissed his creditors with ten cents on a dollar.

It was also shown that the prime mover in favor of Clark was a cousin of his, and the same person who was supposed to have held a large portion of bankrupt property in trust for the said Clark at the time of his failure! Still Barnaby was no more fit for the office, than the petitioners in favor of Clark had represented. There were fifty in Harrowfork eminently qualified to fulfil the duties of post master, and who would give infinitely better satisfaction than either of the new candidates; but of them all, there was no one, who, in the opinion of the petitioners, was better calculated for the office than the present incumbent. It was only a few dissatisfied, mischief-making people, who pretended to consider a change at all desirable. Upton had now been in a year; had shown himself obliging and faithful; and although a few unimportant mistakes, unavoidable under the circumstances, had escaped his eye in the early part of his career, he was now experienced, and no such errors would be likely to occur in future.

The attention of the Department was then called to the fact that the names of John Harmon, Solomon Corwin, Amos Fink, and several others, probably would be found on both the Clark and Barnaby petitions! This inconsistency was easily accounted for. In the first place, John Harmon had always been accustomed, when Crocker was post master, to make himself quite at home in the office. Mr. Upton, however, exercising a stern impartiality, had from the first excluded every outsider from the private room, Harmon not excepted, during the business of opening and assorting the mails. Thereupon Harmon had taken offence, and was ready to sign any petition against Upton, without regard to the source whence it originated. With respect to Corwin and Fink and any others whose names might be found on both the previous petitions, they were easy, good-natured individuals, who could not say "no;" and who might generally be prevailed upon to sign any sort of a paper to which their attention was called.

It was therefore the humble prayer of the petitioners, that no needless change should be made, but that the present post master should be continued in office, at least until some good reason should be assigned for his removal.

Then followed a good show of names designed to impress the Department with the power and influence of the Upton party.

This put a different face upon the matter, and simple justice seemed to require that the actual incumbent should remain unmolested in the enjoyment of the honors and emoluments of his office.

But there came another statement from a fourth party, containing grave and serious charges not only against Barnaby and Clark, but also against Upton, and recommending the removal of the latter, and the appointment of a new candidate, Mr. Ezekiel Sloman, to the vacancy. It was made to appear that Mr. Sloman was the man, of all others, to please the community at large; and for a time his prospects were very good; but some of Upton's friends getting wind of the matter, it was satisfactorily represented to the Department, that although an honest, well-meaning man, the said Sloman was entirely destitute of energy and business tact; that, indeed, he had so little worldly capacity that he was literally supported by the charity of friends; and that in order to relieve themselves of the encumbrance, these friends had united to have him appointed post master.

Thus Sloman was cast overboard. The Upton party exulted. Their opponents were exasperated, and a coalition was formed between the Barnaby and Clark factions.

Aminadab Fogle and John Harmon put their heads together. Both Clark and Barnaby were dropped, and all hands agreed to support a new man named Wheeler. But the main thing was to remove Upton. The following strong point was accordingly made against that individual, in addition to the previous charges.

"Although entirely disinterested in the matter, except so far as the common rights of humanity are concerned, the undersigned consider it their conscientious duty to inform your Honor that the said Upton is decidedly opposed to the present national administration. He has long been at heart an abolitionist of the deepest dye, and of late his fanaticism has shown itself in public. During the recent Presidential campaign, the post-office was made the head-quarters of the Free Soilers, and was, during a large portion of the time, converted into a regular caucus room by the leaders of that party. That your Honor may judge for yourself what this man's political conduct has been, the undersigned take the liberty of calling your attention to the enclosed editorial notice of a Free Soil meeting in which Deacon Upton took an active part. It is clipped from the columns of the "Temperance Goblet," a paper neutral in politics and religion, and entirely independent and impartial on the post-office question.

The following is the newspaper paragraph referred to:

"Next, we were a little surprised to see our respected friend post master Upton take the floor, and treat the audience to a harangue, which as a specimen of eloquence will, we venture to assert, find nothing to compare with it in the orations of Cicero. But it was the matter, more than the manner of the speech, which excited our astonishment. We had always given our friend credit for being a law and order man, *notwithstanding his well known abolition prejudices*," (words in italics underscored with ink by the petitioners,) until the occasion of this public demonstration of the most ultra Garrisonianism. How a man, uniformly discreet, should have suffered his feelings to run away with his judgment in a public discourse, we cannot conceive, unless it be that in the whirlwind of eloquence that bore him away, all consideration of law, patriotism, and duty, were lost sight of. After all, it is not Upton who is to blame, it is the times. He should have lived in Athens, in the palmy days of Grecian oratory. What would Demosthenes have been by the side of the giant Upton? Echo answers "What?"

This proved the decisive blow. Upton was cut off like Hamlet, senior,

"Even in the blossoms of his sin."

Scarce was his removal effected, however, when the eyes of Harrowfork were suddenly opened to the fact that he was "about the best man for post master, that could be had, after all!"

The slanders that had been circulated to his disadvantage, were turned in his favor. Among other instances of dishonest dealing, in the opposition party, the great fraud touching Upton's Abolitionism, was now discovered and exposed. He was proved to be entirely innocent of any such "political heresy;" and it was further shown that the slip of editorial clipped from "The Temperance Goblet," had never appeared in the columns of that paper—that it had been prepared expressly, and privately printed for the dishonest purpose it had served!

But the correction of the false and malicious statements came too late to benefit Upton in his official capacity. He had "gone out with the tide," and the returning waves were ineffectual to bring him in again. He was politically defunct, and a new post master "reigned in his stead."

About the new post master. He was the favorite of no faction, and the appointment came to him as unexpectedly as to the public. This is the way of it.

26

About the time, the "Town Committee," having first endorsed a paper in favor of Wheeler, sent privately to Washington to inform the Post Master General that the said endorsement was a mere formality, to be taken no notice of whatever; and to recommend a new candidate named Foster.

The Department becoming not a little disgusted with the whole business, wrote to a "reliable" man in the vicinity, but not in the town, for advice on the subject. Flattered by the compliment, the "reliable" person drew up an elaborate paper on the subject, demonstrating that the party would be endangered by the appointment of either of the rival candidates, and representing that some such cool-headed and discreet individual as Mr. Walters, (a widower of forty,) against whom no prejudice had been raised, and who would no doubt prove acceptable to the entire community, should receive the commission. This "reliable" man was supposed of course to be quite disinterested. His suggestion was accordingly adopted, and Walters walked into the Post-Office, as Upton walked out.

But little opposition would have been excited against the new incumbent, had the manner of his appointment remained a secret. But the "reliable" man thought it too good to keep. He desired that society should know what an important personage he had become. The dignity of his being consulted by the Department at Washington, would be but half enjoyed privately. He accordingly rode over to Harrowfork, shook hands with the "Selectmen," talked about the post-office, and laughed inwardly, holding his sides and looking suspiciously wise, whenever the subject of the new appointment was broached. He knew a thing or two—*he* could tell a secret if he chose—there was more than one way to settle a quarrel;—he knew the Department, the Department knew him. Ha! ha! ha! and ho! ho! ho! &c.

Horrible doubts racked the brain of John Harmon. He took Aminadab Fogle aside.

"Look here!" said he. "What relation is Judge Ames (the "reliable man") to the new post master?"

"I declare," replied Fogle, "I never thought of that! Walters is Ames' wife's sister's husband's youngest brother! He is dreadful thick, too, with the family, and the talk is he is going to marry Ames' oldest daughter."

"That explains it," said John Harmon; "I knew there was something of the kind at the bottom of it all. Keep dark, and I'll pump the Judge until we get out of him all about the way this rascally appointment has been made."

Already it was "a rascally" appointment.

After Harmon's talk with the Judge, who was but too ready to acknowledge his instrumentality in the matter, it became a "detestable appointment," and an "underhanded proceeding." And scarce had the tail of the Judge's horse disappeared over the bridge that night, when all Harrowfork rang with the discovery that had been made. Little thought the "reliable" man as he went home, chuckling over the joke, what a hornet's nest he had disturbed. But he probably knew something of it the following Sunday, when the widower Walters went over to Amesbury to pay a visit to the Judge's family in general, and his eldest daughter in particular.

The truth is, a deafening hum of indignation had gone up from Harrowfork, and it was universally declared that the new appointment was by far the most objectionable that could possibly have been made!

The result was, the Department, the "reliable" man, and the new post master, individually and collectively, got soundly abused by all hands; and it was not long before a delegation was dispatched to Washington, to expose the fraud, and remonstrate against the continuance of Walters in office. Against the latter, the most serious charges were preferred. It was claimed, among other things, that he had been in town but a few years; furthermore, that he had some time since held the office of post master in a neighboring state, and had resigned to prevent being removed for official delinquencies. It was mainly on this ground that the Post Master General was induced to recall his commission. Scarcely was this done, however, when it was discovered that the unfortunate man had been wronged; that it was another Walters who had been a post master, &c.

Anxious to make immediate reparation, the Department hastened to send on the papers again; but by this time, Walters, indignant at the manner in which he had been treated, refused to accept the office, writing a high-toned and dignified letter on the subject to the Post Master General.

"I do not wish," said he, "to have anything whatever to do with the petty strife of politics. I have not sought, neither do I desire, any public office. Had such been my ambition, my recent experience would be sufficient entirely to eradicate the disease, unless it had become chronic, from the effects of breathing too long the malaria of political society.

"'Some men are born great; some achieve greatness; and others have greatness thrust upon them;' mine was of the last description; but I am thankful that it has been temporary: nor shall I again consent to endure 'the slings and arrows of outrageous Fortune,' in so lofty and exposed a position as that of post master of Harrowfork."

The sharp and independent style of this epistle made Walters quite popular with the Department, and he was again urged to accept the commission, which he again refused.

The trouble was accordingly no nearer a settlement than at the outset. The Department had unwittingly offended everybody, and the "reliable" man was, perhaps, the most violently indignant of all. When applied to a second time, he fired off an explosive epistle at the Post Master General, which would serve as a model for that style of writing.

"He was not the person," he said, "to place himself more than once in a position to be gratuitously insulted." And he was surprised that the Department, after subjecting Walters to the treatment he had received, should again apply to him (the Judge) for assistance. Had he an enemy whom he wished to make the victim of public animadversion and disgrace, he might possibly nominate him to the office. But certainly he could not think of laying such an affliction at the door of his friends. In conclusion, the Post Master General, President, and Company, were politely invited to "look elsewhere for support in future."

The truth is, the Judge's vanity was touched. Having enjoyed the notoriety of procuring the appointment of Walters, he naturally became incensed at the turn affairs had taken, and seized the first opportunity of emptying the vials of his wrath in a quarter where they were expected to produce a sensation. The Administration, however, survived.

Meanwhile Mr. Atkins, editor of the Temperance Goblet, who had *his* special candidate—a speculator named Blake—was playing his cards adroitly. He had a strong ally in Hon. Mr. Savage, M. C., then at Washington. The last-named gentleman, who had previously taken offence at the Post Master General, for having the independence to fill a vacancy in a post-office in his District without consulting him, now, however, came alertly to the rescue, assuring the Department that Blake was the most suitable man that could be chosen. Blake was accordingly honored with the commission which Walters had refused.

Now Blake was a strenuous advocate of the "Maine law." He, accordingly, had for his enemies all the opponents of his favorite doctrine. The "Harrowfork Freeman," an anti-Maine law organ, was particularly bitter against him. The editor of that paper lent his columns to the exposure of the new post master's past course, and in a "scathing article" accused him of having been formerly the proprietor of a large distillery, and of having accumulated the bulk of his property in that business!

On the other hand, Atkins of the Goblet devoted his paper to the defence of his candidate. At the same time Hon. Mr. Savage had become reconciled to the Post Master General, in consequence of the attention paid to his recommendation in the case, and wrote a friendly and familiar letter to the Department, explanatory and apologetic of Blake's course. He alluded to the article in the "Freeman," and expressed a hope that the Department would not be prejudiced by its statements.

This reference, by the way, was the first intimation the Department had, that such an article ever appeared. The honorable member went on to treat the subject as if the general Government and the nation at large stood waiting with breathless anxiety for the issue.

"True," said he, "he was at one time engaged in the manufacture of liquor; but certainly that circumstance should not injure him in the estimation of high-minded and liberal men. It is an honest calling, if honestly followed, and nobody will pretend that Blake has not shown himself upright in all his dealings. For my part, I hold to enlightened views on the subject of eating and drinking; nor do I believe that one citizen has a right to penetrate and criticise another's private life."

Blake was continued in office, whether in consequence of the Honorable member's championship, we cannot say. But certain it was, that in the election struggle which came off soon after, Atkins of the Goblet supported the regular candidate for Congress, who was no other than this same Mr. Savage, of "enlightened views;" and by carrying the mass of the temperance vote, secured his re-election by some forty-five majority!

The Goblet's course in this business appeared not a little mysterious. It had supported Blake for post master—a man whose temperance professions were now regarded as entirely superficial and worthless—and Savage for Congress, a person more than suspected as being a moderate drinker and a man of boasted "liberal principles." Messrs. Harmon and Fogle put their dissatisfied heads together to discover the secret. They were aided and encouraged by the editor of the Freeman, and presently in an article in that paper headed, "How to make Tin Night-Caps out of Pine Shingles," the whole "black history of shameless fraud and double-dealing," as it was called, was revealed to an astounded public. We quote a few paragraphs from the Freeman's article :—

"Here," said the merciless reviewer, with genuine satire, "here is a beautiful instance of love and harmony in political life! Here is prophecy fulfilled. 'The lion and the lamb shall lie down together, and a little child shall lead them.' Savage—rightly named—is the lion. Blake—innocent, harmless, dove-like Blake, who never did anything wrong, is the lamb; and Atkins is the little boy. He leads them into sweet pastures of public office; and gives them to drink of Congress water and post-office pap. O happy trio! O honest and consistent coalition!

"What makes the union appear all the more admirable, is the fact that the most discordant elements have here been made to blend and intermingle. Savage is a moderate drinker, who loves his wine at dinner, and his punch before going to bed. Atkins is a stiff and uncompromising temperance man. One is Maine law, the other is Anti-Maine law. As for Blake, he is sometimes one, sometimes both, and sometimes neither one thing nor the other. But Atkins supports Savage, Savage supports Blake, and they all support each other.

"Now, as our grandmother used to say, 'wherever you see a turnip-top growing, you may be sure that there's a turnip at the bottom of it. Large or small, it's still a turnip.' Now, we have long admired the luxuriance of Savage, Atkins, Blake & Co.'s turnip-tops. We have recently been looking for the turnip, and lo! here it is! Who secured Savage's re-election? Blake, when at the last county convention of the Maine Laws, he advised them not to make an independent temperance ticket for Congress. Who devoted his paper to the cause of the moderate drinker? Atkins. Who got Blake the post-office? Atkins and Savage. But what are Savage and Blake doing for Atkins all this time? Is Atkins so unselfish as to work for them gratis? Nobody believes it! Where then does the milk in the cocoa-nut come from? Let us see.

"In the first place—we have it on the authority of an old lady who knows the genealogy of every family in the county, and can trace most people's ancestry back to Noah—Blake is Atkins's second cousin. There's one point. Now for another. Blake owns three-fourths of the entire Goblet printing establishment, and holds the property in such a way, that he can any day take the paper into his own hands, and manage it to suit himself! Therefore, whoever edits the Goblet, is Blake's tributary. We were going to say tool or slave, but concluded to sacrifice truth to politeness. Thus it happens that Atkins is only as it were Blake's left hand," &c.

After several more paragraphs of the same sort, the author of the annihilating article, who found it very difficult to conclude the subject, being of a very rich and attractive nature, finally summed up all his points, and bound them together with a striking original quotation, attributed to Shakspeare. It was as follows:

"O consistency! thou art a jewel!
Which, like the toad, ugly and envious,
Bears yet a precious secret in his head."

It was this mongrel quotation which damped the Freeman's powder. The Goblet took it up, turning the laugh against its rival; and for months the modern style of rendering Shakspeare was a standing joke. Of course a copy of the Freeman, containing the editorial marked, was sent to the Post Master General; but on reading about the toad at the end of the annihilating article, the Department dismissed the whole subject with a good-natured laugh.

Notwithstanding the truth of the charges against him, Blake was continued in office. 'Twas probably the fun of the thing that saved him.

Then followed a lull. The good people of Harrowfork were worn out with the harassing post-office question, and it was permitted to rest until the approach of the next Congressional election.

Atkins of the Goblet went openly to work to secure the re-nomination of Savage. But in the mean time, a "spy in Washington"—there are always "spies in Washington"—privately gave information to the leading Maine law men in the District, concerning the Honorable member's very equivocal support of temperance principles. Armed with this intelligence, the indignant constituency remonstrated with

Atkins on the inconsistency of his course. He however, "flatly denied" the allegations against Savage.

"Very well," said the constituency; "you may be sincere, but we shall investigate the matter a little."

At the allusion to investigation, Atkins winced, and endeavored to dissuade his friends from such a "needless step."

"We'll have a committee appointed to write Savage a letter, at all events, and demand an exposition of his principles," replied they. "We want to know what sort of a man we are supporting. We went for Savage before, mainly through your influence; now we're determined to make sure it's all right, before we give him a single vote."

"Nonsense, gentlemen," said Atkins; "of course it's all right! Don't go to bothering our candidate with letters. Letters are the devil in politics."

The temperance men, however, were not to be dissuaded, and a letter was written, in which the Hon. member was asked, among other things, if he was or was not "in the habit of using intoxicating liquors as a beverage, while at the seat of Government?"

In reply to this question, the gentleman of "enlightened views" wrote to the committee:—

> "I frankly admit, that in consequence of the bad water at Washington, which has so deleterious an effect upon my health, when I drink it, as to render me for a large portion of the time unfit for business, I have occasionally, by the advice of my physician, resorted to ardent spirits, simply as a remedial agent. Yet this habit has been confined *strictly* to the Capital. Never out of Washington have I indulged in anything of the sort, even as a medicine."

This letter was received with significant nods and winks, expressive of doubts and disapprobation, by the committee; and it was sent to the "Goblet" for publication. In the mean time, however, its author had given Atkins private instructions on the subject; and the "Goblet" declined to publish the letter.

"Gentlemen," said Atkins, when called on for an explanation, "this is an absurd affair from beginning to end. I opposed the proceeding at the outset. I consider the letter perfectly satisfactory; but my readers are tired of these things, and so am I. I must therefore be excused from having anything to do with the affair."

"You will publish the letter, however, as an advertisement?" suggested the committee.

"Not even as an advertisement!"

"Not if paid for?"

"No, not if paid for, gentlemen!" said the imperturbable Atkins.

"Very well," replied the committee, exasperated, "we know who will publish it."

They went across the way to the office of the "Freeman," the "rum paper," as it was called. Harmon, who was of the committee, knew the editor, and took him confidentially aside.

"Atkins," said he, "refuses to print this document; 'twill be just the thing for you, and it will spite him to see it in the Freeman."

"To tell you the truth," said he, "I'm afraid to publish it. 'Twill just suit our moderate drinkers, and I'm not so sure but it would injure *our* candidate with that class of men. On the whole," said he, "I think I won't print it."

Foiled in this quarter, John Harmon bethought him of the "News Courier," a neutral paper published in a neighboring town, which offered to print communications relating to the approaching campaign, provided they were written in a proper spirit, and did not compromise too much its position as a neutral journal.

The Savage letter was accordingly sent to the Courier, and promptly appeared in its columns. But the editor, desiring to keep both scales of the balance as nearly in equilibrium as possible, inserted in the same number of his paper a very profound, scientific treatise, signed "Filter," giving an analysis of the Washington water, showing that its chemical properties were identical with those of the member's own well at home! and strongly questioning the utility of mixing whiskey with it at all, and more especially such whiskey as is too often sold at the seat of Government!

The result was decisive. The Goblet lost popularity and patronage; Atkins lost influence and money; and Savage lost the election. On the other hand, the News Courier gained the favor and support of the temperance people, by its "bold and manly course" in exposing the rottenness of Savage's principles. John Harmon was triumphant; and one of the very leaders of the temperance cause was sent to Congress.

The new member was no other than Judge Ames, the "reliable" man, himself! Reader, be not surprised! Political life is fertile in such unexpected events. The Judge had gained popularity by coming out strongly for the Maine law. The old party to which he belonged had endorsed his nomination, John Harmon electioneered for him, and lent his horse and wagon to bring invalids, old men, and indifferent voters to the polls, on election day; and the Judge was returned by an overwhelming majority.

Then the old question of post master was again revived, and the whole ground gone over again; the contest becoming more personal and desperate than before, and the files of the Department teeming with all sorts of exaggerated petitions and violent remonstrances. The appointing power was made the victim of every kind of imposition and abuse.

In the mean while the new member exercised that better part of valor, called discretion. Popularity rendered him good-natured and conservative; and he lost no time in effecting a reconciliation with the Post Master General, of whom he had so rashly complained. Already, on the other hand he had written to his constituents describing the embarrassment of his situation, and requesting as a particular favor that he might for a brief period at least be excused from any personal interference with the post-office quarrel.

This unexpected communication somewhat disappointed the

enemies of Blake; John Harmon, in particular, was highly exasperated, having previously obtained a promise from Ames that, in case of his election, he would use his influence to have Blake removed.

The antagonistic parties were accordingly left to settle their difficulties as best they could. The battle raged furiously. Fresh petitions, remonstrances, affidavits, and accusations were volleyed at the Department; and at length a special bearer of dispatches was delegated to Washington, to support the charges against Blake, and demand of the Post Master General his reasons for declining immediate action in so plain a case.

Now, the person selected for this important mission was no other than our old acquaintance, Mr. John Harmon. He was intrusted with the business for several excellent reasons. In the first place, he was a ready and vehement talker. Secondly, he was an enthusiast on the post-office question, and a bitter opponent of the Blake faction. Thirdly, he understood human nature, and knew how to manage Ames. Fourthly, and chiefly, he was the author of the most serious charge against Blake. He had a short time before posted a letter containing a twenty dollar bank-note, at the Harrowfork post-office. This letter never reached its destination. Now, Blake knew there was money in that letter; and it could be proved that, not long after its miscarriage, just such a bank-note as the one contained was passed by the post master, "under suspicious circumstances."

This charge was on file among the papers of the Department; and it was thought that Harmon was the most suitable person to agitate the subject.

Mr. John Harmon made a comfortable journey, and arrived at the seat of Government in due season. His first business was to secure lodgings suited to the high character of a delegate from Harrowfork. But Washington was crowded with visitors, and the hotels were filled. Mr. John Harmon was chagrined. He leaned his chin upon his hand, and his elbow upon the counter of the "National." Mr. John Harmon ruminated.

"I don't see but what me'n' you'll hef to go halves, and turn in together," said a voice at his other elbow.

Mr. John Harmon looked up. A stranger, of tall figure, prominent cheek-bones, sallow complexion, dressed in a very new and very stiff suit of clothes, smiled upon him in a decidedly friendly manner.

"There's jest one room, the landlord says'st we can hav' on a pinch," contined the speaker. "It's up pooty high, and an't a very sizable room, at that. I've got the furst offer on't, but I won't mind makin' a team'th you, if you're a mind to hitch on, and make the best on't. What d'ye say?"

Mr. John Harmon said he supposed he would accept his new friend's proposal. But at the same time he hinted to the clerk at the desk that he was from the Hon. Mr. Ames' District.

"If you were the President, himself, we could not do any better by you, under the circumstances," said the clerk.

This assurance served to soothe John Harmon's injured feelings, and he retired to the room in the top of the house, with his new acquaintance.

"Come down on Gov'ment business, I s'pose likely?" suggested the latter.

"Yes," replied John Harmon, "on post-office business."

"I want to know! Glad we fell in," cried the stranger. "I came down on some sich business myself."

"Indeed!" said John Harmon. "You are going to call on the Post Master General, then?"

"Shouldn't be 'tall surprised," remarked the other, rolling up his sleeves over the wash-bowl. "Can't tell exac'ly, though. I wanted to see what was goin' on down here, and git a sight of the big bugs, and hear a little spoutin' in Congress; so I told our folks to hum—says I, I b'lieve I'll scooter off down to Washin'ton, says I, and take a peep into the Dead Letter Office, and see if I can find hide or hair o' that 'ere hundred dollar letter, says I."

"Have you lost a letter containing a hundred dollars?" inquired John Harmon, interested.

The stranger said "'twas jes' so," and went on to relate the circumstances. He also incidentally stated that his name was Forrester Wilcox; that he owned a farm somewhere "down East," comprising over two hundred acres of land, and one hundred and fifty under cultivation; that he had been a member of the Maine legislature, and held the office of "deputy sheriff" in his county. This account of himself impressed John Harmon favorably; and in return for the confidence, he talked Mr. Forrester Wilcox to sleep that night, on the subject of the Harrowfork post-office.

On the following morning, our friends concluded to pay an early visit to the Post-Office Department. They were now on excellent terms with each other; and on arriving at the Department, John Harmon readily accepted an invitation from Forrester Wilcox to accompany him to the Dead Letter Office, before endangering the digestion of his breakfast, by entering upon the perplexing Harrowfork business. Accordingly, as they entered the building, Mr. Wilcox hailed a messenger.

"Look here! you!" said he, "where abouts does a chap go to find the Dead Letters?"

"This way," replied the polite messenger.

The visitors were shown to the left, through the lower main hall of the Department; then turning into another passage, the messenger pointed out the last door on the right, as the one they were in search of.

"Thank ye," said Mr. Wilcox; "I'll do as much for you some time. May as well bolt right in, I suppose?" he added, consulting his companion.

John Harmon said "certainly," and the next moment the two found themselves in the midst of the clerks of that important Bureau. Mr. Forrester Wilson singled out one of the most approachable of them, and addressed him on the subject of the hundred dollar letter.

"I have no recollection of any such letter," said the clerk.

However, for the visitor's satisfaction, he examined the list of returned money letters, for the last quarter. John Harmon, interested for his friend Wilcox, also ran his eye over the list.

"It's not here," said the clerk; "but you may rest assured, that in case it is at any time discovered, it will find its way back to you in safety."

He was about to dismiss the visitors, but John Harmon coughed; John Harmon looked very red. John Harmon was perspiring very profusely. The truth is, among the last letters on the list, he found recorded the identical one, containing the twenty dollar bank note, which Blake was charged with purloining! What to do in the matter, John Harmon was at a loss to know. After some hesitation, however, he asked permission to glance once more at the list. He was accommodated, and presently his finger rested on the important entry.

"I declare," said he, "if there ain't a letter I mailed at Harrowfork! I had no idea of finding it here! Can I get it now, by proving property?"

"It has already been returned to your address," answered the clerk, on learning the circumstances. "You will find it on your return to Harrowfork. It miscarried in consequence of a mistake in the superscription."

"Are you sure it has been sent?" inquired John Harmon.

The clerk was quite sure, and John Harmon instantly withdrew.

"So there's one of your charges agin Blake knocked overboard," suggested Wilcox. "He'll be a little grain tickled to see that 'ere letter come back, I s'pect!"

"No person," answered John Harmon, magnanimously, "no person in the world can be more rejoiced than I am, that Blake is proved innocent of the charge."

Wilcox replied that he was very glad to hear it; and so they parted to meet again at dinner. Whether John Harmon was so greatly rejoiced at the proof of Blake's innocence, will be seen in the sequel.

While the Down Easter went to see the lions about town, our delegate found his way to the apartment of the Post Master General, and inquired for that officer in a manner which said very plainly, "I am John Harmon, of Harrowfork; and I guess now we'll have that little post-office affair settled."

Unfortunately—or rather fortunately, for his own peace of mind, at least, the Post Master General was engaged that morning at Cabinet meeting at the White House, and John Harmon was referred to the First Assistant, who listened patiently to his statement. Our delegate had a speech prepared for the occasion, which he now declaimed in a very high tone of voice, "with a swaggering accent, sharply twanged off," as Sir Toby Belch would have said, and with vehement and abundant gestures.

"I am instructed by my constituents," he said, in conclusion, "to demand of the Department satisfactory reasons for the delay and procrastination to which we have been obliged tamely to submit!"

"You should consider," politely returned the Assistant, "that Harrowfork numbers only one among some twenty-four thousand post-offices in the Union; and that it is a little unreasonable to expect us to bear in mind all the details of an occasional and not uncommon case. We will attend to your business, however, directly."

The papers relating to the Harrowfork Post-Office were sent for, and promptly produced. The delegate seized them without ceremony. The first endorsement that caught his eye, checked his eagerness, and induced reflection.

"I'd like to know, sir," said he, "*what that means?*" as he called the Assistant's attention to the word "Rest," inscribed in formidable characters, very much resembling the hand-writing of the Post Master General.

"If you think," he continued, "or imagine, or flatter yourselves that you're to have any kind of *rest* in this marble building, till that rascally Blake is turned out, you're very much mistaken. Or if it means that you want the *rest* of the temperance men in favor of his removal, I can promise you so much, on my responsibility as a delegate."

The Assistant smiled. He had dealt with persons of John Harmon's temperament before.

"Permit me to inform you," said he, "what that harmless little word signifies. It means nothing more nor less than that, for the present, no action is to take place. Ah!" he added, glancing at the brief upon the papers, "I remember this case very well! It has been from first to last an exceedingly vexatious one to the Department, and these memoranda bring it pretty fully to my recollection."

"Well, sir," interrupted John Harmon, in his declamatory way—"isn't it plain? isn't it perfectly clear? Haven't we the rights of the case, sir?"

"It is not quite so plain—not quite so clear—nor is it easy to determine who has the rights of the case," returned the official. "The most troublesome point at the present time, seems to be this: while, according to the documents, a majority of the citizens of Harrowfork seem to be eager for a removal, both the late member of Congress, and the newly elected one, have written private letters here—I mention this confidentially—in favor of the present incumbent."

"You don't mean Ames?" cried John Harmon. "Ames hasn't come out for Blake?"

"There is a letter on file, over his own signature, in which he represents that Blake is as suitable a man as could be named, and that he had better be continued in office."

The Assistant spoke with seriousness and candor. John Harmon was thunderstruck.

"Just give me a look at that letter!" said he, through his closed teeth. "I want to see it over Ames' own fist, before I believe it! When we promised our support for his election, he agreed to carry out our wishes in regard to the post-office, at all hazards! If he has dared to turn traitor!" muttered John Harmon, revengefully.

"The letter is entirely of a private nature," said the Assistant, "but it is contrary to our wishes to keep any communications secret, that are designed to influence our public acts; and owing to the peculiar circumstances of the case, I am willing to show you the letter,—on condition, however, that its contents shall not be divulged outside the Department."

John Harmon, burning to seize upon the evidence of Ames' treachery, assented, although reluctantly; and the official explored the wilderness of papers, for the document in question. "Here it is," said he, "no!"—glancing at the endorsement—"this is a communication with regard to a letter of your own, containing a twenty dollar note, which Blake is charged with purloining. How is it about that? anything new?"

"Well,—no,—hem!" coughed John Harmon. After discovering the proof of Blake's innocence, in the Dead Letter Office, he rather hoped the subject would not be mentioned; but he was too much absorbed in looking after Ames' honesty, to take very good care of his own. "The matter—hem!" (John's throat was quite musty)—"stands about as it did."

"You have no positive proof of the charge, then?"

"No,—well,—that is, not what would be called legal proof, I suppose. The circumstances were very strong against Blake at the time, but being all in the neighborhood, nobody liked to prosecute. For my part," said John Harmon, nobly, "I'd rather suffer wrong, than do wrong, and I preferred to lose the twenty dollars, to injuring Blake's private character."

The Assistant made a commendatory remark touching this generous sentiment, and passed over the letter. John Harmon wiped the perspiration from his brow, and felt relieved. Whether he was ashamed to confess his own gross carelessness in the matter, and the injustice of his charge, or whether—acting on the principle of doing evil that good might come from it, he determined to make the most of every point established against Blake, without regard to truth—does not plainly appear. We leave the affair to his own conscience. The assistant meanwhile drew Ames' letter out of the "case." In his eagerness to grasp it, John Harmon dropped it upon

Darley fect
VAN INGEN SNYDER

the floor. As he stooped to take it up, his eye caught a glimpse of a visitor who had just entered. John Harmon looked at the visitor, the visitor looked at John Harmon. John Harmon looked first red, then white; the visitor looked first very white, then very red. The delegate was the first to resume his self-possession.

"Well, friend Ames, how do you do?" said he, adroitly shifting the letter from his right hand to the left, and giving the former to the "Honorable" member.

"Very well! Capital!" replied Ames, nervously. "What's the news?"

"Nothing particular," said John Harmon, with a grim smile, sliding the letter into his hat. "Fine weather—Good deal of company at Washington, I find."

"O yes, considerable!" Ames rubbed his hands, and tried to appear at ease. "I am glad to see you here. You must go up to the House with me. How are all the folks at home? How's Harrowfork now-a-days?"

John Harmon answered these questions evasively.

At the same time, the Assistant's countenance betrayed an inward appreciation of unspeakable fun. The member's face grew redder still, and still more red. The truth is, he had that morning received a note from Blake warning him of Harmon's journey to the Capital, and had just left his seat in the House, hastening to the Department, to secure the fatal letter before it betrayed his treachery.

As we have seen, he was just too late.

The Assistant took pleasure in seating the two visitors side by side upon the same sofa, and allowed them to entertain each other. But the conversation was forced, unnatural, embarrassing. At length Ames, resolved upon knowing the worst, plunged desperately into the all-important subject.

"I suppose," said he, "you don't entirely get over the excitement at home about the post-office."

"No, we don't," replied John Harmon, significantly; "and that ain't the worst of it." He bent over the end of the sofa, and deliberately, with the grimmest sort of smile, drew from his hat the Honorable member's private note.

"And, somehow, it don't strike me," he added, glancing his eye over its contents, "that this letter of yours is going to lessen the excitement very materially. I suppose you know that hand-writing?"

He thrust the letter into the Honorable member's face. The Honorable member's face flushed more fiery than before. He stammered, he smiled, he rubbed his handkerchief in his hands, and upon his brow.

"My dear Harmon," said he, blandly, "I see you don't fully understand this business."

"I'm sure I don't," cried John Harmon; "and I'd like to find the honest man who does! Didn't you pledge yourself to use your influence, if elected, to have Blake removed?"

"Don't speak so loud!" whispered the Honorable member, who didn't at all fancy the humorous smile on the Assistant's face. "It's all right, I assure you. But this isn't exactly the place to talk over the affair. Come with me to my lodgings, and we'll discuss the matter."

Not averse to discussion, John Harmon consented to the proposal.

"I beg your pardon," said the Assistant Post Master General, "but that paper,—I cannot suffer that to be removed."

It was the fatal letter. John Harmon wanted it; the Honorable member wanted it still more; but the Assistant insisted, and the document was left behind.

Now, the Honorable member was in what is commonly termed a "fix." Like too many such politicians, who, nevertheless, as Mark Antony says, are "all honorable men," he had found it convenient to adopt the "good Lord, good devil" policy, using two oars to row his boat into the comfortable haven of public office.

Accordingly, while gently drawing figmative wool over the visual organs of the radical temperance people, he had managed, at the same time, by private pledges, to conciliate Atkins,

Blake & Company, and secure the silence of the Goblet. Once elected, he did not fail to look forward to a future election, in view of which he considered it expedient to smile upon one faction with one side of his face, and grin upon the opposition with the other.

For this double-dealing, honest, honest Iago,—we mean honest John Harmon—called the member to account.

How the affair was settled is not generally known. But one thing is positive. The Honorable member and the delegate from Harrowfork suddenly blossomed into excellent and enduring friends; and not long after, Mr. John Harmon became the occupant of a snug berth at the seat of Government, supposed to have been obtained through the influence of the Honorable member from his District.

"How about Blake and the post-office?" inquired Mr. Forrester Wilcox, the morning he left Washington.

"I've concluded," replied John Harmon, candidly, "that the post-office is well enough as it is. Blake turns out to be a passable kind of post master after all, and I don't really think 'twill be worth while to make any change for the present."

And this was the answer the worthy delegate made to all persons, who, from that time forward, interrogated him on the subject.

Shortly after, his very Honorable friend, the member from his District, being now decidedly averse to political letter-writing, went home on a flying visit, and passing through Harrowfork, took pains to make himself agreeable to all parties. Among other nice and prudent acts, he privately consulted Blake. The post master listened to his advice, and immediately on the member's return to Washington, appointed as an assistant in his office, a young man of strict temperance principles, who was quite popular with the opposition, and who had for some time acted as Secretary of the "County Association for the Suppression of Intemperance."

This appointment seemed to cast oil upon the troubled waters. And so the matter rests at the present date.

Ames is still in Congress; John Harmon continues to enjoy his comfortable quarters at the seat of Government. Tim Blake remains the efficient post master of Harrowfork, with the young man of strict temperance principles for his assistant; and Atkins still edits the Goblet.

This powerful organ has of late regained something of its former popularity and patronage; but whether it will support Ames at the next Congressional election, depends upon Blake; whether Blake retains his office, depends upon Ames; whether Ames maintains his position and influence at home, depends in a very great measure upon honest John Harmon, who, like the Ghost in Hamlet,

> "Could a tale unfold, whose lightest word would harrow up"

the political soil of Harrowfork, in a manner dangerous to the Constitution and the Union.

CHAPTER XXI.

UNJUST COMPLAINTS

Infallibility not claimed—"Scape-Goats"—The Man of Business Habits—Home Scrutiny.

A Lady in Trouble—A bold Charge—A wronged Husband—Precipitate Retreat.

Complaints of a Lawyer—Careless Swearing—Wrong Address—No Retraction.

A careless Broker—The Charge repulsed—The Apology—Mistake repeated—The Affair explained—A comprehensive Toast.

INFALLIBILITY is not claimed by those connected with the Post-Office Department, and it cannot be denied that mistakes sometimes occur through the carelessness or incompetency of some clerk or other official. But if there is a body of men who perform the duties of scape-goats more frequently than any other, those men are post masters, and post-office clerks.

Whoever takes this responsible station with the expectation that a faithful discharge of his duty will protect him from all suspicion and blame, cherishes a pleasing dream that may at any moment be dispelled by the stupidity, or carelessness, or rascality of any one among the many-headed public, whose servant he is.

When it is considered that in the selection of persons to fill the important office of post master, the Department makes every effort to secure the services of competent and honest men, and that they, in the appointment of their clerks, generally endeavor to obtain those of a like character, it may reasonably be supposed that at least as high a degree of accuracy and integrity can usually be found inside of post-office walls, as without its boundaries.

I cannot, indeed, claim for this corps of officials entire immaculacy. Could I justly do so, they would be vastly superior in this respect to mankind at large. But without setting up any such high pretensions, I would suggest that those connected with the post-office receive a greater share of blame for failures in the transmission of letters than justly belongs to them. Many people seem to think that nobody can commit a blunder, or be guilty of dishonesty in matters connected with the mails, but post masters or their employés.

Acting on this impression, such persons, when anything goes wrong in their correspondence, do not stop to ascertain whether the fault may not be nearer home, but at once make an onslaught upon the luckless post-office functionary who is supposed to be the guilty one.

The investigation of some such unfounded charges, resulting in placing the fault where it belonged, has brought to light curious and surprising facts, respecting the atrocious blunders sometimes committed by the most accurate and methodical business men. Such men have been known to send off letters with no address, or a wrong one; and even (as in one case which will be found in this chapter) to persist in attempting to send a letter wrongly directed. They have been known to mislay letters, and then to be ready to swear that they had been mailed. The blame of these and similar inadvertencies has been laid, of course, upon somebody connected with the post-office.

Mr. A. is a man of business habits; *he* never makes such mistakes, and indignantly repudiates the idea that any one in his employ could be thus delinquent. So the weight of his censure falls on the much-enduring shoulders of a post-office clerk.

Besides the class of cases to which I have alluded, which

arise from nothing worse than carelessness or stupidity, many instances occur in which the attempt is made by dishonest persons to escape detection, by throwing the blame of their villany upon post-office employés. Cases like the following are not uncommon.

A merchant sends his clerk or errand-boy to mail a letter containing money. This messenger rifles it, reseals it, and deposits it in the letter box. On the receipt of the letter by the person to whom it is addressed, the robbery comes to light; and, as the merchant is naturally slow to believe in the dishonesty of his messenger, he at once jumps at the conclusion that the theft was committed after the letter entered the post-office. In such cases, and in those of which I have been speaking, it would be well to establish the rule that scrutiny, like charity, should "begin at home."

Letters are sometimes mailed purporting to contain money for the payment of debts—when in fact they contain none—with the intention of making it appear that they have been robbed in their passage through the mails. In short, the cases are numberless in which, through inadvertence or design, censure is unjustly thrown upon the employés of the post-office; and the investigations of this class of cases forms no unimportant branch of the duties of a Special Agent.

It has been the pleasing duty of the author, in not a few instances, to relieve an honest and capable official from the load of suspicion with which he was burdened, by discovering, often in an unexpected quarter, where the guilt lay.

THE BITER BIT.

The following case, which might properly be entitled "The Biter Bit," displays still another phase of the subject in hand.

A lady of a very genteel and respectable appearance, called one day on a prominent New England post master, with a letter in her hand, which she insisted had been broken open and resealed. She handed the letter to the post master, who examined it, and appearances certainly seemed to justify her assertion. She further declared that she well knew which clerk in the office had broken it open, and that he had previously served several of her letters in the same way. Upon hearing this, the post master requested her to walk inside the office, and point out the person whom she suspected.

Such an unusual phenomenon as the appearance of a lady inside the office, produced, as may be supposed, a decided sensation among the clerks there assembled. Nor was the sensation diminished in intensity when the post master informed them, that the lady was there for the purpose of identifying the person who had been guilty of breaking open her letters!

This announcement at once excited the liveliest feelings of curiosity and solicitude in the mind of almost every one present, and each one, conscious of innocence, indulged in conjectures as to who that somebody else might be, whom the accusing Angel (?) was to fix upon as the culprit.

All their conjectures fell wide of the mark. After looking about for a moment, the lady pointed out the last man whom any one in the office would have suspected of such an offence —one of the oldest and most reliable of their number.

"That is the person," said she, indicating him by a slight nod of the head; "and if he persists in making so free with my letters, I will certainly have him arrested. Why my letters should always be selected for this purpose, I cannot imagine; but if any more of them are touched, he will wish he had let them alone."

This direct charge, and these threats, produced a greater commotion among his fellow clerks, than in the mind of the gentleman accused. Waiting for a moment after she had spoken, he broke the breathless silence that followed her words, by saying calmly,—"Mrs. ———, I believe?"

"That is my name, sir."

"Have you concluded your remarks, madam?"

"I have, sir, for the present."

"Then, madam, I will take the liberty to inform you that *your husband* is the person on whom you ought to expend your indignation. He has, at different times, taken several of your letters from the office, opened and read them, and after resealing, returned them to the letter box, having made certain discoveries in those letters, to which he forced me to listen, as furnishing sufficient ground for his course, and justifying former suspicions! He earnestly requested me never to disclose who had opened the letters, and I should have continued to observe secrecy, had not your accusation forced me to this disclosure in self-defence. If you wish to have my statement corroborated, I think I can produce a reliable witness."

The lady did not reply to this proposition, but made a precipitate retreat, leaving the clerk master of the field, and was never afterwards seen at that post-office.

In the summer of 1854, among the complaints of missing letters made at the New York post-office, was one referring to a letter written by a young lawyer of that city, directed as was claimed, to a party in Newark, N. J. Enclosed was the sum of twenty-five dollars in bank-notes.

The writer of the letter was annoyed by the circumstance, to an unusual degree, and caused a severe notice of censure upon the Post-Office Department, to be inserted in one of the leading New York journals. A formal certificate was also drawn up, duly sworn to, and forwarded to Washington.

It read as follows:—

State of New York,
City and County of New York, ss.

John B. C——, of said city, Counsellor at Law, being duly sworn, doth depose and say that on the 19th day of July instant, he enclosed the sum of $25 in a letter addressed to Capt. John M——, Newark, N. J., and deposited the same in the post-office in the city of New York. That the said enclosure and deposit of the letter was made in the presence of one of the principal clerks of the said post-office, whose attention deponent particularly called to the fact at the time. That deponent is informed, and believes that the said clerk's name is John Hallet.

Sworn before me this
10th day of August, 1854.
(Signed) Henry H. M——,
Comr. of Deeds.

The complainant was visited by the Special Agent, and the bare suggestion that the failure might have been owing to some error in the address of the letter, was received with much indignation. *He* didn't do business in that way, and the post-office and its clerks couldn't cover up their carelessness or dishonesty, by any such inventions.

The reader ought to have been present in the post master's room, some few months subsequently, when this infallible (?) individual called, in response to a notice that his letter had been returned from the Dead Letter Office!

Secretary.—"Good morning, Mr. C———."

C.—"Good morning, sir. I have received a notice to call here for a letter."

Secretary.—"Yes, sir, that is the one referred to, (placing the unlucky missive before him). Is that address in your hand-writing?"

C.—"Why,—y-e-s, it's mine sure—I couldn't dispute that."

Secretary.—"It seems to be directed to Newburg, N. Y., instead of to Newark, N. J."

C.—"I have nothing to say. I could have sworn that the address was correct."

Secretary.—"You did so swear, I believe. Mistakes will happen, but I think the least you can do, will be to retract the article you published censuring us, for what you were yourself to blame."

The amazed limb of the law made no further reply, but left the office gazing intently on the letter, and in his bewilderment getting the wrong door, as he had originally got the wrong address upon the letter.

No such correction was ever made, however, and like hundreds of similar faults, for which others are alone responsible, the charge yet stands against the Post-Office Department, and those in its employ.

Some years since, a letter containing drafts and other remittances to a considerable amount, was deposited in the New York office, to be transmitted by mail, having been directed (as was supposed) to a large firm in Philadelphia. This letter would pass through the hands of a clerk, whose duty it was to separate all those deposited in the letter box, and arrange them according to their respective destinations. He discovered that it was directed to *New York*, yet though he had heard of the firm to which it was addressed, he thought it might have been so directed for some particular purpose, and accordingly placed it in the "alphabet," for delivery to the proper claimant. On the day after this, Mr. D., of the firm of D. & A., well known brokers in Wall Street, called at the office and stated that his clerk had deposited such a letter to be mailed in time to go to Philadelphia the same day, but that he had been advised that it had not been received.

The clerk in attendance was somewhat perplexed by this statement, but suggested the probability that *his* clerk, in the hurry of business, had directed it wrong.

Mr. D. replied that this could not be, for he saw all his letters before they were confided to the charge of his clerk, and as the one in question had not been received, it must have been mailed incorrectly through the ignorance or carelessness of the clerk assigned to that duty; and indeed went so far as to intimate that it might have been detained purposely. This insulting remark induced the post-office clerk to express his perfect indifference concerning such a groundless conjecture, and to state, as his opinion, that the charge of ignorance, carelessness, or sinister design, would eventually be found to rest on the shoulders of Mr. D. or his clerks.

Against this turning of the tables, that gentleman indignantly protested, and the post master, who overheard the altercation, appeared vexed and displeased at the supposed delinquency of his clerk. A general search was commenced in the office, in order, if possible, to settle the disputed point. In the course of this investigation, the "pigeon-hole" designed for letters corresponding with such a name as that of the Philadelphia firm, was examined, and the letter in question was found, directed "New York," instead of "Philadelphia."

Upon this being known, Mr. D. made many apologies, begged to be exonerated from all intention to charge criminality upon any one, took his letter and retired, much disconcerted and chagrined.

He went to his office and poured out sundry vials of wrath upon the head of his luckless clerk, to whom he attributed the atrocious blunder which had been committed. The affair, however, did not end here.

On the following day a letter was deposited in the post-office, at about one o'clock, in time for the Philadelphia mail, *directed precisely as before!* viz. addressed to the Philadelphia firm, but directed "New York," and happened to fall under the eye of the clerk who had been cognisant of the error of the day previous. This second instance of gross inadvertence, or something worse, on the part of somebody, was rather too much for the equanimity of the post master, who at once sent for Mr. D., and showed him the letter, which seemed as if it was under the influence of some mischievous enchanter. As the words "New York," in the superscription, stared D. in the face, he in turn became enraged, and was about to leave the office with the fell design of discharging his clerk *instanter*. The post master then requested him, before he left, to sit down and alter the direction of the letter from "New York" to "Philadelphia," which he did. The letter was mailed accordingly, and duly received.

A few days afterwards, the post-office clerk met Mr. D., and said to him, "I suppose you have turned off your clerk for his mismanagement in relation to the letter about which so much trouble was made in our office."

"Ah!" replied he, "I believe I shall have to confess that *I* was the only one to blame in the matter. My clerk was perfectly innocent. On returning home with the letter, I laid it down with the intention of having the mistake in the direction rectified, but having something else to call off my attention just then, it was mixed with the letters for city delivery, and was taken to the office with them by my clerk."

Thus all this trouble and vexation was caused by the carelessness of a man who was accustomed to system and accuracy in the transaction of his business; and the above related facts may lead even persons of this description not to be too confident of their own freedom from error, when any mistake like that just mentioned occurs.

I can give no better summary of the whole subject under consideration, than that which is found in some remarks made by Robert H. Morris, Esq., on the occasion of his retirement from the office of post master of New York, in May, 1849, at a dinner prepared for the occasion.

During the evening Mr. Morris said,

"Gentlemen, please fill your glasses for a toast. As I intend to toast a man you may not know, I deem it necessary, before mentioning his name, to tell you what sort of a man he is.

"He rises at 4 o'clock in the morning and works assiduously during the whole day, until 7 o'clock in the evening—goes wearied to bed, to rise again at 4 o'clock, and again to work assiduously.

"If the gentlemen of the press—and there are some among us—incorrectly direct their newspapers for subscribers, it is the fault of the man I intend to toast, if the papers do not reach those to whom they should have been addressed.

"If a publishing clerk omits to address a newspaper to a subscriber, it is the fault of the man I intend to toast that the subscriber does not get his paper.

"If a man writes a letter and seals it, and neglects to put any address upon it, it is the fault of the man I will toast, if the letter does not reach the person for whom it was intended.

"If an officer of a bank addresses a letter to Boston instead of New Orleans, it is the fault of the man I shall presently toast, if the letter is not received at New Orleans.

"If a merchant's clerk puts a letter in his overcoat, and leaves that coat at his boarding-house, with the letter in his pocket, the man I will toast is to blame because the letter has not reached its destination.

"If a merchant shuts up a letter he has written, between the leaves of his ledger, and locks that ledger in his safe, the man I will toast has caused the non-reception of that letter.

"If a poor debtor has no money to pay his dunning creditor, and writes a letter that he encloses fifty dollars, but encloses no money, having none to enclose, the man I will toast has stolen the money.

"If a *good, warm-hearted, true* friend, receives a letter from a dear (?) but poor friend, asking the loan of five dollars; and, desiring to be considered a good, warm-hearted, true friend, and at the same time to save his five dollars, writes a letter saying 'dear friend, I enclose to you the five dollars,' but only wafers into the letter a small corner of the bill,—the man I will toast has stolen the five dollars out of the letter, and in pulling it out, tore the bill.

"If a rail-road-bridge is torn down or the draw left open, and the locomotive is not able to jump the gap, but drops into the river with the mail, the man I will toast has caused the failure of the mail.

"This, gentlemen, is the stranger to you, whom I will toast. I give you, gentlemen—A POST-OFFICE CLERK!"

CHAPTER XXII.

PRACTICAL, ANECDOTAL, ETC.

The wrong Address—Odd Names of Post-Offices—The Post-Office a Detector of Crime—Suing the British Government—Pursuit of a Letter Box—An "Extra" Customer—To my Grandmother—Improper Interference—The Dead Letter—Sharp Correspondence—The Irish Heart—My Wife's Sister.

GIVING the wrong State in an address, is a disease as common among letters, as hydrophobia among dogs. A draper's clerk in C—— sent a remittance to Boston which did not arrive there. The draper was obliged to send the amount (three hundred and fifty dollars) again, which he did personally, to prevent mistakes. This too failed to arrive, but the first was soon received by him from the Dead Letter Office, having died at Boston in *New York*, instead of *Massachusetts!* The merchant drank gunpowder-tea, and gave his clerk a "blowing up." The latter person, however, was in some sort avenged, not long after, for Coroner John Marron reported that the second letter, written and mailed by the merchant himself, had died of the same disease that carried off the first, and forwarded the body to him.

It should here be mentioned, for the benefit of the uninitiated, that the gentleman referred to, is the Third Assistant Post Master General, embracing the Superintendence of the Dead Letter Office. His duties may be considered as in some respects analogous to those of a Coroner, as he, or those in his bureau, in the case of defunct money letters, ascertain the causes of death, and send the remains to surviving friends.

The omission of the name of the State from the address of a letter, often causes much uncertainty in its motions.

There are, for instance, seven Philadelphias besides the one in Pennsylvania, twenty-three Salems, as many Troys, and no end of Washingtons, Jeffersons, and other names distinguished in the history of the country.

There are three New Yorks, and eleven Bostons. Indeed the majority of the names of the post-offices are at least duplicated, and often repeated many times, as we could easily show; but two or three more specimens of this will suffice. Twenty-three Franklins, twenty Jacksons, and sixteen Madisons, will help to perpetuate the memories of the distinguished men who once bore those names.

The danger of a letter's miscarrying in consequence of the omission of the name of the State on its direction, is of course reduced to nothing, when there is no other post-office in the country with the same name as the one addressed, especially if there is any oddity about the name. Thus, were we to direct a letter to "Sopchoppy," it would be likely to find the place rejoicing in that euphonious title, even were the State (Florida) omitted in the address; although it would often involve the trouble of consulting the list of post-offices. "Sorrel Horse," also, could not fail to receive whatever might be sent to it.

A teetotaler would not be surprised to find "Sodom" in "Champaign County;" and while on this subject we would say that temperance views seem to have prevailed in naming post-offices. We have two named Temperance, and three Temperancevilles, to balance which, besides the above Sodom, there appear only "Gin Town," and "Brandy Station," one of each.

One given to speculation on such matters, would be curious to know what must be the state of society in "Tight Squeeze." Is the "squeeze" commercial or geographical? Do hard times prevail there as a general thing, or is there some narrow pass, leading to the place, which has originated the name? There may be some tradition connected with the subject; at least a moderately lively fancy might make something even of such an unpromising subject as "Tight Squeeze."

Far different must be the condition of things in "Pay Down." This favored place is doubtless eschewed by advocates of the credit system, and here Cash must reign triumphant.

Some villages seem to aspire to astronomical honors. There are in our social firmament, one Sun, one Moon, and two Stars; also one Eclipse, and a Transit, whether of Venus or not is unknown. So it appears that the "man in the Moon," is not altogether a fictitious character, but may be a post master.

The twenty-five thousand names contained in the list of post-offices would furnish many other curiosities as noticeable as those just cited, and we refer those who are desirous of entering more largely into the subject, to that work.

It is sufficient for us to have called the attention of the public to the necessity of exactness and sufficient fulness in the address of letters, to insure their delivery at the place where they are intended to go. Much vexation and real inconvenience would be obviated, if more care were exercised in this respect, and the Dead Letter Office would have fewer inquests to make.

THE POST-OFFICE AS A DETECTOR OF CRIME.

The mails, as we have seen, afford facilities to the rogue for carrying out his designs as well as to the honest man in the prosecution of his business. But the post-office has been made, accidentally or purposely, the instrument of bringing to light criminals who had hitherto remained undetected; and whose deeds had no such connection with the mails as those which have thus far been described in this work.

A striking instance of this has been kindly furnished me by the Cincinnati Post Master, relating to a case which has excited the horror of the whole country. I refer to the Arrison case, most of the circumstances of which are doubtless familiar to my readers.

It will be recollected that the man Arrison was guilty of murdering the steward of the Cincinnati Hospital, and his wife, by means of a box, containing explosive materials, which took fire by the action of opening it. Arrison immediately absconded, and his place of retreat remained undiscovered for some time; but he was destined to be betrayed by a chain of circumstances, hanging upon an accident of the most trifling description.

A letter came to the Cincinnati office from Muscatine, Iowa, addressed to "P. F. Willard, Cincinnati, Ohio." The Muscatine postmark was so placed as to cover the P. in the address in such a manner as to make it resemble a C. There being a young lawyer in the place by the name of C. F. Willard, the letter was very naturally placed in his box. Upon opening and reading the document, he found that its contents were of the most mysterious character, and totally incomprehensible. Finding thus that it was not intended for him, he very properly returned it to the office with the request that it should be handed to the post master. This gentleman calling to mind the circumstances of the Arrison case, and being familiar with some of the names connected therewith, came to the conclusion, after reading the letter, that Arrison was the writer, and thereupon gave the information which led to his discovery and arrest.

SUING THE BRITISH GOVERNMENT.

A clerk stationed at the "General Delivery" window of the post-office, dispensing epistolary favors to the impatient throng without, was suddenly confronted by a countenance flaming with wrath; which countenance was part and parcel of the individual, now first known to fame by the name of Mike Donovan, who had elbowed his way through the crowd, and now stood before the astonished official, demanding justice. Handing him a foreign letter, marked "24 cents," Mike exclaimed in a tone of righteous indignation,

"Here, sir, is a letther that I paid twinty-four cints for, out of me own pocket, and the letther is from Pat Cosgrove, me cousin in ould Ireland, and Pat is as honest a boy as iver saw daylight, and Pat, he says inside of the letther that he paid the postage, and so some raskill has chated me, and I mane to make him smart for't; and I'd be obleiged to ye if ye'd tell me who to *sue*. Bedad, it isn't me that's goin to put up wid such rashcality."

Here he brought down his shillalah on the floor, to the imminent danger of his neighbor's toes, with an emphasis strongly suggestive of his fixed determination to exact the uttermost farthing from his unknown defrauder.

The clerk informed him if any mistake had occurred, the British Government was the delinquent, and therefore the party to be sued.

"Is it the British Government?" inquired Pat.

"Certainly," was the reply, "that's where you must look for your twenty-four cents."

Mike settled his hat over his eyes, and walked out of the office with an air of defiance to the world in general, and the British Government in particular.

PURSUIT OF A LETTER BOX.

Timothy Boyle, entering the post-office one morning, and perceiving a clerk "taking a limited view of society" through the aperture technically called "general delivery," naturally supposed that the duties of this functionary included receiving as well as delivering, and accordingly handed him a letter adorned with the lineaments of the Father of his Country, (not Tim's,) and bearing upon its exterior this general exhortation to all whom it might concern,—"With spede."

The clerk directed Tim to deposit the document in the letter box.

"And where *is* the letther box?"

"Follow this railing," said the young man, "and you will find it round the corner;" meaning thereby the corner of the tier of boxes, which was surrounded by a neat railing.

On the strength of these instructions, Tim turned on his heel, dashed into the main street, ("with spede," as per letter,) and walked on vigorously till he arrived at a corner, which happened to be occupied as a tailor's shop.

"I want to put this letther in the box," said Tim, after looking about him in vain for any sign of such a receptacle.

"What box?" asked the tailor.

"What box would I put it in but the letther box?" replied Tim.

"Who sent you here after a letter box?" said the tailor; "you must be a natural fool to suppose that we have any such thing here."

"Natheral fule or not, sir, I was towld by the clark at the post-office that I'd find the box round the corner, and shure this is a corner I've come to, and if it isn't here, I don't know where I'll find it."

"You'd better go back to the post-office," said the tailor, "and see whether the clerk can make you understand where to put your letter."

So the unlucky Tim left the tailor's shop with the impression that he had been made a goose of by the post-office clerk, and by "nursing his wrath to keep it warm," he succeeded in bringing it to the boiling point, by the time that he again entered the office.

"And it's a purty thrick ye've bin a playin' me, Misthur Clark," he vociferated, "sendin' me to a tailor's shop for a letther box! Bad luck to ye, what for did ye put me to all this throuble?"

The clerk blandly explained to Mr. Boyle that the "throuble" was caused by his own impetuosity, not to say stupidity, and finally succeeded in describing the locality of the letter box in such a lucid manner, that even Tim was guided by his direction to the much desired spot, and it is to be hoped that the letter in question underwent no more such vicissitudes, before it reached its destination.

AN "EXTRA" CUSTOMER.

An Irish dame entered the post-office at ——, and walking up to the post master with a letter in one hand, and a three cent piece in the other, she committed them both to his charge, inquiring, "will the letther go?"

"Certainly it will," was the reply.

"But is it in time for the extra?"

"In time for the *what?*" asked the mystified post master.

"Is this letther in time for the *extra?*" repeated the woman.

"What do you mean by extra," rejoined the official.

"I mane, is the *baggage* put up?" replied the persevering questioner.

The post master, seeing that the good woman was so thoroughly posted up in all the details of letter-sending, informed her categorically that the letter *would go*, inasmuch as it was in time for the "extra," and the "baggage" was *not* "put up."

Hereupon the inquisitive lady, having been fully satisfied in her own mind that the epistle would not fail of the "extra," sailed out of the office a happier, if not a wiser woman.

TO MY GRANDMOTHER.

A little bright eyed, flaxen-haired boy, was one day observed to enter the vestibule of the post-office at Washington, with a letter in his hand, and to wait very modestly for the departure of the crowd collected about the delivery window. As soon as the place was cleared, he approached the letter box and carefully deposited his epistle therein, lingering near as if to watch over the safety of the precious document. His motions attracted the attention of the clerk stationed at the window, whose curiosity induced him to examine the superscription of the letter just deposited by the little fellow. The address on the letter was simply, "To my dear Grandmother, Louisiana;" doubtless some good old lady, whose memory, in the mind of her innocent grandchild, was redolent of cake and candy, and all the various "goodies" which grandmothers are generally so ready to supply, to say nothing of the various well meant offices of kindness, to which their sometimes blind affection prompts them. "Look here, my little man," said the clerk, "what is your grandmother's name, and where does she live?"

"Why, she's my grandma, and she lives in Louisiana."

"Yes, I see that on the letter, but it will never get to her if her name isn't put on, and the place where she lives."

"Well, please put it on, sir."

"But I shall not know what her name is, unless you tell me."

"Why, sir, she's my grandma,—don't you know her? She used to live at my house."

After the display of considerable ingenuity on the part of the clerk, and a good deal of innocent evasion by the child, the old lady's name and place of residence were finally ascertained, and added to the address; after which the little one went on his way, rejoicing in the assurance given by the clerk that now his "dear grandmother" would certainly receive the important epistle from her darling.

IMPROPER INTERFERENCE.

A letter was once sent from the Dead Letter Office at Washington, containing rail road scrip to a considerable amount. The letter had been mailed in a Southern town, and miscarried, and it was returned to the post master of that town for delivery to the writer. It so happened that the writer of the epistle had failed in business, and on the arrival of the letter the post master informed one of his creditors, and an attachment was laid on the letter by the Sheriff.

The writer reported the case to the Department, when a peremptory order was sent requiring the post master to return the letter at once to the Dead Letter Office at Washington. It was sent, and the return mail brought the post master's dismissal from office and the appointment of his successor.

The post-office was worth $1200 a year, and the discharged post master had abundance of time to count up the profits that might have been made by acting up to the good old rule, "Let every man mind his own business."

THE DEAD LETTER.

The following is contributed by "Dave," of the Columbus (Ohio) post-office.

During my term of service at the General Delivery of this office, it was my custom, upon receiving dead letters from Washington City, to make a list of the names of the persons to whom they were addressed, and stick it up in the lobby of the office, with a notice, "Call for Dead Letters."

One day an elaborate specimen of Erin's sons, whose brawny fist and broad shoulders seemed to denote a construction with an eye single to American rail roads, lounged into the office, and up to the board containing the aforesaid list. He looked at it a moment and burst into tears. I spoke to him through the window, and asked him what was the matter.

"Oh! Mr. Post Master, I see ye have a daid letther for me. I spect me sester in Ireland's daid, and it's not a wake since I sint her a tin pound note to come to Ameriky wid—and kin ye tell me how long she's bin daid, Mr. Post Master?'

I asked him his name, found the "letther," and after a request from him to "rade it, sir, and rade it aisy if you plaze," opened it and told him not to cry; that his sister was not dead, but that it was a letter written by himself and directed to *Michael Flaherty*, BOSTON, CHICAGO.

"And is Michael daid, Mr. Post Master?"

"No, I guess not," said I.

"Well, who *is* daid, sir?"

I explained to him that letters not taken from the office to which they were addressed within a certain time, were sent to what was called the Dead Letter Office at Washington City, and from thence, if containing anything valuable, to the persons who wrote them.

"God bliss ye for that, sir, but Michael lives in Chicaga."

I told him I would not dispute that, but Boston and Chicago were two distinct cities, and the letter was addressed to both, and that Boston being the first named, it had been retained there, and his friend had not received it.

"Sure and I thought Boston was in Chicaga! and that's what ye call a daid letther, is it? Faith and I thought it was Bridget and not the letther, was daid. Ye see, Mr. Post Master, Michael he writ home to the ould folks that he lived in Chicaga, that he had married a nice American lady, that she was a sea-cook on a stameboat, and that they called her a nager. So whin I started for Ameriky, the ould modder, Michael's modder, she give me these illegant rings (the letter contained a pair of ear-rings,) to give Michael's wife for a prisint. When we landed at Boston, I wrote Michael the letther, tould him I was going to Columbus to live, put on the name—Michael Flaherty, Boston, Chicaga, and put it in the post,—and sure here it is, and Michael's sea-cook nager niver got it. Bad luck to the ship that fetched me to Boston, Mr. Post Master."

After offering to "trate me for the trouble" he had caused me, he left, and ever after, when he mailed a letter he brought it to me to put on the address, "Because he didn't understand these daid letthers."

SHARP CORRESPONDENCE.

One of the Peter Funk "Gift-Enterprise" firms in a large city, sent a package of tickets to a post master in Maine, the postage upon which was fifteen cents unpaid. They got the following hard rap over the knuckles, from the indignant official:—

"I herewith return your tickets. You must be fools as well as knaves, to suppose that I will aid you in swindling my neighbors, and *pay all the expenses myself.*"

To which he in a few days received the annexed "settler:"—

Sir,

"We perhaps owe you an apology for sending the parcel postage unpaid.

As we infer from the phraseology of your note, that you are willing to swindle your neighbors if we will pay all the expenses, please give us your lowest terms on which you will act as our agent.

P. S. All communications shall be strictly confidential."

This note was promptly returned, with the following endorsement across its face, by the post master:—

"It seems you are not only fools and knaves, but blackguards also. Ask my neighbors if they think I would "swindle" them either at my own expense or that of any one else."

To which this answer came back by next mail:—

"We *have* inquired of your neighbors long ago, and that's the reason we applied to you in the first instance."

Here follows the post master's final reply:—

"I acknowledge the corn. Send us your street and number, so that

I can call on you when I come to the city, and I may conclude to aid your "Enterprise."

But that was the last thing that the "Gift" gentleman could think of doing. In fact, secrecy as to his locality, was quite essential in keeping out of the clutches of the Police.

THE IRISH HEART.

Many of the reading public will remember the sad accident which occurred in Hartford, Conn., in the year 1853, when by the bursting of a boiler connected with a car factory, several of the workmen were killed. Among the killed were two Irishmen, brothers, each of whom left a widow, with an infant child. These men had been industrious and faithful toward their employers, and kind in their own households, so that when they were taken away in such a sudden and shocking manner, their sorrowing widows felt a double stroke, in the loss of affectionate hearts, and in the deprivation of many of the comforts which the hand of affection had hitherto supplied. Their little ones, too, required much of their attention, and often seriously interfered with their efforts to provide for the daily wants of their desolate households.

About six months after the accident, the Hartford post master received from the Department at Washington a "dead letter," which had been written by these brothers to a female relative in Ireland, enclosing a draft for ten pounds sterling, to defray the expenses of her passage to America.

This anxiety on the part of these children of Erin who had come to this land of promise, to furnish their relatives and friends whom they had left behind, with the means of following them, is a striking manifestation of that ardent attachment to home and its circle of loved ones, which leads them to undergo every sacrifice in order to effect a reunion with those for whose presence they long with irrepressible desires, as they go about, "strangers in a strange land." They have often been known to submit to the severest privations for the sake of bringing over a sister, a brother, or some other relative, without whom the family circle would be incomplete. All this is but one aspect of the "Irish heart," whose warmth of affection and generous impulses should put to shame many, who without their ardent unselfishness, coolly laugh at the blunders and *mal apropos* speeches of its possessors, and attribute that to shallowness, which is in truth but a sudden and sometimes conflicting flow of ideas. As the mad poet McDonald Clark once wrote in an epigram on an editor who had accused him of possessing "zigzag brains,"

> "I can tell Johnny Lang, by way of a laugh,
> Since he's dragged in my name to his pen-and-ink brawl,
> That some people think it is better by half
> To have brains that are 'zigzag,' than no brains at all!"

"By their works ye shall know them." It is comparatively easy to utter the language of affection, and to express a vast deal of fine sentiment; and much of this spurious coin is current in the world. But when one is seen denying himself almost the necessaries of life, in order to accumulate a little fund for the benefit of some one near to his heart, though far away, we feel that there can be no deception here. Like the widow's mite, it has the ring of pure gold.

The letter referred to, (which was sent back from Ireland in consequence of some misdirection,) was full of kind feeling, and manifested on the part of the writers a firm and simple trust in the goodness of Providence. The post master sent word to the widows that this letter was in his possession, and accordingly was visited by the bereaved women, whose tears flowed fast as they gazed upon the record which recalled so vividly the kindnesses of their departed husbands. The little sum enclosed, as they stated, was the result of the united efforts of the two families, who cheerfully joined in this labor of love. How many a recollection of unmurmuring self-denial, with the hope that made it easy; how many a remembrance of bright anticipations of the happiness to be enjoyed, when the beloved one, for whose sake these efforts were made, should be received within their family circle; how many such things must have been brought to mind by the sight of the missive, so freighted with affection and memories of the past!

The post master informed the widows that by returning the draft to the office from which it was purchased, they might obtain the money on it; but they replied that since it had once been dedicated to an object sacred both to the departed and their survivors, it must go back to Ireland, and fulfil its mission.

So these poor stricken women, to whom ten pounds was a large sum, (even larger than when the letter was first sent,) and who much needed the comforts it would purchase, sent back the draft, and have since had the happiness of meeting their relative in America, and seeing the wishes of their husbands faithfully carried out.

This is but one of many constantly recurring instances of generosity and devotion which come to the knowledge of post masters; and while we have put on record some of the blunders of an impulsive people, our sense of justice as well as inclination, has prompted us to make public the foregoing incidents, so forcibly illustrating the warm attachments that grace the IRISH HEART.

MY WIFE'S SISTER.

The most ridiculous errors and omissions sometimes occur on the part of persons applying to post masters for missing letters. The following amusing correspondence will illustrate this phase of post-office experience:—

New York, 29th Jan. 1855.

Post Master New York.

Dear Sir,

A week ago last Monday, I mailed two letters, both having enclosures, but of no intrinsic value, directed to my wife's sister in New Haven, Conn., neither of which have ever reached their destination.

Very respectfully yours,

W. B. H———.

The above letter was forwarded to the post master of New Haven, after having been read by the New York post master. It was soon returned with the following pertinent inquiries :—

Post Office, New Haven, Conn., Feb. 1, 1855.

Solus ! ?

Well, that is a fix ! What is that name ? Is it Jonathan or Wm. B. Haskell, or Hershel ? Who'd he marry ? How many sisters did his wife have ? What were their names ? Who are their friends and relations in New Haven ? Is the lady here on a visit ? Or, like a careful matron, has she come here to educate her children ? Egad, I don't know ! My library is wofully deficient in genealogy, and I shall be obliged to "give it up." Who can tell me the name of "my wife's sister ?"

Yours truly,

L. A. T———.

The New Haven post master's letter was then sent to Mr. H., with the annexed note :—

Post Office, New York, Feb. 2, 1855.

Mr. Wm. B. H——.

Dear Sir,

By direction of the post master, I forwarded your letter of inquiry to the post master at New Haven.

He returns the letter to this office with a request that the name of your "wife's sister" may be given to him, as he has been unable to discover it, although possessed of a large library embracing many works of a genealogical character. The P. M. at New Haven is inclined to the belief that it will be difficult to find the letter sent to his office, unless the name of the party addressed is given to him. In this belief the P. M. at New York joins, and the two P. M.'s hold concurrent opinions on this subject.

With all due apologies for the seemingly gross ignorance of the post masters in this matter,

I am very respectfully

Your Obedient Servant,

Wm. C——,

Secretary.

CHAPTER XXIII.

RESPONSIBILITY OF POST MASTERS.

CASES sometimes occur of the loss of letters apparently by the carelessness of post masters or their clerks; and in view of such cases, an important question arises; namely, to what extent a post master is responsible for the consequences of such carelessness?

The subject is not free from difficulties. In many cases it would be hard to say what constitutes culpable carelessness.

It is common in country towns for persons to take from the post-office the mail matter of their neighbors, especially when they live at a distance from the office, as an act of accommodation to them; and many letters are thus safely delivered every day.

Now should a valuable letter in this way come into the possession of some dishonest person, and be retained by him, it would seem severe, if not unjust, to prosecute the post master for the loss; since in committing it unawares to improper hands, he did but act in accordance with ordinary usages, countenanced by the community.

It would undoubtedly be a safer way of doing business, to insist upon an order in every case where a letter is delivered to any other person than the one to whom it is addressed, or some one usually employed by him for this purpose. But the country post master who should rigidly insist upon this rule, would receive "more kicks than coppers" for his good intentions; and indeed, cases like the one supposed are few and far between.

In cities, also, something like the following might and does frequently happen. A person known to be in the employ of another, comes to the post-office, and says he is sent by his employer for his letters, and the clerk in attendance, believing his statement, gives them to him. He robs the letters and disappears. In this case, it hardly seems that the clerk was guilty of a culpable degree of negligence.

Here is another instance of the manner in which a letter may go to the wrong person, where the fault is not chargeable to post-office employés. In the list of advertised letters, one is found for John Smith. An individual calls for the letter, claiming to be the identical John, and receives it; but a day or two after the "Simon Pure" appears, and is indignant at learning that his letter has already been appropriated, or that the clerk knows nothing about it, having forgotten the circumstance. Of course the clerk, in such a case, might require the supposed John Smith to identify the letter as far as was possible, by mentioning the place from which he expected it; but many supposable circumstances might destroy the conclusiveness of this evidence of identity, such as the acquaintance of the false John with the real one, and his knowledge of the place whence he received most of his correspondence. Besides, the real claimant might not be able to tell where the letter was mailed, for his correspondent might have written from some other place than the one where he usually lived.

But it is needless to multiply instances. Those that we have mentioned, and many others which will readily occur to the reader, will suffice to show that the number of cases in which a post master can justifiably be prosecuted, is very limited by the nature of the circumstances.

On the other hand, a proper diligence requires of the post master not only the obvious precaution of securing reliable assistants, but a care in relation to the minutiæ of his office which shall prevent the mislaying of letters, by carelessness *within*, or their abstraction by theft from *without*. The boxes and delivery window should be so arranged as to render the interior of the boxes inaccessible to outsiders, and of course no one should be admitted within the enclosure, under any ordinary circumstances.

I am aware that these hints are unnecessary to the great body of post masters in this country; yet it can do no harm to mention such things, as it appears by the following report that post masters are sometimes held to answer before a court, for the want of diligence in discharging the duties of their office.

The suit was brought in 1849, by Moses Christy of Waterbury, Vermont, against Rufus C. Smith, post master at that place, for the loss of a letter containing fifty dollars, mailed at Salisbury, Mass., Nov. 23, 1849, by Moses True, Jr.

Moses True, Jr., testified that he carried the letter to the Salisbury post-office, and showed the money to the post master, who counted it, and it was then enclosed in the letter, and left with the post master, who testified that he mailed it in the ordinary way, and forwarded it to Waterbury by the usual course. The letter not being received by Christy, application was made for it to the post master, but nothing could be found of it. The post-bill, however, which accompanied it, was found in the Waterbury office.

It was shown that a son of Christy and one other person were in the habit of calling at the post-office for his letters; but they both swore that they did not remember receiving the letter in question, and that if it was taken out by either of them, it was, in the absence of Christy, laid upon his desk or placed in a private drawer.

It was further proved that the Waterbury office was kept in a room about sixteen feet square, divided in the centre by the boxes and a railing, which separated the part devoted to the office business, from the portion appropriated to the use of the public; that the boxes were so arranged that the box of Moses Christy could easily be reached through the "delivery;" and that persons were frequently allowed to pass behind or near one end of the counter within the enclosure, to transact business with the post master.

There was no evidence to show that any persons, other than the office assistants, were permitted to go behind the railing at the time the letter in question arrived at the office.

It appeared that the post master employed several persons as assistants in the Summer and Autumn of 1849, but there was no evidence to show that any of these persons were regularly appointed and sworn. It further appeared by Christy's postage account, that one or two letters were charged to him on the 24th of November, 1849, and he produced four or five letters, which, by the ordinary course of the mails, would have been received on that day.

We here copy from "Vermont Reports," Vol. 8, p. 663 :—

The defendant requested the Court to charge the jury as follows :— 1. That the defendant does not in any manner stand as an insurer in relation to the business of his office, and is only held to ordinary diligence in the discharge of the duties of his office, and can only be made liable for losses occasioned by a want of such diligence, and that the burden of proof is upon the plaintiff, to establish the fact of the want of such diligence. 2. That in order to establish the fact of want of ordinary diligence, the plaintiff must show some particular act of negligence in relation to the letter in question, and that the loss was the direct consequence of the particular negligence proved. 3. That although there may have been official misconduct on the part of the defendant, yet unless it be shown that the plaintiff's loss was the result of such misconduct, he cannot recover. 4. That if the letter were by mistake delivered to the wrong person, stolen by a stranger, or embezzled by a clerk, the defendant is not liable, unless he has been negligent, and the loss was the direct consequence of his negligence. 5. That it is not sufficient, to entitle the plaintiff to recover, merely to show that a letter was received at the office, and that the person to whom it was directed has not received it. 6. That the post master is not liable for the negligence of his deputies, unless he is guilty of negligence in appointing wholly unsuitable persons. 7. That the defendant being a public officer, he would not be liable in an action of trover, unless, at the time the letter was called for, he had the letter in his possession or control, and withheld it, or had actually appropriated the letter, or money, to his own use.

The Court charged the jury in accordance with all the foregoing requests, except the second and sixth. In relation to the second request the Court charged the jury, that it was not necessary, in order to enable the plaintiff to recover, that he should show a particular act of negligence in relation to the letter in question; but that, if the plaintiff had shown a general want of common care and diligence on the part of the defendant, either in the construction of his places of deposit for letters, so that they were unsafe, or in the management of the post-office, in permitting persons to go behind the railing who had no legal right to go there, and had also satisfied them that the letter and money in question were lost in consequence of such negligence or misconduct of the defendant, then the defendant should be liable. In reference to the sixth request the Court charged the jury, that as there was no proof that any of the persons who were employed by defendant in the office had ever been appointed or sworn as assistants, they were to be regarded as mere clerks, or servants of the defendant, and that if, through negligence or want of common care and diligence on the part of such clerks or servants, the money and letters were lost, the defendant would be liable therefor

Verdict for plaintiff. Exceptions by defendant.

The decision was sustained in the Supreme Court.

If the report of the above case shall have the effect to render any class of post masters more careful of the custody of correspondence, and in the general management of their offices, the object of its insertion will have been answered.

CHAPTER XXIV.

OFFICIAL COURTESY, ETC.

The post-office clerk who fails to do his duty thoroughly, is like a light-house keeper, who now and then allows his light to go out, or become dim. Sometimes no harm may result; but it may be that the helmsman of some gallant ship laden with precious goods, and far more precious lives, seeing no light to direct him through the angry storm, steers blindly onward, and is wrecked upon the very spot whence the guiding star should have beamed.

Not only is it the duty of those connected with post-offices to exercise the utmost carefulness and exactness, in order that mail matter may promptly reach the persons for whom it is intended, but sometimes much caution and discretion are required from them, that letters may not fall into hands for which they were not designed.

There are other qualifications scarcely less desirable for post-office employés than exactness and caution. Patience and courtesy toward the various individuals constituting that public which it is the duty of these officials to serve, go very far in carrying out the idea of the post-office,—that of being a convenience to the community.

We have elsewhere shown that the life of a post-office clerk is not passed upon a bed of roses, and we would here call his attention to the truth that many annoyances must be expected by him in the course of his experience. The ignorance and consequent pertinacity of those who apply for letters, frequently try his patience to the utmost.

A person, for instance, anxiously expecting a letter, and not understanding that the mail by which it would come arrives only once a day, inquires at the office half a dozen times on the same day, and it is not very wonderful that the clerk in attendance should give short answers to the persevering applicant, or even omit to search for the letter. Yet, even in a case like this, much allowance should be made for the possible circumstances of the person in question. He may be waiting for news from a sick child, or for some other information of the utmost importance to him, and it is surely hard enough to be disappointed in such expectations, without being obliged to suffer the additional pain of a harsh response.

Of course post-office clerks seldom know the peculiar circumstances of those who apply for letters; but the exercise of patience and mildness toward all, would be sure to spare the feelings of those who often rather need sympathy than rough words.

Many who carry on little correspondence, and therefore have little occasion to be informed respecting post-office matters in general, often make blunders which are very annoying; but it is to be remembered that those in charge of the post-office, were employed for this, (among other things which contribute to the perfection of this branch of public service,) namely, to bear with all classes of correspondents, and to maintain a uniform courtesy toward every one. This would render it possible for even the most timid to approach the "delivery window," without experiencing the sensation of looking into a lion's den, as has sometimes (but I trust seldom) been the case.

On the other hand, it is reasonable that those who avail themselves of the conveniences of the post-office, should take pains to inform themselves on those points which it is necessary they should know, in order to avoid giving inconvenience to themselves, and unnecessary trouble to those appointed to serve them.

The times of opening and closing mails, and similar matters, should be known, that the post-office may not bear the blame due to negligence outside its walls.

Cases now and then occur, similar to the following, which happened but a few years ago.

A letter came into the Windsor, Vermont, post-office, containing a draft on the Suffolk Bank for three hundred dollars, and directed "Johnson Clark, Windsor, Ct." The "Ct.," however, was written so indistinctly as to resemble "Vt.;" and as there was a person by the name of Johnson Clark (as we shall call him) in the latter place, the letter was handed to him.

When he looked at the post-mark, (that of a town some twenty or thirty miles distant,) he remarked, "I can't imagine who can have been writing to me from there," and after opening and reading it, he returned it to the post master, saying that it was not for him.

But his honesty was only of a transient nature, for he could not keep the money out of his thoughts, and he soon began to think that he had been rather hasty in returning the letter, when, for aught he knew, he could have retained its contents with impunity. For was not the letter directed to Johnson Clark? And may not one take possession of a letter directed to himself?

This course of thought and these queries were followed by the determination to recover the letter, and appropriate the contents.

Clark accordingly went to the post master the next day, and stated that he had heard, the evening before, of the death of a relative who had been living at the West, and who had left him a small legacy, namely, the sum contained in the letter. On the strength of these representations, the post master gave him the document, without, so far as appears, making any attempt to verify his statement. The inheritor of legacies proceeded forthwith to the Bank in the village, and obtained the money on the draft, endorsing it, as is customary. It only required his own name to be written, and where was the harm? thought he.

A few days after this, the person who had written the letter came to Windsor, Vt., having been informed by his correspondent at Windsor, Ct., that it had not reached him; and thinking it possible that it might have gone astray.

On his arrival at the former place, he soon ascertained that the Vermont Dromio had taken possession of his letter.

This worthy found that the name of Johnson Clark was not a spell potent enough to protect him in the enjoyment of his unrighteous gain. He was sent to the State Prison for two years.

In this instance, the post master was clearly guilty of carelessness in allowing Clark to obtain the letter on the pretext that he offered. As there was a well known town in Connecticut of the name of Windsor, prudence would have required a closer examination of the address, after the letter was returned by Clark. And the story by which Clark imposed upon him, was sufficiently lame in some particulars to have called for a closer investigation of its truth. If the post master had requested to be allowed to read that part of the letter which referred to the pretended legacy, a refusal on the part of Clark to permit it, would of course have created a strong suspicion that he was playing a dishonest game, and would have justified the post master in withholding the letter until further proof could be obtained as to the identity of Johnson Clark with the one for whom the epistle was designed.

Cases similar to the above are not unfrequent; and in all such instances, those who rely on a name identical with that of some other person, as a shield for attempted dishonesty, have found their defence fail them in the hour of need.

The matter seems too plain to need elucidation; yet not a few persons, equally compounded of folly and knavery, have actually supposed that the possession of a name like that of another man, would enable them to keep on the shady side of the law in making free with his purse also.

This accidental resemblance of name has often been used for dishonest purposes in other ways than the one just described.

Snooks manufactures a patent medicine which is beginning to obtain some celebrity, when some obscure Snooks starts up with *his* pill, or elixir. The innocent public, ready to swallow pills and stories bearing the name of Snooks, makes no distinction between the two personages; and the "original Jarley" is compelled to share his honors and emoluments with his upstart namesake. Trickery like this can seldom be reached by law, but the appropriator of the contents of a letter under circumstances like those above detailed, is dealt with like any other kind of robbery.

CHAPTER XXV.

IMPORTANCE OF ACCURACY.

AFTER giving "outsiders" the share of blame which rightly belongs to them for the delay, miscarrying, and loss of valuable mail matter, a balance remains due to the post masters and post-office clerks.

We have elsewhere expressed our views respecting dishonesty in these officials, and shall consequently confine our present remarks principally to carelessness and other similar faults, which can hardly be called crimes, but which often produce effects as disastrous as those which are the result of evil intention. These faults, indeed, differ only in degree from what are termed crimes; for neglect of duty, is on a small scale, a species of dishonesty.

There is, perhaps, no situation in which a lack of promptness and accuracy in the transaction of business may be productive of so great evil, as in that of a post-office employé. Those engaged in ordinary branches of business have some idea of the relative consequence of the matters about which they are occupied from day to day. They can generally know what is the actual importance of any given transaction, so that, if they are disposed to be negligent, they may, if they choose, avoid incurring the guilt and blame which would follow unfaithfulness in great things.

But the post-office clerk seldom has the power of making such a discrimination. The letter which is carelessly left over to-day, may go to-morrow, but too late to save the credit of a tottering house, or to render the instructions it may contain, of any avail. In the rapid course of commercial transactions, what is wisdom one day, may be folly the next, and thus it not unfrequently happens that the best contrived plans may be ruined by the delay or non-arrival of a letter.

The following instance will illustrate this.

Before the passage of the late Postal Treaty with Great Britain, a clerk in one of our large cities was sent to the post-office to mail a letter, containing an order for goods on an English house. The clerk pocketed the twenty-four cents which he had been intrusted with for the purpose of pre-paying the letter; therefore agreeably to the postal arrangements then existing, it could not go by steamer, but was sent by a sailing vessel.

Consequently the order was delayed, and therefore was not executed as promptly as the firm sending it had expected; and when the goods arrived they had fallen in value to such an extent, that the firm in question incurred by the operation a loss estimated at at least ten thousand dollars.

CHAPTER XXVI.

Post Masters as Directories—Novel Applications—The Butter Business.

A Thievish Family—"Clarinda" in a City—Decoying with Cheese—Post Master's Response.

A Truant Husband—Woman's Instinct.

EDITORS are supposed by many to be walking encyclopedias, with the record of the entire range of human knowledge inscribed on the tablets of their brains; and there are those who in like manner seem to consider post masters as living Directories, able at short notice to inform any one who chooses to ask, where Smith lives, and what business Jones is in, or what is the price of guano, (an inquiry actually made by letter, of a New York post master.)

In short, these Government officers are often called upon to serve the public in a sphere which Congress never contemplated in the various enactments it has passed respecting the duties of post masters, and the details of the postal system.

A few specimens of letters received by different post masters, may not be uninteresting, as illustrating this phase of post-office life.

Here is one from an individual desirous of entering into a mercantile transaction in the "botter" line, and receiving the post master's endorsement of some good "commish marchan", who could be interested in the business.

G———, Pennsylvania, January 29, 1855.

Postmaster will pleze to give this letter to a good Commish Marchan what he could pay for fresh botter everry weak if a man would cent a hundred up to 3 hundred paunts my intension is to go in sutch bisnis You will plese rite me back to this present time.

Yours Respectful

J. S.

If the "fresh botter" was "cent everry *weak*," as was proposed, it must undoubtedly have been very much sought after, as possessing the negative, but important merit of not being *strong*.

Our next specimen was received by the post master of one of the cities in Western New York, and is unique both as regards its object, and its orthography, or rather cacography, which appears like "fonotipy" run mad.

North S——, Nov. 19, 1854.

Dear friend it is with plaisure that I take my pen in hand to inform you of a famly moveing from this place the wider stacy and her to girls they are poor and haf to work for their liveing clarinda is the girl that workes the most from home mr sam shirtleff says that she has worked for him and she stole pork and cheese and the pork hid between the bed blankets and they found it and weid it and thaught a rat had braught it there and the cheese she carid home with her they sent to ladies there a visiting and sent a peic of cheese with them and they got tea and had cheese uporn the table and they sliped a peice of the cheese in thir laps and compard it togather and it was the same cind it was a large inglich cheese that shirtleff bought she has also worked to mr alford blax and his brother the old batchlor his mother was old and generly done the niting she nit seventeen pare of socks and layed them up for her boys when she got old and coldent nit no more and they was all taken away by her to pare afterwords was found at the store and she sed that she had took them they owed her five dolars yet and they wont pay her till she delivers the socks and she dare not make no fuss for fear they will bring her out she worked to mr cringlands and she hooked a paro of whitc kid gloves and a hym book and a pocket handkerchief and the gloves she traded away to the store for a dress by giveing a pare of socks to boot and she worked to truman buts this sumer she had taken a pare of stockin which they found in her sunday bonet and they lost to shiling in money and then they discharged her bengman grene bought a set of dishes and they lost to platters out of the set they lost sope and buter out of their sular she borrowed of mister spicer a silver pen which coast a do.ar and after he was dead she denied haveing it and she told it herself that she sold it for half a dolar and a pennife and the pennife was fifty cents they borrowed a pale of wheat flour and when they carid it home and put to thirds rie The pepole most look out for them in the trincket line mr sir post master plese answer this as soon as you can and oblidge your friend much yours with respect

Direct your leter silas stickney North S——, N. Y.

The zeal of Silas, if he was actuated by no sinister motives—no spite toward "the wider stacy and her to girls," especially "clarinda," whose exploits form the burden of his complaints—this zeal is highly commendable, and united with it there is a fulness of specification in the catalogue of "clarinda's" misdemeanors which equals in richness and effect anything that even the fertile brain of Dickens could conceive.

The ingenious device of sending ladies to the suspected domicil under color of a friendly visit, but provided with a touchstone in the shape of "a peic of cheese," wherewith to detect the other piece supposed to have been purloined by some one of the thievish family, was worthy of a Vidocq; and the triumphant issue of the case, when their worthy Committee of Investigation "sliped a peic of cheese in their laps" and settled its identity with the "inglich cheese" which the victimized "shirtleff" had purchased, showed the power of genius, attaining great ends by the use of simple means

This epistle developes a new ramification of the postal system. A post master entreated to act as a conservator of public morals; to exert all his powerful influence against "clarinda," who proved treacherous to "mr sam shirtleff" in the matter of pork and cheese; and abstracted from "mr alford blax and his brother the old batchlor, the seventeen pare of socks" that their mother had "nit" to comfort their nether extremities when she, by reason of the infirmities of age, "coldent nit;" and filched "sope and buter" out of "bengman grenes sular;" to say nothing of the "pare of stockin" which were secreted in her "sunday bonet," and "to shilling," the loss of which occasioned her discharge from the service of "truman buts."

Upon this unfortunate post master was thrown the charge of seeing that the city received no detriment from the demoralizing influence of Clarinda!

This gentleman, not willing to be outdone by his correspondent in his devotion to the public good, indited the following reply:—

B—— Post-Office, Dec. 13, 1854.

Mr. Silas Stickney.

Dear Sir:

I am in receipt of yours of the 19th ult., and in reply would say that I cannot too highly commend your solicitude in behalf of good morals, and your discretion in selecting the post master of this place to carry out your benevolent designs toward its inhabitants. The corrupting influence of small villages upon large towns is a thing much to be lamented, and it grieves me to think that the unsophisticated inhabitants of this place are to be exposed to the machinations of the "widow stacy and her to girls." It will be, sir, like the Evil One entering the garden of Eden, where all was innocence and purity!

If in the course of my official duties, I find it feasible to ward off impending danger from this immaculate town, be assured that I shall not fail to do so.

Yours, &c.,
W. D——, P. M.

But post masters are made confidants in graver matters than these. They are not unfrequently called upon by deserted wives to look up their truant husbands, and by desolate husbands to aid them in recovering frail partners, who have been unfaithful to their marriage vows, and have forsaken the "guides of their youth."

Letters of this description are principally from the more illiterate class of community; yet amid the crooked chirography and bad spelling, there sparkles so much tender affection, sometimes for the guilty one, sometimes for the innocent children, who are suffering from the unprincipled conduct of a parent, that these cases command the warmest sympathy of those whose aid is invoked, although the requests thus made relate to matters entirely out of their sphere, and consequently they are seldom able to afford much assistance to the parties in trouble.

I will here give an extract from this class of letters, as illustrating the above remarks. The following is from a letter received by the post master of a city in Ohio, from a woman who had been deserted by her husband five years previous. She requested the post master to read it to her husband, in case he should find him, so it is written *at* the latter person. In the postscript, (which is generally supposed to contain the pith of female correspondence,) she says,—

"You would shed tears If you onley could see wat a smart peart little boy you have hear what a sham It Is to think that A sensable man should leave a wife and a child that Is got as much sense as he has—and people say he is as much like you as he can be he has got the pretys black eyes I have ever seen In any ones head he has an eye like a hawk."

Thus is the *argumentum ad hominem* supplied by woman's instinct. Fatherly pride was called upon to effect that to which conjugal affection was inadequate.

CHAPTER XXVII.

A Windfall for Gossipers—Suit for Slander—Profit and Loss—The Resuscitated Letter—Condemned Mail Bag—An Epistolary Rip Van Winkle.

IN country villages, where few events happen to interrupt the monotony of every day life, the occurrence of an out-of-the-way incident is like seed sown in a fertile soil, producing a fruitful crop of speculations and surmises, and affording food for conversation for many a day to the eager gossip-hunters who abound in such small places.

About thirty years ago, the quiet town of Lebanon, in the State of Connecticut, was enlivened by one of these occurrences, which brought a new influx of curiosity-mongers to the blacksmith's shop; covered all the barrels, boxes, and counters in the store with eager disputants, and gave new life to the Sewing Society, and its auxiliary "tea-fights." The cause of this unwonted moving of the waters, was on this wise:

Mr. Jonathan Little, a well known New York merchant, while on a summer visit to Lebanon, his native place, mailed at that office a letter directed to the firm of which he was a member, and containing bank-notes to the amount of one thousand dollars. The letter failing to arrive at its destination, and Special Agents being as yet unknown, Mr. Little advertised in several papers, describing the money lost, and offering a reward for its recovery. This, however, produced no results, and the tide of speculation and discussion rose to its highest pitch.

The loss of the bewildering sum of one thousand dollars naturally stimulated the imaginative powers of the Lebanonians, and, hurried away by his zeal, or perhaps by a wish to appear sagacious, Mr. Roger Bailey, the brother of the Lebanon post master, while in conversation with several persons, incautiously asserted that Amasa Hyde, the post master at Franklin, (the next town to Lebanon on the route to New York,) had taken the letter, adding, "He's just such a fellow."

The by-standers were rather astonished at this bold charge, impeaching as it did the integrity of a man whose character had always been above suspicion. That "bird of the air" which is always ready to "carry the matter," soon diffused the information that Amasa Hyde was supposed to be the delinquent. This gentleman being indisposed to leave his reputation at the mercy of "thousand-tongued Rumor," which personage could not easily be brought before a jury, instituted inquiries for the purpose of discovering the originator of these injurious reports. He succeeded in tracing them to their source, and sued the unwary Bailey for slander. Mr. B., by the verdict of the jury, was compelled to pay some seven hundred dollars and costs, for the pleasure of expressing his opinion.

This, however, is but an episode in the history of the lost letter. After a while the excitement died away, and Mr. Little found it necessary to place the thousand dollars to the account of "Profit and Loss," especially the latter.

The theory was once advanced by an acute genius, and applied to the case of a tea-kettle inadvertently dropped into the ocean, that "a thing isn't lost when you know where it is." But the subject in hand seems to show that a thing isn't always lost, if you *don't* know where it is. For, about two years after the occurrences above mentioned, the missing letter came to light with all its valuable contents. And this resuscitation took place, not in Lebanon, nor in Franklin, but in the New London post-office!

It appears that the mail bag which contained the letter, was found, on its arrival at New London, so much worn as to be unsafe, and was accordingly condemned by the post master and thrown aside as useless, having first, of course, been emptied of its contents, as was supposed. Two years subsequently, a quantity of old mail bags and other rubbish was removed from the office, and the letter in question took the opportunity to drop out, and return, an epistolary Rip Van Winkle, to the world whence it had retired for so long a time.

CHAPTER XXVIII.

VALENTINES.

Their Origin—Degeneration—Immoral Influence—Incitement to Dishonesty.

WHO Saint Valentine was, is not much to the purpose in this place. We will give him credit for having been, however, a very excellent and highly respectable individual. We must therefore utterly protest against the custom which has obtained of late years, making him the tutelary Saint of innumerable silly lovers, mean mischief-makers, and vulgar letter-writers generally.

Unfortunately for the reputation of this inoffensive Bishop, the day noted in the calendar as sacred to his blessed memory, happens to be that on which, according to the auld-wives' legends of Merrie England, there is a universal marrying and giving in marriage among the feathered tribes. The Fourteenth of February seems rather bleak for a grand wedding festival at which any birds but snow birds are expected to attend; but we suppose we must respect the tradition. It seems early too for imitative lads and lasses, who should wait until the warm spring approaches;

"When the South-wind in May days,
With a net of shining haze,
Silvers the horizon wall,
And with softness touches all—
Tints the human countenance
With a color of romance;"

and when all nature is bathed afresh in light and love, and inspired with new life.

But, says a French writer, the divine faculty which distinguishes man from the brutes, is the capacity to drink when he is not thirsty, and to make love at all seasons of the year. Whether this "divine faculty" is a God-gift, or a perversion and abuse, the legitimate fruit of the sad tree of knowledge of good and evil, we will not stop to discuss. Man has it in full exercise; and however the birds may grumble at being obliged to hurry up their matrimonial cakes under the very beard and brow of winter, Cupid will be found—like the classical clothes-brusher and job-waiter — "*nunquam non paratus*,"—always ready at your service.

The probability is that the human custom of choosing mates about this time, is more ancient than the notion touching the pairing of birds, and that the latter is a mere fable, suggested by the former. Some commentator on Shakspeare has traced it back "to a pagan custom of the same kind during the Lupercalia feasts of Pan and Juno, celebrated in the month of February by the Romans. We are further told that, the anniversary of St. Valentine happening in this month, the pious promoters of Christianity placed this custom under his patronage in order to indicate the notion of its pagan origin." Unhappy St. Valentine! But we must remember that formerly there was something sweet and poetical in the choosing of mates. Now we are thrilled with tender emotions when poor Ophelia sings her

"Good morrow to St. Valentine's-day."

But somehow, romance dies out in our material age; and beautiful superstitions give place either to cold practical knowledge, or degenerate into farcical caricatures. What a difference between the rapturous and bashful exchange of vows pledged by the youth and maidens in good old times, before reading and writing came in fashion, and the celebrated Valentine composed by the younger Mr. Weller! The vulgarization of the custom has been gradual. Instead of the song-singing invitations to love, under cold windows,

"All in the morning betime,"

lovers began, in the course of human progress, to indite gentle missives to their sweethearts, and to receive autograph replies. This improved method was eagerly adopted by all such as dared not give verbal utterance to their sweet passion, as well as by those who had private malice to vent, and sneaking insults to offer. Then arose the manufacture and merchandise of Valentines, which has of late become so important a branch of industry.

From early in February until late in March, our toy shops and periodical and fancy "depots" appear to traffic mainly in these exceptionable articles. Their windows flame with the vulgar trash. On every corner "Valentines!" "Valentines!" stare us in the face. Some are very choice and costly; we see now and then one inlaid in a rich casket, and prized at twenty-five or even fifty dollars. Others are made of fine fancy paper, adorned with flowers in water colors, or prettily filigreed; with a scroll in the center for the verses expressive of the sender's sentiments.

But the softer heads that indulge in these expensive trifles, are comparatively few. A cheaper luxury satisfies our economical sentimentalists. All kinds of coarsely ornamented note-paper, and large square awkward envelopes, find their ready patrons. Every taste is suited, from the sickliest fastidiousness, to the most clownish ambition for flashy colors and tawdry designs.

In opposition to the sentimental Valentines, we have the gross caricatures which have done more than anything else of this kind to disgust the common sense and good taste of community. It would seem that only the most vulgar minds could be attracted by these; yet the large traffic in them shows that vulgarity is an extensive element in the popular character. No matter how indelicate and disgusting one of these specimens of low invention may be, some fool will be found to purchase it, and send it to another individual whom he either wishes to insult or expects to amuse.

In this way all sorts of printed immoralities obtain circulation. In this way cowards take revenge for imaginary slights or dignified rejections. In this way, for about two or three weeks in each year, some altogether harmless and well-meaning people have been subjected to gross annoyances and serious taxes for postage. Thanks to the law-makers, the advance pay requisition will hereafter put a stop to that species of petty swindling.

Year after year the same foolish figures and senseless mottos are forwarded from the same simpletons to the same victims. We know a musician who for three successive seasons has received that witched caricature, representing a shape—

> "If shape it could be called that shape had none,—"

all nose and moustache, blowing a trombone considerably larger than himself.

Our dentist usually enjoys a visit from a caricature suited to *his* profession—a tooth-drawer with his little head in a vast chasm representing a young lady's mouth. He has learned to expect it; he good-naturedly looks for it, about Valentine's day; and merely opening it when it comes, to see that it is the right one, he quietly tosses it into the fire.

This Valentine sending is a custom like that of a certain drunken revel once popular in Denmark,—"More honored in the breach than in the observance." It is ignored by good society. And as for the victimized, it is a mark of common sense to bestow every Valentine into the grate, unopened, as soon as received.

It is estimated that not less than half a million of these worse than worthless missives pass through the post-offices annually. The cost to the parties purchasing them, forms an aggregate of about $200,000. Over and above this expense is the postage, which is sometimes double, triple, or even four or five times the ordinary rates of single letter postage. Formerly many were unpaid, and often persons to whom they were addressed, indignantly refused to take them from the office. Thus were the mails not only uselessly encumbered with the vile trash, but quantities of the "rejected addresses" were subjected to the formality of visiting the Dead Letter Office, where they finally met with that destruction they so clearly merited. This abuse of the post-office privileges is unworthy of any nation above the capacity of monkeys.

The immoralities circulated and encouraged by Valentines cannot be estimated. Statistics would fail to arrive at the amount of vice engendered by this pernicious breed. One of the worst evils that owe their origin to this cause, is the temptation laid in the way of post-office clerks. A Valentine is often the first provocation to crime. Numerous instances have come under the observation of the writer, in which persons convicted of robbing the mails, trace back their transgressions to no more serious a fault than that of peeping into one of these silly missives. They are often carelessly sealed, and easily opened by third parties without discovery.

Imagine a young man intrusted with the care of a village post-office. He is interested in Miss A. He believes she encourages his sentiments. He hopes her proud father will some day encourage him as an eligible suitor for his daughter's hand. Still he is subject to desponding and jealous doubts. And when, one evening in the middle of February, a Valentine addressed to his paragon strikes his eye as he is assorting the mails, an indescribable pang shoots through his heart. He wonders who sent it. Tom Bellows is at first suspected, but the handwriting differs from Tom's. "Can it be Robert Cartwright?" says the distressed clerk. "He is partial to Miss A., and she seems pleased with him. What can he be writing to her?"

Such thoughts perplex the young man's brain. The Valentine is not taken from the office that evening; and when all is quiet, he draws it once more out of the box, and again examines the superscription. It is certainly Cartwright's writing. "O dear!" sighs the clerk, "how easy I could open it, and nobody know it!" Aching with curiosity, but calling moral principle and self-denial to his aid, he returns the missive to the box, and goes to bed. But sleep is out of the question. He is awake, thinking about the Valentine, and those supposed to be immediately interested therein. "I wonder if I *could* open it!" he says to himself. "I've half a mind to try."

He gets up, strikes a light, and a moment later the Valentine is in his hand. "If it comes open," says he, "I'll seal it again without reading it. I only want to see if it can be done without having it show afterwards." Instantly he starts back. The Valentine is open! Really, he did not mean to do it; it came open so much easier than he expected! Although it is night, and he is alone, he cannot help looking over his shoulder to assure himself that the grim individual watching him, exists only in his imagination. "Well," thinks he, "it's done, and who knows it? What's the harm, as long as I'm going to seal it up again?—and after all, I don't see that it will be much worse just to see if there is any name to it, provided I don't read the rest."

Thus excusing himself, he profanes the sacred interior of the missive, and finds the suspicious signature—"Robert." Trembling at the temptation to read more, he hastily folds the sheet, and returns it to the envelope. But the next moment it is out again, and he is reading with flushed cheek and burning eye, the tender words that Robert C. has written to Miss A.

"All this hath a little dashed his spirits;" and he returns to bed feverish and restless. In spite of his reason, which keeps saying stoutly, "what's the harm? nobody will know it," he suffers greatly in conscience. But the Valentine is taken from the office, and the profanation of its mystery remains unsuspected. And in a few days another Valentine appears, addressed to Robert Cartwright. The hand-writing, although disguised, is alarmingly like Miss A.'s. By this time the clerk's jealousy has eaten up his conscience.

"There's no more harm in opening two than in opening one," whispers the devil in his ear.

"I believe you," says the clerk; "but I may yet be found out."

"No danger," says the devil; "only be careful."

He is too ready to adopt the suggestion. He is excusable, he thinks, under the circumstances. The Valentine is accordingly opened and read. Deliberation and forethought add gravity to the offence. The clerk has unconsciously blunted his moral perceptions, and weakened his moral strength; and he is now prepared to open regular letters passing through his hands. At first it is jealousy and rivalry that tempt his curiosity. Then other matters of interest entice him, until one day he discovers, in no little consternation, that he has thrust his fingers into a nest of bank-notes!

"Well, after all," says he, "Mr. B. is rich; he won't mind the loss; it's only a trifle with him. While to me, the sum is considerable. If I don't keep up appearances with Bob Cartwright, I might as well be out of the world. I've a right to live; and destroying this letter and appropriating its *contents*, is just nothing at all, if I don't get found out. But I'm safe enough—I'm the very last person to be suspected."

The career of this young man need not be traced further.

Nor need the subject of Valentines be pursued. We have written enough to show that they are the offspring of weak sentimentalism or foolish buffoonery; an encumbrance to the mails, an annoyance to those who receive them, a tax to all parties, and a temptation to post-office clerks; and withal, imbecilities and immoralities which all worthy citizens should take every occasion to discountenance, and banish from civilized society.

CHAPTER XXIX.

THE CLAIRVOYANT DISCOVERY.

A SHORT time after the detection of the New Haven mail robber, a gentleman from the town of W. called upon the post master at Hartford, to say that he had some weeks since mailed a letter at the post-office in the town where he resided, addressed to a firm in Hartford; and containing a sum of money, and that the letter had never been received.

On examining his records, the post master ascertained that no bill had been received from the office where the letter was mailed corresponding with the date of the mailing, and that consequently the letter, so far as his records could show, had never reached his office.

As the time of this loss happened at the period when the mail robber was committing depredations from day to day, and as the post-bill was missing, the Hartford post master expressed the opinion that the letter had very probably fallen into the hands of the mail robber, although New Haven was off the route on which the letter should go, and the package of letters could not have got there without having been missent.

This theory was entirely unsatisfactory to the gentleman who mailed the letter, and he left Hartford with the conviction that he would be compelled to endure the loss of his money with such philosophy as he could summon to his aid.

But hope soon succeeds fear, as daylight follows darkness,

and before many days the gentleman in search of his money again called at the post-office in Hartford, that being the important port in his voyage of discovery.

It was very evident that his mind was somewhat "exercised," and the ominous tone in which he requested the post master to meet him immediately, at room No. —— at the hotel where his name was entered, made it clear that a revelation of no slight importance was about to be made.

The post master told him he would accompany him immediately, and started with his eager friend for the appointed place. During their walk nothing was said on the great subject-matter, probably because it was deemed too solemn in its nature to be broached amid the bustle and jar of a crowded street.

The hotel was soon reached, and the communicator of the "latest intelligence" ascended the stairs to the room where the gentleman accompanying him would be called on to listen to the disclosures about to be made, and take such action thereon as circumstances might seem to require.

After pointing solemnly to a chair, declaring by such dumb show that he desired the post master to be seated, and then taking a chair himself and sitting thereon so as to face the person with whom he was conversing, he deliberately asked—

"Do you believe in clairvoyance?"

What an unexpected question! And how should such a question be noticed? Certain it was that among all the laws in relation to the Post-Office Department, and the rules and regulations for its government, minute and circumstantial as they were, not one word could be found instructing the officers of this branch of Government what they should do in the matter of clairvoyance. Even Ben Franklin himself, who was "*par excellence*" the electrical Post Master General, had never issued an order bearing on this subtle subject. And here, in this hotel room, where, at a great many different times, a great many different kinds of spirits had entered a great many different kinds of persons, this official in a great business Department, dealing constantly with the practicalities of life, and without law, rules, or regulations to tell him what he should do in the emergency, was met with the question proposed, in a sepulchral voice,—"Do you believe in clairvoyance?"

Was it his duty to discuss with the questioner the "Odic force," and "Biology" and "Psychology," and all the other theories connected with the doctrines of spiritualism? Must post masters be also masters of mental science, and of things in heaven and earth never dreamed of in the philosophy of the great mass of mankind? Because they have to deal with the transmission of intelligence to different parts of the earth, must they also take charge of intelligence coming from unknown regions, "out of space, out of time?"

The question, however, was before him, and the post master replied that he had heard of some strange things connected with clairvoyance.

Seemingly satisfied with this reply, the gentleman went on to say that he had been very anxious to know what had become of his letter, and had therefore consulted a clairvoyant.

Some locations are blessed with a gifted seer, or more generally *seeress*, whose mind at inspired intervals is a complete "curiosity shop" of the universe—who can tell the whereabouts of a lost thimble or teaspoon, who can inform the anxious inquirer who committed the last murder, and who can describe to eager listeners the manner in which people conduct voiceless conversation in Saturn, and how they fight in Mars, and how they make love in Venus. Or the gifted one, descending rapidly to earth, can prescribe a remedy for any ill that flesh is heir to,—and all these wonders are performed for a moderate pecuniary compensation, and with the praiseworthy object of aiding and enlightening "suffering humanity."

Our inquiring friend was so fortunate as to reside in one of these localities, and his mission to the post master was that of rehearsing the discoveries of the Priestess.

He stated that the information given by the clairvoyant lady was so minute and distinct as to leave a strong impression of its truthfulness on his mind. That she traced the letter from the time it was put in the office—saw it placed in the mail bag, saw the bag taken from the office, saw every station where it stopped—saw it taken into the Hartford office—saw it opened there, saw a clerk take the letter, open it, and on finding that it contained a number of bank-bills, put said letter in a drawer of his, and then lock the drawer.

Farther than this, the Seeress declared that said clerk wore large whiskers, and a large gold ring, and that he resided in Front Street.

In addition to these facts the lady declared that the letter thus opened, with the bills still in it, was yet remaining in the locked drawer of the delinquent clerk.

Having carefully repeated this train of circumstantial evidence, pointing so distinctly to a certain culprit, the gentleman then commenced interrogating the head of the Hartford post-office :—

"Have you, sir," said he, "a clerk in your employment who wears whiskers ?"

The witness was compelled, on the part of some of his clerks at least, to plead guilty to this first count in the indictment from an invisible Grand Jury. As whiskers are not an expensive article of luxury, even post-office clerks can afford to wear them.

"Have you," continued the counsel for the unknown prosecutor, "a clerk who wears large whiskers *and* a large gold ring ?"

The reply to this query was not equally satisfactory, for the witness averred that his clerks were decidedly not given to jewelry; and as to gold, they felt that they could invest it more usefully than in the purchase of mammoth finger-rings.

"Have you," continued the pertinacious querist, "a clerk who lives in Front Street ?"

Here again the answer was not gratifying, for the witness

declared that to the best of his knowledge, no clerk of his had, whether with or without whiskers, or whether with or without a stupendous finger-ring, made Front Street illustrious by residing therein.

Notwithstanding the discrepancy, the gentleman went on with his inquiries:—

"Have you a clerk in your employment who has a drawer of which he keeps the key?"

The reply to this question was such as to meet the wishes of the querist, and he was told that there was more than one such clerk in his office.

"Then," said the gentleman, "I demand that you have those drawers opened, and their contents examined!"

Notwithstanding the urgent desire of the person who had reposed such confidence in the revelations of the female informer, the post master peremptorily declined to take a single step implying a doubt as to the integrity of his clerks, on the mere strength of clairvoyant testimony.

Argument was in vain, and the disappointed letter seeker left Hartford, thinking in all probability that General Pierce would have done better to have given the charge of the office there to some person more willing to accommodate the public!

Some time after this, the Special Agent met the post masters of New Haven and Hartford, in pursuance of instructions from the Department, for the purpose of distributing the funds taken from the depredator, among those who had lost by the robberies.

On examining the money found on the person of the robber, there were discovered the seven bank-bills, all of one denomination, lost by our clairvoyant-seeking friend! The bills not only agreed with his description, but, what made the case still stronger, was the fact that no other bills of the same denomination and bank were claimed by any other party.

How it was that "the Spirits" gave the distinguished seeress such a complete tissue of falsehoods, will probably remain unknown until the "new philosophy" becomes better understood, or until the Spirit of Franklin, who it is said presides over communications from the upper spheres, appoints some Special Agent to investigate the causes of failure.

The gentleman who unexpectedly regained his money, may still entertain his old affection for clairvoyance, but he cannot deny that the poet was right when he exclaimed,

> "Optics sharp it needs, I ween,
> To see what is not to be seen."

CHAPTER XXX.

POETICAL AND HUMOROUS ADDRESSES UPON LETTERS.

THE exterior, as well as the interior of a letter is sometimes made the vehicle of sentiment, affection, wit, fun, and the like, which, thus riding as outside passengers, display their beauties to the gaze of those connected with post-offices. In such instances, it may be that the writer's ideas, gushing from his pen, have overflowed their bounds, and spread themselves upon the usually dry surface of the epistle. It must be a pleasing relief to post-office clerks, wearied with the monotonous task of turning up innumerable names, to find the flowers of fancy and imagination supplanting the endless catalogue of Smiths and Browns which ordinarily meet their eyes. Below are a few specimens of these embellished addresses.

The first is probably from some home-sick miner. It was mailed at San Francisco, California. His wife and children have no doubt derived, long ere this, the pleasure which he anticipated for them, in the perusal of the letter:—

Go, sheet, and carry all my heart;
(I would that thou couldst carry me,)
Freighted with love thou wilt depart
Across the land, across the sea.

O'er thee will bend a loving face,
To thee will listen little ears;
Thou wilt be welcomed in *my place*,
And thou wilt bring both smiles and tears.

Across the land, across the sea,
  Thy homeward course thou wilt pursue,
I may not see them welcome thee,
  Yet know I well their hearts are true.

Then swiftly go, thou ocean steed;
  Roll on, ye rapid iron wheels,
Bearing away, with careless speed,
  The message that my soul reveals.

The address followed, in plain prose.

Rail road, steamboats, horses, stages,
All of you are paid your wages,
All of you, for nothing better
Than to take this little letter.
Should the document miscarry,
Uncle Sam will see "old Harry!"
To prevent this dread collision,
I present unto your vision
State, county, and between, the town,
Indiana, Nashville, Brown.
For Mrs. Jane Eliza Brent,
This is enough,—now "let her went."

Here is a specimen in a less elevated strain:—

Robber, shouldst thou seize this letter,
  Break it not; there's nothing in't,
Nought for which thou wouldst be better:
  Note of bank, or coin from mint.

There is nothing but affection,
  And perhaps a little news;
When you've read this, on reflection,
  Take or leave it as you choose.

If you should conclude to leave it,
  I would like to have it go
To Seth Jones, who will receive it
  In the town we call Glasgow,
    And the state of old Kentucky,
    (There's no rhyme for that but "lucky.")

The following seems to have been the superscription to a dun, written "more in sorrow than in anger."

A hard old hoss is Charley Cross,
  And I don't care who knows it;
He's borrowed an X, and never expects
  I'll dun him, so he goes it.

He'll find he's mistaken, and won't save his bacon,
  Unless he sends me the tin:
In the city of Penn, somewhere is his den;
  I can't tell what *state* he is in.

Perhaps he's "slewed," or may be, pursued
  By some other man he owes,
Whichever it is, when this meets his phiz,
  My account he had better close.

The street and number were subjoined; but it is to be feared that the "old hoss" proved hard-bitted, and would have nothing to do with "*checks*," except those in his favor.

Post master dear,
I greatly fear
That this letter never will go
To him I write,
Unless to your signt
The name I plainly show.

'Tis Thomas Brown,
The name of his town
Is Hartford; the county the same,
Land of steady habits,
Famed for onions and rabbits,
The place whence once I came.

This is apparently an outpouring of the sorrows of a victim to the Maine law, and was mailed in that state:—

Oh John O'Brien, half of you is better than the whole,
For that would be a Demi-John, my sorrow to console.
Oh dear O'Brien, briny tears into my whiskers roll,
To think that you live in New York, while here is not a soul
To stand treat; or in other words, to "pass the flowing bowl."

All flesh is grass: all paper's rags,
(So it is said by wicked wags.)
But I would like to pass along
Among th' epistolary throng,
Till I reach the town of Kent
Nor to a paper mill be sent,
And come to an untimely end,
Before I find my writer's friend;
Whose name is Putnam, or Sam Put,
In the old State Connecticut.

This is going to my tailor,
  A *trust*-worthy man is he;
Like a clock, for ever *ticking*,
  He keeps his account with me.

To send my bill I here request him
  For the br—ches he has made:
Thanks to good old uncle Samuel,
  He must send it on *pre-paid.*

(The address was in prose.)

When you C this letter,
You'd better letter B.
For it is going over
Unto Tom McG.
In the town of Dover,
State of Tennessee.

Address on a Valentine:

Mr. Post Master, keep this well,
for every line is going to tell
how much I love my Bill Martell,
Syracuse, N. Y.

I want this letter to go right straight
To Wilmington city in Delaware State,
To Daniel B. Woodard, a cooper by trade;
He can make as good barrels as ever were made.

Swiftly hasten, Postman's organ,
  Bear this onward to its fate,
In New York to George C. Morgan;
  John Street, No. 78.

East 10th Street, City of New York,
  Two hundred fifty-three—
Is where of all this little work,
  This moment ought to be.

And could I to the lightning's wing
  Or telegraphic wire,
Attach it by a silken string,
  'Twould be my fond desire.

But since to do the swift exploit
  Each other power must fail,
I send to Emily Bailey Hoyt,
  With pleasure—in the mail.

I know a man, his name is Dunn!
  He lives in splendid style:
But if he'd pay—say half his debts,
  He'd lose 'bout all his "*pile.*"

He stops in Charlestown, old Bay State,
  Quite near to Bunker Hill,
Where many a brave man met his fate,
  Dispensing Putnam Pill.

A VALENTINE ADDRESS.

Lizzie, they say the little birds
  Are making matches now;
(Warranted to keep in any climate.)
A good example they have set
  Which I would like to follow;
So if you have a heart to let,
  I hope to know to-morrow.

On the river Hudson,
  In the town of Troy,
Lives Miss Sarah Judson
  Full of life and joy.

'Tis for that sweet creature
  This epistle's meant;
If it does but reach her,
  I shall be content.

The following address was found on a missive which passed through the New York office on or about the 14th of February, and was secured with a seal representing Cupid taking aim at one of his victims with a revolver:

Cupid's mother has supplied him
  With "six shooters" for his bow;
When he'd arrows I defied him;
  Now, alas! he's laid me low.

Here I send, done up in paper,
  Fanny May, my heart to you.
I think you will keep it safer
  Than I've done,—so now adieu.

The town and state were in prose.

Send this, Post Master, if you are willing,
To John M. P——, a darned old villain.
Let it go without Postage Bounty,
To Union Valley, Cortland County.

Take me along in haste I pray,
To John O'Donnel without delay.
The postage is paid, there is no excuse
If I'm not delivered at Syracuse.

Let nought impede thy progress,
  While on thy journey going,
And quickly may'st thou be received,
  By John, or Pardon Bowen,
Albany, N. Y.

Miss Kate May,
Somewhere in New York City.
I hope to goodness she will receive
this missive.

John M. Simpson, Dedham,
Mill Village,
Mass.
in care of John Lee,
the man that speaks through
his nose or with the crucket foot.

For Nevel Kelly, Degrau St.,
next shanty to the river in the rear
of the grave-stone yard,
Brooklyn, N. Y.

New Haven, post-office
State of Connecticut
Brown Street
Number 58
For elen Rumford
under care of mister allen
And if the main law folks up there don't like the name of *Rum*ford
i can't help it.

---

for
Brigded Livingston no 16 post
office city Hartford, State of
Cannada or three-ways to No 39
America.

To Thos. Walsh 362 3rd Avenue
or if not there (New York
To the care of America
Jerrimiah O Droyer—No—173
South street South Troy New York
To be forwarded
To Mary Dohorty (For Thos. Walsh
(in haste America

To Mr. Leedfara, who runs the ferry
over across to Long Island for Mary
Maguire New York.

Mistress Crovor Keeps
a stand in the
hutson dippo—New York
lives in reed street.

Direct this letter to
315 Second floor
Back room for Kate
Barrey washington street
New York
in heast.

To the Lady that wears a white cloak Straw
Bonnett trimmed with Blue & wears a blue
veil, brown or striped dress
No — Bleeker street
New York.

To Don Tom Rigan
and Monseer Birch—

To New York city straight let this 'ere letter go
Right to der corner of der Bowery and Grand
Into Jim Story's place which every one must know
Onto I forgot his name's old oyester stand.
The *blades* it's intended for are hearty and frisky,
You'll find backe of der bar, where yer give dis letter.
The postman may find himself a cocktail der better.

P. O. No 9 Albany Street
Boston State of Mass for Michael
Ryan tailor and if he do not
live here i expect that the
Person who will live here will
forward this letter to him
if they chance to know
where he live.

Mister John Shane
Syracuse
No 152 Salina Street
your parents are here,
and state New York city
North America.

William Doger Syracuse
Corner of James and Warren
street undago county state
of new york—america—
care for John Burk or
Jeremiah Burk paid
or Else where

The American Girl who
wants a place, 329 Sixth
Avenue, up two flights of
Stairs, Back Room.

Thadeus M. Guerai Esqr.
son of Pat Guerai, Late Manager
of the Devon estate, County
Limerick Ireland, and husband
of Sarah Coburn Harding;
Niece of Major Harding
of Harding Grove, County
Limerick Ireland—
Care of B. Douglass & Co.
Charlestown
S. C.

33 *

CHAPTER XXXI.

ORIGIN OF THE MAIL COACH SERVICE.

THE greatest improvement in the English mail service, during the eighteenth century, was the introduction of mail coaches. This was brought about by the energy and perseverance of JOHN PALMER, ESQ. Like most of those who introduce great improvements, he was an "outsider," one unacquainted by business habits and associations, with the postal service.

At that time (about 1783) stage coaches, with passengers, traversed the country over all the principal roads, and ran from five to seven miles an hour. The mails, however, had *never* had any better conveyance than that of a horse or a gig, managed by a man or boy. The whole mail service was on a most irregular footing; mail robberies were frequent, and the speed did not average over three and a half miles an hour.

Mr. Palmer's plan was, to have the mails transferred to the stage coaches, that the swiftest conveyance which the country afforded should carry the mails. For so obvious an improvement, we would suppose that there would be little or no opposition. Parliamentary Committees were appointed, Post Masters General reported, and all the officials were against it! Statesmen took it up; the proposition was debated in Parliament; and, after many years of persevering labor, Mr. Palmer saw his plan adopted.

But opposition did not end here. There were more reports

against it, and those who opposed at first from ignorance, and a belief that no improvement would result, now kept up their opposition from a dread of being thought false prophets. But there were those who appreciated the improvement, and Mr. Palmer got a pension from Government of three thousand pounds a year for life, and afterwards a grant of fifty thousand pounds, for the benefit his improvement in the mail service had been to the revenue of the country.

We have, from a well known post-office reformer,* a nice piece of sarcasm for the special benefit of those who *oppose* great improvements, and then deny their value after they have been adopted and proved.

A report from the English Post Master General says: "From a comparison of the gross produce of inland postage for four months, and from every other comparison they have been able to make, they were perfectly satisfied that the revenue has been very considerably decreased by the plan of mail coaches."

This report gives the opinions of the Lords of the Treasury, and enlarges on the innumerable inconveniences which the change had occasioned. The great post-office reformer, forty years after this, makes the following comment:—

"Heavy must be the responsibility on those who thus persisted in folly and mischief; and wonderful is it that Mr. Palmer should have been able to beguile the Government and the legislature into sanctioning his mad career! Who was the statesman, unworthy of the name, that thus gave the rein to audacity; that thus became, in his besotted ignorance, the tool of presumption? Who stood god-father to the vile abortion, and insisted on the admission of the hideous and deformed monster into the sacred precincts of Lombard Street, the seat of perfection? His name—alas! that the lynx should be guided by the mole! that Samson should be seduced by Delilah! Palinurus allured by a dream!—his name was WILLIAM PITT."

---

* Rowland Hill, Esq.

CHAPTER XXXII.

EVASION OF THE POST-OFFICE LAWS.

Before the adoption of the present rates of postage, much ingenuity was displayed in making newspapers the vehicles of such information as should legitimately have been conveyed by letters. Various devices were employed to effect this object.

As the law strictly prohibited writing upon papers, requiring that such newspapers should be charged with letter postage, the problem was, to convey information by their means without infringing the letter of the law.

Sometimes a sentence or a paragraph was selected, some of the letters of which were crossed out in such a manner that the letters left legible conveyed the meaning which the operator intended. By such transmuting process, pugnacious editorials were converted into epistles of the mildest and most affectionate description, and public news of an important character not unfrequently contracted into a channel for the conveyance of domestic intelligence.

As the constructions of the law on this subject, by the officers of the Department, became more and more stringent, the most amusing and ingenious inventions to get beyond their reach were resorted to.

For instance, marking an advertisement or other notice, with a pen or pencil, having been declared a violation of law, attention was sometimes called to such notices, by cutting round them on three sides, thus making a sort of flap, and doubling it back on the side left uncut. In one case, which now occurs to the author, a notice served in that way, thus producing a hole in the paper, had the strikingly appropriate caption of "A good Opening!"

The vacancy produced in the paper, in such a case, of course attracted the attention of the person who received it, and *that* advertisement was sure to be read, if no other.

Hieroglyphics were sometimes employed for conveying contraband ideas. The following will answer as a specimen of this class of attempted evasions. It was neatly drawn on the margin of a newspaper which came to a Western post-office, from a town in New England.

The meaning will of course be readily understood by the reader—"Children all well!"

Such specimens of the fine arts are seldom attempted under the present low rates of postage, as the saving of two cents would hardly pay for the required time or labor. But there are those even now-a-days, who, for that paltry consideration, are found willing to compromise their consciences, if indeed they have any, by resorting to some of the less laborious methods, in attempting to carry out their prudential designs.

CHAPTER XXXIII.

POST OFFICE PAUL PRYS.

LEGISLATIVE enactments have been found no less necessary, to defend the sacredness of private correspondence from the prying eye of curiosity, than from the plundering hand of dishonesty.

There are many who would recoil from the thought of robbing a letter of its pecuniary contents, but feel no compunction at violating its secrecy for the sake of indulging an idle or a malicious inquisitiveness, if the commission of the deed can be concealed. This may not be called a common evil, and yet it exists; and it is one against which Acts of Congress have been levelled almost in vain, for there is perhaps hardly any portion of the laws of that body relative to the protection of correspondence, through the mails, about which there is felt so great a degree of security.

This violation of the first principles of decency and propriety, not unfrequently leads to results more disastrous than those which are caused even by robbery itself. The person, too, who indulges himself in this disgraceful practice, cannot be sure that he will always keep clear of more serious misdemeanors. He who pries into letters for one purpose, may be led to pry into them for another. When one has become accustomed to tampering with letter seals, he has broken through a powerful restraint to crime, and has laid himself yet more open to the assaults of temptation.

Sometimes a state of things exists in a neighborhood which clearly shows that some unauthorized person is acquainted with the contents of many of the letters passing through the post-office, before the rightful owners have received them. Secrets of the utmost importance are suddenly blazed abroad, and those of less consequence are used to inflict much annoyance upon the persons whom they concern. Those in charge of the post-office become the objects of suspicion, and the inhabitants of the infected district, if they are unable to obtain positive proof of unlawful meddling with their correspondence, at least show, by their endeavors to prevent their letters from going through the dangerous channel, that they have lost their confidence in the integrity of the post master, or of his assistants.

For instance,—Farmer Haycroft's daughter had settled the preliminaries of a treaty of the most tender description with a young gentleman of a neighboring city, though without the knowledge and contrary to the wishes of the parental potentates on both sides. Their happiness, it is clear, depended on preserving their secret inviolate. Should it come to the ears of their "potent, grave, and reverend *Seniors*," a storm of wrath might be expected like that which is seen when two clouds, heavily charged, unite in pouring out their burden of lightning, wind, and rain.

Therefore, in order to avoid such a consummation, interviews were not risked, as being too hazardous, but a correspondence was carried on under fictitious names.

Much solicitude was felt by the inquisitive matron who presided over the *Pryington* Post-Office, to know who "Elizabeth Greene" (the *nom de guerre* of the Haycroftian damsel) could be. So she cross-questioned the boy who inquired for letters for the aforesaid Elizabeth, but he was decidedly non-committal. And, as a last resort, she sent her servant-maid to follow the unwary messenger, and see where he went. She returned with the exciting intelligence that Jane

Haycroft met him and received from his hands the letter which the boy had just taken from the office.

This information but aggravated the thirst for knowledge which raged in the breast of the post mistress, and she inwardly resolved that she would in some way unravel the mystery that lurked under the name of "Elizabeth Greene."

The town was shortly after astonished with the news of the proposed "match," and as the post-office dame was not supposed to deal in *clairvoyance*, the inference was natural that some less creditable but more certain method had been adopted to bring the important fact to light.

The detection of supposed guilt in cases of this kind was formerly very difficult, and heretofore the Special Agents had rather undertake the investigation of a dozen cases of mail robbery than to attempt to unearth one of these moles, working under ground, and gnawing at the roots of their neighbor's reputation and happiness. For these Paul Prys generally leave but few traces behind them by which they may be ferreted out, however strong the grounds of suspicion may be.

Tests have been devised, however, by which these dealers in contraband knowledge may be unerringly pointed out and detected in their contemptible occupation. A letter may be opened, read, and resealed never so carefully, yet by means of these tests the opening can be satisfactorily proved, and the opener brought to justice, at least so far as a removal from office can answer the ends of punishment.

A knowledge of this secret plan rests solely with the Post Master General and his Special Agents, and it can only be communicated to the latter under the most positive injunctions of secrecy. It will be applied in all cases where there is reasonable ground for believing that correspondence has been tampered with.

The legal penalty for this offence is five hundred dollars fine, and imprisonment for twelve months.

CHAPTER XXXIV.

SPECIAL AGENTS.

THE institution of Special Agents did not originate in this country. At a comparatively early period it constituted a part of the British postal system, and these Agents are termed "Post-Office Surveyors." This corps of officials has ever been considered by the English Government one of the most important adjuncts of the Post-Office Department.

In the early history of the Department in our own country persons were occasionally employed, in cases of emergency, to act as its representatives, and to exercise temporary supervision over some of the various branches of the mail service; but the Special Agent system, as it now exists, was first organized in the year 1840, while the Hon. Amos Kendall was at the head of the Department.

The number of Special Agents in the United States has been gradually increased since their first establishment, and is now eighteen, suitably distributed throughout the country, each one having a district assigned him as the particular field of his operations, but to act elsewhere if so ordered.

It is not the intention to enter into an argument for the purpose of proving the usefulness of this branch of the Department. If this has not been shown by the facts recorded in the former part of this volume, as well as by the many prominent and familiar cases all over the country, which have been so successfully conducted by other members of the corps, it would be in vain to attempt it now. I would only say a few words respecting the power of this system, to *prevent* crime.

There are some persons in the world of firm principles and unbending rectitude, who need not the aid of outward circumstances for the maintenance of an upright character. But perhaps the majority of mankind require some external helps in the way of restraints, from public opinion, and even the threatenings of the law. On such the fear of detection frequently acts in a most salutary manner, deterring from the commission of crime, and sometimes leading to a higher motive for right conduct than apprehension of punishment.

In more than one instance, after the conclusion of some important case of depredation, I have been informed that money-letters, passing upon other routes than the ones under suspicion, and even at a considerable distance, have been regarded with a reverence never felt for them before. A portly envelope was considered a sort of Trojan horse, filled with the elements of destruction, ready to overwhelm the explorer of its treacherous recesses. This extraordinary caution was owing, of course, to the knowledge (which often gets out in spite of the utmost endeavors to prevent it) that the Special Agent was abroad; and when once a person has been thoroughly impressed with the danger of tampering with the forbidden thing, he does not soon nor easily yield to the whisperings of the tempter.

The duties of a Special Agent of the Post-Office Department involve a constant and vigilant supervision of all its interests. This embraces a much wider range of action, and requires much higher qualifications on the part of those who undertake it, than any simply "detective" service. It is believed that neither Congress nor the public generally attach such a degree of importance to the office in question as it really possesses, both in itself and in the estimation of the Department. This is perhaps owing to the fact that so great a proportion of its duties have of late been connected with the investigation of cases of depredation upon the mails. This has given the corps of Special Agents the apparent character of mere "detective officers," while in truth they are much more than this.

The qualifications which a Special Agent should possess are numerous and diverse; some, indeed, not often found in connection with one another. A high degree of shrewdness and tact is required, in order to estimate probabilities rightly, and to pursue investigations in such a way as to avoid attracting attention or exciting alarm. And an essential pre-requisite to success is a good knowledge of human nature. To calculate beforehand with correctness what a given person will do under certain circumstances, and thus to anticipate his movements, and make him subservient to the execution of your plans; to vary the mode of approach to suspected persons, according to the combinations of circumstances and the shades of character existing in the case in hand; to do all this, and much more of a like description, demands no small knowledge of the workings of the human mind.

It is comparatively an easy matter to follow up a mail robber when once upon his track, (though there is often nicety even in this,) but to collect the scattered rays of suspicion and conjecture, and to bring them together into one focus, throwing its revealing glare upon the criminal, requires a higher order of intellect than any after operations. And the caution which is always necessary in the conducting of these cases, in order to secure a successful result, is called for not only for the sake of detecting the guilty, but in order that the innocent may not suffer blame.

It often happens that circumstances of the strongest kind indicate the guilt of some person, who, notwithstanding, is entirely free from all connection with the crime. Never, perhaps, is a stronger temptation to hasty and indiscreet procedures offered than by such a state of things. Yet he who is guided by discretion, is not led away by the dazzling hope of immediate success in his investigation, but, aware how fallacious are sometimes the strongest appearances, he considers the question before him with coolness and deliberation, fully conscious of the priceless value of character, and reluctant to make any movement that might unjustly throw a shadow upon it.

From the nature of their employment, Special Agents are constantly brought in contact with the most intelligent and prominent men in the community, who justly expect to find the Post-Office Department represented by men of gentlemanly bearing, fair education, correct deportment, and sound discretion. The absence of any of these qualities, especially of all of them, would lower the standing of the Department with those whose good opinion is most valuable, and would naturally cause speculations on the reasons why persons so deficient in the qualities necessary to make them acceptable to people of discernment, should have been appointed to such a responsible post.

It would hardly be just to hold the Department responsible for the existence of all such evils, as there is always danger that the influence and diplomacy of politicians may be used for the purpose of securing appointments to persons who are unfit for them. If the time ever comes when politicians shall act upon truly patriotic principles, then we may reasonably expect that the appointing of subordinate officers of this Department will be left to those in whose power the law has placed it, undisturbed by pressure from without.

The duties of a Special Agent are often made more difficult by the thoughtlessness or curiosity of those whom he meets in the course of his official business. The maintenance of secrecy is absolutely necessary to much success in his plans. It is perfectly obvious that the measures taken to detect a rogue should be concealed from him, and it is generally no less important that he should not know that any one is on his track. The public at large, however, seem to think themselves at liberty to inquire of an Agent all about his plans; where he is going, whom he is in pursuit of, and any other matters that curiosity may suggest. Often have I been saluted, on entering an omnibus or a railroad car, with the question, "Well, H——, who has been robbing the mails now?" thus making the person of the Agent known to all within hearing, and perhaps to some from whom it were very desirable to keep such knowledge. I received a similar salutation once from a thoughtless acquaintance, in the presence of a delinquent post-office clerk whom I was watching, and to whom I was before unknown.

In country places, also, Agents are often brought to their wit's end for answers to the questions proposed, which shall be satisfactory to the querist, and keep within the bounds of truth. Sometimes they find themselves compelled, in anticipation of this annoying curiosity, to take refuge in a mercantile character, inquiring the price of butter, and other "produce." At other times, with parental solicitude, they inform themselves of the comparative merits of different boarding-schools; or they, in pursuance of their own policy, discuss policies of "Life Insurance." I was once indebted to the system alluded to for my escape from the fangs of an inquisitive landlord. In the investigations of the case then in hand, it was of the utmost importance that the presence of an Agent of the Department, on that route, should not be known. So when mine host commenced his inquiries, I informed him that I had thought of delivering a lecture on Life Insurance, and asked him whether he supposed that an audience could be got together in the village. He appeared very much interested in the matter, and offered to guarantee at least five hundred hearers for the proposed lecture. One evening, while I was in my room employed in preparing decoy letters, he called upon some errand, and, observing me at work among some papers, he said:

"Ah, at work on your lecture, are you? Well, I won't disturb you."

We went so far as to make some arrangements for the printing of hand-bills, &c., but the mental illumination which the inhabitants of the village had in prospect, was extinguished by my disappearance, accompanied by a culprit, whom it was more important to secure than even an "audience of five hundred." During the examination of the criminal, my worthy host inquired of me, with a sagacious wink, how the "Life Insurance" business flourished?

It may not be out of place here to allude to an erroneous idea respecting the powers of Special Agents, which prevails to some extent, namely, that the Agents are permitted by the Department to open letters addressed to other persons, where the interests of justice seem to require it. This is contrary to the truth. An Agent has no more power or right than any other person to open letters not belonging to him, for whatever purpose he may wish to do so. Should he see fit to break a seal, he does it at his own responsibility. The law makes no exceptions in his favor. And the Department cannot confer this power of opening letters, because no such power has been given it. The Post Master General is as accountable to the laws as any private citizen.

CHAPTER XXXV.

ROUTE AGENTS.

THIS is the designation of a very useful and indispensable class of officials, who were hardly known to the service in this country previous to the year 1839. Their introduction appears to have been contemporaneous with the employment of railroads for the transportation of the U. S. mails, and a necessary consequence of the adoption of this mode of conveyance.

The number of these Agents has been progressively increased in proportion with the extension of railroads, and they are now employed upon nearly all these roads in this country, as well as upon many of the steamboats which carry the mails.

Since 1847, they have increased as follows:—

In 1848	there	were	47
1849	"	"	61
1850	"	"	100
1851	"	"	127
1852	"	"	209
1854	"	"	260
1855	"	"	295

By the terms of contract with each railroad company, it is required to furnish a suitable car for the use of the mail or Route Agent when so requested by the Department. The

Agent occupies this traveling post-office, or mail car, receives and delivers mails along the route; assorts, and gives the proper direction to all mail matter passing through his hands; mails such letters, prepaid *by stamps*, as are handed him, and accompanies the mails in their transit between the post-office and the railroad station or steamboat, at the terminus of the route.

It is too often the case that persons of influence, in proposing a candidate for this responsible post, greatly undervalue the nature and importance of the duties to be performed, supposing that they involve merely the mechanical labor of delivering mail bags at the different post-office stations upon the route. The fact is, that the successful working of our postal machinery depends in no small degree upon the active, faithful, and intelligent discharge of the Route Agents' duties. In New England especially, and perhaps in some other sections of the country, a very large proportion of the correspondence passes through the hands of these officials, at some stage in its progress.

Much care, and a thorough knowledge of the topography of the sections of the country through which the route lies, as well as that of more distant portions, are therefore required for giving letter and other packages a direction by which they will reach their destination in the shortest possible time. And that essential preliminary, the ascertaining where a given package is to go, is a matter not always easy of accomplishment. For the most skilful interpreters of the species of chirography known as "quail tracks," are often taxed to their utmost capacity of learning and experience, in the endeavor to decipher the outside addresses of packages which they are required to "distribute" without loss of time.

Furthermore, in consequence of the improvements constantly progressing in many parts of the country, and the frequent changes in railroad, steamboat, and stage connections, resulting from that and other causes, what would be correct "distribution" one day, might not be so the next. The old adage, "The longest way round is the shortest way home," is often literally true in the sending of mail matter, for steam occupies less time in accomplishing a circuitous route of a hundred miles, than horses in passing over a direct one of twenty.

On the other hand, it sometimes happens that a long route by stage should be adopted, instead of a short one by railroad, owing to a want of the proper railroad connections.

When all these demands upon the vigilance and ability of the Route Agent are exercised, it will be obvious that it would be difficult to estimate the amount of injury that the public might receive from the employment of a careless, inefficient, or illiterate person in this position.

Among the Post Master General's instructions to Route Agents is one requiring them to receive and mail all letters written after the closing of the mail at the places where the writers reside, and before its departure. This privilege—intended solely for the accommodation of those who are prevented by unavoidable circumstances from depositing their letters in the post-office—has of late been used, or rather abused, to a degree never dreamed of by the Department. This abuse, in many cases, has proceeded to an extent which would seem to warrant the withholding of the privilege.

Tardy and indolent correspondents, who can save a few steps by taking their letters to a mail car or steamboat, instead of to the proper place of deposit, a post-office, find the hard-worked Route Agent an invention admirably calculated to facilitate the indulgence of their lazy habits, and do not scruple to avail themselves of the opportunity to the utmost extent.

There is also a numerous class who entertain feelings of hostility toward their post master for various reasons; not unfrequently from the failure of their own attempts or those of their friends to obtain the office which he holds. These persons show their resentment by withholding their mail matter from the post-office, and thus cheating the incumbent out of his lawful commissions. In carrying out this plan, they make the Route Agent an innocent accessory, by placing all their correspondence in his car just before the departure of the train, thus unnecessarily increasing his labor for the sake of gratifying their own malice.

Another class, fully persuaded of the truth of the principle that "seeing is believing," and unwilling to trust in anything less reliable than their own eyes, deposit their letters with the Agent rather than in the post-office, in order to avoid the innumerable perils which might beset them in their passage from the custody of the post master to that of the Agent! These cautious persons are not satisfied without ocular demonstration of the departure of their letters, so that if the letters should fail to reach their destination, they would still have the pleasing consciousness that they had done all in *their* power to avoid such a catastrophe.

Still another class confide their letters to the Route Agent, from a belief that letters, especially valuable ones, will thus go forward more safely and expeditiously. But this is an incorrect idea, for in the first place the pressure of other indispensable duties, such as receiving, assorting, and delivering mails, may occupy so much of the Agent's time that he will find it impossible to mail all the letters handed him, in which case they would often suffer at least a day's delay. And as to the supposed additional safety of money-letters, when sent in this way, it may be remarked that in case of a serious collision happening to the train while the letters were still loose, the chances of their loss from destruction or theft, would be much greater than if they were properly secured in a locked mail-pouch. Important losses have occurred in this way, and of course they may happen at any time.

In behalf of the Route Agents, whose duties, at best, are sufficiently arduous, the public are earnestly requested to exercise the privilege referred to only in accordance with its original intention, namely, in reference to letters which *cannot* with due diligence be mailed in the ordinary way.

Another important regulation contained in the Route Agents' instructions, is that which forbids the admission within the mail car of any one except those officially connected with the Department. The strict enforcement of this rule is well for all concerned, and should be cheerfully acquiesced in by the railroad companies and the public at large.

Nor should its application in individual cases be construed, as has sometimes been done, into a distrust of the honor or honesty of the person refused admittance. It is done simply in pursuance of a wholesome and reasonable requirement, and with the view to confine responsibility to those upon whom it is placed by the Department, and to guard against hindrances to the faithful and accurate discharge of their duty.

The faithfulness of one of the Route Agents, in respect to a compliance with Instructions, was a few years since tested by the Post Master General in person, who happened to be travelling *incog.*, so far as those on that train were concerned.

Just as the cars were about to leave one of the stations, Judge HALL, then Post Master General, presented himself at the door of the mail apartment, when the following conversation occurred:—

Post Master General.—Good morning, sir; I would like a seat in your car to avoid the dust.

Agent.—Well, I would like to accommodate you, but you see what my Instructions say, (at the same time pointing to the printed Circular posted up in the car, with the signature of "N. K. HALL" attached.)

P. M. General.—Yes, that is all well enough, but Mr. Hall probably did not mean to exclude honorable gentlemen who would not interfere with the mails, or annoy you with conversation.

Agent.—(Scanning the person of his unknown visiter pretty closely)—Suppose he didn't, what evidence have I that you are an honorable gentleman? Besides, I am a strict constructionist, and the order says no person is allowed here except those connected with the Department.

Judge Hall insisted upon staying, however, and deliberately took a seat in the only chair on the premises. Whereupon the Agent proceeded to call the baggage-master to assist in forcibly ejecting this persevering customer; and he certainly would have *gone out,* had he not without loss of time presented his card to the incensed Agent, just in time to prevent so ludicrous a denouement.

He was warmly commended for his faithfulness, and highly enjoyed the visit of his distinguished guest during the remainder of his stay.

CHAPTER XXXVI.

DECOY LETTERS.

THOSE who may have perused the preceding pages of this work, will require no further comment on the nature and utility of decoy letters. But as some persons are met with who, without much reflection, condemn their use under all circumstances, it may be well to offer a few remarks in defence of this practice.

It is very clear that decoy letters can never injure honest men. These missives trouble no one who does not unlawfully meddle with them, and it can hardly be claimed that they offer any greater temptations to the dishonestly inclined than any other class of money-letters. It is of course impossible for any one to distinguish between a decoy letter and a genuine one, and he who faithfully discharges his duties in reference to other letters, will never find out by his own personal experience, that there are such things as decoys.

It should not be forgotten that these devices are employed for the public good, and that the security of a vast amount of property, as well as the removal of unjust suspicion, often depends upon the detection of some delinquent post-office employé. In such a case, it would surely be foolishly fastidious to object to the adoption of a method of effecting the desired end, which accurately distinguishes between the innocent and the guilty, and which does injustice to no one.

In the defence of criminals tried in the United States

Courts, for mail robbery, whose detection has been effected by means of decoy letters, especially in cases where there seems to be no other ground of defence, it is frequently insisted on very eloquently, that as the law of Congress on this subject provides against the embezzlement of letters "intended to be conveyed by post," no offence is committed by the purloining of decoys, inasmuch as this class of epistles are not *bonâ fide* letters, and are not intended to be conveyed in the mail, within the true intent and meaning of the statute.

This position has been overthrown, however, as often as it has been assumed, and it is believed that the decisions on this point, of all the United States Judges before whom the question has been raised, have been uniform throughout the country.

In a recent important trial in the city of New York, before his Honor Judge Betts, the decoy system received a severe hetchelling from the learned counsel for the prisoner, and after the evidence had been laid before the jury, the Court was asked to dismiss the case and the culprit, on the ground that the offence provided against in the twenty-first section of the Act of 1825, had not been committed.

But his Honor took a very different view of the matter, as will appear by the following extract from his decision:—

Judge Betts remarked to the jury that the facts upon which the indictment is found being uncontroverted, the question of the prisoner's guilt depends solely upon points of law.

When facts are ascertained, it is the province of the Court to determine whether they come within the provisions of the law sought to be applied to them; and, although in criminal cases the jury gives a general answer, covering both the law and fact, to the inquiry whether the accused is guilty or not guilty, it is not to be supposed they will, in a case resting wholly upon a question of law, render a verdict in opposition to the instructions of the Court. The defence of the accused assumes that the twenty-first section above recited, in order to a conviction under it, demands affirmative proof from the prosecution that the letters were *intended to be conveyed by post,* according to their address: And it is urged that such proof not being made, but on the contrary, the evidence being that the writer of the letters did not intend they should be so delivered, but meant to take them out of the mail himself, to prevent their delivery, if they were not embezzled in the office in this city, the acts done by the accused are no offence under the statute.

I think that construction of the statute cannot be maintained in respect to letters actually in the mail, and especially in this case, where the letters had been conveyed by post and came into this office by the mail from other offices.

It is a presumption of law, and not a matter of proof, that letters so circumstanced, were intended to be conveyed by post. The question of intention is no longer referable to the private purpose of the writer, whatever might be the fact when letters are given to persons employed in the Post-Office Department, out of the office, for the purpose of being put into it or conveyed by mail.

When, however, a letter already in the mail is purloined, (1 McLean R. 504; 2 Id. 434,) or is embezzled by a carrier on the route, (1 Curtis R. 367,) it is, in judgment of law, intended to be conveyed by post, within the meaning of the statute, and the private purpose and intention of the person who put it in the mail, is in no way material, and need not be proved.

Nor indeed, if the accused can prove, or it is made to appear upon the evidence of the prosecution, that the letter was placed in the mail or came into a post-office, prepared and intended as a decoy, and was not intrusted to the mail in the way of bonâ fide correspondence, is the criminality of taking it thereby absolved: even if the evidence advances another stage, and shows that the decoy was aimed at and intended for the particular person caught by it, (*The United States* v. *Laurence*, 2 McLean R. 441; *The United States* v. *Foye*, 1 Curtis R. 307–8.)

These decisions enforce the manifest policy of the statute. The post-office establishment, and the enactments maintaining the security of its action and the fidelity of persons employed in it, compose a great national measure, and the laws governing and protecting it are to be construed so as to subserve the public good, and not with a view to what might be a reasonable rule in transactions between individuals. But I apprehend that even in individual transactions, the agents of a bank, a merchant's clerk, or a domestic servant could not protect themselves against a criminal or civil charge of appropriating the effects of their employers, by proof that the property had been placed within their reach by its owner, in distrust of their honesty, and for the purpose of testing it.

The method adopted by the Department to detect offenders under this law, does not appear to me objectionable in the point of view pressed by the counsel for the accused. No further temptation or facility to the commission of the offence is thereby placed before such offenders than must necessarily be presented in the daily business of their trusts. These packages were in every respect the same in appearance, and with only the same indications of enclosing money, as ordinary letters by which remittances are made. And it seems to me when it comes to be understood by persons handling such packages in the mail or destined for it, that a watchful eye may be following each package from office to office, and noticing everything done to it, that the apprehension of such supervision may act almost with the force of a religious consciousness of accountability, in awing wicked purposes and preventing criminal actions.

I am persuaded that letters would rarely be intercepted in their transmission by post, if every person concerned in mailing or carrying them, could be impressed with the idea that each package enclosing valuables, may be but a bait seeking to detect whoever may be dishonest enough to molest it, and to become a swift witness for his conviction and punishment.

The jury convicted the prisoner, and on the 29th day of December, 1854, he was sentenced to ten years' imprisonment.

SUPPLEMENTARY CHAPTER.

PRACTICAL INFORMATION.

THE design of the author, in the preparation of the present volume, would be but imperfectly answered, were he to fail to communicate that practical information which it is very desirable that the public at large should possess, both for their own sake and that of those connected with the mail service. For, an accurate knowledge of the requirements of the law upon leading points, would obviate much of the disappointment and unpleasant feeling to which mistaken views on the subject give rise. There are popular errors on many matters connected with post-office regulations which are every day causing trouble and vexation, and which can only be corrected by presenting the facts as they are.

This information is not accessible to the public in general; at least, it is out of the way, and is not kept before the people. The Department publishes, at irregular intervals, an edition of its laws and regulations for the use of post masters, each of whom is supplied with a copy; and this, with the exception of the ordinary newspaper record of the laws as they are passed, is the only source of information upon this subject open to people in general. The detail of regulations established by the Department, seldom finds its way into the papers, and correspondents are left to acquire their knowledge respecting it by (sometimes sad) experience.

It is the intention of the author to supply these deficiencies in part at least, avoiding, however, all laws and regulations likely to be changed by legislation, or the constructions put upon them by the chief officers appointed from time to time to administer those laws.

Post masters being already provided with the official instructions pertaining to their duties, a repetition here is deemed unnecessary farther than a knowledge of the laws and regulations may be essential to the public.

For the items of information presented below, the author relies in part on the suggestions of his own experience, but they are mainly compiled from the established regulations of the Post-Office Department, and such of the decisions of its chief officers as are likely to remain permanently in force :—

MISSING LETTERS, ETC.

That the loss or delay of letters, valuable or otherwise, is often caused by the dishonesty or carelessness of those to whose custody they are committed, must be acknowledged. Still, in a large proportion of such cases, the cause is to be found in some one or a combination of those curious omissions and mistakes to which all correspondents—but more especially men deeply involved in business pursuits—are so liable. The records of the Dead Letter Office, if consulted, would present a list of delinquents in this particular, embracing the names of hundreds of individuals and firms, ranking as the most exact and systematic persons in the community.

A similar examination of the official reports of the Special Agents and post masters, would further show to what an extent such losses are attributable to a want of fidelity and proper care on the part of persons employed to convey letters to and from the post-office. Suggestions as to the remedies are hardly called for.

So far as relates to misdirections, as they are most apt to occur with persons and mercantile houses of extensive correspondence, an excellent precaution may be found, in requiring the post-office messenger, after the letters have been prepared for the mail, to enter in a book kept for that purpose, the full outside address of each letter, with the date of mailing. In case any one of them is incorrectly addressed, and fails to reach its intended destination, a reference to the book of superscriptions will show where the missing document was sent, and lead to its immediate recovery. If correctly addressed, that fact would appear, and materially aid in an official investigation.

This, together with the adoption of a greater degree of care than is at present exercised, in the selection of persons to act as private letter carriers, would greatly reduce the number of losses, mishaps, and complaints in connection with the mails. Where it is possible, but one person should be sent to the post-office.

The name of the writer or firm, written or printed on the letter, is an advantage in case of miscarriage.

When a valuable letter is missing from any cause, the fact should be at once reported to the post master, in writing, with full particulars, and a search made by the complainants, of the pockets of any spare overcoats about the premises.

Where letters are delivered by a public letter carrier, or penny post, a locked box or some other safe place of deposit for the letters thus left, should be provided. A neglect of this precaution, is the cause of many annoyances and losses.

The address of letters intended for delivery in cities, should include, if possible, the occupation, street and number of the party addressed.

When a letter is, by mistake or owing to a duplicate name, delivered to the wrong person, it should be immediately returned to the post-office with a verbal explanation, and not be dropped into the letter box. If inadvertently opened by the party taking it from the office, the fact should be endorsed on the back of the letter, with the name of the opener.

Experience has shown that locked letter boxes or drawers opening on the outside, especially in cities and large towns, are unsafe, as depositories of letters, especially those containing articles of value.

No letters should be given to Route Agents upon the cars or steamboats, except such as cannot be written before the closing of the mail at the post-office. Under no circumstances can Route Agents receive letters that are not pre-paid *by stamps.*

When there are good grounds for believing that letters are opened and read from motives of curiosity, complaint should be made in writing to the Chief Clerk of the Post-Office Department, Washington. A secret plan for the certain detection of *prying* delinquents has recently been devised.

Two or more letters directed to different persons, cannot be sent by mail in one envelope or packet, without subjecting the sender to a fine of ten dollars. This does not apply to any letter or packet directed to a foreign country.

Costly and delicate articles of jewelry or other valuables, should not be placed in a letter, as they are liable to serious injury in the process of stamping.

It is a violation of law to enclose a letter or other thing (except bills and receipts for subscription,) or to make any memorandum in writing, or to print any word or communication, after its publication, upon any newspaper, pamphlet, magazine, or other printed matter. The person addressed must pay letter postage, or the sender be fined five dollars.

If a letter is deposited in a post-office, and the enclosure accidentally omitted, or it becomes necessary to alter or add to the contents, it is much better to *write another letter*, than to trouble those in the office to look for the original one. In large places, especially, a successful search for it, even immediately after its deposit, would consume much valuable time, and such a request is altogether unreasonable, when the remedy suggested is so simple and cheap.

On calling or sending for a letter known to have been advertised, the fact should always be stated, otherwise only the *current* letters are examined.

Although it is strictly the duty of post masters and other agents of the Department, to correct or report such errors in the mail service as may come to their knowledge, it is, nevertheless, desirable that any private citizen should inform the Department of continued neglect or carelessness in the execution of mail contracts or mismanagement in a post-office.

Legal provision has been made by Congress, by which letters may be sent *out* of the mail in cases of emergency. By the use of the Government envelope, *with the stamp printed thereon*, and constituting a part thereof, letters may be so sent, provided the envelope is duly sealed, directed, and addressed, and the date or receipt or transmission of such letter written or stamped thereon. The use of such envelope more than once, subjects the offender to a fine of fifty dollars.

A letter or ordinary envelope with a postage stamp *put on* by the writer, *cannot* go out of the mail (except by private hand,) for the reason that the law confines the matter entirely to the envelopes furnished by the Department. Were the privilege extended to the other kind of stamps, there being no way to cancel them, by their re-use, extensive frauds upon the revenue would be the result.

A singular notion seems long to have prevailed that it is no violation of law to send an *unsealed* letter outside of the mail. This makes no difference whatever. Even if the paper written upon is not folded, it is a letter.

Where bundles of newspapers are sent in the mail to "clubs," without the names of the subscribers upon the papers, the post master is under no official obligation to address them. Still the Department enjoins a spirit of courtesy and accommodation towards publishers and the public, in all such matters.

A person receiving a letter from the post-office by mistake, or finding one in the street or elsewhere, can under no pretence designedly break the seal without subjecting himself to a severe penalty.

A printed business card or the name of the sender, placed upon the outside of a circular, subjects it to double postage; and for any writing, except the address, letter postage is charged.

The following are among the established rules and regulations of the Department founded upon existing statutes of Congress:—

Only the dead letters containing enclosures of value, are required by law to be preserved and returned to their owners; but if the writer of a letter not containing an enclosure of value desires to have his letter preserved, it will be done if he pre-pay the letter and mark the words "to be preserved," in large characters, on the sealed side. Upon the return of his letter he will be required to pay the postage from Washington.

The masters of steamboats under contract with the Department, will deliver into the post-offices (or to the route or local agent of the Department, if there be any,) at the places at which they arrive, all letters received by them, or by any person employed on their boats, at any point along the route.

Masters or managers of all other steamboats, are required by law, under a penalty of thirty dollars, to deliver all letters brought by them, or within their care or power, addressed to, or destined for, the places at which they arrive, to the post masters at such places: *except letters relating to some part of the cargo*, and left unsealed. All letters not addressed to persons to whom the cargo, or any part of it, is consigned, are therefore to be delivered into the post-office, to be charged with postage.

Every master of a vessel from a foreign port is bound, immediately on his arrival at a port, and before he can report, make entry, or break bulk, under a penalty not to exceed $100, to deliver into the post-office all letters brought in his vessel, directed to any person in the United States, or the Territories thereof, which are under his care or within his power, except such letters as relate to the cargo or some part thereof.

Stage coaches, railroad cars, steamboats, packetboats, and all other vehicles or vessels performing regular trips at stated periods, on a post route between two or more cities, towns, or places, from one to the other, on which the United States mail is regularly conveyed under the authority of the Post-Office Department, are prohibited from transporting or conveying, otherwise than in the mail, any letter, packet, or packets of letters, (except those sealed and addressed and prepaid by stamped envelopes, of suitable denominations,) or other mailable matter whatsoever, except such as may have relation to some part of the cargo of such steamboat, packetboat, or other vessel, or to some article at the same time conveyed by such stage, railroad car, or some vehicle, and excepting also, newspapers, pamphlets, magazines, and periodicals.

A newspaper, pamphlet, circular, or other printed sheet, if in a wrapper, should be so folded and wrapped that its character can be readily determined; and so that any prohibited writing, marks, or signs upon it may easily be detected. If closely enveloped and sealed it is chargeable with letter postage.

No post master or other privileged person can authorize his assistant, clerk, or any other person to write his name for the purpose of franking any letter, public or private.

The personal privilege of franking travels with the person possessing it, and can be exercised in but one place at the same time.

No post master or privileged person can leave his frank behind him upon envelopes to cover his correspondence in his absence.

Money and other valuable things, sent in the mail, are at the risk of the owner. But, if they be lost, the Department will make every effort in its power to discover the cause, and, if there has been a theft, to punish the offender.

Letters can be registered on the payment of the registry fee of five cents for each letter.

Post masters, assistants, and clerks, regularly employed and engaged in post-offices, and also post riders and drivers of mail stages, are by law exempt from military duty and serving on juries, and from any fine or penalty for neglect thereof.—*Act of* 1825, *sec.* 35 ; *Act of* 1836, *sec.* 34.

A post master will suffer no person whatever, except his duly sworn assistants, or clerks and letter carriers, who may also have been sworn, to have access to the letters, newspapers, and packets in his office, or whatever constitutes a part of the mail, or to the mail locks or keys.

If no special order upon the subject has been made in regard to his office, a post master is allowed seven minutes only to change the mail.

If the mail be carried in a stage, coach, or sulky, it will be the duty of the driver to deliver it as near the door of the post-office as he can come with his vehicle, but not to leave his horses, and he should not be permitted to throw the mail on the ground.

Post masters will not suffer newspapers to be read in their offices by persons to whom they are not addressed; nor to be lent out in any case, without permission of the owners.

If newspapers are not taken out of the office by the person to whom they are addressed, the post master will give immediate notice to the publishers, and of the cause thereof if known.

Packets of every description, weighing more than four pounds, are to be excluded, except public documents, printed by order of either House of Congress, or such publications or books as have been or may be published, procured, *or purchased*, by order of either House of Congress, or joint resolution of the two Houses, and legally franked.

Newspapers and periodicals to foreign countries (particularly to the continent of Europe) must be sent in narrow bands, open at the sides or end; otherwise they are chargeable there with letter postage.

Drop and box letters, circulars, free packets containing printed documents, speeches, or other printed matter, are not to be advertised.

If newspapers are carried out of the mail for sale or distribution, post masters are not bound to receive and deliver them. Pamphlets and magazines for immediate distribution to subscribers cannot be so carried without a violation of the law of Congress.

The great mails are to be closed at all distributing offices not more than one hour before the time fixed for their departure ; and all other mails at those offices, and all mails at all other offices, not more than half an hour before that time, unless the departure is between 9 o'clock, P. M., and 5, A. M., in which case the mail is to be closed at 9, P. M.

Postage stamps and stamped envelopes, may be used in pre-payment of postage on letters to foreign countries, in all cases where such pre-payment can be made in money.

A letter bearing a stamp, cut or separated from a stamped envelope, cannot be sent through the mail as a pre-paid letter. Stamps so cut or separated from stamped envelopes lose their legal value.

It is expected that a disposition to accommodate will prompt a post master to search for and deliver a letter, on the application of a person who cannot call during the usual office hours.

No person can hold the office of post master, who is not an actual resident of the city or town wherein the post-office is situated, or within the delivery of the office.—*Sec.* 36 *of Act of* 1836.

Letter postage is to be charged on all hand-bills, circulars, or other printed matter which shall contain any manuscript writing whatever.

When the mail stops over night where there is a post-office, it must be kept in the office.

Any person wishing a letter mailed direct, and not to be remailed at a distributing office, can have his directions followed by writing the words "mail direct" upon the letter.

The use of canvas bags of any kind, for any other purposes than the conveyance of mail matter, subjects every person so offending, to all the penalties provided in the 4th section of the Act of 1852. Contractors, mail carriers, and others in the service of the Department, are by no means free from censure in this respect, and increased vigilance in the detection of such practices, and the prompt and indiscriminate punishment of the offenders, have recently been enjoined by the Post Master General.

Some of the laws are often violated by persons not connected with the post-office, and it is proper, therefore, that all classes should be made acquainted with the penalties which attach to such offences. For this reason the following extracts from the laws are here inserted :—

Act of 1825.

SEC. 9. *And be it further enacted*, That if any person shall, knowingly and wilfully, obstruct or retard the passage of the mail, or of any driver or carrier, or of any horse or carriage, carrying the same, he shall, upon conviction for every such offence, pay a fine not exceeding one hundred dollars; and if any ferryman shall, by wilful negligence, or refusal to transport the mail across any ferry, delay the same, he shall forfeit and pay, for every ten minutes that the same shall be so delayed, a sum not exceeding ten dollars.

SEC. 21. *And be it further enacted*, That if any person employed in any of the departments of the post-office establishment, shall unlawfully detain, delay, or open any letter, packet, bag, or mail of letters, with which he shall be intrusted, or which shall have come to his possession, and which are intended to be conveyed by post; or, if any such person shall secrete, embezzle, or destroy any letter or packet intrusted to such person as aforesaid, and which shall not contain any security for, or assurance relating to money, as hereinafter described, every such offender, being thereof duly convicted, shall, for every such offence, be fined, not exceeding three hundred dollars, or imprisoned, not exceeding six months, or both, according to the circumstances and aggravation of the offence. And if any person, employed as aforesaid, shall secrete, embezzle, or destroy any letter, packet, bag, or mail of letters, with which he or she shall be intrusted, or which shall have come to his or her possession, and are intended to be conveyed by post, containing any bank-note or bank post bill, bill of exchange, warrant of the Treasury of the United States, note of assignment of stock in the funds, letters of attorney for receiving annuities or dividends, or for selling stock in the funds, or for receiving the interest thereof, or any letter of credit, or note for, or relating to, payment of moneys, or any bond, or warrant, draft, bill, or promissory note, covenant, contract, or agreement whatsoever, for, or relating to, the payment of money, or the delivery of any article of value, or the performance of any act, matter, or thing, or any receipt, release, acquittance, or discharge of, or from, any debt, covenant, or demand, or any part thereof, or any copy of any record of any judgment or decree in any court of law, or chancery, or any execution which may have issued thereon, or any copy of any other record, or any other article of value, or any writing representing the same; or if any such person employed as aforesaid, shall steal, or take, any of the same out of any letter, packet, bag, or mail of letters, that shall come to his or her possession, such person shall, on conviction for any such offence, be imprisoned not less than ten years, nor exceeding twenty-one years; and if any person who shall have taken charge of the mails of the United States, shall quit or desert the same before such person delivers it into the post-office kept at the termination of the route, or some known mail carrier, or agent of the General Post-Office, authorized to receive the same, every such person, so offending, shall forfeit and pay a sum not exceeding five hundred dollars for every such offence; and if any person concerned in carrying the mail of the United States, shall collect, receive, or carry any letter, or packet, or shall cause or procure the same to be done, contrary to this act, every such offender shall forfeit and pay, for every such offence, a sum not exceeding fifty dollars.

SEC. 22. *And be it further enacted,* That if any person shall rob any carrier of the mail of the United States, or other person intrusted therewith, of such mail, or of part thereof, such offender or offenders shall, on conviction, be imprisoned not less than five years, nor exceeding ten years; and, if convicted a second time of a like offence, he or they shall suffer death; or, if, in effecting such robbery of the mail, the first time, the offender shall wound the person having custody thereof, or put his life in jeopardy, by the use of dangerous weapons, such offender or offenders shall suffer death. And if any person shall attempt to rob the mail of the United States, by assaulting the person having custody thereof, shooting at him or his horse or mule, or threatening him with dangerous weapons, and the robbery is not effected, every such offender, on conviction thereof, shall be punished by imprisonment, not less than two years nor exceeding ten years. And, if any person shall steal the mail, or shall steal or take from, or out of, any mail, or from, or out of any post-office, any letter or packet; or, if any person shall take the mail, or any letter or packet therefrom, or from any post-office, whether with or without the consent of the person having custody thereof, and shall open, embezzle, or destroy any such mail, letter, or packet, the same containing any article of value, or evidence of any debt, due, demand, right, or claim, or any release, receipt, acquittance, or discharge, or any other article, paper, or thing, mentioned and described in the twenty-first section of this act; or, if any person shall, by fraud or deception, obtain from any person having custody thereof, any mail, letter, or packet, containing any article of value, or evidence thereof, or either of the writings referred to, or next above-mentioned, such offender or offenders, on conviction thereof, shall be imprisoned, not less than two, nor exceeding ten years. And, if any person shall take any letter or packet, not containing any article of value, nor evidence thereof, out of a post-office, or shall open any letter, or packet, which shall have been in a post-office, or in custody of a mail carrier, before it shall have been delivered to the person to whom it is directed, with a design to obstruct the correspondence, to pry into another's business or secrets; or shall secrete, embezzle, or destroy any such mail, letter, or packet, such offender, upon conviction, shall pay, for every such offence, a sum not exceeding five hundred dollars, and be imprisoned not exceeding twelve months.

SEC. 23. *And be it further enacted*, That if any person shall rip, cut, tear, burn, or otherwise injure, any valise, portmanteau, or other bag, used, or designed to be used, by any person acting under the authority of the Post Master General, or any person in whom his powers are vested, in a conveyance of any mail, letter, packet, or newspaper, or pamphlet, or shall draw or break any staple, or loosen any part of any lock, chain, or strap, attached to, or belonging to any such valise, portmanteau, or bag, with an intent to rob, or steal any mail, letter, packet, newspaper, or pamphlet, or to render either of the same insecure, every such offender, upon conviction, shall, for every such offence, pay a sum not less than one hundred dollars, nor exceeding five hundred dollars, or be imprisoned not less than one year, nor exceeding three years, at the discretion of the court before whom such conviction is had.

SEC. 24. *And be it further enacted*, That every person, who, from and after the passage of this act, shall procure, and advise, or assist, in the doing or perpetration of any of the acts or crimes by this act forbidden, shall be subject to the same penalties and punishments as the persons are subject to, who shall actually do or perpetrate any of the said acts or crimes, according to the provisions of this act.

SEC. 45. *And be it further enacted*, That if any person shall buy, receive, or conceal, or aid in buying, receiving, or concealing, any article mentioned in the twenty-first section of this act, knowing the same to have been stolen or embezzled from the mail of the United States, or out of any post-office, or from any person having the custody of the said mail, or the letters sent or to be sent therein; or if any person shall be accessory after the fact to any robbery of the carrier of the mail of the United States, or other person intrusted therewith, of such mail, or of part thereof, every person, so offending, shall, on conviction thereof, pay a fine not exceeding two thousand dollars, and be imprisoned and confined to hard labor for any time not exceeding ten years. And such person or persons, so offending, may be tried and convicted without the principal offender being first tried, provided such principal offender has fled from justice, or cannot be found to be put on his trial.

Act of 1836.

SEC. 38. *And be it further enacted*, That if any person shall be accessory after the fact, to the offence of stealing or taking the mail of the United States, or of stealing or taking any letter or packet, or enclosure in any letter or packet sent or to be sent in the mail of the United States, from any post-office in the United States, or from the mail of the United States, by any person or persons whatever, every person so offending as accessory, shall, on conviction thereof, pay a fine not exceeding one thousand dollars, and be imprisoned for a term not exceeding five years; and such accessory after the fact may be tried, convicted, and punished in the district in which his offence was committed, though the principal offence may have been committed in another district, and before the trial of the principal offender: *Provided*, such principal offender has fled from justice, or cannot be arrested to be put upon his trial.

Sec. 28, *Act of* 1825.

* * * And if any person shall counterfeit the hand-writing or frank of any person, or cause the same to be done, in order to avoid the payment of postage, each person, so offending, shall pay, for every such offence, five hundred dollars.

Sec. 5, *Act of* 1845.

And be it further enacted, That if any person or persons shall forge or counterfeit, or shall utter or use knowingly, any counterfeit stamp of the Post-Office Department of the United States issued by authority of this act or by any other act of Congress, within the United States, or the post-office stamp of any foreign Government, he shall be adjudged guilty of felony, and, on conviction thereof in any court having jurisdiction of the same, shall undergo a confinement at hard labor for any length of time not less than two years, nor more than ten, at the discretion of the court.

Sec. 11, *Act of* 1847.

* * * And any person who shall falsely and fraudulently make, utter, or forge any postage stamp with the intent to defraud the Post-Office Department, shall be deemed guilty of felony, and on conviction shall be subject to the same punishment as is provided in the twenty-first section of the act approved the third day of March, eighteen hundred and twenty-five, entitled "An act to reduce into one the several acts establishing and regulating the Post-Office Department."

Act of 1851.

Sec. 3. * * * And any person who shall forge or counterfeit any postage stamp provided or furnished under the provisions of this or any former act, whether the same are impressed or printed on or attached to envelopes or not, or any die, plate, or engraving therefor, or shall make or print, or knowingly use or sell, or have in his possession with intent to use or sell, any such false, forged, or counterfeited die, plate, engraving, or postage stamp, or who shall make or print, or authorize or procure to be made or printed, any postage stamps of the kind provided and furnished by the Post Master General as aforesaid, without the especial authority and direction of the Post-Office Department, or who, after such postage stamps have been printed, shall, with intent to defraud the revenues of the Post-Office Department, deliver any postage stamps to any person or persons other than such as shall be authorized to receive the same, by an instrument of writing duly executed under the hand of the Post Master General, and the seal of the Post-Office Department, shall, on conviction thereof, be deemed guilty of felony, and be punished by a fine not exceeding five hundred dollars, or by imprisonment not exceeding five years, or by both such fine and imprisonment.

SEC. 4. * * * And if any person shall use or attempt to use in prepayment of postage, any postage stamp which shall have been before used for like purposes, such person shall be subject to a penalty of fifty dollars for every such offence, to be recovered in the name of the United States, in any court of competent jurisdiction.

Sec. 30, *Act of* 1825.

* * * If any person employed in any department of the post-office, shall improperly detain, delay, embezzle, or destroy, any newspaper, or shall permit any other person to do the like, or shall open, or permit any other to open, any mail, or packet, of newspapers, not directed to the office where he is employed, such offender shall, on conviction thereof, forfeit a sum not exceeding fifty dollars, for every such offence. And if any person shall open any mail or packet of newspapers, or shall embezzle or destroy the same, not being directed to such person, or not being authorized to receive or open the same, such offender shall, on conviction thereof, pay a sum not exceeding twenty dollars for every such offence. And if any person shall take, or steal, any packet, bag, or mail of newspapers, from, or out of any post-office, or from any person having custody thereof, such person shall, on conviction, be imprisoned, not exceeding three months, for every such offence, to be kept at hard labor during the period of such imprisonment. If any person shall enclose or conceal a letter, or other thing, or any memorandum in writing, in a newspaper, pamphlet, or magazine, or in any package of newspapers, pamphlets, or magazines, or make any writing or memorandum thereon, which he shall

have delivered into any post-office, or to any person for that purpose, in order that the same may be carried by post, free of letter postage, he shall forfeit the sum of five dollars for every such offence.

Act of 1845.[1]

SEC. 9. *And be it further enacted,* That it shall not be lawful for any person or persons to establish any private express or expresses for the conveyance, nor in any manner to cause to be conveyed, or provide for the conveyance or transportation, by regular trips, or at stated periods or intervals, from one city, town, or other place, to any other city, town, or place, in the United States, between and from and to which cities, towns, or other places, the United States mail is regularly transported, under the authority of the Post-Office Department, of any letters, packets, or packages of letters, or other matter properly transmittable in the United States mail, except newspapers, pamphlets, magazines, and periodicals; and each and every person offending against this provision, or aiding and assisting therein, or acting as such private express, shall, for each time any letter or letters, packet or packages, or other matter properly transmittable by mail, except newspapers, pamphlets, magazines, and periodicals, shall or may be, by him, her, or them, or through his, her, or their means or instrumentality, in whole or in part, conveyed or transported contrary to the true intent, spirit, and meaning of this section, forfeit and pay the sum of one hundred and fifty dollars.

SEC. 10. *And be it further enacted,* That it shall not be lawful for any stage coach, railroad car, steamboat, packetboat, or other vehicle or vessel, nor any of the owners, managers, servants, or crews of either, which regularly perform trips at stated periods on a post route, or between two or more cities, towns, or other places, from one to the other of which the United States mail is regularly conveyed under the authority of the Post-Office Department, to transport or convey, otherwise than in the mail, any letter or letters, packet or packages of letters, or other mailable matter whatsoever, except such as may have relation to some part of the cargo of such steamboat, packetboat, or other vessel, or to some article at the same time conveyed by the same stage coach, railroad car, or other vehicle, and excepting also, newspapers, pamphlets, magazines, and periodicals; and for every such offence, the owner or owners of the stage coach, railroad car, steamboat, packetboat, or other vehicle or vessel, shall forfeit and pay the sum of one hundred dollars; and the driver, captain, conductor, or person having charge of any such stage coach, railroad car, steamboat, packetboat, or other vehicle or vessel, at the time of the commission of any such offence, and who shall not at that time be the owner thereof, in whole or in part, shall, in like manner, forfeit and pay, in every such case of offence, the sum of fifty dollars.

SEC. 11. *And be it further enacted*, That the owner or owners of every stage coach, railroad car, steamboat, or other vehicle or vessel, which shall, with the knowledge of any owner or owners, in whole or in part, or with the knowledge or connivance of the driver, conductor, captain, or other person having charge of any such stage coach, railroad car, steamboat, or other vessel or vehicle, convey or transport any person or persons acting or employed as a private express for the conveyance of letters, packets, or packages of letters, or other mailable matter, and actually in possession of such mailable matter, for the purpose of transportation, contrary to the spirit, true intent, and meaning of the preceding sections of this law, shall be subject to the like fines and penalties as are hereinbefore provided and directed in the case of persons acting as such private expresses, and of persons employing the same; but nothing in this act contained shall be construed to prohibit the conveyance or transmission of letters, packets, or packages, or other matter, to any part of the United States, by private hands, no compensation being tendered or received therefor in any way, or by a special messenger employed only for the single particular occasion.

SEC. 12. *And be it further enacted*, That all persons whatsoever who shall, after the passage of this act, transmit by any private express, or other means by this act declared to be unlawful, any letter or letters, package or packages, or other mailable matter, excepting newspapers, pamphlets, magazines, and periodicals, or who shall place or cause to be deposited at any appointed place, for the purpose of being transported by such unlawful means, any matter or thing properly transmittable by mail, excepting newspapers, pamphlets, magazines, and periodicals, or who shall deliver any such matter, excepting newspapers, pamphlets, magazines, and periodicals, for transmission to any agent or agents of such unlawful expresses, shall, for each and every offence, forfeit and pay the sum of fifty dollars.

[The 8th section of the Act of August 31, 1852, provides that letters enclosed in "Government Envelopes," so called, having the stamp *printed* thereon, may be conveyed *out of the mail. Provided*, That the said envelope shall be duly sealed, or otherwise firmly and securely closed, so that such letter cannot be taken therefrom without tearing or destroying such envelope; and the same duly directed and addressed, and the date of such letter, or the receipt or transmission thereof, to be written or stamped, or otherwise appear on such envelope.]

* * * "And if any person shall use, or attempt to use, for the conveyance of any letter, or other mailable matter or thing, over any post-road of the United States, either by mail or otherwise, any such stamped letter envelope which has been before used for a like purpose, such person shall be liable to a penalty of fifty dollars, to be recovered, in the name of the United States, in any court having competent jurisdiction."—*Sec.* 8, *Act of* 1853.

[Newspapers for subscribers may go in or out of the mail; but pamphlets, magazines, &c., if intended to supply regular subscribers, must go in the mail.—*Act of* 1847.]

Act of 1847.

SEC. 2. *And be it further enacted,* That all moneys taken from the mails of the United States by robbery, theft, or otherwise, which have come or may hereafter come into the possession or custody of any of the agents of the Post-Office Department, or any other officers of the United States, or any other person or persons whatever, shall be paid to the order of the Post Master General, to be kept by him as other moneys of the Post-Office Department, to and for the use and benefit of the rightful owner, to be paid whenever satisfactory proof thereof shall be made; and upon the failure of any person in the employment of the United States to pay over such moneys when demanded, the person so refusing shall be subject to the penalties prescribed by law against defaulting officers.

SEC. 13. *And be it further enacted,* That it shall not be lawful to deposit in any post-office, to be conveyed in the mail, two or more letters directed to different persons enclosed in the same envelope or packet; and every person so offending shall forfeit the sum of ten dollars, to be recovered by action *qui tam,* one half for the use of the informer, and the other half for the use of the Post-Office Department: *Provided,* That this prohibition shall not apply to any letter or packet directed to any foreign country.

Act of 1852.

SEC. 3. *And be it further enacted,* That if any person shall steal, purloin, embezzle, or obtain by any false pretence, or shall aid or assist in stealing, purloining, embezzling, or obtaining by any false pretence, or shall knowingly and unlawfully make, forge, or counterfeit, or cause to be unlawfully made, forged, or counterfeited, or knowingly aid or assist in falsely and unlawfully making, forging, or counterfeiting any key suited to any lock which has been or shall be adopted for use by the Post-Office Department of the United States, and which shall be in use on any of the mails or mail bags of the said Post-Office Department, or shall have in his possession any such mail key or any such mail lock, with the intent unlawfully or improperly to use, sell, or otherwise dispose of the same, or cause the same to be unlawfully or improperly used, sold or otherwise disposed of, or who being employed in the manufacture of the locks or keys for the use of the said Post-Office Department, whether as contractor or otherwise, shall deliver or cause to be delivered any finished or unfinished key or lock used or designed by the said Post-Office Department, or the interior part of any such mail lock, to any person not duly authorized under the hand of the Post Master General of the United States and the seal of the said Post-Office Department to receive the same, (unless such person so receiving the same shall be the contractor for furnishing such locks and keys, or engaged in the manufacture thereof in the manner authorized by the contract, or the agent for such manufacturer,) such person so offending shall be deemed guilty of felony, and, on conviction thereof, shall be imprisoned for a period not exceeding ten years.

Sec. 4. *And be it further enacted,* That if any person shall steal, purloin or embezzle any mail bags in use by or belonging to the Post-Office Department of the United States, or any other property in use by or belonging to the said Post-Office Department, or shall, for any lucre, gain, or convenience, appropriate any such property to his own, or any other than its proper use, or for any lucre or gain shall convey away any such property to the hindrance or detriment of the public service of the United States, the person so offending, his counsellors, aiders, and abettors, (knowing of and privy to any offence aforesaid,) shall, on conviction thereof, if the value of such property shall exceed twenty-five dollars, be deemed guilty of felony, and shall be imprisoned for a period not exceeding three years; or if the value of such property shall be less than twenty-five dollars, shall be imprisoned not more than one year, or be fined not less than ten dollars, nor more than two hundred dollars, for every such offence.

Act of 1855.

Sec. 2. *And be it further enacted,* That it shall not be lawful for any post master or other person to sell any postage stamp or stamped envelope for any larger sum than that indicated upon the face of such postage stamp or for a larger sum than that charged therefor by the

Post-Office Department; and any person who shall violate this provision shall be deemed guilty of a misdemeanor, and, on conviction thereof, shall be fined in any sum not less than ten nor more than five hundred dollars. This act to take effect and be in force from and after the commencement of the next fiscal quarter after its passage. *Provided,* That nothing herein contained shall be so construed as to alter the laws in relation to the franking privilege.

SEC. 3. *And be it further enacted,* That for the greater security of valuable letters posted for transmission in the mails of the United States, the Post Master General be and hereby is authorized to establish a uniform plan for the registration of such letters on application of parties posting the same, and to require the pre-payment of the postage, as well as a registration fee of five cents on every such letter or packet to be accounted for by post masters receiving the same in such manner as the Post Master General shall direct: *Provided however,* That such registration shall not be compulsory; and it shall not render the Post-Office Department or its revenue liable for the loss of such letters or packets or the contents thereof.

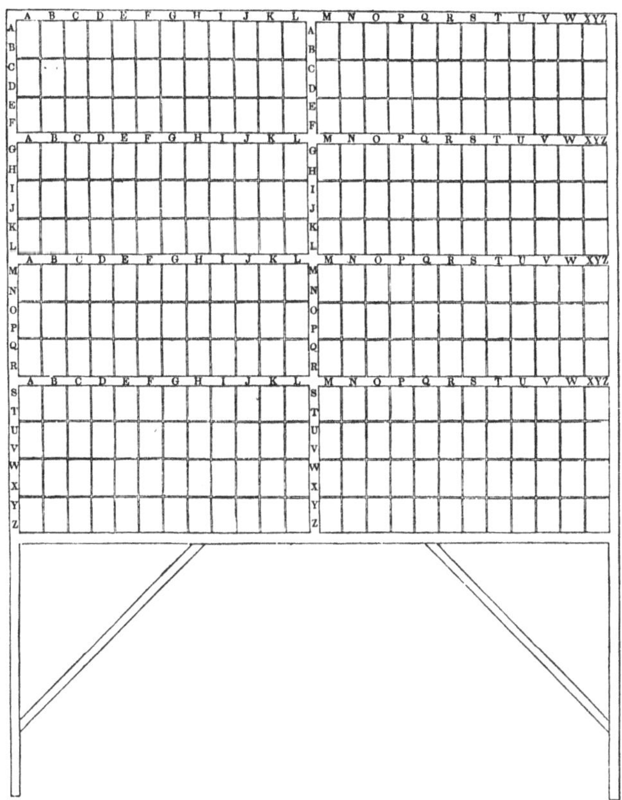

IMPROVED LETTER CASE.

The delivery of letters can be greatly facilitated by means of a very simple improvement in the letter case for the "general delivery," which has already been adopted to some extent, with the most satisfactory results.

In the early history of post-offices, the old-fashioned letter case divided off in alphabetical order, or by vowels, answered a tolerable purpose, and so it would now in very small offices,—but as population increased, and fifty or more letters had to be overhauled before the applicant could receive an answer, some relief both for post masters and the public became absolutely indispensable, and various trifling changes and improvements were adopted—but none of them were found to be "up to the times," till the introduction of the labor and time saving invention called the "Square of the Alphabet." It is believed to have been originally planned and adopted in the post-office at Providence, R. I. Since then, the dimensions of the case and the arrangement of the boxes have been varied to suit the amount of business in the comparatively small number of offices that have introduced it. But the size and plan exhibited in the prefixed diagram, is believed to be the most convenient and simple, and well suited to places varying in population, from five thousand to fifty thousand.

The practical advantage is, that by the division of the letters when placed in the pigeon holes, at least four applications can be correctly answered, where one can be under the old plan of crowding a large number of letters together. And where this improved case occupies a position opposite the "general delivery" window, many individuals soon learn the location of the box where their letters should be, and in case it is empty, inquiry becomes unnecessary.

The rows of letters of the alphabet running horizontally, from left to right, represent the surname, and are several times repeated for convenience, and as an aid to the eye in tracing given initials; while the perpendicular rows of letters stand for the Christian name, and are used doubly, to reduce the size of the case. Where it is necessary, however, the Christian initials can also be placed singly, by enlarging the case, or making it in two sections, using only half of the alphabet for each, placing the two sections in an angular form, or backing one against the other, and putting the entire frame on an upright shaft turning upon a pivot at top and bottom, near the general delivery, so as to admit of turning the case, as the locality of the initials inquired for may require.

The plan for example works thus:—John Jones calls for a letter. The person in attendance glances at the J. on the horizontal line, and then runs the eye to the range of the J. on the perpendicular line, and that is the box in which Jones' letter ought to be. One for Isaac Jones would be in the same place, in a case constructed after the above arrangement.

Its dimensions are as follows:—

Size of the entire case, 5 feet 1¼ inches, by 4 feet 2½ inches.

Size of pigeon holes or letter boxes, 3¾ by 2¼ inches.

Thickness of outside of case and lettered shelves, ¾ of an inch.

Intermediate shelves, ¼ inch thick.

Upright partitions of boxes, ⅛ inch thick—partitions cut out concave in front.

The legs or supports of the case should be about 2 feet in length, and "white wood" is considered the best material for the entire case.

Paint can be used for the lettering, or letters printed upon paper, and pasted on separately, will answer the purpose.

THE END.